MUNICIPAL COURT

PRACTICAL SKILLS SERIES

By the Honorable David A. Keyko, P.J.M.C.

THE NEW JERSEY INSTITUTE FOR CONTINUING LEGAL EDUCATION
One Constitution Square, New Brunswick, New Jersey 08901-1500
908-249-5100

Copyright © 1994 by the
NEW JERSEY INSTITUTE FOR CONTINUING LEGAL EDUCATION
All Rights Reserved

The PRACTICAL SKILLS SERIES textbooks are published primarily for use as integral components of the Skills Training Course which the New Jersey Institute for Continuing Legal Education administers on behalf of the New Jersey Supreme Court pursuant to R. 1:26 of the Rules Governing the Courts of the State of New Jersey. The PRACTICAL SKILLS SERIES consists of 17 practice oriented textbooks which are provided to each Skills Training Course registrant. These textbooks are designed to assist newly admitted practitioners in resolving many of the practical problems commonly experienced in the first few years of New Jersey law practice.

The PRACTICAL SKILLS SERIES is not intended to be a substitute for a practitioner's independent legal research and analysis. Instead, these textbooks are intended to augment or supplement a Skills Training Course registrant's own research and analysis.

NEW JERSEY INSTITUTE FOR CONTINUING LEGAL EDUCATION
is the non-profit, continuing education service of the
NEW JERSEY STATE BAR ASSOCIATION
in cooperation with
Rutgers—The State University of New Jersey and Seton Hall University

INTRODUCTORY MATERIAL
About the Author iv
Introduction 1
Courtroom Decorum 2
Applicability of Court Rules 4

JURISDICTION
General Comments 5
Over Juveniles 6
    Exhibit 1: Motion to Transfer to Family Part/Order to Transfer to Family Part 7
    Exhibit 2: Order for Dismissal 9
By Waiver of Indictment & Trial by Jury 10
    Exhibit 3: Waiver of Indictment & Trial by Jury 11
Limitations of Actions 12

PRETRIAL
The Initial Interview 13
    Exhibit 4: Municipal Court Interview Sheet 14
    Exhibit 5: Letter of Representation to Municipal Court 16
Notice in Lieu of Complaint 17
    Exhibit 6: Notice in Lieu of Complaint 18
Representation of Indigents 19
    Exhibit 7: Application to Establish Indigency 20
First Appearance, Arraignments 22
    Exhibit 8: Municipal Court Complaint/Warrant 23
    Exhibit 9: Municipal Court Complaint/Summons 24
Bail 25
    Exhibit 10: Statewide Bail Schedule 28
    Exhibit 11: Record of Property Pledged as Security for Bail 29
    Exhibit 12: Recognizance 31
    Exhibit 13: Assignment of Bail 33
    Exhibit 14: Authorization to Apply Bail Against Fines 34
Preparation for Trial 35
    Exhibit 15: Letter Requesting Defendant's Driving Abstract 36
Violations Bureau/Municipal Mandatory Penalties 37
    Exhibit 16: Statewide Violations Bureau Schedule 38
    Exhibit 17: Minimum Mandatory Fines and Penalties 53
Deposition & Discovery 58
    Exhibit 18: Letter Requesting Discovery 61
    Exhibit 19: Letter Requesting Discovery from State Police 63
    Exhibit 20: Request for Examination of Evidence from State Police 65
    Exhibit 21: Sample Lab Report 66
Search Warrants 67
Motions 67
Motions to Suppress 69
    Exhibit 22: Notice of Motion to Suppress Evidence 70
    Exhibit 23: Order to Suppress Evidence 72
Plea Bargaining 73

TRIAL
Interpreters 77
Juvenile Witnesses 77
Trial 77
Objections 79
Contempt 79
"Legal Issues in Drunk Driving Cases" 80
"How to Lose Your Municipal Court Case" 91

i

SENTENCING
Statement in Defense or Mitigation 94
    Exhibit 24: Statement in Defense or Mitigation of Penalty 95
Sentencing 97
    Exhibit 25: Community Service Program Background Statement, Time Guidelines and Participant Eligibility & Exclusion Criteria 99
    Exhibit 26: Standard Conditions for Adult Criminals on Probation 102
Motions Concerning Sentencing 103
Motion to Reduce or Change Sentence or for New Trial 103

APPEAL
Direct Appeal 103
    Exhibit 27: Notice of Appeal 106
    Exhibit 28: Affidavit of Filing 107
    Exhibit 29: Notice of Appeal to Municipal Court 108
    Exhibit 30: Notice of Appeal to Municipal Prosecutor 109
    Exhibit 31: Notice of Appeal to Superior Court 110
    Exhibit 32: Notice of Appeal to County Prosecutor 111
    Exhibit 33: Order Staying Sentence 112
Interlocutory Appeals 113

POST-SENTENCE
Expungement 113
    Exhibit 34: Verified Petition for Expungement 117
    Exhibit 35: Affidavit of Service 120
    Exhibit 36: Order to Show Cause 122
    Exhibit 37: Order for Expungement 123

SUBSTANTIVE LAW
Traffic Violations 125
    General Comments 125
        Exhibit 38: Traffic Complaint and Summons 126
        Exhibit 39: Accident Report 130
        Exhibit 40: Accident Report Code Explanation 132
        Exhibit 41: Order for Payment of Fines and Costs 133
        Exhibit 42: Summons When Defendant Failed to Appear Originally and Failed to Pay Costs and Fines 135
    Driver's License 137
        Exhibit 43: Explanation of Driver's License Codes 138
        Exhibit 44: Photo Driver's License 139
        Exhibit 45: Julian Calendar 140
    Point System 142
        Exhibit 46: Motor Vehicle Point System 143
    Driver's Abstract 147
        Exhibit 47: Explanation of Event Codes on Driver's Abstract 148
        Exhibit 48: Complete Listing of Municipal Court Codes 149
        Exhibit 49: Sample Driver's Abstract 154
        Exhibit 50: Manual of Abbreviations Used on Driver's Abstracts 160
    Unlicensed Driver 169
    Driving While License or Registration is Suspended or Revoked 170
        Exhibit 51: Sample Notice of Proposed Suspension 172
        Exhibit 52: Mailing List 174
        Exhibit 53: Order of Suspension by Division of Motor Vehicles 175
        Exhibit 54: Order of Suspension by Municipal Court 176
    Failure to Maintain Liability Insurance 178
        Exhibit 55: Insurance Card 180

Other Violations
    Consumption of Alcohol While a Driver or Passenger in a Motor Vehicle 181
    Disorderly/Petty Disorderly & Local Ordinance Violations 182
        Exhibit 56: Disorderly/Petty Disorderly Persons "Ticket" Summons 183
    Non-Driving Alcohol Offenses 184
        Exhibit 57: Amendment to N.J.S.A. 33:1-81 185
    Drug Offenses 188

OTHER
Victim-Witness Rights in New Jersey 189
Alcohol Treatment Rehabilitation Act 199
    Exhibit A: Request by Defendant to be Examined 204
    Exhibit B: Court Referral 205
    Exhibit C: Order of Temporary Commitment and Stay of Proceedings 206
    Exhibit D: Client-Probation Department Participation Agreement 207
    Exhibit E: Probation Referral Agreement 208
    Exhibit F: Order of Dismissal of Charges Pursuant to ATRA 209
    Exhibit G: Notice of Motion for Medical Examination 210
    Exhibit H: Order that Defendant Submit to Medical Examination 211
    Exhibit I: Notice of Motion for Alcohol Treatment 212
    Exhibit J: Order for Alcohol Treatment 213
    Exhibit K: Defendant's Certification 214

APPENDICES
A: Court Rules: Part 7 and Applicable Rules of Part 3 215
B: Breathalyzer Handbook & Certifications 254

ABOUT THE AUTHOR

David A. Keyko has served as a Municipal Court Judge since 1973 and presently presides in twelve municipalities in Gloucester and Camden Counties. He also serves, since January, 1986, as Presiding Judge of the Municipal Courts of Camden County. Judge Keyko is past President of the Camden County Conference of Municipal Court Judges and the 1988 President of the Gloucester County Conference of Municipal Court Judges. He has been Chairman of the Supreme Court Committee of Municipal Court Education since its inception in 1982, as well as serving as a member of the Supreme Court Committee on Municipal Courts, the Supreme Court Committee on Complementary Dispute Resolution, the Supreme Court Task Force on Municipal Court Improvement and the Supreme Court Committee on Plea Agreements in the Municipal Court.

Judge Keyko is the author of "Drunk Driving—A Judge's Perspective" (N.J.S.B.A. Journal, November, 1983) and "Administering Justice in a New Way" (New Jersey League of Municipalities, March, 1983), as well as Editor of the *New Jersey Municipal Judges Benchbook*. A graduate of Drew University and the University of Texas School of Law, he is admitted to the District of Columbia Bar and is a member of the American Judges Association and the National Conference of Special Court Judges. Judge Keyko has also been selected to appear in "Who's Who in American Law" for the last several years as well as "Who's Who in the East".

INTRODUCTION

The Municipal Courts of the State of New Jersey may well be considered the most important courts in our judicial system. If the average citizen in this state ever appears in any court, it will more likely than not be in the Municipal Court. Furthermore, the penalties which may be imposed by the court are significant in that they include incarceration, community service, fines, restitution, probation and revocation of driver's licenses, and other sanctions. For the 1992 court year, 6,617,505 cases were concluded by the 537 Municipal Courts of this state as compared to 1,026,846 cases concluded by the Superior Court. The Municipal Courts of this state suspended 93,227 drivers' licenses as part of a sentence, and the total revenue collected by the municipal courts in fines, costs, bail forfeitures and VCCB penalties amounted to $220,165,928.

To the average Municipal Court defendant, his or her day in court is just as important and equally frightening as that of a Superior Court litigant. Despite this fact, "seasoned" attorneys often shun appearances in the Municipal Court leaving the practice of Municipal Court law to the younger attorney and a few experienced specialists.

Practice in the Municipal Courts offers unparalleled opportunity to the young attorney for several reasons. First, it is relatively easy to attract clients requiring representation given the large number of complaints filed annually. Secondly, municipal court practice affords the young attorney the opportunity to develop his or her skills by learning to think and act quickly "on his or her feet". Such experience and exposure is invaluable. Lastly, the potential fees to be earned by establishing a municipal court practice can be substantial.

Municipal court practice may be as challenging to the counselor with many years experience who is called upon to represent a long standing client.

Since the early 1980's, as a result of increased public and governmental attention to traffic safety, drunk driving, insurance costs and increased enforcement by state and local police, the caseloads of municipal courts have increased tremendously, resulting in a greater number of clients requiring and desiring the services of counsel. It is likely that this condition will continue to escalate in the years to come. Given the substantial minimum penalties which may be incurred by defendants for many motor vehicle and some non-indictable offenses, the need for quality representation has increased; and the private citizen, desiring the services of an attorney, deserves to receive competent and qualified representation. Lack of preparation is no longer tolerable to the client, the court, or the public interest.

It is hoped that this practice manual will serve both newly admitted and experienced attorneys with a sound practical and technical background necessary to prepare counsel for appearances in the Municipal Court.

COURTROOM DECORUM

Municipal Court is most likely the only court with which the average citizen will be involved. Accordingly, the impression created by an attorney upon the members of the public in attendance at Municipal Court is the most readily remembered. It is, therefore, important that the attorney make the proper appearance and impression. The attorney should dress in the same fashion as he or she would for an appearance in the Superior Court keeping in mind that not only will he or she be "sized up" by the Municipal Court Judge, but also the audience. A disheveled or sloppy appearance does little to impress your client, the audience or the Judge, and is, rightly or wrongly, translated as a lack of concern for not only yourself, but also for your work. This observation may appear to be somewhat elementary, but frequently attorneys who have worked all day in their offices sometimes feel that they may act and dress less formally for the Municipal Court. Case law would seem to indicate that a Municipal Court Judge, or any other Judge, may not comment on an attorney's dress or appearance, but Judges are human too and what may offend an objective observer may well have a similar, unspoken, effect on the Judge.

One of the most important and practical approaches which should be employed prior to appearing before a Judge for the first time is to learn as much as possible about the Judge's likes, dislikes, or inclinations. This is easily accomplished by calling another attorney who has had experience before the Judge in question. For example, some Judges will frown upon an attorney approaching the Judge prior to court for the purpose of introduction, while others would prefer to make the attorney's acquaintance in chambers prior to the opening of court. Some Judges may have particularly strong feelings about such violations as shoplifting, drinking in public, etc., and this information may prove to be valuable to the attorney in the strategy or presentation of the case. The attorney would be well advised to learn of the "propensities" of the particular Judge before whom he or she is about to appear.

Always be on time for the calling of the docket, or list of cases. If it is necessary for you to appear at a later time because of other commitments, notify the Judge or Court Clerk in advance requesting permission to arrive at a later time and confirm by letter. Do not forget to advise your client of this arrangement so that the client does not sit in the courtroom feeling abandoned until your arrival.

Always address the Judge in court or in chambers as "Your Honor" or "Judge" to show respect. Even though you may be more familiarly acquainted with the Judge because of his or her law practice and cases you might have had together, it is recommended that you use the appropriate title of respect so that observers, police, other attorneys or prosecutors do not get the wrong impression of an impermissible degree of familiarity which may later serve as the basis for a claim of prejudice or favoritism.

There is nothing inappropriate in speaking with witnesses or the police officer prior to court. Remember, however, that the officer is not compelled to discuss anything with you. If the officer chooses not to speak with you, do not pursue it. Also, it is not advisable to use the content of your informal pretrial conversations during trial in an effort to embarrass the officer. The officer will not forget, and your reputation for fair play and reasonableness will be severely affected as the officer will most likely share his unpleasant experience with other members of the police force. You should never attempt to do so without justifiable cause. You should be skillful enough and properly prepared to impeach the officer or other witnesses without using informal pretrial conversations. It is absolutely necessary that you exercise good judgment in your relations with police officers if you anticipate return visits to the court. While it is your responsibility to vigorously represent your client, do not let your zeal interfere with the exercise of good common sense.

Similar good sense should be exercised in your relations with the municipal prosecutor. More likely than not, the same prosecutor will be in attendance on your return visits and the fewer unnecessary enemies you cultivate, the better. Most prosecutors will usually be willing to discuss your case, any special discovery or evidentiary problems involved, or stipulations to be entered upon the record. It is frequently a long night for the prosecutor and whatever ground rules you are able to establish in an effort to expedite your case are often well received, keeping in mind that your primary responsibility is to your client. Developing a reputation with the prosecutor, police officers and the Judge as a capable, but reasonable advocate is the ultimate goal.

It is exceptionally bad form for an attorney to be talking to the client or another attorney while court is in session. Refrain from waiting until the night of court to talk to your client or to clear up last minute details. If it is necessary to do so, wait until a recess is called, or take your client outside the courtroom. Also remember, this is serious business to your client and you should not banter back and forth with other attorneys as if it were a meeting of old friends at a social. Your client and your case are your only concerns and you should act accordingly.

Since all Municipal Courts use a sound recording device of one sort or another, it is usually necessary to remain seated even when addressing the court due to the location of the microphone. Nevertheless, it is advisable that an attorney should always stand while addressing the court unless the court indicates that it is not necessary, or you ask permission not to stand.

When your case is called, speak distinctly and directly into the microphone and state, as follows: "Your honor, John Jones of the Firm of Smith and Jones of Camden City representing the defendant, Richard Roe. We waive a reading of the complaint(s) and enter pleas of...." Even though you have previously entered your appearance in writing with the clerk of the court, you should still state your appearance and plea for the audio record. Do not mumble and do not fail to state your name and office location, it may be the only free publicity you will get.

While the trial is in progress, the testifying witness should be given your undivided attention as to the content of the testimony. Do not allow yourself to be drawn into an argument with the witness or officer. Keep your temper in check and stick to your prepared case strategy. There is no reason why your trial demeanor should be any different than that displayed in the Superior Court. Be sensitive to the Judge's reactions and glance frequently in the direction of the judge to measure his or her interest. Keep in mind that in Municipal Court, the only person you have to convince is the Judge, not the prosecutor, the audience, or the police officer. This is another reason why you should attempt to learn as much as possible about the Judge's predispositions prior to your appearance.

Perhaps the most thankless job in the judicial system is that of the Municipal Court or Violations Clerk. They are frequently part-time, usually underpaid, and most always overworked. The last thing they need, or will tolerate, is an abusive attorney. In dealing with Court personnel, always be pleasant and cordial. When you make a request and the Clerk refuses it, it is because the Clerk is complying with the Judge's generally established procedures. Except where circumstances make it impossible, always request postponements well in advance so that the Clerk will have sufficient time to notify the witnesses, officers, or other parties involved, if the postponement is granted. If it is on short notice, it would be appropriate for you to undertake the responsibility of notifying the parties to ease the burden of the Clerk. Never argue with, or "pull rank" on the Court Clerk. If you feel the urge to do so, you are talking to the wrong person; call the Judge. The best approach to take in dealing with court personnel is to treat them courteously and with respect. "You can attract more bees with honey...."

Although Municipal Court proceedings are taped, recordings are sometimes unsatisfactory or inaudible. In those circumstances where it is necessary to bring your own court stenographer to transcribe a record, perhaps for use in a subsequent negligence trial, review the court rule carefully, (R. 7:4-5a to c), and notify the Judge and Court Clerk of your intention to use a stenographer. The stenographer's presence is not then mistakenly construed as an attempt at intimidation, or an effort at showmanship. It is always improper to threaten an appeal prior to, or while the trial is in progress.

In summary, the best advice which can be given concerning how to comport oneself in Municipal Court is to use your good common sense, know the facts and applicable law, be prepared, and put yourself in the place of the Judge while keeping in mind that you must represent your client's interests. With this in mind, an appearance in Municipal Court can be a truly productive and rewarding experience.

APPLICABILITY OF COURT RULES

Practice in the Municipal Courts is governed by Part 7 of the New Jersey Rules of Court. Part 7 applies to both traffic (Rule 7:6) and non traffic matters. Frequent reference is made to Part 3 (Rules Governing Criminal Practice) in sections of Part 7. Because Court Rules are subject to revision by the Supreme Court, it is necessary to insure familiarity with the changes which are published in the New Jersey Law Journal. Further, procedures may vary from county to county or between vicinages as a result of special procedures or programs approved by the Supreme Court. One such example is that some counties still provide that preliminary hearings on indictable matters be conducted in the Municipal Court, whereas other counties do not provide for preliminary hearings. These counties, instead, may operate pursuant to an approved pre-indictment "screening" process, such as Central Judicial Processing Court, or direct review by the County Prosecutor administratively, without appearance prior to indictment. Therefore, applicability of the Court Rules depends, to a degree, upon local practice as approved by the Supreme Court.

JURISDICTION OF THE MUNICIPAL COURTS

General Comments

Municipal Courts have jurisdiction of such actions as herein described provided that the offense alleged occurred within the territorial boundaries of the municipality (N.J.S.A. 2A:8-20) "and any premises or property situated or located partly within and partly without the municipality or municipalities." Provided further that in the event an offense is committed in one municipality in the presence of an officer, he may arrest in a second municipality outside his territorial jurisdictional limits. *State v. Mc Carthy,* 123 N.J. Super. 513 (Cty. Ct. 1973), also *State v. O'Donnell,* 192 N.J. Super. 128 (App. Div. 1983). In the event a traffic offense occurs between two municipalities, including roads or highways serving as boundary lines between said municipalities, either municipality may exercise jurisdiction. N.J.S.A. 39:5-3. In those instances involving offenses on interstate bridges, for example, between Pennsylvania and New Jersey or New York and New Jersey, interstate compacts provide for jurisdiction in either state's Municipal Court. See e.g., N.J.S.A. 32:4-6; *State v. Holden,* 46 N.J. 361 (1966).

Pursuant to N.J.S.A. 2A:8-21 the Municipal Courts exercise jurisdiction in the following:

1. Violations of motor vehicle or traffic laws, usually contained in N.J.S.A. 39:1-1 *et seq.*;

2. Violations of Fish and Game Laws (N.J.S.A. 23:1-1 *et seq.*);

3. Petty disorderly and disorderly persons offenses, primarily contained in Title 2C;

4. Violations of the ordinances of the municipality wherein the Municipal Court is located or of the municipalities to which its jurisdiction extends;

5. Offenses as to which no indictment by grand jury is required;

6. Offenses of an indictable nature where indictment and trial by jury are waived, and the Judge of the Municipal Court is an attorney at law, and where such offenses do not compel a penalty in excess of one year imprisonment, a $1,000 fine or both with the permission of the county prosecutor (N.J.S.A. 2A:8-22);

7. Violations of the "poor" laws (Chapters 1 and 4 of Title 44), including certain types of Domestic Relations problems and emergent issuance of Temporary Restraining Orders;

8. Violations of the truancy laws in Titles 18A and violations of Chapter 6 and 17 of Title 9, Children;

9. Such other violations as are specifically designated by statute or ordinance including failure to remit or report unemployment taxes, failure to report and remit Sales and Use Taxes, transportation of hazardous wastes, smoking in schools by juveniles and such other issues as time to time are enacted by the legislature;

10. Notices in Lieu of Complaint pursuant to R.7:3-2.

The Municipal Court is the court of original jurisdiction in indictable offenses in that bail in such cases is usually set by the Municipal Court Judge except as to specified capital offenses. See R.7:5-1 *et seq.* It should be noted that the Superior Courts have concurrent jurisdiction with the Municipal Court. Court rules also specifically provide for the transfer of non-indictable matters arising out of a family relationship upon motion to Superior Court, Family Part. See R.7:4-2(j), R.5:1-2(c)(3), and R.5:1-3(b)(2).

Frequently, indictable offenses are downgraded, after administrative review in the county prosecutor's office, to a lesser offense, such as a disorderly or petty disorderly persons offense, and returned to the Municipal Court for disposition.

Given the above, it is obvious that the Municipal Court has a wide range of jurisdiction over a number of topics which will expose the attorney to a variety of subject matters.

Jurisdiction of Juveniles

Pursuant to N.J.S.A. 2A:4A-23, violations of Chapters 3, 6, or 8 of Title 39 by a juvenile of or over the age of 17 years, but under 18 years, do not constitute delinquency. Such violations are therefore cognizable in the Municipal Court regardless of whether the defendant was ever licensed or ever possessed a permit to drive. Also cognizable in the Municipal Court are violations, by a juvenile of any age, of Chapters 3 and 4 of Title 39 relating to ownership and operation of motorized bicycles and violations of Article 3 or 6 of Chapter 4 of Title 39 relating to pedestrians and bicycles. N.J.S.A. 39:4-203.3 provides that any juvenile who violates Title 39 sections dealing with pedestrians may be fined not more than $10.00. Non-traffic matters which would be a violation of Title 2C or local ordinances, when committed by a juvenile are under the jurisdiction of the Family Part of the Superior Court. N.J.S.A. 2A:4-3a *et seq.* For the purposes of disorderly and petty disorderly offenses and ordinance violations, a defendant is considered an adult if he or she is one day short of becoming 18 years of age.

If representing an adult defendant in an incident in which a juvenile has also been charged in juvenile court, it is necessary to delay proceeding in the adult case(s) until such time as the juvenile matter has been resolved. The purpose is to prevent or avoid the necessity of a juvenile defendant being called to testify in the adult matter while the juvenile still has a case pending in the Superior Court, Family Part, thus preventing the juvenile's rights from being compromised. Once the juvenile matter has been resolved, the case against the adult defendant may proceed. In those instances where both juveniles and adults are defendants in the same case arising out of the same or closely related set of facts, the adult case should be transferred upon formal motion to the Superior Court, Family Part. See R.7:4-2(j). (See Sample Forms, **Exhibits 1 and 2**). In the alternative, the adult case should be delayed until such time as the juvenile matter is concluded. You should promptly notify the Municipal Court Judge or Court Clerk in the event you receive a trial notice in Municipal Court while the juvenile case remains outstanding so that the matter may be postponed by the Municipal Court with only minimal inconvenience. Of course, the preferable course of action would be to try both the juvenile and the adult in the Superior Court in the interests of judicial economy, avoidance of double jeopardy issues, and in accordance with the "one case, one controversy" theory. However, the aforementioned practice is not very often followed.

N.J.S.A. 2A:4A-27 provides that any juvenile 14 years of age or older charged with delinquency may elect to have the case transferred to the appropriate court having jurisdiction as if the accused had been an adult.

EXHIBIT 1

_____

STATE OF NEW JERSEY   :   SUPERIOR COURT OF NEW JERSEY
:   CHANCERY DIVISION—FAMILY PART
          Plaintiff,   :   CAMDEN COUNTY
:
:
:   DOCKET NO._____
:
:   MOTION TO TRANSFER TO FAMILY PART
vs.   :   RELATED FAMILY_____
:   MUNICIPAL COURT DOCKET NO.:
:
:   _____
:
         Defendant.   :

_____

PLEASE TAKE NOTICE that the_____ will

move before the Chancery Division, Family Part, Camden County on_____

_____ for an order transferring the above captioned

municipal court complaint to the Family Part for further hearing.

_____   _____
         Date   Movant

EXHIBIT 1 (Continued)

STATE OF NEW JERSEY	:	SUPERIOR COURT OF NEW JERSEY
	:	CHANCERY DIVISION—FAMILY PART
Plaintiff,	:	CAMDEN COUNTY
	:	
	:	DOCKET NO. FO-04-
	:	
	:	ORDER TO TRANSFER MUNICIPAL COURT
	:	COMPLAINT TO THE SUPERIOR COURT
vs.	:	OF NEW JERSEY CHANCERY DIVISION
	:	FAMILY PART—COUNTY OF CAMDEN
	:	
	:	RELATED FAMILY_____
Defendant.	:	MUNICIPAL COURT DOCKET NO._____

This matter having come before the court on Motion of_____

and it appearing that the above captioned municipal court matter is appropriately cognizable in the Family Part and for good cause shown, it is on this _____ day of _____, 19_____

ORDERED that the above captioned matter be transferred to the Superior Court of New Jersey, Chancery Division Family Part of the County of Camden.

DATED:_____   _____
                                                                                              Judge

EXHIBIT 2

STATE OF NEW JERSEY :	SUPERIOR COURT OF NEW JERSEY
:	CHANCERY DIVISION—FAMILY PART
Plaintiff, :	CAMDEN COUNTY
:	
:	DOCKET NO.:_____
:	
vs. :	RELATED FAMILY:_____
:	
:	ORDER FOR DISMISSAL
:	
Defendant. :	

This matter having come before the court on its own motion and the court having made findings of facts and conclusions of law, and for other good cause shown, It is on this _____ day of _____, 19_____

ORDERED that the above-captioned matter be dismissed for the following reason(s):_____
_____

Dated:_____   _____
                                                                                        Judge

Waiver of Indictment and Trial by Jury

Municipal Courts also have jurisdiction over such offenses occurring within their territorial jurisdiction which are ordinarily indictable when the defendant has waived his or her right to indictment and trial by jury and the County Prosecutor consents in writing. N.J.S.A. 2A:8-22. The defendant and/or his or her attorney must simply, to effectuate such a waiver, sign the reverse side of the original CDR-1 (**Exhibit 3**). The following are the types of matters in which indictment and trial by jury may be waived:

1. Crimes enumerated in Chapters 17, 18, 20 and 21 of Title 2C of the New Jersey Statutes provided that the injury or loss to the victim is under $500.00 (N.J.S.A. 2A:8-22a).

2. Other indictable offenses where the penalty that may be imposed does not exceed a fine of $1,000.00 or imprisonment for a term not exceeding one year (N.J.S.A. 2A:8-22b).

The decision to waive indictment and trial by jury should be made in light of the following considerations:

1. The inclination or personality of the Municipal Court Judge in such offenses.

2. The possible sentence which could be imposed in the Municipal Court as opposed to that which the defendant might receive in the Superior Court.

3. Whether the defendant has a prior criminal record and whether such record is known or will be made known to the Municipal Court Judge.

4. Whether the defendant might qualify for Pretrial Intervention if the matter remains in the Superior Court.

Because this waiver requires the prior consent of the County Prosecutor, it is necessary to give advance notice to the Municipal Court and the County Prosecutor.

EXHIBIT 3

_____
_____
_____
_____

CO-DEFENDANT(S)

DOCKET No. _____	
DEFENDANT _____	
Municipal Court of _____	
County of _____	
State of New Jersey	

To: _____ Reason _____
To: _____ Reason _____
To: _____ Reason _____
To: _____ Reason _____

ADJOURNMENTS

EXHIBITS

for STATE _____
_____
_____
_____

for DEFENDANT _____
_____
_____
_____

WITNESSES
NAME AND ADDRESS

for STATE _____
for DEFENDANT _____

COUNSEL

for STATE
Name _____
Address _____

for DEFENDANT
Name _____
Address _____

WAIVER OF INDICTMENT BY GRAND JURY AND TRIAL BY JURY

The defendant herein, being advised of the nature of the charge against him and of his rights to indictment by grand jury and trial by jury, hereby waives prosecution by indictment and trial by jury and requests to be tried before this court.

Dated: _____

_____
Signature of Defendant

Signed in the presence of: Approved

_____
Judge

Limitation of Actions

When a client consults an attorney, most particularly with respect to a motor vehicle violation signed by a private citizen, the attorney should be especially certain that the complaint has been signed within the time prescribed by the applicable statute of limitations. If the client is advised to sign a counter-complaint, it must also be completed within the time period provided. Any complaint signed subsequent to the expiration of the applicable statute of limitations, would be subject to dismissal. Prosecutions for offenses are subject to the following limitations:

1. N.J.S.A. 2C:1-6a provides that prosecutions for murder or manslaughter may be commenced at any time.

2. N.J.S.A. 2C:1-6b(1) provides that a prosecution for a crime must be commenced within five years after it is committed.

3. N.J.S.A. 2C:1-6b(2) provides that a prosecution for a disorderly persons or petty disorderly persons offense must be commenced within one year after it is committed.

4. N.J.S.A. 39:5-3 provides that process for the appearance of a person charged with a motor vehicle offense must issue within thirty days of the commission of the offense with the following exceptions:

    A complaint may be made at any time within one year after a violation of Sections 39:3-12 (securing a driver's license by having another person take the driver's license examination, or taking a driver's examination for another applicant); 39:3-34 (applying for a driver's license or registration certificate, or learner's permit while one's driver's license or registration certificate has been suspended or revoked); 39:3-37 (giving fictitious name or address, or making any intentional misstatement of fact in an application for a registration of a motor vehicle or a driver's license); 39:4-129 (leaving the scene of an accident, failure to exhibit license and registration to anyone involved in an accident or failure to give assistance to those injured in an accident); or 39:10-24 (any violation of Chapter 39 which does not provide a specific penalty, misrepresentation on title papers, receiving a motor vehicle or a title paper in violation of Chapter 39, forging or counterfeiting a part of title papers or misrepresenting the description of a motor vehicle). A complaint for operating without insurance, (N.J.S.A. 39:6B-2), may be filed within six months of the date of offense where indicated.

    Complaints charging operation of a motor vehicle while driver's license has been refused, suspended or revoked must be filed within 90 days of the date of offense. N.J.S.A. 39:5-3.

THE INITIAL INTERVIEW

Whether the client accused of a traffic or disorderly persons offense is new to your office or one of long standing, the initial interview concerning a Municipal Court appearance is equally important. For this reason, it is essential that the initial interview be conducted in your office rather than on the courthouse steps. Your office atmosphere will serve to impress upon your client the seriousness of the offense and will also demonstrate that you consider it so. There will also be less opportunity for distraction and the client will be more secure in that his or her confidence will be held inviolate. No matter how accomplished you have become in the handling of Municipal Court matters, an appointment should be made with the client in your office well in advance of the hearing date.

The primary objective of the initial interview is to gather the facts of the case. You may accomplish this by asking the appropriate questions, including those which the Judge or prosecutor may ask. By assuming this adversarial role toward your client, he or she will become familiar with what to expect in cross examination by the prosecutor. If you choose to employ this technique you should first inform your client of your intentions and explain that it is done in an effort to prepare him or her for trial. This technique also provides an opportunity to teach your client how to properly answer questions and not volunteer information. Inadequate preparation of the client and witnesses may easily result in surprise and embarrassment to both you and your client.

While you are attempting to gather the facts of the case you should, at the same time, be making every effort to establish a rapport with your client, put him or her at ease and gain his or her confidence. Answer all of the client's questions honestly and realistically. Give the client a brief idea of the procedures which will be followed in the Municipal Court. Do not be afraid to offer information such as directions to the courthouse, where to park, where to meet, and a description of the physical layout of the building and courtroom. Although you may be familiar with these details, it is unlikely that your client is and the more advance knowledge your client has, the more at ease the client will feel.

The importance of the client being absolutely truthful with the attorney should also be stressed. Any intentional distortion of the facts or unintentional omissions may seriously handicap any effort to successfully represent the client. Where necessary, advise the client of the necessity of providing photographic or documentary evidence which may be helpful and instruct him or her to obtain and have this evidence in his or her possession at the time of trial, or prior thereto. It is recommended that you give your client a list of what is required and retain a copy of this list in your files to insure that all necessary documents have been obtained.

Once you have ascertained the facts of the case, discuss them with your client and explain how the particular law applies. Be honest with your client in regard to the strengths and weaknesses of his or her case as well as those of the State.

Lastly, the attorney should discuss the fee arrangement in a straightforward manner and set the fees while determining the time and method of payment. It is perfectly proper to establish a flat fee or an hourly rate with retainer, but it is improper to set forth a fee on the basis of result. *See*, Rules of Professional Conduct 1.5(d)(2). It is not advisable to send a letter of representation to the court without having been retained, i.e. being paid. Many Judges will require an attorney to represent a client in Municipal Court even when the fee has not been paid if the attorney has obtained a postponement for the client or has sent in a letter of representation. The fact that you are unpaid or have a fee dispute with your client is not a matter of the court's concern. **Exhibit 4** is a sample interview sheet which you may modify for your particular needs. **Exhibit 5** is a sample of a letter of representation which should be sent to the court as much in advance of your appearance as possible.

EXHIBIT 4

INTERVIEW SHEET
MUNICIPAL COURT

DATE: _____

1. Name _____ 2. S.S.#: _____

    Address _____ Dr. Lic. #: _____

    _____ Tag #: _____

    _____ Height: _____ Weight: _____

    Phone ( ) _____ Eye Color _____

    How long at present address? _____

3. Occupation: _____

4. Name, address, phone number of employer and how long employed? _____
   _____

5. Single: _____ Married: _____ Divorced: _____ Separated: _____ Widowed _____

6. Spouse's Name: _____

7. Number of children or other dependents:

    Children: _____

    Dependents: _____

8. Has bail been posted? If so, amount $ _____ posted by _____

9. If anyone else was arrested and charged, list names and addresses: _____
   _____
   _____

10. Present offense(s), list charges: _____
    _____
    _____

    Ticket # _____ Summons #: _____ Warrant #: _____

11. Court: _____ Date of Appearance: _____

12. Complete description of alleged offense: (include date, times, weather conditions, place of incident and names of all people present) _____
    _____
    _____

13. Witnesses: (names, addresses and phone #) _____
    _____
    _____

EXHIBIT 4 (Continued)

14. Notes:_____
_____
_____

15. Prior convictions (include description of each charge, date of conviction, and place of conviction):
_____
_____

16. Other attorneys involved:_____
_____

17. Injuries or property damage:_____
_____
_____

18. Fee agreement:_____
19. Referred by:_____
20. Other:

Attorney to do:

Retainer letter/fee agreement_____

Letter of Representation_____

Request Discovery_____

Expert's Report_____

Subpoena _____

Videotape _____

Request Driver's Abstract _____

Visit Scene _____

Review law and possible penalties _____

Investigate _____

Interview witnesses _____

Accident report _____

Hospital _____

Other _____

Client to do:

Obtain Photographs _____

Copy of Complaints & Summons _____

Written Description of Events _____

Estimate _____

Other _____

EXHIBIT 5

MARTIN J. QUEENAN
ATTORNEY AT LAW

422 High Street
P.O. Box 295
Burlington, N.J. 08016

December 2, 1982

Jean DiBiasi, Court Clerk
Winslow Township Municipal Court
Route 73
Braddock, N.J. 08037

Re: State vs. Charles B. Murray
Summons Nos. 6782 & 6783

Dear Mrs. DiBiasi:

Please be advised that I represent **Charles B. Murray** in regard to the above captioned matter.

Please enter my appearance as attorney for **Charles B. Murray** _____. At this time we are entering a plea of **Not** Guilty.

Kindly address all communications to me.

Very truly yours,

Martin J. Queenan, Esquire

MJQ/kd

cc: Joseph A. Marressa, Esquire, Mun. Pros.

NOTICE IN LIEU OF COMPLAINT

R. 7:3-2 provides that if the offense charged may constitute a minor neighborhood or domestic dispute, a notice may issue to the person or persons charged, requesting their appearance before the court, or such persons designated by the court and approved by the Assignment Judge, in order to determine whether a complaint should issue or other appropriate action be taken.

The types of matters which may be placed on a Notice in Lieu of Complaint are minor offenses, including some disorderly persons offenses, such as:

1. Family disputes;
2. Simple assaults (non-injury);
3. Trespasses;
4. Obstruct, molest, hinder or otherwise interfere;
5. Creating a disturbance;
6. Noise complaints;
7. Dog and other animal complaints;
8. Annoying phone calls;
9. Shoplifting;
10. Larceny under $200.00;
11. Neighborhood disputes;
12. Merchant/Customer disputes;
13. Landlord/Tenant disputes;
14. Malicious destruction of property;
15. Property disputes.

The Notice in Lieu of Complaint is a standard form (see **Exhibit 6**). The proceedings when such a notice is filed are informal. It is not necessary that the proceedings be recorded or that they be conducted with the same formality as if a complaint had issued. Legal representation of the parties involved and cross-examination of witnesses may or may not be permitted at the discretion of the court since the judge may not impose criminal type sanctions, but is only interested in a solution to these societal problems. The court may only make recommendations to be followed in an attempt to solve the problem informally or may suggest that a formal complaint be filed. If a formal complaint is issued, the municipal judge may, at his own discretion and properly so, disqualify himself from hearing the formal complaint.

Some communities have established Community Resolution Dispute Committees or Arbitration Panels specifically for the purpose of handling these types of matters. If appropriate, the attorney should inquire as to whether or not referral to such a committee or panel is an option. The committee may only either make recommendations to resolve the dispute or recommend that a formal complaint should issue. If either the complainant or the defendant is unwilling to follow any recommendations the committee may make, the matter will be referred to the municipal court.

EXHIBIT 6

MUNICIPAL COURT OF THE
_____ OF _____, COUNTY OF ESSEX,
STATE OF NEW JERSEY

Notice in Lieu of Complaint, Rule 7:3-2

TO_____

OF_____

_____, N.J.

Please take notice that you have been informally charged by

_____ of _____

_____, N.J., with the commission of a (Neighborhood/Domestic) dispute, to wit:

You are therefore hereby notified to appear before a hearing officer of the Community Dispute Resolution Project at _____, in said municipality at _____ m. on the _____ day of _____, 19_____, so that it may be determined whether or not a complaint should be issued. A copy of the Project's guidelines is enclosed.

Dated:

_____
Judge

REPRESENTATION OF INDIGENTS

In those instances where it appears that a defendant before the court, if convicted, faces the probability of incarceration, a substantial fine, loss of driving privileges, or other consequences of magnitude, and that the defendant is indigent, the court, upon request, must appoint counsel without charge. *Rodriquez v. Rosenblatt*, 58 N.J. 281 (1977). **Exhibit 7** is a sample of the current application used to determine indigency. In the alternative, a Judge may make a determination of indigency based upon oral questioning on the record. *State v. Abbondanzo*, 201 N.J. Super. 181 (App. Div. 1985), provides that prior to or at the trial of any criminal case where a jail sentence may follow a conviction, the judge must first advise the *pro se* defendant of the exposure to incarceration before determining that the defendant effectively waived the right to counsel. See also *State v. Lach*, 213 N.J. Super. 466 (App. Div. 1986).

Not all municipalities employ a municipal public defender and it is very possible that a recently admitted attorney will be appointed to represent an indigent free of charge. Some municipalities which do not have a public defender may provide a minimum stipend to the appointed attorney, but in other courts the attorney will be required to present an indigent without being compensated.

An attorney appointed to represent an indigent may be excused if the client does not cooperate or respond.

All attorneys licensed to practice in the State of New Jersey have a responsibility to undertake representation of an indigent as assigned by the court. *Madden v. Delran Tp.*, 126 N.J. 591 (1992). The attorney, however, may be excused for good cause, such as the existence of a conflict of interest. An additional serious consideration arises in those instances where the attorney may have restricted his or her practice to tax law, securities regulation, or the like, and does not feel competent to represent a defendant in Municipal Court. If this is the case, it should be brought to the attention of the Judge promptly with a request to be excused from this service. It, however, has been determined that it is contemptuous for an attorney to refuse to represent an indigent without cause. *State v. Frankel*, 119 N.J. Super. 579 (App. Div. 1972).

It would appear that assigned counsel's responsibility does not end with the disposition of the Municipal Court matter, but that the assigned counsel shall also advise the defendant regarding his or her right to appeal. If the defendant wishes to appeal, the assigned counsel must prepare and file the Notice of Appeal and an application for assignment of counsel on appeal. Representation of a defendant for the original trial does not include representation upon appeal or any subsequent application for post conviction relief unless further assigned by a Superior Court Judge. R. 3:27-2. The attorney is under no obligation to represent the defendant in other matters in the same or another Municipal Court, unless so ordered by the Judge. If the client makes an attempt to "adopt" you as his or her private free attorney, the client should be promptly and firmly informed of the extent of assigned counsel's responsibility.

N.J.S.A. 40:6A-1 *et seq.* provides that in the event the municipality incurs and pays an expense in excess of $150.00 for the representation of an indigent, the municipal attorney may file a notice with the Clerk of the Superior Court as to the amount of the lien to be placed against the defendant for reimbusement to the municipality.

EXHIBIT 7

APPLICATION TO ESTABLISH INDIGENCY (FORM 5A)

PUBLIC DEFENDER   ASSIGNMENT OF COUNSEL   PAY FINE IN INSTALLMENTS

COURT_____ COUNTY_____

NAME (Please Print)_____

CHARGES_____ IND.#/COMP.#_____ TRAF. TIC. #_____

HAVE YOU EVER BEEN KNOWN BY, ARRESTED UNDER OR USED ANY OTHER NAME?
SPECIFY_____

ADDRESS_____ APT./FLOOR_____ PHONE_____
       (Street)

_____ JAIL_____ BAIL (amt. posted)_____
(Municipality)   (State)   (Zip)

HEIGHT_____ WEIGHT_____ RACE_____ SEX_____

DATE OF BIRTH_____ PLACE OF BIRTH_____ SOCIAL SECURITY #_____

ARE PRESENTLY ON PROBATION?_____ OR PAROLE?_____ (Specify)

MARRIED_____ SPOUSE'S NAME_____ NUMBER OF CHILDREN_____

ARRESTING AGENCY_____ WHERE ARRESTED_____ DATE OF ARREST_____

NAMES OF PERSONS ARRESTED WITH YOU_____

DO YOU HAVE ANY OTHER PENDING CHARGES IN ANY JURISDICTION? (Specify)_____

ARE YOU PRESENTLY EMPLOYED?_____

PRESENT JOB OR LAST EMPLOYER_____
                          (Name & Address)

MONTHLY EMPLOYMENT EARNINGS _____ DO YOU RECEIVE CHILD SUPPORT? ____
OR ALIMONY? _____

IS THE CHILD SUPPORT BY COURT ORDER?____ AMOUNT OF SUPPORT OR ALIMONY_____

IS SPOUSE AND/OR CHILDREN EMPLOYED? _____ WHERE_____

SALARY_____

OTHER INCOME (Welfare, Soc. Sec. VA, Unemp. Ins., Disability, Work. Comp., Stocks, Bonds, etc.)
Specify Type & Value:_____

DO YOU OWN PERSONAL PROPERTY (Auto, jewelry, furs, motorcycles, trucks, etc.) Specify type & value:_____

DO YOU OWN A HOUSE OR LAND?_____ DO YOU RENT?_____

ADDRESS_____ VALUE (If you own) _____
MONTHLY RENT OR MORT._____

MAJOR DEBTS, LOANS, BILLS_____

NAME(S) OF BANKS WHERE YOU HAVE ACCOUNT(S):_____

AMOUNT_____ CASH ON HAND_____

EXHIBIT 7 (Continued)

HAVE YOU EVER BEFORE BEEN REPRESENTED BY AN ATTORNEY?_____
IF SO NAME _____

DATE OF REPRESENTATION _____

CERTIFICATION R. 1:4-4(b)

I certify that the foregoing statements made by me are true. I am aware that if any of the foregoing statements made by me are willfully false, I am subject to punishment.

_____   _____
              DATE   DEFENDANT'S SIGNATURE

If defendant is charged with a non-indictable offense(s) only, the judge is to make the determination as to indigence. However, if the defendant is charged with an **indictable** offense, have him check the Public Defender box, complete the application, and then refer it to the Office of the Public Defender.

FIRST APPEARANCES, ARRAIGNMENTS

The initial process in the Municipal Court is either a warrant or summons. **Exhibit 8** is a complaint/warrant or CDR-2 and **Exhibit 9** is a complaint/summons or CDR-1, both of which are used for non-traffic offenses.

The arraignment consists of reading the complaint or stating the substance of the charge to the defendant and must be done in open court. R. 7:4-2(a)(1). After the reading of the complaint, the defendant shall be called upon to plead thereto provided the offense is within the jurisdiction of the Municipal Court and will be tried there. If the matter is beyond the jurisdiction of the Municipal Court, the arraignment will be held in the Superior Court after an indictment has been returned. R. 3:9-1.

When representing a defendant who wishes to plead not guilty, an attorney may, at or before arraignment, file a statement that the defendant has received a copy of the Complaint, has read it or had it read or explained to him, understands the substance of the charge and enters a plea. R. 7:4-2(a)(2).

A defendant may plead either guilty or not guilty, but the court, in its discretion, may refuse to accept a plea of guilty. The court shall not accept a guilty plea without first addressing the defendant personally and determining whether the plea was made voluntarily and with an understanding of the nature of the charge and consequences of the plea. The Court must also be satisfied a factual basis for the plea exists. If the defendant refuses to plead or stands mute the court shall enter a plea of not guilty. R. 7:4-2(b).

Pursuant to R. 3:9-1, arraignments are conducted in the Superior Courts on indicted matters. The Municipal Court will usually conduct a "first appearance" on indictable matters where the court will explain the charges and ascertain whether the defendant has obtained counsel. If the defendant has not obtained counsel, the defendant is advised of the right to apply for a Public Defender and of the right to remain silent. The Municipal Court will also inform the defendant of the existence of the Pretrial Intervention program. At this time, it may also be appropriate to request a bail reduction, if bail has not yet been posted. Some municipal courts will allow an attorney to enter a letter of representation and waive the first appearance.

EXHIBIT 8

The State of New Jersey vs. W366642

POLICE CASE NO.	
COURT	
COUNTY OF	N.J.
COURT CODE NUMBER	
COURT DOCKET NUMBER(S) C—	

Defendant / Alias _____
Address _____
City, State _____ SS No _____
Date of birth _____ Date of arrest _____

Number of co-defendants _____ Dr. Lic.# _____ SBI No _____

COMPLAINT

Complainant: _____ (NAME OF COMPLAINANT) of _____ (IDENTIFY DEPARTMENT OR AGENCY REPRESENTED)

Residing at _____ (ADDRESS OF PRIVATE CITIZEN COMPLAINANT)

Upon oath says that, to the best of (his) (her) knowledge, information and belief, the named defendant on or about the _____ day of _____, 19 _____, in the _____ of _____ [MUNICIPAL CODE NO] _____ County of _____ N.J did;

Charge Number 1 N.J.S.	Charge Number 2 N.J.S.	Charge Number 3 N.J.S.
Charge Number 1 As Amended N.J.S.	Charge Number 2 As Amended N.J.S.	Charge Number 3 As Amended N.J.S.

Subscribed and sworn to before me this _____ day of _____, 19 _____

Signed _____ (NAME AND TITLE OF PERSON ADMINISTERING OATH)
Signed _____ COMPLAINANT

To any peace officer or other authorized person: Pursuant to this warrant, you are hereby commanded to arrest the named defendant and bring (him)(her) forthwith before this court to answer the foregoing complaint.

Bail has been fixed by _____ in the amount of $ _____ (Specify condition of release, e.g. R.O.R.)
Date Warrant Issued _____
Court Appearance Date _____ Time _____ (AM)(PM) _____
SIGNATURE OF JUDGE OR CLERK

COURT ACTION (Wherein judgment or Conditional Discharge is entered in this court)

DATE OF FIRST APPEARANCE

CHARGES	WAIVER INDT JURY	PLEA	DATE OF PLEA	ADJUDICATION OF COND DISCH	DATE	COND DISCHARGE TERM	JAIL TERM	SUSP	FINE	SUSP	COSTS	SUSP	PROBATION TERM	SUSP
Number 1														
Number 2														
Number 3														

OTHER COURT ACTION | Total DEDR Penalty Amount: | Total Violent Crimes Penalty Amount:

| DATE | DEFENDANT DISCHARGED AS TO PROBABLE CAUSE PROSECUTOR GIVEN PRIOR NOTICE | Total Lab Fee | Restitution | DL. Susp. | Institution to Which Sentenced |
| DATE | COMPLAINT REFERRED TO PROSECUTOR | Community Service | Conditional Disch. Fee | | JAIL TIME CREDIT |

Other (specify) _____

BAIL INFORMATION

| DATE | AMOUNT BAIL SET | REL ON BAIL | R.O.R. | COMMITTED DEFAULT | COMMITTED WITHOUT BAIL | PLACE COMMITTED |

SURETY COMPANY - PERSON POSTING BAIL - RELEASED IN CUSTODY OF - ADDRESS

PROSECUTING ATTORNEY AND DEFENSE COUNSEL INFORMATION

| PROSECUTING ATTORNEY | NONE 1 | STATE 2 | COUNTY 3 | MUNICIPAL 4 | OTHER 5 | DEFENSE COUNSEL | NONE 1 | RETAINED 2 | PUBLIC DEFENDER 3 | ASSIGNED 4 | OTHER 5 |

MISCELLANEOUS INFORMATION

List Companion CDR numbers (Including Co-defendants).

JUDGE _____ DATE _____

NJ / CDR-2 (REV. 2-90) ORIGINAL

24/Municipal Court

EXHIBIT 9

The State of New Jersey vs. S287743

POLICE CASE NO.	
COURT	
COUNTY OF	N.J.
COURT CODE NUMBER	
COURT DOCKET NUMBER(S) C—	

Defendant / Alias _____
Address _____
City, State _____ SS No. _____
Date of birth _____ Date of arrest _____

Number of co-defendants _____ Dr. Lic.# _____ SBI No. _____

COMPLAINT

Complainant: _____ (NAME OF COMPLAINANT) of _____ (IDENTIFY DEPARTMENT OR AGENCY REPRESENTED)

Residing at _____ (ADDRESS OF PRIVATE CITIZEN COMPLAINANT)

Upon oath says that, to the best of (his) (her) knowledge, information and belief, the named defendant on or about the _____ day of _____, 19___, in the _____ of _____ [MUNICIPAL CODE NO] County of _____ N.J. did;

Charge Number 1 N.J.S.	Charge Number 2 N.J.S.	Charge Number 3 N.J.S.
Charge Number 1 As Amended N.J.S.	Charge Number 2 As Amended N.J.S.	Charge Number 3 As Amended N.J.S.

Subscribed and sworn to before me this _____ day of _____, 19___.

Signed _____ (NAME AND TITLE OF PERSON ADMINISTERING OATH) Signed _____ (COMPLAINANT)

You are hereby summoned to appear before this court to answer the above complaint. If you fail to appear on the date and at the time stated, a warrant will be issued for your arrest.

Date summons issued _____ Date to appear _____ Time _____ (AM)(PM)

_____ (SIGNATURE OF PERSON ISSUING SUMMONS) / (TITLE)

COURT ACTION (Wherein judgment or Conditional Discharge is entered in this court)

DATE OF FIRST APPEARANCE

CHARGES	WAIVER INDT/JURY	PLEA	DATE OF PLEA	ADJUDICATION OR COND DISCH	DATE	COND DISCHARGE TERM	JAIL TERM	SUSP	FINE	SUSP	COSTS	SUSP	PROBATION TERM	SUSP
Number 1														
Number 2														
Number 3														

OTHER COURT ACTION Total DEDR Penalty Amount: _____ Total Violent Crimes Penalty Amount: _____

DATE	DEFENDANT DISCHARGED AS TO PROBABLE CAUSE PROSECUTOR GIVEN PRIOR NOTICE	Total Lab Fee	Restitution	DL. Susp.	Institution to Which Sentenced
DATE	COMPLAINT REFERRED TO PROSECUTOR	Community Service	Conditional Disch. Fee		JAIL TIME CREDIT

Other (specify) _____

BAIL INFORMATION

DATE	AMOUNT BAIL SET	REL ON BAIL	R.O.R.	COMMITTED DEFAULT	COMMITTED WITHOUT BAIL	PLACE COMMITTED

SURETY COMPANY - PERSON POSTING BAIL - RELEASED IN CUSTODY OF - ADDRESS

PROSECUTING ATTORNEY AND DEFENSE COUNSEL INFORMATION

PROSECUTING ATTORNEY	NONE	STATE	COUNTY	MUNICIPAL	OTHER	DEFENSE COUNSEL	NONE	RETAINED	PUBLIC DEFENDER	ASSIGNED	OTHER

MISCELLANEOUS INFORMATION

List Companion CDR numbers (Including Co-defendants).

_____ JUDGE   _____ DATE

NJ / CDR 1 (REV. 2-90)   ORIGINAL

BAIL

The purpose of bail is to insure the defendant's appearance in court on the return date of the complaint. The posting of bail is usually required in those instances where a warrant or initial process has issued. Charges placed on summonses do not normally require bail. The following guidelines are set forth in R. 3:3-1(b) to determine whether a summons or warrant should issue.

Whenever an application for a warrant or summons is made before a Judge or Clerk authorized to issue a warrant, a summons should issue unless the Judge, Court Clerk or Deputy Court Clerk finds any of the following conditions:

1. The accused is charged with murder, kidnapping, aggravated manslaughter, manslaughter, robbery, aggravated sexual assault, sexual assault, aggravated criminal sexual contact, aggravated assault, aggravated arson, arson, burglary, violations of the Controlled Dangerous Substances Act, excluding minor possessory offenses, any crime involving the possession or use of a firearm, or conspiracies or attempts to commit such crimes;

2. The accused has previously failed to respond to a summons;

3. The Judge, Court Clerk or Deputy Court Clerk has reason to believe that the defendant is dangerous to himself or herself, to others or to property;

4. There are one or more outstanding arrest warrants for the accused;

5. The whereabouts of the accused are unknown and an arrest warrant is necessary to subject him to the jurisdiction of the court.

6. The Judge, Clerk, or Deputy Court Clerk has reason to believe that the accused will not appear in response to a summons.

Pursuant to R. 3:26-2 and R. 7:5-1 *et seq.*, the Municipal Court Judge has the authority, with limitations, to set bail in criminal cases. Bail for the following offenses may not be set in Municipal Court, but must be established by the Superior Court:

1. Murder
2. Kidnapping
3. Manslaughter
4. Aggravated Manslaughter
5. Aggravated Sexual Assault
6. Sexual Assault
7. Aggravated Criminal Sexual Contact
8. A person arrested in an extradition proceeding

It is not unusual for an attorney's initial contact or entry into a case to result from the defendant or the defendant's relatives' request to make an application for, or to arrange for, the posting of bail or a reduction of bail. In those instances where the Municipal Court Judge has the authority to set bail, the Judge may also reduce same upon application of the attorney or defendant. This request may be made in open court. Although technically all Municipal Court Judges have the authority to reduce bail set by any other Municipal Court Judge within the same county, it is rarely done. As a matter of courtesy, you should first attempt to contact the Municipal Court Judge who originally set bail to make an application for a bail reduction. Bail may also be reduced by the Judge of the municipality in which the defendant resides, the theory being that this Judge is in a better position to assess whether the defendant will appear on the trial date. This provision is also rarely invoked as a matter of practice.

The Superior Court also has concurrent jurisdiction to reduce any bail set by the Municipal Court Judge or to release the defendant on his or her own recognizance. If a defendant is committed to jail because bail was denied, only a Superior Court Judge may thereafter admit the defendant to bail. Given that the primary purpose of bail is to insure the defendant's appearance in court, Municipal and Superior Court Judges are usually amenable to seriously consider an attorney's request to reduce bail. However, it should again be noted that once an attorney has made an appearance or request to reduce bail, the attorney may be compelled to continue representing the defendant throughout the proceedings regardless of whether the attorney has been paid to do so. It is, therefore, not a good practice to attempt to enter a case for the sole purpose of reducing bail.

For indictable offenses some counties or vicinages have established a "bail schedule" which is utilized by Municipal Court Judges, Clerks, Deputy Clerks or police officers "in charge" for the purpose of setting bail. This schedule which may vary from county to county is merely a guideline and is not sacrosanct. A Municipal Court Judge, at his or her discretion, may set a bail which is either higher or lower than that which is set forth on the bail schedule, taking into account the nature of the crime charged, the defendant's character and previous criminal record, as well as any other relevant circumstances. **Exhibit 10** is the statewide municipal bail schedule. (N.J.S.A. 2A:162-1 *et seq.*)

Bail for crimes of the fourth degree or a disorderly persons offense or petty disorderly persons offense shall not exceed $2,500 unless the court finds that the person arrested represents a serious threat to the physical safety of the persons involved or to potential evidence, or unless the court feels that bail of $2,500 will not reasonably insure the defendant's appearance. The court shall place on the record the specific reasons for imposing bail in excess of $2,500 for offenses of the fourth degree or less.

Aside from bail, a defendant may be released on his or her own recognizance for a stated amount. Bail may also be obtained solely upon the signature of an individual surety or the posting of a real estate bond. A sample real property bond form is shown in **Exhibit 11** and sample recognizance is shown in **Exhibit 12**. Bail may also be arranged through a professional bail bondsman. A list of the approved bondsmen may be obtained directly from the Court Clerk, or by reference to the New Jersey Lawyer's Diary.

The ten percent bail program, in which the defendant is required to post only 10% of the stated bail with a minimum of $25.00, originally began as a pilot program. Due to its success, however, it is now effective almost statewide. The result of the 10% program has been to minimize the need for professional bail bondsmen, although bail bondsmen are still available.

Even though the 10% bail program has been heartily endorsed by the Supreme Court of New Jersey, the Judge retains the discretion to exclude a defendant from participating in this program for sound reasons and sufficient findings. The state has the burden of proving grounds for excluding the defendant from the 10% program and such proofs must rise to the level of a "preponderance of the evidence." *State v. Casavina*, 163 N.J. Super. 27 (App. Div. 1978). Out-of-state defendants are entitled to 10% bail, but admission to the program may be refused at the discretion of the Judge.

When bail is set in the Municipal Court for an indictable offense, the bail is forwarded to the County Clerk and held there until the charges have been resolved. If the charge is downgraded to a non-indictable offense and is returned to the Municipal Court for hearing and disposition, the bail is also returned to the Municipal Court.

Almost all, if not all, counties have a "bail visit" in their respective county jails to review the bail of defendants who remain in jail awaiting the posting of bail. The visit is usually conducted by the bail unit of the County Probation Department. This procedure facilitates releasing defendants on a lower bail or their own recognizance to avoid holding them in jail for an inappropriate period of time.

If bail is posted, it is not improper for an attorney to obtain an "Assignment of Bail" from the owner of the bail monies to insure payment of attorney's fees. With an Assignment of Bail, as shown in **Exhibit 13,** the bail essentially becomes the property of the attorney. It is not advisable, however, that an attorney post bail for a client. Such posting may raise an ethical question as to whether the attorney has a personal and financial interest in the outcome of the matter.

Once the case has been decided, posted bail may also be used to satisfy monetary fines or costs, provided that the bail is the property of the defendant. **Exhibit 14** is an Authorization to Apply Bail Against Fines and Costs and Waiver of Rights. If the bail is the property of another, it may not be applied toward, or in satisfaction of, fines and costs unless the owner of the bail consents.

If the defendant fails to appear after posting 10%, the amount posted may be forfeited by the court, and technically the defendant then becomes indebted to the court for the remaining 90%. If 10% bail has been posted by someone other than the defendant, only the defaulting defendant is liable for the remaining 90%. *State v. Moncrieffe,* 158 N.J. Super. 528 (App. Div. 1978). In the event that the defendant does not appear, the bail may be forfeited and the matter may be dismissed pursuant to R. 7:4-2(i), or a new warrant with another bail may be issued.

Additionally, the Judge may impose conditions on bail or on release, such as entering into a drug or alcohol program, not harassing the complainant, or reporting telephonically to the Probation Department on a weekly basis.

EXHIBIT 10

RANGE

	Minimum	Maximum
Disorderly Person Offenses and Contempt	$250.00	$500.00
Ordinance Violation	$200.00	$500.00
Petty Disorderly Persons	$125.00	$250.00

Traffic Offenses

1. Where no minimum penalty provided by law — $25.00 — $100.00

2. Where statute provides a minimum mandatory fine, bail may not exceed the minimum penalty.

The court for good cause shown may impose a lower or higher bail and R. 3:26-4(a) (10% bail) shall apply unless otherwise directed by the Assignment Judge.

EXHIBIT 11

OFFICE OF THE
SHERIFF OF GLOUCESTER COUNTY

RECORD OF PROPERTY PLEDGED AS SECURITY FOR BAIL.

PROPOSED SURETY:

Book _____ Page _____ of the records of Gloucester County of Deed and Property offered for Security by

Name_____

Address_____

Name_____

Address_____

Description:

Assessed Valuation:_____

Mortgages of record affecting above premises:_____
_____

Judgments of record in County Clerk's Office:_____
_____

Taxes—Amounts and Years:_____

Water Rents:_____

Mechanics Liens or Attachments:_____

Pending Bail Bonds:_____

Other Liabilities:_____

EXHIBIT 11 (Continued)

This is to certify that the information as stated above is the result of a search of indices in the Gloucester County Clerk's Office against_____

_____

_____ from_____ to _____

_____
Title Examiner

Bail_____

Defendant_____

Date_____

Accepted   )
Not Accepted)_____

EXHIBIT 12

The State of New Jersey

vs.

_____
Defendant

_____
Charge

MUNICIPAL COURT
_____ of _____

County of _____

RECOGNIZANCE
(r.1 13.3(b) R 3:36-4(a) r 3:26-5)

☐ Real Property Bond   ☐ 10% Cash Deposit

State of New Jersey,   )
) ss.   ☐ R.O.R.   ☐ Corporate Surety   ☐ Full Cash Bail
County of _____   )

(check applicable)

We, the undersigned, jointly and severally acknowledge ourselves to be indebted to the State of New Jersey in the sum of _____ Dollars ($ _____) to be made and levied of our and each of our goods, moneys, chattels and real estate if default be made in the following conditions, to wit:

The Conditions of this Recognizance are that the Defendant shall personally be and appear at all stages of the proceedings and until the final determination of the cause and that the Defendant and Surety agree to immediately notify the Court of change of address; and if the Defendant and Surety comply with these Conditions, then this Recognizance is to be void.

We, the undersigned, principals and sureties, do hereby acknowledge that by entering into this Recognizance that they submit themselves to the jurisdiction of this Court; that they irrevocably appoint the Clerk of the Court having jurisdiction of this cause as his agent upon whom papers affecting each of their liability on the Recognizance may be served; that each of them waive a Jury Trial; that the Liability of the Principal and Surety may be enforced by Motion of this action, if one is pending without the necessity of an independent action; and that the Motion may be served on the Principal and Surety by mailing it by ordinary mail to the Clerk of the Court, who shall forthwith mail a copy thereof by ordinary mail to the Principal and Surety at the address stated herein.

The said Principal and Surety further acknowledge that Execution may issue thereon or payment secured as provided by the Rules Governing the Courts of the State of New Jersey or by other laws of the State of New Jersey.

If a 10% Cash Bail Deposit has been posted by a surety other than the defendant, the liability of the surety posting such 10% Cash Bail Deposit is hereby limited to the amount of the deposit.

EXHIBIT 12 (Continued)

This Recognizance is signed, sealed and delivered this _____ day of _____ 19 ____.

_____ (L.S.)   _____
Defendant, as Principal   Address of Defendant

_____ (L.S.)   _____
Surety   Address of Surety

APPROVED AND ADMITTED TO BAIL:

_____
(Judge) (Clerk) (Other Authority)

If Corporate Surety affix Corporate Seal and Power of Attorney.

I have been advised that the posting of a 10% Cash Deposit of the Full Amount of Bail is available to me.

By_____   _____
(Authorized Agent)   (Signature of Defendant)

EXHIBIT 13

_____
_____
_____
_____
_____

STATE OF NEW JERSEY,	:	SUPERIOR COURT OF NEW JERSEY
	:	LAW DIVISION, CRIMINAL
Plaintiff,	:	COUNTY
v.	:	
	:	
Defendant(s).	:	ASSIGNMENT OF BAIL

STATE OF NEW JERSEY
                     ss.
COUNTY OF

Bail having been set in the total amount of _____ DOLLARS ($) on the above mentioned matter, and the defendant(s) having posted the total of _____ DOLLARS ($), as ten percent (10%) of the bail under the prevailing system, by and through _____, it is the intention of the undersigned to assign _____ DOLLARS ($), as counsel fees to _____, upon the release of said funds at the completion of the above captioned matter either by the Clerk of the Municipal Court of _____ or by the _____ County Clerk, with the check being made out in the attorney's name.

_____
(Signed by Defendant/Owner of Bail)

Sworn to and subscribed before me
this   day of   , 19   .

_____

EXHIBIT 14

MUNICIPAL COURT OF MOUNT EPHRAIM
121 S. Black Horse Pike • Mount Ephraim, NJ 08059
(609) 931-0994

AUTHORIZATION TO APPLY BAIL AGAINST FINE(S) AND COSTS and WAIVER OF RIGHTS

STATE OF NEW JERSEY
v.

_____
DEFENDANT

Docket No. _____

Summons No. _____

I am the Defendant and have not appeared in the above municipal court where I was charged with the following offenses(s);

By signing this paper, I understand that:
1. I give up my right to a trial and plead guilty.
2. I give up my right to have a lawyer.
3. For other than a non-traffic or parking offense, a record of my conviction will be sent to the Division of Motor Vehicles of the State of New Jersey and will become part of my driving record. If I received my license to drive from another state, a record of my conviction, for other than a non-traffic or parking offense, will be sent to the Commissioner of Motor Vehicles of that state.
4. I admit that I have failed to appear in Court and may be subject to a penalty for additional costs of $_____ ($50 for a non-taffic or parking offense, $25 for a moving offence, $15 for a parking offense, unless the judge otherwise orders) for the issuance of a bench warrant, $10 for the issuance of a Failure to Appear notice, in addition to the fines and costs listed in the statewide violations schedule or the violations schedule adopted by the above Municipal Court.

I request and authorize the Municipal Court Administrator to apply the bail posted against fines and costs owed. I further certify that the address and driver's license number given below are correct.

Date _____

_____
DEFENDANT (Signature)

_____
MAILING ADDRESS

_____

_____
DRIVER'S LICENSE NO.

Administrative Office of the Courts
CP0109 (1/88)

White: Defendant Copy
Canary: Court Copy

from Municipal Record Service (609) 547-2444

PREPARATION FOR TRIAL

The success or failure of a Municipal Court attorney in the trial of contested cases is, in large part, controlled directly by the attorney's preparation. There is no substitute for preparation and no excuse for not being prepared.

The first step in preparing for trial is to become familiar with the facts of the case. An attorney's unfamiliarity with the facts will become evident and prove embarrassing during the trial. Prior to trial, take detailed notes as the client relates the incident. Interview available witnesses. In the event a favorable witness will not appear voluntarily, the witness should be subpoenaed, but not without first interviewing the witness, for obvious reasons. If the witness appears involuntarily, his testimony may be affected.

Prepare the client for the court appearance by reviewing the testimony and explaining the procedure which the court will follow so that the client's unfamiliarity is not so overwhelming so as to distract him. The attorney should try his or her best to put the client and witnesses at ease.

It may be necessary for the attorney to do further investigation, such as requesting discovery or visiting the scene of the accident and taking photographs. The attorney may request that the client provide the necessary photographs of the vehicle or the scene, but try to have photographs accurately reflect the conditions which existed on the day of the offense, especially as to weather conditions, time of day, traffic volume, etc. If the client is charged with driving while under the influence and a videotape was made at arrest, view the videotape in the presence of the client, prior to trial. It will be necessary to contact the police department directly to arrange for a pre-trial viewing of the videotape, for which there is no charge.

Even though the attorney may have handled ten, twenty, or one hundred similar cases involving an alleged violation of a specific statute or regarding a specific location, the attorney should always reread the statute or revisit the scene with the specific facts in mind. The attorney also should list the elements of the offense which the state must prove and the attorney's observations. In doing so, the attorney should also reread the annotations and applicable case law to insure familiarity with any possible defenses the client may have. The attorney should also review the case from the point of view of the prosecution to determine its weaknesses and prepare the client accordingly. If there have been postponements, make sure you again review the testimony and law prior to trial.

In the event documentary evidence is required, such as an insurance card, registration, etc., make sure it is available at the time of trial. A copy of the client's driving abstract also should be obtained in traffic cases and a letter requesting an abstract is illustrated in **Exhibit 15**. When requesting an abstract, the attorney should specify that he or she wants a ten-year abstract, otherwise he or she will be sent a three-year abstract. Courts are sent ten-year abstracts. If the facts dictate the use of an expert the attorney should review the case prior to trial and make arrangements to insure the expert's attendance.

If the attorney has located an important reported case which is relevant to the pending case, it would be appropriate to provide a copy to the court with the appropriate underlinings or highlighting for the Judge's use. If defense counsel plans to cite an unpublished opinion, he or she must not only provide a copy to the prosecutor and court, but must also, without demand, provide copies of any other unpublished opinions which are relevant in that they are in opposition to the case.

EXHIBIT 15

NEW JERSEY DIVISION OF MOTOR VEHICLES
Abstract Department
137 East State Street
Trenton, New Jersey 08666

                                        Re: James Smith
                                                123 Main Street
                                                Madison, New Jersey
                                                DL #S1234 46789 10525

Dear Sir:

Enclosed is my check for $_____. I ask that you forward to my office at the above address a certified copy of the above named's driving abstract for the last ten (10) years along with a certified mailing list and notice suspension, if applicable.

Your cooperation in this matter is most appreciated.

                                                                      Very truly yours,

cc: Mr. James Smith

VIOLATIONS BUREAU/MUNICIPAL MANDATORY PENALTIES

Pursuant to R. 7:7-1 the Municipal Courts may establish a Violations Bureau for the purpose of accepting appearances, waivers of trial, pleas of guilty and payments of fines and costs in non-indictable offenses. All Municipal Courts have established a Violations Bureau. The limits on types of offenses which may be disposed of through the Violations Bureau are described in R. 7:7-3 and a Violations Schedule has been approved and published. The Schedule sets forth those violations, with the accompanying fines and costs, which may be paid directly through the Violations Bureau of the Municipal Court (see **Exhibit 16**). These are also listed in the New Jersey Lawyers Diary. If a plea of not guilty, or in some instances, a guilty plea, is enterd before a Municipal Court Judge, the Judge is not limited to those fines and costs as set forth in the schedule. The Schedule is applicable only if paid through the Violations Bureau.

If the defendant has several summonses, it may be advisable to pay the uncontested summonses through the Violations Bureau prior to trial because the fines and costs set forth in the Schedule are minimums. In those instances, however, where a plea of guilty may adversely affect the defense to a contested summons, such as pleading guilty to speeding or careless driving where a drunken driving summons is contested on the grounds of failure to prove operation, the attorney should not have the defendant plead guilty to the lesser offense, nor should the defendant plead guilty to a lesser included offense.

Each violation on the schedule has a maximum penalty prescribed in Title 39 which does not appear on the schedule. The attorney should be familiar with the maximum penalties so that a Judge does not impose a sentence in excess of the maximum. There are other violations where a minimum mandatory penalty is also prescribed, but are not payable through the Violations Bureau. These are embodied in **Exhibit 17**. These can also be found in the New Jersey Lawyers Diary.

In addition, each Municipal Judge has the authority to establish a Violations Schedule for frequently violated local ordinances, such as failure to license a dog, local parking violations, etc. Such schedules are subject to approval by the Assignment Judge and must be posted in the Violations Bureau.

The penalties for violations of many sections of Title 39 are set forth elsewhere in Title 39 and not in the section as charged. Following are the two main penalty provisions in Title 39:

N.J.S.A. 39:4-104 provides: "A person violating a section of this article shall, for each violation, be subject to a fine of not less than $50.00 or more than $200.00 or imprisonment for a period not exceeding 15 days, or both, except as herein otherwise provided."

And N.J.S.A. 39:4-203 reads:

> For a violation of a provision of this chapter or any supplement thereto for which no specific penalty is provided, the offender shall be liable to a penalty of not more than $50.00 or imprisonment for a term not exceeding 15 days or both; except that for a violation of a section of article 11, 13, 14, or 17 of this chapter or any supplement thereto for which no specific penalty is provided, the offender shall be liable to a penalty of not less than $50.00 or more than $200.00 or imprisonment for a term not exceeding 15 days or both.

38/Municipal Court

EXHIBIT 16

REV. 9/1/93

NOTICE

Pursuant to *R.* 7:7-3, the following Violations Bureau Schedule has been amended on August 26, 1993, to be effective September 1, 1993, and shall be prominently posted at the location of each Violations Bureau.

STATE OF NEW JERSEY
STATEWIDE VIOLATIONS BUREAU SCHEDULE
MOTOR VEHICLE SECTION

TITLE 39		PENALTY
3-4	Driving or parking unregistered motor vehicle	$33.00
3-9a	Failure to notify change in name	21.00
3-9a	Failure to endorse license	37.00
3-10	Driving with an expired license (When paying through the Violations Bureau the defendant is required to attach a photocopy of a valid driver's license to the summons.)	33.00
3-11	Conditional license violation	37.00
3-17	Failure of possession of driver's license and/or registration (Non-resident motorists)	33.00
3-20	Excess weight	$517
	Plus $100 for each 1,000 lbs. or fraction thereof	
3-20	Speed Violation Same Penalties as *N.J.S.A.* 39:4-98	
3-29	Failure of possession of driver's license and/or registration and/or insurance identification card. (Note—If violation is for more than one offense involving license, registration or insurance card, they are separate offenses and the Penalty indicated is for each offense.)	33.00
3-29	Refusal to exhibit driver's license and/or registration and/or insurance identification card (Note—If a violation is for more than one offense involving license, registration or insurance card, they are separate offenses and the Penalty indicated is for each offense.)	33.00
3-32	Failure to replace lost, destroyed or defaced driver's plates	33.00
3-33	Display of unclear, indistinct license plates—(Limited to this portion of Statute only.)	33.00
3-36	Failure to notify complete change of address	21.00
3-38	Use of other marker (Limited to this portion of Statute only.)	42.00
3-44	Vehicle in unsafe condition	33.00
3-47	Improper lighting equipment; altering equipment	33.00
3-49	Headlights	33.00
3-50	Improper use of emergency lights (Limited to subsections (a) and (b) only.)	33.00
3-51	Improper auxiliary driving lamps	33.00

EXHIBIT 16 (Continued)

TITLE 39

Section	Description	Penalty
3-52	Improper additional lighting equipment and use thereof	33.00
3-53	Spot lamps	33.00
3-54	Special restrictions on lights	33.00
3-55	Improper operation with alternate road lighting equipment	33.00
3-56	Operating without front lighted lamps	33.00
3-57	Improper single beam lighting	33.00
3-58	Improper multiple beam headlights	33.00
3-59	No light beam indicator	33.00
3-60	Improper use of high and low headlight beams	33.00
3-61	Lamps and reflectors required on particular vehicles	33.00
3-61.1	Mounting of lamps and reflectors	33.00
3-61.2	Combination of lighting devices and reflectors; prohibited combinations	33.00
3-61.3	Stop lamps: construction, placement and use	33.00
3-61.4	Overhanging loads; placement and use of red lamps and flags	33.00
3-62	Unlighted lamps on parked vehicle	33.00
3-64	Emergency warning light equipment	33.00
3-64.3	Signals to flash simultaneously when stopped for transacting business	33.00
3-65	Lamps on other vehicle and equipment	33.00
3-66	Maintenance of lamps	33.00
3-69	Horns and warning devices	33.00
3-70	Noisy muffler	33.00
3-71	Mirrors	33.00
3-72	Tire Equipment	33.00
3-73	Tire chains	33.00
3-74	Obstruction of windshield for vision	33.00
3-75	Safety glass requirement	33.00
3-76.2	Safety belt equipment	33.00
3-76.2a	Failure to Use a Child Passenger Restraint when transporting a Child under the age of five	37.00
3-76.2f	Failure to wear seat belt (N.J.S.A. 39:3-76.2j)	37.00
3-76.3	Motorcycles; height of handle bar grips	33.00
3-76.4	Muffler systems for motorcycles	33.00
3-76.5	Footrests and helmet for motorcycle passenger	67.00
3-76.6 to 3-76.10	Motorcycle operation and equipment violations	33.00
3-79.1	Device to prevent throwing of dirt on following vehicles (buses, trucks, trailers)	33.00

EXHIBIT 16 (Continued)

TITLE 39   **PENALTY**

Section	Description	Penalty
3-81*	Use of stud tires—(Limited to this portion of Statute only)	42.00
3-84	Excess weight and dimensional restrictions N.J.S.A. 39:3-84.3 Dimensional violation:	167.00
	Weight violation: According to excess pounds per Statute, but not less than (minimum)	67.00
4-10 to 4-14.2	Bicycles and roller skates	33.00**
4-15 to 4-25.1	Horses and Horse-Drawn vehicles	33.00
4-26 to 4-30	Machinery, vehicles or apparatus of unusual size or weight (Fine to be paid to agency charged with maintenance of road upon which violation occurs).	67.00
4-32 to 4-37.1	Pedestrian violations	33.00**
4-38 to 4-45	Street cars	33.00
4-46	Commercial vehicle—Display of owner's name (Fine to be forwarded to Motor Vehicle Division)	21.00
4-53	Leaving vehicle with engine running	33.00
4-54	Trailers—equipment required, towing, etc. Dimensional restrictions See N.J.S.A. 39:3-84 Excess Weight See N.J.S.A. 39:3-20 & 3-84 as applicable***	42.00
4-55	Action on steep grades and curves	33.00
4-56	Delaying traffic	33.00
4-56.6	Abandonment of vehicle on private property (First paragraph)	37.00
4-57	Failure to comply with direction of officer	33.00
4-58	Vehicle loaded obstructing view	33.00
4-59	Hitch-hiking	33.00
4-60	Soliciting trade or contributions on highway	33.00
4-61	Tailboard riding	33.00
4-62	Leaving curb	33.00
4-64	Throwing matter from vehicles	217.00
4-65	Letting off or taking on persons	33.00

*By regulation of the Director of Motor Vehicles, stud tires shall not be used on a highway earlier than November 15 or later than April 1 of each year.

**The appropriate penalty under the Violations Bureau Schedule is $21 ($10 + $10 court costs + $1 ATS Surcharge) when committed by a juvenile under the age of 17. N.J.S.A. 39:4-203.3.

***If N.J.S.A. 39:3-84 is the applicable statute, the appropriate penalty under the *Violations Bureau Schedule* is $0.02 per pound of the total excess weight if the total excess weight is 10,000 lbs. or less and $0.03 per pound of the total excess weight if the total excess weight is more than 10,000 lbs. but in no event less than $67 ($50 + $15 court costs + $1 ATS surcharge). See N.J.S.A. 39:3-84.3j.

EXHIBIT 16 (Continued)

TITLE 39		PENALTY
4-66	Emerging from alley, driveway or garage	33.00
4-66.1	Yield right-of-way when entering or leaving highway to or from private road or driveway	33.00
4-67	Obstructing passage of vehicles	33.00
4-68	Doors of streetcar or autobus closed	33.00
4-69	Riding on part of truck, bus or vehicle not intended for passengers	33.00
4-71	Driving on sidewalk	33.00
4-72	Stopping on signal from driver of horse	33.00
4-76	Overweight vehicles on bridges (interstate) (Fine to be forwarded to Director of Motor Vehicles) Same Penalties as *N.J.S.A.* 39:3-84	
4-77	Loading so as to spill	37.00
4-78	Carrying metals (Noise)	33.00
4-79	Backing vehicle to curb to unload	33.00
4-80	Disobedience of traffic officer	67.00
4-81	Failure to observe traffic signal	67.00
4-82	Failing to keep right	67.00
4-82.1	Driving on safety island	67.00
4-83	Keeping to right at intersection	67.00
4-84	Passing to right—vehicles moving in opposite directions	67.00
4-85	Passing to the right when overtaking; passing when in line, signals, etc.	67.00
4-85.1	One-way traffic	67.00
4-86	Passing to left of center, on grade or curve	67.00
4-87	Failing to give overtaking vehicle right of way	67.00
4-88	Driving in marked lanes	67.00
4-89	Following: space between trucks (less than 100 ft. outside business or residence district), except to pass	67.00
4-90	Right-of-way at intersection	67.00
4-90.1	Entering or leaving limited access highways improperly	67.00
4-91	Right-of-way emergency vehicles	67.00
4-92	Clearance for, following or parking near emergency vehicles	67.00
4-92.1	Clearance for fire apparatus returning to fire station	67.00
4-94	Railroad employee unnecessarily blocking highway with train	67.00
4-97	Careless driving where no accident involving personal injury (Note—Accident resulting in *personal injury* cannot be paid through the Violations Bureau, *R.* 7:7-3(2) and (5).)	67.00
4-97.1	Slow Speed as blocking traffic	67.00

EXHIBIT 16 (Continued)

TITLE 39   **PENALTY**

4-98   Speeding

(minimum)

Exceeding the limit by:	Penalty
1-15 miles per hour	$67.00
16-20 miles per hour	77.00
21-25 miles per hour	87.00
26-30 miles per hour	97.00
33-35 miles per hour	107.00
36-40 miles per hour	117.00
etc.	etc.

NOTE: Court costs and a $1 ATS surcharge are included on the above penalties. See page 20 of this schedule for allocation of penalty between fine, costs, and $1 ATS surcharge.

4-100	Rate of speed across sidewalk (4 mph)	67.00
4-115	Turns at controlled intersection	67.00
4-116	Special right or left turn	67.00
4-117	Special pedestrian signals—(pedestrian violation)	67.00
	(motorist violation)	67.00
4-119	Failure to observe flashing traffic signals	67.00
4-122	Failure to obey signal of police	67.00
4-123	Right and left-hand turns	67.00
4-124	Failure to turn as indicated by buttons or markers at intersection	67.00
4-125	U-turn on curve or grade or where view obstructed or "No U-Turn" sign	67.00
4-126	Failure to signal before starting, turning or stopping	67.00
4-127	Backing or turning in street	67.00
4-127.1	Stopping at railroad crossing (under certain circumstances)	67.00
4-127.2	Failure to stop for gate at approaches to movable span bridge	67.00
4-128	Failure to make full stop at railroad gate or crossing (buses, school buses, fuel trucks)	37.00
4-135	Parking: direction and side of street; angle parking and one-way street parking	33.00
4-136	Parking on highway; removing disabled vehicle	33.00
4-137	Vehicle without driver; brakes set; motor stopped, etc.	33.00
4-138	Improper parking	
	a. Within intersection	33.00
	b. On a crosswalk	33.00
	c. Safety (bus) zone	33.00
	d. In front of driveway	33.00
	e. Within 25 ft. of crosswalk	33.00
	f. On a sidewalk	33.00
	g. "No Parking" area established by State Highway Department	33.00
	h. Within 50 feet of "Stop" sign	33.00
	i. Within 10 feet of fire hydrant	33.00
	j. Within 50 feet of railroad	33.00

EXHIBIT 16 (Continued)

TITLE 39

		PENALTY
	k. Within 20 feet of driveway entrance to fire station or 75 feet on opposite side of street (when properly signposted)	33.00
	l. Alongside or opposite street excavation or obstruction, causing traffic obstruction when properly signposted	33.00
	m. Double parking	33.00
	n. On a bridge, elevated structure, underpass or immediate approaches (except where space for parking is provided)	33.00
4-139	Loading or unloading for unreasonable period of time	33.00
4-144	Failure to obey "Stop" or "Yield Right-of-Way" signs	67.00
4-145	Failure to yield to vehicle entering Stop or Yield intersection after stopping	67.00
4-208	Improper parking on state property	33.00
4-215	Failure to obey signals, signs or directions	33.00
8-1	Failure to have inspection	33.00
8-4	Failure to make repairs	33.00
8-6	Failure to display approval certificate	33.00

(Fines for inspection violations are forwarded to Division of Motor Vehicles)

N.J.S.A. 54:39A-10 Failure to exhibit identification marker or card—Motor Fuels Use Tax Act (Fine to be forwarded to Division of Motor Vehicles)   30.00

EXHIBIT 16 (Continued)

REV. 9/1/93

GARDEN STATE PARKWAY REGULATIONS
(Coding under New Jersey Administrative Code)

REGULATION NO.
N.J.A.C.   **PENALTY**

Regulation	Description	Penalty
19:8-1.2	Speed limits Same Penalties as *N.J.S.A.* 39:4-98	
19:8-1.3	Retarding traffic	$67.00
19:8-1.4	Uniform direction of traffic	67.00
19:8-1.5	Passing	67.00
19:8-1.6	U-Turns prohibited	67.00
19:8-1.7	Use of median strip and roadside areas prohibited	67.00
19:8-1.8	Parking, Standing, Stopping	33.00
19:8-1.9	Limitations on use of Parkway	
	(a) No vehicle shall enter or leave the Parkway except at access points designated	67.00
	(b) Use of the Parkway and entry thereon by the following is prohibited at all times;	
	1. Pedestrians except on sidewalks, footpaths, and other areas specifically designated	33.00
	2. Vehicles drawn by animals	33.00
	3. All bicycles other than motorcycles	33.00
	4. Animals led, ridden, unattended or driven on the hoof other than horses on bridle paths and leashed dogs in permitted areas	33.00
	5. Vehicles containing animals or poultry not properly confined	33.00
	6. Vehicles whose condition, equipment or tires create a probable hazard to such vehicles or others	33.00
	7. Farm implements and farm machinery whether self-propelled or towed	33.00
	8. Vehicles with improperly secured attachments or loads	33.00
	9. Vehicles with deflated pneumatic tires, metal or solid tires, or caterpillar treads	33.00
	10. Construction equipment other than trucks except by special permit from Authority	33.00
	11. Vehicles, or combination of vehicles, including any load exceeding maximum dimensions: Height—13'6"; Width—8'0"; Length—55'0"	167.00
	12. Motor vehicle in tow or motor vehicles pushing or being pushed on travel portion of road, except the moving of disabled vehicles under State Police direction	33.00
	13. Vehicles with loads extending more than four (4) feet beyond the rear or front of the body	33.00
	14. Vehicles carrying anything on the top, sides, front or rear with lateral projection in excess of twelve (12) inches or vertical projection in excess of twenty-four (24) inches from body of vehicles	33.00
	15. All vehicles except cars, campers, omnibuses, and vehicles entitled to toll-free passage under *N.J.A.C.* 19:8-3.2 (Toll-free passage) are prohibited from the Parkway north of Interchange 105.	33.00

EXHIBIT 16 (Continued)

N.J.A.C.		PENALTY
19:8-1.10	Violation of Civil Defense Regulations	33.00
19:8-1.11	Load limit of structures	42.00
19:8-1.13	Failure to obey traffic control device	67.00
19:8-2.1	Littering	37.00
19:8-2.3	Display of posters prohibited	33.00
19:8-2.4	Parades and Demonstrations prohibited, picnics prohibited, except at designated sites	42.00
19:8-2.5	Hunting and Trapping prohibited	33.00
19:8-2.7	Fires prohibited	33.00
19:8-2.8	Soliciting of alms or contributions prohibited	33.00
19:8-2.9	Hitch-hiking and loitering prohibited	33.00
19:8-2.10	Sales and distribution prohibited	33.00
19:8-3.1	Refusal to pay or evading payment of tolls	42.00

STATUTORY PROVISIONS IN ADDITION TO REGULATIONS

N.J.S.A.		PENALTY
27:12B-18	(b) Careless driving where no accident involving personal injury Same Penalty as *N.J.S.A.* 39:4-97	
	(d) Slow speed so as to impede or block traffic	$67.00
	(f) Failure to obey directions of police officer or traffic device	67.00

NEW JERSEY TURNPIKE REGULATIONS
(Coding under New Jersey Administrative Code)

REGULATION NO.

N.J.A.C.		PENALTY
19:9-1.2	Speed limits Same as *N.J.S.A.* 39:4-98	
19:9-1.3	Traffic Control Devices	67.00
19:9-1.4	Uniform direction of traffic	67.00
19:9-1.5	U-Turns prohibited	67.00
19:9-1.6	Parking, Standing or Stopping	33.00
19:9-1.7	Use of median strip prohibited	67.00
19:9-1.8	Violations of Air Raid precautions	33.00
19:9-1.9	Limitations on use of turnpike	
	1. Pedestrians	33.00
	2. Bicycles	33.00
	3. Motorcycles during adverse weather conditions	33.00
	4. Vehicles drawn by animals	33.00
	5. Animals led, ridden or driven	33.00
	6. Vehicles loaded with animals or poultry not properly confined	33.00
	7. Vehicles with deflated pneumatic tires or with tires in unsafe condition	33.00
	8. Farm implements and machinery whether self-propelled or towed	33.00

EXHIBIT 16 (Continued)

N.J.A.C.		PENALTY
	9. Passenger vehicles or passenger vehicle drawn trailers with improperly secured loads, including loads on top or sides with lateral or horizontal projection in excess of 12" or vertical projection in excess of 24"	33.00
	12. Dimensional specifications	167.00
	14. Vehicles towed by other vehicles, unless in accordance with regulations	33.00
	15. Vehicles with loads extending more than four (4) feet	33.00
	16. Vehicles with improperly secured loads	37.00
	17. Vehicles loaded or operated so that contents may be scattered on roadway	37.00
	18. Vehicles unable to maintain speed of at least 35 mph on level grade	33.00
	19. Vehicles in such condition as to create hazard to other vehicles or to persons	33.00
	20. Certain vehicles banned during adverse weather conditions	33.00
	21. Specified towing violations	33.00
	23. Commercial vehicles overloaded with hay or straw	37.00
19:9-1.10	Littering	37.00
19:9-1.11	Commercial vehicles loaded as to spill, not covered by tarpaulin	37.00
19:9-1.13	Hitch-hiking, loitering	33.00
19:9-1.14	Failure to follow prescribed towing regulations	33.00
19:9-1.17	Turnpike project	67.00
19:9-1.18	Violation of maximum sound levels	107.00
19:9-1.19	Tolls	42.00
19:9-1.20	Records	42.00

STATUTORY PROVISIONS IN ADDITION TO REGULATIONS

N.J.S.A.		PENALTY
27:23-25	Refusal to pay or evading payment of tolls	$42.00
27:23-26	Careless driving where no accident involving personal injury Same Penalty as *N.J.S.A.* 39:4-97	
27:23-27	Slow speed so as to impede or block traffic	67.00
27:23-28	Failure to obey directions of police officer or traffic device	67.00

ATLANTIC CITY EXPRESSWAY—REGULATIONS

REGULATION NO.

N.J.A.C.		PENALTY
19:2-2.1	Speed limits Same Penalty as *N.J.S.A.* 39:4-98	
19:2-2.2	Retarding traffic	$67.00
19:2-3.1	Failure to comply with signs or signals	67.00
19:2-3.2	Uniform direction of traffic	67.00
19:2-3.3	Use of Passing Lane	67.00
19:2-3.4	U-Turns prohibited	67.00
19:2-3.5	Use of median strip and roadside areas	67.00

EXHIBIT 16 (Continued)

N.J.A.C.		PENALTY
19:2-3.6	Parking, Standing or Stopping of vehicles	33.00
19:2-3.7	No vehicle shall enter or leave Expressway except at access points designated	67.00
19:2-3.8	Violation of Civil Defense Regulation	33.00
19:2-4.1	Pedestrian violations	33.00
19:2-4.2	Animals led, ridden or driven on the hoof	33.00
4.3(a)	Restricted vehicles:	
	1. Vehicles drawn by animals	33.00
	2. Bicycles, with or without motors, motor scooters and motorcycles	33.00
	3. Vehicles with livestock not properly confined	33.00
	4. Farm implements or machinery, either self-propelled or towed	33.00
	5. Construction equipment other than trucks	33.00
	6. Vehicles with deflated pneumatic tires, metal or solid tires, or caterpillar treads	33.00
	(Deflated pneumatic)	33.00
	7. Vehicles in tow except as provided in Regulation 4.3	33.00
	8. Vehicles with improperly secured attachments or loads	33.00
	9. Vehicles including any load exceeding maximum dimensions: Length—55'0"; Width—8'0"; Height—13'6"	167.00
	10. Vehicles with loads extending more than four feet (48 inches) beyond the front or rear of the body, or with lateral projections in excess of 12 inches or vertical projections of 24 inches (passenger vehicles only)	33.00
	11. Vehicles whose condition, equipment or tires are considered unsafe for operation	33.00
	12. Vehicles performing emergency or repair service unless acting under contract or permit from the Authority	33.00
19:2-4.6	Tampering with or misusing Emergency Call Box System	33.00
19:2-5.1	Littering	37.00
19:2-5.3	Unauthorized advertising devices and posters	33.00
19:2-5.4	Parades, demonstrations and picnics prohibited	33.00
19:2-5.5	Igniting fires or fireworks prohibited (Court appearance required for use, display or discharge of firearms or weapons)	33.00
19:2-5.6	Hunting, trapping and fishing prohibited	33.00
19:2-5.7	Sales and distribution prohibited	33.00
19:2-5.8	Soliciting of alms prohibited	33.00
19:2-5.9	Hitch-hiking and loitering prohibited	33.00
19:2-6.1	Refusal to pay or evading payment of tolls	42.00

STATUTORY PROVISIONS IN ADDITION TO REGULATIONS

N.J.S.A.		PENALTY
27:12C-37	(B) Careless driving where no accident involving personal injury Same Penalty as N.J.S.A. 39:4-97	
	(D) Slow speed so as to impede or block traffic	$67.00
	(F) Failure to obey directions of police officer or traffic device	67.00

EXHIBIT 16 (Continued)

NOTE: The Penalty listed for the following violations namely:

- Regulation and Registration of Power Vessels (with the exceptions of *N.J.S.A.* 12:7-45) (Speed of power vessels (wash or wave)) and *N.J.S.A.* 12:7-48 (Mooring, grounding or abandoning hulk or derelict)
- Boating Regulations
- Water Skiing
- Personal Watercraft

include a $50.00 VCCB assessment and a $75.00 SNSF assessment as part of the total penalty. The SNSF and VCCB assessments apply to these petty disorderly persons or disorderly persons offenses. (See *N.J.S.A.* 12:7-34.51 and Chapter 220, Laws of 1993). Accordingly, when processing a payment through the Violations Bureau, $50.00 should be allocated for forwarding to the Violent Crimes Compensation Board with the monthly report, and $75.00 should be allocated for forwarding to the Safe Neighborhood Services Fund.

REGULATION AND REGISTRATION OF POWER VESSELS

Statute No. N.J.S.A.		PENALTY
12:7-34.4	Registration of Power Vessels	$190.00
12:7-34.9	Possession and exhibition of license	155.00
12:7-34.38	Numbering of Vessels	190.00
7-34.39(b)	Certificate of number not in possession	190.00
7-34.39(c)	Assigned number not displayed	190.00
7-34.45(a)	Failure to report change of address	155.00
7-34.45(b)	Failure to report change of owner	155.00
7-34.47(c)	Manufacturers' and dealers' numbers, display	190.00
7-34.47c	Display of tax exemption decal	155.00
12:7-45	Speed of power vessels (wash or wave)	65.00
12:7-48	Mooring, grounding or abandoning hulk or derelict	65.00

BOATING REGULATIONS

N.J.A.C.		PENALTY
7:6-1.3	Numbering pattern	190.00
7:6-1.4	Display of numbers on vessels	190.00
7:6-1.8	Transfer of certificate	155.00
7:6-1.15	Display of validation sticker	155.00
7:6-1.16	Numbering of manufacturers' dealers' boats	190.00
7:6-1.17	Numbering of livery boats	190.00
7:6-1.19	Change in address	155.00
7:6-1.21	Renewal of registration	155.00
7:6-1.23	Lifesaving device	190.00

EXHIBIT 16 (Continued)

N.J.A.C.		PENALTY
7:6-1.24	Rotating or sequential flashing light not permitted	190.00
7:6-1.25	Siren shall not be permitted	190.00
7:6-1.26	Muffling device	190.00
7:6-1.27	Use of cutouts	190.00
7:6-1.30	Transversing race course	190.00
7:6-1.31	Speed (wash and wave)	190.00
7:6-1.33	Anchoring near aid to navigation	190.00
7:6-1.34	Anchoring in channels	190.00
7:6-1.36	Riding on vessels in such position as to endanger life or limb	190.00
7:6-1.37	Water-skiing	190.00
7:6-1.38	Finding, recovery of boat; department to be notified	190.00
7:6-1.42	Diving or swimming	190.00

WATER SKIING

7:6-3.1	Beaver Dam Creek, Point Pleasant and Brick Town, Ocean County	190.00
7:6-3.2	Deal Lake, Monmouth County	190.00
7:6-3.3	Grinnel Lake, Sussex County	190.00
7:6-3.4	Indian Lake, Morris County	190.00
7:6-3.5	Paulinskill Lake, Sussex County	190.00
7:6-3.6	Grover's Mill Pond, Mercer County	190.00
7:6-3.7	Lake Mohawk, Sussex County	190.00
7:6-3.8	South Branch of Kettle Creek, Ocean County	190.00
7:6-3.9	Shrewsbury and Navesink Rivers and adjacent areas; tidal waters	190.00

PERSONAL WATERCRAFT

7:6-9.3	(a) Operation between sunrise/sunset, restricted visibility	190.00
	(b) Operation—Point Pleasant Canal	190.00
	(c) Operation—Cape May Canal	190.00
	(d) Proceeding at an unsafe speed	190.00
	(e) Operation—airborne/leaving the water while crossing wake of another vessel within 100 feet of vessel creating the wake	190.00
	(f) Operation—within 50 feet of bathing beach	190.00
	(g) Operation—above idle speed within 50 feet from person in water	190.00
	(h) Towing a waterskier or any device	190.00
	(i) Operation—failure to wear a U.S. Coast Guard Approved Type I, II, III or V Hybrid Personal Flotation Device	190.00

EXHIBIT 16 (Continued)

REV. 9/1/93

**STATE OF NEW JERSEY
STATEWIDE VIOLATIONS BUREAU SCHEDULE
PAYMENT OF STATUTORY PENALTY—R. 4:70-4(a)**

A. FOR PENALTIES INVOLVING TITLE 39 OFFENSES OR THE OPERATION OF A MOTOR VEHICLE

1. Where the statutory penalty does not exceed $50 for each offense, including where the minimum statutory penalty does not exceed $50 for each offense, the defendant at any time before the hearing date, upon presentation of the signed plea of guilty and waiver of trial endorsed on the summons, may pay the penalty and in addition appropriate court costs in the Violations Bureau subject to the limitations prescribed in R. 7:7, including the limitation when the summons is marked to indicate that a court appearance is required.

2. Where the statute provides simply for a **MAXIMUM** penalty not in excess of $50, it may be disposed of by payment through the Violations Bureau of one-half the maximum penalty plus appropriate court costs.

3. Where the statute provides for a **MINIMUM** penalty not in excess of $50, even though the maximum exceeds $50, it may be paid through the Violations Bureau by a payment of the minimum penalty plus the appropriate court costs.

4. Where the statute provides for a **FIXED PENALTY ONLY,** not in excess of $50, it may be paid through the Violations Bureau by a payment of the penalty fixed by statute plus the appropriate court costs.

5. Appropriate court costs shall be established as follows: Where one-half of the **MAXIMUM** penalty is less than $15, court costs shall be $9.50. See item 2 above. For example, if the statute provides for a maximum penalty of $20, the amount to be paid through the Violations Bureau is $21—$10 (one-half of the maximum penalty established by the statute) plus $9.50 court costs, $1.00 ATS Surcharge and $.50 EMT Surcharge. Where the **MINIMUM** penalty is less than $15, court costs shall be $9.50. See item 3 above. For example, if the statute provides for a minimum penalty of $10, the amount to be paid through the Violations Bureau is $21—the $10 minimum penalty plus $9.50 court costs, $1.00 ATS Surcharge and a $.50 EMT Surcharge. Where the **FIXED PENALTY** is less than $15, court costs shall be $9.50. See item 4 above. For example, if the statute provides for a fixed penalty of $10, the amount to be paid through the Violations Bureau is $21—the $10 fixed penalty plus $9.50 court costs, $1.00 ATS Surcharge and $.50 EMT Surcharge.

   Otherwise, the amount of court costs shall be $15.50. For example, if the statute provides for a **MAXIMUM** penalty of $50, the amount to be paid through the Violations Bureau is $42—$25 (one-half of the maximum penalty established by the statute) plus $15.50 court costs, $1.00 ATS Surcharge and $.50 EMT Surcharge. If the statute provides for a **MINIMUM** penalty of $35 for a violation, the amount to be paid through the Violations Bureau is $52—the $35 minimum plus $15.50 court costs, $1.00 ATS Surcharge and a $.50 EMT Surcharge. If the statute provides for a **FIXED PENALTY** of $35, the amount to be paid through the Violations Bureau is $52—the $35 fixed penalty plus $15.50 court costs, $1.00 ATS Surcharge and $.50 EMT Surcharge.

   (Note that R. 4:70-4(a) applies to all offenses involving a statutory penalty not just to Fish and Game offenses. These offenses come under the Penalty Enforcement Law, N.J.S.A. 2A:58-1 et seq. It includes, for example, such violations as Weights and Measures, N.J.S.A. 51:1-29, Cigarette Tax Act, N.J.S.A. 54:40A-24, Fish and Game, N.J.S.A. 23:1-2, Conservation and Development, N.J.S.A. 13:9-44.10, Consumer Fraud Act, N.J.S.A. 56:8-14, Motor Fuel Retail Act, N.J.S.A. 56:6-4.1).

*NOTE: The $1 ATS Surcharge would not apply to Title 5A violations.

EXHIBIT 16 (Continued)

REV. 9/1/93

B. FOR ALL OTHER NON TITLE 39 OFFENSES AND NON-MOTOR VEHICLE OFFENSES

1. Where the statutory penalty does not exceed $50 for each offense, including where the minimum statutory penalty does not exceed $50 for each offense, the defendant at any time before the hearing date, upon presentation of the signed plea of guilty and waiver of trial endorsed on the summons, may pay the penalty and in addition appropriate court costs in the Violations Bureau subject to the limitations prescribed in R. 7:7, including the limitation when the summons is marked to indicate that a court appearance is required.

2. Where the statute provides simply for a **MAXIMUM** penalty in excess of $50, it may be disposed of by payment through the Violations Bureau of one-half of the maximum penalty plus appropriate court costs.

3. Where the statute provides for a **MINIMUM** penalty not in excess of $50, even though the maximum exceeds $50, it may be paid through the Violations Bureau by a payment of the minimum penalty plus the appropriate court costs.

4. Where the statute provides for a **FIXED PENALTY ONLY,** not in excess of $50, it may be paid through the Violations Bureau by a payment of the penalty fixed by statute plus the appropriate court costs.

5. Appropriate court costs shall be established as follows: Where one-half of the **MAXIMUM** penalty is less than $15, court costs shall be $10. See item 2 above. For example, if the statute provides for a maximum penalty of $20, the amount to be paid through the Violations Bureau is $20— $10 (one-half of the maximum penalty established by the statute) plus $10 court costs. Where the **MINIMUM** penalty is less than $15, court costs shall be $10. See item 3 above. For example, if the statute provides for a minimum penalty of $10, the amount to be paid through the Violations Bureau is $20—the $10 minimum penalty plus $10 court costs. Where the **FIXED PENALTY** is less than $15, court costs shall be $10. See item 4 above. For example, if the statute provides for a fixed penalty of $10, the amount to be paid through the Violations Bureau is $20—the $10 fixed penalty plus $10 court costs.

Otherwise, the amount of court costs shall be $15. For example, if the statute provides for a **MAXIMUM** penalty of $50, the amount to be paid through the Violations Bureau is $40— $25 (one-half of the maximum penalty established by the statute) plus $15 court costs. If the statute provides for a **MINIMUM** penalty of $35 for a violation, the amount to be paid through the Violations Bureau is $50—the $35 minimum plus $15 court costs. If the statute provides for a **FIXED PENALTY** of $35, the amount to be paid through the Violations Bureau is $50— the $35 fixed penalty plus $15 court costs.

(Note that R. 4:70-4(a) applies to all offenses involving a statutory penalty not just to Fish and Game offenses. These offenses come under the Penalty Enforcement Law, N.J.S.A. 2A:58-1 et seq. It includes, for example, such violations as Weights and Measures, N.J.S.A. 51:1-29, Cigarette Tax Act, N.J.S.A. 54:40A-24, Fish and Game, N.J.S.A. 23:1-2, Conservation and Development, N.J.S.A. 13:9-44.10, Consumer Fraud Act, N.J.S.A. 56:8-14, Motor Fuel Retail Act, N.J.S.A. 56:6-4.1).

ALLOCATION OF PENALTY BETWEEN FINE, COSTS AND $1 ATS SURCHARGE

The total penalty indicated on the Statewide Violations Bureau Schedule for each **traffic and parking offense** includes the fines, costs, and $1 ATS Surcharge and a $.50 EMT Fund assessment. For each **such** offense, where the maximum fine or penalty allowable by the statute is less than $15, $9.50 shall be the amount of the costs, $1 shall be the ATS Surcharge and a $.50 EMT Fund assessment, and the balance shall be the fine. For each **such** offense, where the maximum fine or penalty allowable by the statute is at least $15, $15.50 shall be the amount of the costs, $1 shall be the ATS Surcharge, and a $.50 EMT Fund assessment, and the balance shall be the fine. (Where the fine is $15 it will be raised to $16 to comply with the policy that costs will not exceed fines). The payment of the statutory penalties pursuant to R. 4:70-4(a) is addressed on page 18 of this Schedule.

EXHIBIT 16 (Continued)

REV. 9/1/93

FAILURE TO APPEAR ON RETURN DATES

1. When a supplemental notice is sent, costs will be $10 additional.

2. When a Notice of Proposed Suspension for a parking violation is sent, $10 penalty will be added to the penalty due.

3. When an Order to Suspend is issued for a parking violation, $15 will be added to the penalty.

4. When a **warrant** is issued, unless the judge otherwise orders, the amount of the bail indicated on the warrant shall be as follows: **Parking offenses**—the amount of the penalty plus $15. **All other listed offenses**—The amount of the penalty plus $25.

   (Note: Under the provisions of N.J.S.A. 39:5-9, costs not to exceed $25 may be deducted from forfeited bail in traffic cases.)

5. By executing the form of **Authorization to Apply Bail Against Fine(s) and Costs and Waiver of Rights,** a defendant against whom a warrant has been issued waives the rights to a lawyer and a trial, enters a plea of guilty to the offense charged, and authorizes the municipal court administrator to apply the bail posted toward the payment of fines and costs owed. This form may be used only for traffic offenses, including parking offenses. Furthermore, it may be used only in those instances in which the offense charged is payable through the Statewide Violations Bureau Schedule or the Violations Bureau Schedule adopted by the municipal court.

COURT APPEARANCE MANDATORY

For any offense not listed on this Schedule (see next session on **ORDINANCE VIOLATIONS**), a court appearance is required unless the court authorizes defense by affidavit in accordance with the provisions of R. 7:6-6. For offenses involving traffic accidents resulting in personal injury, a court appearance is also required.

ORDINANCE VIOLATIONS—Ordinance violations, including parking and nonparking traffic offenses and other ordinance violations, may be listed on a separate Violations Bureau Schedule subject to the approval of the Assignment Judge.

APPEARANCE OF DEFENDANT IN CERTAIN CASES

The officer issuing the summons may, where in the opinion of the officer circumstances indicate the defendant should appear in court, check the complaint and summons "Court Appearance Required" in which event the case may not be processed in the Violations Bureau.

Dated: **AUGUST 27, 1993**

Robert D. Lipscher
Administrative Director of the Courts

EXHIBIT 17

MINIMUM MANDATORY FINES AND PENALTIES RELATING TO MOTOR VEHICLES

(NOTE: STATUTE SHOULD BE CONSULTED IN EACH CASE)
COURT COSTS ARE **NOT** INCLUDED

9.a	Failure to notify change in name	$10
9.a	Failure to endorse license	$20
39:3-10	Defendant driving without a license who has never been licensed in N.J. or elsewhere	$200

and no license issuance for at least 180 days

3-12	Illegal securing of driver's license	$200-500

or not less than 30 days **nor** more than 90 days imprisonment **or** both

3-20	Weight in excess of limitation permitted by certificate of registration	$500

plus $100 per 1,000 lbs. or fraction thereof

	Excess speed	See 39:4-98
3-20.1	Misuse of registration of empty trucks	$25-100

and suspension or revocation of the privilege

3-27.17	Unauthorized use of "Disabled Veteran" plates	$25-50
3-27.21	Improper use of "Commuter Van" plates	$25-50
3-27.27	Misuse of "Street Rod" plates	$25-50
3-35	Lending or using registration certificate or plates	$25-50
3-37	Falsifying application on examination	$200-500

or not more than 6 mos. imprisonment **or** both

3-38	Counterfeiting plate or marker	$50-100

or not more than 6 mos. driver's license revocation

	Using other than issued marker	$25-50
	Using counterfeit plate	$50-100

or not more than 6 mos. driver's license revocation **or** both

3-39a	Loaning license	$25-100
3-39c	Operator who exhibits driver's license of another	$200

or imprisonment for up to 60 days **or** both

3-39d	Exhibiting driver's license of another for purposes of identification	$25-100
3-40	Driving after license has been suspended, First offense	$500

and up to 6 mos. additional license suspension

	Second offense	$750

and not more than 5 days imprisonment **and** up to 6 mos. additional license suspension

	Third offense	$1,000

and 10 days imprisonment **and** up to 6 mos. additional license suspension
Note: In addition to above penalties for violation of 39:3-40, in case of accident resulting in personal injury to another person include 45 days imprisonment

	Offense during suspension for drunken driving	$500

and possible imprisonment for up to 90 days **and** 1 to 2 yrs. additional suspension of driver's license **"notwithstanding"** the above penalties
The judge should consult the statute.
Also, see penalties under 39:4-50a

3-70.2	Air pollution	$25-100
3-76.2a-d	Restraint or safety belt for child under age 5	$10-25

(may be suspended if defendant can prove possession and use of approved restraint)

3-76.2f	Failure to wear seat belt	$20
3-76.5	Footrests and helmet for motorcycle passenger	$50-100
3-79.8	Prohibition of supplying fuel to vehicle without label	$25
	Subsequent offense	$50

EXHIBIT 17 (Continued)

3-80	Equipment with rubber tires	$50-100
	Subsequent offense	$100-200
3-81	Projection from tires	$25-50
3-84.3i	Violation of dimensional limitations	$150-500
3-84.3j	Violation of weight limitations	$50
4-14.3g	Operating a moped while under the influence	See penalties under 4-50a
4-14.3h	Second violation of any provision of Chapter 4 by moped operator under age 17	

      30 day suspension of moped operating privileges
 Subsequent offense: Suspension of moped operating privileges until age 17

4-48	Operating or using a vehicle without consent of owner	$100
4-49	Tampering with motor vehicle	$10-50
	Subsequent offense	$50-100

      or not more than 30 days imprisonment **or** both

4-49.1	Operation of a motor vehicle while in possession or in motor vehicle, any narcotic drugs	$50

      and 2 yrs. suspension of driver's license

39:4-50a	Operating under the influence	$250-400

  and 12 to 48 hrs. detainment (per I.D.R.C. requirements); **and** in court's discretion not more than 30 days imprisonment; **also** 6 mos. to 1 yr. suspension of driver's license

  Second offense. (If second offense occurs more than 10 yrs. after first conviction shall treat as a first offense.) $500-1,000

  and 30 days community service **and** 48 hrs. to 90 days imprisonment **and** 2 yrs. suspension of driver's license

  Third or subsequent offense. (If third or subsequent offense occurs more than 10 yrs. after second conviction shall treat as a second offense.) . $1,000

  and 180 days imprisonment (may be lowered by up to 90 days serving community service) **and** 10 yrs. suspension of driver's license

  Surcharge for Drunk Driving Enforcement Fund (imposed on each conviction) $100

4-50.2	Refusal to undergo breathalyzer test	$250-500

      and 6 mos. suspension of driver's license

	Subsequent offense	$250-500

      and 2 yrs. suspension of driver's license

4-51a	Driving while drinking an alcoholic beverage	$200
	Second or subsequent offense	$250

      or 10 days community service

4-52	Racing on highway	$25-100
	Subsequent offense	$100-200
4-53	Leaving vehicle with engine running	$10-25
4-54	Dimensional restrictions	See 39:3-20 and 39:3-84.3 as applicable
	Excess weight	See 39:3-20 and 39:3-84.3 as applicable
4-56.1	Willful abandonment of motor vehicle	$200-500

      and 1 to 5 yr. suspension of driver's license

	Subsequent offense	$500-1,000

      and 5 yrs. suspension of driver's license

4-56.5	Abandonment of motor vehicle	$100-500
	Subsequent offense	$500-1,000

    and suspension of driver's license for not more than 5 yrs.

4-56.8	Failure of towing service to tow disabled vehicle	$25-50
4-63	Placing injurious substances on highway	$100-500

    and may forfeit right to operate a motor vehicle for 30 days

4-64	Throwing or dropping debris from a vehicle	$100-500
4-76	Driving overweight vehicle on interstate bridge	See penalties under 39:3-84.3

EXHIBIT 17 (Continued)

4-80	Failure to obey directions of officer	$50-200
	or up to 15 days imprisonment, **or** both	
4-81	Failure to obey traffic control device	$50-200
	or up to 15 days imprisonment, **or** both	
4-82	Failure to keep to right	$50-200
	or up to 15 days imprisonment, **or** both	
4-82.1	Failure to drive on right-hand roadway	$50-200
	or up to 15 days imprisonment, **or** both	
4-83	Failure to keep to right at intersection	$50-200
	or up to 15 days imprisonment, **or** both	
4-84	Failure to pass to right when proceeding in opposite direction	$50-200
	or up to 15 days imprisonment, **or** both	
4-85	Failure to pass to left when overtaking	$50-200
	or up to 15 days imprisonment, **or** both	
4-85.1	One-way traffic	$50-200
	or up to 15 days imprisonment, **or** both	
4-86	Failure to overtake and pass properly	$50-200
	or up to 15 days imprisonment, **or** both	
4-87	Failure to give overtaking vehicle right of way	$50-200
	or up to 15 days imprisonment, **or** both	
4-88	Failure to obey regulations when driving in marked lanes	$50-200
	or up to 15 days imprisonment, **or** both	
4-89	Following vehicle too closely	$50-200
	or up to 15 days imprisonment, **or** both	
4-90	Failure to yield right of way at intersection	$50-200
	or up to 15 days imprisonment, **or** both	
4-90.1	Entering or leaving limited access highways improperly	$50-200
	or up to 15 days imprisonment, **or** both	
4-91	Failure to yield right of way to emergency vehicles	$50-200
	or up to 15 days imprisonment, **or** both	
4-92	Failure to comply with regulations concerning emergency vehicles	$50-200
	or up to 15 days imprisonment, **or** both	
4-92.1	Following fire department vehicle too closely	$50-200
	or up to 15 days imprisonment, **or** both	
4-94	Railroad employee unnecessarily blocking highway with train	$50-200
	or up to 15 days imprisonment, **or** both	
4-94.1	Failure to comply with regulations for limited access highway	$50-200
	or up to 15 days imprisonment, **or** both	
4-96	Reckless driving	$50-200
	or up to 60 days imprisonment, **or** both	
	Second subsequent offense	$100-500
	or up to 3 mos. imprisonment, **or** both	
4-97	Careless driving	$50-200
	or up to 15 days imprisonment, **or** both	
4-97a	Motor Vehicles operation causing property damage	$50-200
	or up to 15 days imprisonment, **or** both	
4-97.1	Slow speed as to impede traffic	$50-200
	or up to 15 days imprisonment, **or** both	
4-98	Speeding	$50-200
	or up to 15 days imprisonment, **or** both	
4-100	Speeding across sidewalk	$50-200
	or up to 15 days imprisonment, **or** both	
4-115	Failure to make proper right or left turn	$50-200
	or up to 15 days imprisonment, **or** both	
4-116	Special right or left turn	$50-200
	or up to 15 days imprisonment, **or** both	

EXHIBIT 17 (Continued)

4-117	Special pedestrian interval:	
	pedestrian violation	$50-200
	motorist violation	$50-200
	or up to 15 days imprisonment, or both	
4-119	Failure to observe flashing traffic signals	$50-200
	or up to 15 days imprisonment, or both	
4-122	Failure to obey police whistle of police officer	$50-200
	or up to 15 days imprisonment, or both	
4-123	Failure to make proper right and left turns	$50-200
	or up to 15 days imprisonment, or both	
4-124	Failure to turn as indicated by buttons or markers at intersection	$50-200
	or up to 15 days imprisonment, or both	
4-125	U-Turn on curve or grade or where view obstructed or "No-U-Turn" sign	$50-200
	or up to 15 days imprisonment, or both	
4-126	Failure to signal before starting, turning or stopping	$50-200
	or up to 15 days imprisonment, or both	
4-127	Backing or turning in street	$50-200
	or up to 15 days imprisonment, or both	
4-127.1	Failure to stop at railroad crossing	$50-200
	or up to 15 days imprisonment, or both	
4-127.2	Failure to stop at approaches to movable span bridges	$50-200
	or up to 15 days imprisonment, or both	
4-128.1	Passing school bus while picking up or discharging	$100
	or up to 15 days imprisonment or community service, or both	
	Subsequent offense	$250
	or up to 15 days imprisonment, or both	
4-129a	Leaving the scene of accident involving injury or death	$100-1,000
	or 30 days imprisonment, or both, and not less than 6 mos. forfeiture operation of motor vehicle	
	Subsequent offense	$500-2,000
	and 3-6 mos. imprisonment, and forfeiture operation of motor vehicle	
39:4-129b	Leaving scene of accident involving damages to attended vehicle or property	$25-100
	or not more than 30 days imprisonment, or both	
	Subsequent offense	$100-200
	or 30 to 90 days imprisonment, or both	
4-129d	Leaving the scene of accident involving damages to unattended vehicle or property	$25-100
	or not less than 30 days imprisonment, or both	
	Subsequent offense	$100-200
	or 30 to 90 days imprisonment, or both	
4-130	Report of accident	$25-100
	or not more than 30 days imprisonment, or both	
	Subsequent offense	$100-200
	or 30 to 90 days imprisonment, or both	
4-132	Damages reported by repairman	$100-500
	or 30 to 90 days imprisonment, or both	
4-144	Failure to obey "Stop" or "Yield Right of Way" signs	$50-200
	or up to 15 days imprisonment, or both	
4-145	Failure to yield to vehicle entering stop or yield intersection after stopping	$50-200
	or up to 15 days imprisonment, or both	
4-201	Parking in space for handicapped contrary to county resolution, ordin. or reg.	$50
4-208	Parking on State property	$1-15

EXHIBIT 17 (Continued)

5B-29	Transportation of hazardous materials	$50-5,000
	Second offense	$100-10,000*
	Third **or** subsequent offense	$250-25,000*
5C-1	Attempting to or agreeing to operate a motor vehicle in a speed racing event	$25-100
	Subsequent offense	$100-200
	or not more than 90 days imprisonment, **or** both	
5E-23	Bulk Commodities Transportation Act (where no other penalty provided) for first offense. Not more than $200 for subsequent offense. Each day of violation is a separate offense.	$25-100
6B-2	Liability Insurance Coverage (first offense)	$300
	and a period of community service as determined by the court, **and** 1 yr. forfeiture of right to operate motor vehicles	
	Subsequent offense	$500
	and 14 days imprisonment **and** 30 days community service (terms of service determined by the court) **and** 2 yrs. forfeiture of right to operate motor vehicles	
8-18	Affixing approval sticker without inspection or conformity to standards	$1,000-1,500
	and suspension of reinspection center's license for 1 to 3 years	
	Subsequent offense	$2,000-3,500
	and permanent revocation of reinspection center's license	
9-2	Hours of duty of operator	$25
	Subsequent offense	$50
10-10	Delivery of certificate of ownership	$25
10-12	Duplicate certificate, false application	$200-500
	or not more than 30 days imprisonment, **or** both	
39:10B-2	Identification of motor component parts: Violation of record maintenance requirements	$25-100
	or up to 90 days imprisonment, **or** both	
11-3 and -9	Operation of junk yards	$25-100
	or up to 90 days imprisonment, **or** both	
39:12-12	Driving schools	$100-250
	or not less than 10 days imprisonment, **or** both	
	Subsequent offense	$250-500
	or not less than 30 days imprisonment, **or** both	
39:12-15	Non-use of seat belts in drivers' school (instructor and student)	$25
	Subsequent offense	$50
N.J.S.A. 4:22-25.1	Report of injury to certain animals by motorist required	$5-25
	Subsequent offense	$25-50
	and ten days in jail	
27:12B-18	Parkway Regulations (19:8-1.9(b)11.) Dimension Violations	$150-500
27:12C-37	Atlantic City Expressway Regulations (19:2-4.3(a)9) Dimensional violations	$150-500
27:23-29	Turnpike Regulations (19:9-1.9(a)12) Dimensional violations	$150-500

*Municipal Court has jurisdiction under $5,000 provided in N.J.S.A. 39:5B-25 *et seq.* N.J.S.A. 39:5B-29.

DEPOSITION AND DISCOVERY

Rule 3:13-2 governing deposition is applicable to actions in the Municipal Court, but due to the nature of these proceedings depositions are rarely utilized in the Municipal Court.

Depositions may be taken if it appears to the Municipal Court Judge that a material witness may be unable to attend or may be prevented from attending the trial. Upon motion and notice to the parties, the court may order that the testimony of such witness be taken orally by deposition and that any designated books, papers, documents or tangible objects, not privileged, be produced at the same time and place. R. 3:13-2(a). The deposition may be taken at the request of either the prosecution or the defense, and the time and place should be agreed upon by all parties. However, if they cannot agree, the court may make the designation. A transcript of all depositions shall be filed with the Municipal Court Clerk. R. 3:13-2(a).

The deposition may be used at trial, so far as admissible under the rules of evidence, if the court finds that the appearance of the witness cannot be obtained because he is dead, or is unable to attend due to age, sickness, infirmity, or imprisonment, is out of state, or because the party offering the deposition was unable to procure his appearance by subpoena. Once a part of a deposition has been offered into evidence, any party may require that any other part or the entire deposition be offered. R. 3:13-2(b).

The discovery rights of both the defendant and the state have been drastically enlarged by R. 3:13-3, as amended, which provides that upon written request by the defendant, the prosecuting attorney shall permit the defendant to inspect and copy or photograph any relevant:

1. Books, tangible objects, papers or documents obtained from or belonging to him;

2. Records of statements or confessions, signed or unsigned, by the defendant or copies thereof, and a summary of any admissions or declarations against penal interest made by the defendant that are known to the prosecution but not recorded;

3. Grand jury proceedings recorded pursuant to R. 3:6-6;

4. Results or reports of physical or mental examinations and of scientific tests or experiments made in connection with the matter, or copies thereof, which are within the possession, custody or control of the prosecuting attorney;

5. Reports or records of prior convictions of the defendant;

6. Books, papers, documents, or copies thereof, or tangible objects, buildings or places which are within the possession, custody or control of the state;

7. Names and addresses of any persons whom the prosecuting attorney knows to have relevant evidence or information including a designation by the prosecuting attorney as to which of those persons he may call as witnesses;

8. Records of statements, signed or unsigned, by such persons or by co-defendants which are within the possession, custody or control of the prosecuting attorney and any relevant record of prior conviction of such persons;

9. Police reports which are within the possession, custody or control of the prosecuting attorney;

10. Warrants, which have been completely executed, and the papers accompanying them, including the affidavits, transcripts or summaries of any oral testimony, returns and inventories;

11. Names and addresses of each person whom the prosecuting attorney expects to call to trial as an expert witness, his or her qualifications, the subject matter on which the expert is expected to testify, a copy of the report, if any, of such expert witness, or if no report is prepared, a statement of facts and opinions to which the expert is expected to testify and a summary of the grounds for each opinion. If this information is requested and not furnished, the expert witness may, upon application by the defendant, be barred from testifying at trial.

Pursuant to R. 3:13-3(b), a defendant who seeks discovery shall permit the State to inspect and copy or photograph:

1. Results of reports of physical or mental examinations and of scientific tests or experiments made in connection with the matter, or copies thereof, which are within the possession, custody or control of defense counsel;

2. Any relevant books, papers, documents or tangible objects, buildings or places or copies thereof, which are within the possession, custody or control of defense counsel;

3. The names and addresses of those persons known to the defendant whom he or she may call as witnesses at trial and their written statements, if any, including memoranda reporting or summarizing their oral statements;

4. Written statements, if any, including any memoranda reporting or summarizing the oral statements, made by any witnesses whom the State may call as a witness at trial;

5. Names and addresses of each person whom the defense expects to call to trial as an expert witness, his or her qualifications, the subject matter on which the expert is expected to testify, and a copy of the report, if any, of such expert witness, or if no report is prepared, a statement of the facts and opinions to which the expert is expected to testify and a summary of the grounds for each opinion. If this information is requested and not furnished the expert may, upon application by the prosecutor, be barred from testifying at trial.

Those documents not subject to discovery include a party's work product, such as internal reports, memoranda or documents made in connection with the investigation, prosecution or defense of the matter. Also, any statements of the defendant made to defendant's attorney or agents is not subject to discovery by the State. R. 3:13-3(c).

The court may, upon motion and for good cause shown, order that the discovery be denied, restricted or deferred. In determining the motion, the court may consider the protection of witnesses and others from physical harm, threats of harm, bribes, and other intimidation, protection of confidential relationships and privileges recognized by law or any other relevant consideration. R. 3:13-3(d).

The defendant has ten days to request discovery and the prosecutor has ten days to respond to a discovery request. Once the prosecutor complies with the defendant's request, the defendant has twenty days to provide discovery to the State. The State does not have to request discovery. R. 3:13-3(e). Once discovery has been provided, each party has a continuing duty to disclose promptly any additional material or witnesses subject to discovery that may come to their attention. If a party fails to comply with this order, the court may require the party to permit the discovery of material not previously disclosed, grant a continuance, prohibit the non-complying party from introducing into evidence the material not disclosed, or such other order as the Court deems appropriate. R. 3:13-3(f).

Pursuant to R. 7:4-2(g), discovery is afforded in those instances where the defendant may be subject to imprisonment or other consequences of magnitude. In all other instances, the court may at its discretion order discovery, upon application of either party.

Discovery requests are directed to the Municipal Prosecutor. However, the best practice to follow is to forward a copy of the discovery request to the appropriate law enforcement agency. It is appropriate to forward a copy of the request to the Court to verify the request and the date thereof.

If the defense intends to have an expert testify on the defendant's behalf, defense counsel should include the proposed expert's curriculum when defense counsel gives reciprocal discovery. This information will avoid the likelihood of the prosecutor's challenge to the expert's credentials.

Exhibit 18 is an example of a sample letter from defense attorneys requesting discovery. **Exhibits 19 & 20** are requests for discovery in matters involving the State Police. **Exhibit 21** is a sample lab report.

EXHIBIT 18

James E. Gabel
ATTORNEY AT LAW
121 WEST JERSEY AVENUE
PO BOX 68
PITMAN, NEW JERSEY 08071

May 7, 1986

Andrew Weber, Esquire
West Deptford Municipal Prosecutor
24 Newton Ave.
Woodbury, New Jersey 08096

    RE: State vs. John Doe

Dear Mr. Weber:

    Please be advised that this office has been consulted by John Doe, Defendant in the above-captioned matter, with regard to charges in violation of 39:4-50 and 39:4-97 issued on April 25, 1986. I hereby request the following items as pretrial discovery in accordance with the Rules of Court and the applicable case law: (please refer to R 3:13-4 and R 7:4-2(g)).

    1. Statement as to probable cause. (See *Delaware v. Prouse,* 440 U.S. 648 (1979);

    2. Name and address of all proposed expert witnesses;

    3. Name and address of any medical personnel that may have examined the Defendant;

    4. Copies of any and all reports of proposed expert witnesses;

    5. Copies of any other results or reports of physical or mental examinations and of specific tests or experiments made in connection with this matter;

    6. All records of statements or confessions, whether written or oral, made by Defendant;

    7. All records or reports of prior convictions of this Defendant, if any, including but not limited to certified abstracts proof of mailings or other official notices;

    8. Any and all photographs or drawings in evidence with reference to this matter as well as an offer of proof as to the authentication of same.

    9. Name and address of any person who is known to have relevant evidence and/or any information, including designation as to which of those persons may be called by the State as witnesses against the defendant;

    10. All police reports made at any time in connection with this matter including the time and date said report was prepared.

    11. Time, date and place at which it is convenient for my office to examine any tangible evidence expected to be introduced against this defendant, including but not limited to any video or sound recordings made in connection with this matter by the State.

EXHIBIT 18 (Continued)

12. All laboratory reports made in connection with this matter.

13. All evidence that the State intends to present to establish the chain of evidence in this matter.

14. Copies of any official documents which the State wishes to introduce to show the qualifications of any witness or the proper operation of any equipment used in preparation of the State's case including but not limited to licenses, certifications, and calibration records;

15. Any and all evidence not specifically requested above which the State intends to introduce at time of trial.

It is understood that any discovery not granted may be excluded at the time of trial on defense counsel's motion. It is further understood that reciprocal discovery will be given to the State in accordance with 3:13-3(b) only upon receipt of a written request for same.

Please bill my office directly for any costs involved in compiling the above information. Your prompt and considerate attention to this matter is greatly appreciated.

Sincerely,

James E. Gabel

JEG/sf

cc: West Deptford Police Department
West Deptford Municipal Court

EXHIBIT 19

REPORT REQUEST INFORMATION

DATE OF REQUEST: _____

To obtain copies of state police accident reports, photographs and drinking-driving reports, this form must be completed and returned to the **APPROPRIATE AUTHORITY INDICATED ON THE REVERSE SIDE.** Please provide the necessary information in Sections A & B and return with the proper fee(s). **DO NOT SEND CASH. COPIES OF REPORTS WILL NOT BE GIVEN TO ANYONE APPLYING IN PERSON AT DIVISION HEADQUARTERS OR STATE POLICE STATIONS.**

SECTION A

Requesting Firm/Company/Agency, etc.:_____

Address:_____

Telephone Number: (   )_____

Name of Requesting Party:_____

IF KNOWN, CHECK TYPE OF REPORT REQUESTED

Accident Report
Drinking-Driving Report Folio
Criminal Investigation Report
Laboratory Report
Other—Explain:_____

Operations Report
Aircraft/Boating Accident
Accidental Injury/Death
Traffic Summons

SECTION B

**DRIVER INFORMATION EXCHANGE/REPORT REQUEST INFORMATION
INSERT INFORMATION WHERE APPLICABLE
NOTE: THE BELOW INFORMATION MUST BE COMPLETED BY PARTIES INVOLVED IN A MOTOR VEHICLE ACCIDENT AND WHEN REQUESTING COPIES OF STATE POLICE REPORTS.**

Name:_____   Name:_____

Address:_____   Address:_____

City, State, Zip:_____   City, State, Zip:_____

Date/Time:_____

Location of Incident:_____

Insurance Company Policy Number:_____

Type Vehicle:_____   Registration Number:_____

Report Case Number:_____   Violation/Statute:_____
(Enclose copy of Traffic Summons)

Trooper Name/Badge Number:_____

Station:_____

Remarks:_____
_____
_____

EXHIBIT 19 (Continued)

State of New Jersey
DEPARTMENT OF LAW AND PUBLIC SAFETY
DIVISION OF STATE POLICE

RECORDS AND IDENTIFICATION SECTION
POST OFFICE BOX 7068
WEST TRENTON, NEW JERSEY 08628 - 0068
(609) 882 - 2000

CARY EDWARDS
Attorney General

COLONEL C. L. PAGANO
Superintendent

PROCEDURES FOR OBTAINING COPIES OF STATE POLICE ACCIDENT REPORTS, PHOTOGRAPHS, AND DRINKING—DRIVING REPORTS

(Pursuant to Title 53:2-3R.S., the following Rules & Regulations have been promulgated by the Superintendent of State Police)

I. Accident Reports
  A. For accidents occurring on NON TOLL roads, contact or write to: Division of State Police, Criminal Justice Records Bureau, P.O. Box 7068, West Trenton, New Jersey, 08628-0068 - Telephone: (609) 882 - 2000, Ext. 2234 or 2504
   1. Complete reverse side of this form and return with the proper fee(s).
   2. Requests for accident reports must be accompanied by a check or money order made payable to **New Jersey State Police** in accordance with the rates outlined herein.
   3. FEES:
      a. 1 to 3 pages .... $ 10.00
      b. Each additional page .... $ 2.00 each
      c. Over 6 pages .... No additional cost

  B. For accidents occuring on TOLL roads, contact or write to the appropriate toll road authority for accident and fee information.
   1. New Jersey Turnpike Authority .... Checks or money orders to be made payable to:
      New Brunswick, New Jersey 08903   **New Jersey Turnpike Authority**
      Telephone: (201) 247 - 3333

   2. Garden State Parkway .... Checks or money orders to be made payable to:
      P.O. Box 20   **Garden State Parkway (or)**
      Woodbridge, New Jersey 07095   **New Jersey Highway Authority**
      Telephone: (201) 442 - 8600

   3. Atlantic City Expressway Authority .... Checks or money orders to be made payable to:
      P.O. Box 389   **New Jersey Expressway Authority (or)**
      Hammonton, New Jersey 08037   **Atlantic City Expressway Authority**
      Telephone: (609) 561 - 6505

II. Photographs
  A. All requests for photographs will be made to: Division of State Police, Criminal Justice Records Bureau.
   1. Prior to the release of photographs, there must be verification that the case is closed.
   2. Complete reverse side of this form and return with the proper fee(s).
   3. Photographs must be purchased in complete sets: no individual photographs will be released.
      Requests must be accompanied by a check or money order made payable to: **New Jersey State Police.**
   4. FEES:
      a. One to ten photographs .... $ 5.00 each
      b. Additional photographs .... $ 3.00

III. Drinking-Driving Reports
  A. All requests for drinking-driving reports will be made to: Division of State Police, Criminal Justice Records Bureau.
   1. Complete reverse side of this form and return with the proper fee(s).
   2. Requests for drinking-driving reports must be accompanied by a check or money order made payable to: **New Jersey State Police.**
   3. FEES:
      a. Drinking-Driving cases .... $ 10.00 each

NOTE: Reports will not be available to anyone applying in person. This form must be completed on the reverse side and forwarded with the proper fees.

Sincerely yours,

Clinton L. Pagano

Colonel C.L. Pagano
Superintendent

New Jersey Is An Equal Opportunity Employer

S.P. 275 (Rev. 10/88) (S.O.P. F25)

EXHIBIT 20

REQUEST FOR EXAMINATION OF EVIDENCE

Submitting Agency (Case Number): A1608697/E-86-78

Laboratory Number: 73123H

STATE OF NEW JERSEY
DEPARTMENT OF LAW AND PUBLIC SAFETY
DIVISION OF STATE POLICE
SPECIAL AND TECHNICAL SERVICES SECTION
POST OFFICE BOX 7068
☐ WEST TRENTON, NEW JERSEY 08625
(609) 882-2000

APR 15 [stamp] '86

(Laboratory Use Only)

☐ North Regional Lab. / ☒ South Regional Lab. / ☐ East Regional Lab.
State Highway 46 / Post Office Box 126 / Sea Girt Avenue
Little Falls, NJ 07424 / Hammonton, NJ 08037 / Sea Girt, NJ 08750
(201) 256-7790 / (609) 561-2060 / (201) 449-0303

CRIME: Possession of Narcotics Paraphernalia 24:21-46
COUNTY OF: Camden

VICTIM: STATE OF NEW JERSEY
SUSPECT: Edward W. Brown — Age 20, Sex M, Race 1B

SUBMITTING AGENCY (Address): N.J.S.P./A.C. Expressway A160

FORWARD REPLIES TO: N.J.S.P./A.C. Expressway P.O. Box 389 Hammonton, NJ
Telephone Number: 561-6505

INVESTIGATED BY: Tpr. R.J. Blaker #3957
DELIVERED BY: [signature] 3957

BRIEF HISTORY OF CASE: (Include Date and Location, if Applicable)

On 3-29-86, while on routine patrol, the listed suspect was stopped for a violation of the drinking driving law, at MP 40.5 WB A.C.E., in Winslow Twsp., Camden Co., and was found to be in possession of a green plastic gram scale, with a white powder substance, believed to be Cocaine, located in the bowl of said scale. It should be noted that said substance is only residue.

EXAMINATION REQUESTED ON SPECIMENS LISTED BELOW:

Request trace analysis be performed for narcotic content. Winslow Twsp. court date scheduled for 5/21/86.

Item #	Code	LIST OF SPECIMENS *SOURCE OF EVIDENCE CODE (V - Victim S - Suspect SC - Scene)
1	S	1) Large manilla envelope containing: 1 green plastic gram scale.

DRUG ☒
TRACE ☐
BIO/CHEM ☐
TOX ☐
ABC ☐
EQUINE ☐

FOR ADDITIONAL INFORMATION USE FORM 631A AND ATTACH

Page 1 of 1 Pages

P. 631 (Rev. 4-83)

EXHIBIT 21

NEW JERSEY STATE POLICE
SPECIAL AND TECHNICAL SERVICES SECTION
FORENSIC SCIENCE BUREAU
LABORATORY REPORT

Regional Laboratory	Laboratory No
☐ Central ☐ North ☒ South ☐ East	73123H

Submitting Agency	Agency No.
NJSP A.C. EXPRESSWAY	A1608697 / E-86-78

CASE: ☐ Supplemental Report ☐ Supplemental Report to Follow

Date of Report: 4/30/86

Specimens in this case were submitted to the Forensic Science Bureau for examination. See attached *Request for Examination of Evidence (S.P. 631)* for list of specimens.

Results of Examination — DRUG ANALYSIS

Specimen Number	Methamphetamine	Controlled Dangerous Substance (CDS)	CDS Schedule	Weight
1	X	X	II	Tr

Analyst: *Nancy S. Bredbenner*
NANCY S. BREDBENNER
SENIOR FORENSIC CHEMIST

PAGE 1 OF 1 PAGES

267

SEARCH WARRANTS

Municipal Court Judges have the authority to issue search warrants where the property being sought is within their territorial jurisdiction. R. 3:5-1. Searches may also be authorized in writing or telephonically as long as the provisions established in *State v. Valencia*, 93 N.J. 126 (1983), have been fulfilled.

Any challenge to the validity of a search warrant authorized by a Municipal Court Judge or the execution thereof must be directed to the Superior Court in the County in which the matter is pending regardless of whether the offense alleged or to be charged is within the jurisdiction of the Municipal Court. R. 3:5-7(a). These challenges shall be made in the usual form of a motion to suppress and must be made within thirty days of the initial plea, or later if it can be shown that the defendant could not have reasonably made it within such time.

Of course, Judges of the Superior Court also have the authority to issue search warrants. However, the discussion is limited herein as it is more properly dealt with in a more in-depth study of prior case law which is almost always constantly changing.

MOTIONS

There are three types of motions which may be made in a Municipal Court matter: a) motions before trial; b) motions at the conclusion of trial and; c) motions which may be made before, during and after trial. See R. 7:4-2(e) and R. 3:10-1 *et seq*. These motions may be presented orally and informally, but affidavits and oral testimony may be presented when required.

A motion as to the failure of the complaint to state a violation of law, lack of jurisdiction, and to sequester witnesses should be made prior to trial commencing.

Any defense which can be determined witout trying the general issue, such as a motion to dismiss for lack of jurisdiction or motion to dismiss for failure to give defendant notice of the offense alleged, may be raised before trial. R. 3:10-1. A defense of double jeopardy and all other defenses based on defect in the prosecution or complaint must be made by motion before trial. A failure to raise these motions before trial is deemed a waiver thereof, but the court may, for good cause shown, grant relief from that waiver. R. 3:10-2.

The defense that the complaint fails to charge an offense and the defense that the complaint is based on a statute or ordinance which is unconstitutional or invalid may be raised by motion only before trial or within ten days after a guilty verdict or within such further time as the court may fix during that ten day period. R. 3:10-3. These defenses shall not be considered during trial.

A defense of lack of jurisdiction may be made at any time during the pendency of proceedings except during trial. R. 3:10-4.

If a motion is denied, the defendant shall be permitted to plead if he has not already done so. If the motion is sustained, the court shall order the complaint dismissed and may also hold the defendant in custody or continue his bail pending the filing of a new complaint.

Motions to dismiss on the grounds that the offense was *de minimus* must be directed to the Assignment Judge.

At the conclusion of the state's case, defense counsel usually will make a motion to dismiss for failure to prove a prima facie case. The standard of proof required at this juncture, based on the testimony and evidence presented, resolving all inferences favorable to the state, is that the state has failed to prove the case beyond a reasonable doubt.

SEARCH WARRANTS

Municipal Court Judges have the authority to issue search warrants where the property being sought is within their territorial jurisdiction. R. 3:5-1. Searches may also be authorized in writing or telephonically as long as the provisions established in *State v. Valencia*, 93 N.J. 126 (1983), have been fulfilled.

Any challenge to the validity of a search warrant authorized by a Municipal Court Judge or the execution thereof must be directed to the Superior Court in the County in which the matter is pending regardless of whether the offense alleged or to be charged is within the jurisdiction of the Municipal Court. R. 3:5-7(a). These challenges shall be made in the usual form of a motion to suppress and must be made within thirty days of the initial plea, or later if it can be shown that the defendant could not have reasonably made it within such time.

Of course, Judges of the Superior Court also have the authority to issue search warrants. However, the discussion is limited herein as it is more properly dealt with in a more in-depth study of prior case law which is almost always constantly changing.

MOTIONS

There are three types of motions which may be made in a Municipal Court matter: a) motions before trial; b) motions at the conclusion of trial and; c) motions which may be made before, during and after trial. See R. 7:4-2(e) and R. 3:10-1 *et seq.* These motions may be presented orally and informally, but affidavits and oral testimony may be presented when required.

A motion as to the failure of the complaint to state a violation of law, lack of jurisdiction, and to sequester witnesses should be made prior to trial commencing.

Any defense which can be determined witout trying the general issue, such as a motion to dismiss for lack of jurisdiction or motion to dismiss for failure to give defendant notice of the offense alleged, may be raised before trial. R. 3:10-1. A defense of double jeopardy and all other defenses based on defect in the prosecution or complaint must be made by motion before trial. A failure to raise these motions before trial is deemed a waiver thereof, but the court may, for good cause shown, grant relief from that waiver. R. 3:10-2.

The defense that the complaint fails to charge an offense and the defense that the complaint is based on a statute or ordinance which is unconstitutional or invalid may be raised by motion only before trial or within ten days after a guilty verdict or within such further time as the court may fix during that ten day period. R. 3:10-3. These defenses shall not be considered during trial.

A defense of lack of jurisdiction may be made at any time during the pendency of proceedings except during trial. R. 3:10-4.

If a motion is denied, the defendant shall be permitted to plead if he has not already done so. If the motion is sustained, the court shall order the complaint dismissed and may also hold the defendant in custody or continue his bail pending the filing of a new complaint.

Motions to dismiss on the grounds that the offense was *de minimus* must be directed to the Assignment Judge.

At the conclusion of the state's case, defense counsel usually will make a motion to dismiss for failure to prove a prima facie case. The standard of proof required at this juncture, based on the testimony and evidence presented, resolving all inferences favorable to the state, is that the state has failed to prove the case beyond a reasonable doubt.

Motion to Suppress

Prior to June 9, 1989, all motions to suppress evidence had to be filed in the Superior Court. Effective June 9, 1989, amendments to Rules 3:5-7, 3:24(d) and 7:4-2(f) now allow for motions to suppress in the case of warrantless searches to be filed with the municipal court. A notice of motion must also be served on either the municipal prosecutor, county prosecutor or deputy attorney general, depending on which one is prosecuting the case on behalf of the state.

Motions to suppress evidence obtained through the use of a search warrant are still heard in the Superior Court.

The reason for the change with regard to warrantless searches was based in part upon the recent large influx of drug related cases into the municipal court. The growing number of suppression motions arising from these cases was becoming unduly burdensome on the Superior Court calendar, hence the shift of these motions to the municipal court.

The current Court Rules applicable to municipal court practice can be found in this book in Appendix A. A sample notice of motion and a sample order follow as **Exhibit 22 and 23.**

EXHIBIT 22

PUFF & AIMINO
122 Delaware Street
P.O. Box 684
Woodbury, New Jersey 08096
(609) 845-0011
Attorney for Defendant

STATE OF NEW JERSEY : CAMDEN COUNTY
                                    MUNICIPAL COURT
        Plaintiff(s), : TOWNSHIP OF WINSLOW

vs. :
                                    SUMMONS NOS. 12371, 12372,
                                  : 12373, S682331
        Defendant.   Criminal Action
                                  :
                                    NOTICE OF MOTION TO
                                    SUPPRESS EVIDENCE

TO: Samuel Asbell, Esq.
       Camden County Prosecutor
       518 Market Street
       Camden, NJ 08101-1217

TAKE NOTICE that the undersigned will apply to the above named Court, at 5th & Mickle Boulevard, Hall of Justice, Camden, New Jersey, 08101, on such date and time as the Court shall assign, or as soon thereafter as counsel may be heard, for an Order suppressing all evidence obtained by the State during and as a result of the warrantless, illegal and unconstitutional motor vehicle stop and the subsequent seizure of the Defendant, _____ conducted by the Officer of the Township of Winslow Police Department, said motor vehicle stop and subsequent search and seizure having been conducted and effected without probable cause or reasonable suspicion to stop and/or search and seizure.

Defendant will rely on his Brief, to be submitted after the State has submitted its Brief and within three (3) days prior to the date of the hearing, pursuant to R. 3:5-7(b).

EXHIBIT 22 (Continued)

Defendant requests oral argument.

A proposed form of Order is attached.

> PUFF & AIMINO
>
> _____
> Michael A. Aimino
> Attorneys for Defendant

DATED: May 6, 1988

PROOF OF SERVICE

On May 6, 1988, I, the undersigned, mailed to: Samuel Asbell, Camden County Prosecutor, located at 518 Market Street, Camden, New Jersey 08101, Attorney for Plaintiff, State of New Jersey, by regular mail, the following:

Notice of Motion to Suppress Evidence and proposed form of Order to Suppress Evidence

I certify that the foregoing statements made by me are true. I am aware that if any of the foregoing statements made by me are willfully false, I am subject to punishment.

DATED: May 6, 1988

_____
HENRIETTE LUGO, Secretary

72/*Municipal Court*

EXHIBIT 23

PUFF & AIMINO
122 Delaware Street
P.O. Box 684
Woodbury, New Jersey 08096
(609) 845-0011

STATE OF NEW JERSEY : CAMDEN COUNTY
                                                 MUNICIPAL COURT
          Plaintiff(s), : TOWNSHIP OF WINSLOW

vs. :

                                                 SUMMONS NOS. 12371, 12372,
                                             : 12373, S682331

          Defendant. : Criminal Action

                                                :

                                                ORDER TO SUPPRESS EVIDENCE

This matter having been brought before the Court on motion of Michael A. Aimino, attorney for Defendant, _____ for an Order requesting the relief set forth in the Motion filed herewith, and the Court having considered the matter and good cause appearing,

IT IS, on this _____ day of _____, 1988, ORDERED:

1. That all evidence obtained during and as a result of the warrantless, illegal and unconstitutional motor vehicle stop and subsequent search and seizure of the Defendant, _____, including but not limited to: (a) any statements or admissions made by the Defendant to the officers of the Township of Winslow Police Department during or after the arrest; and (b) Any alleged controlled dangerous substances found as a result of the stop are hereby suppressed and may not be entered into evidence by the State of the time of trial.

PAPERS FILED WITH THE COURT:

(   ) Movant's pleadings

(   ) Reply papers

                                                                                                      J.S.C.

PLEA BARGAINING

New Jersey permits plea bargaining in certain municipal court matters. The following is a directive from the Supreme Court of New Jersey to all Municipal Court Judges implementing plea bargaining in Municipal Court. Guidelines for Operation of Plea Agreements in the Municipal Courts of New Jersey can be found following Rule 7:4-8 in Appendix A.

SUPREME COURT OF NEW JERSEY

ROBERT N. WILENTZ
CHIEF JUSTICE

313 STATE STREET
PERTH AMBOY, NEW JERSEY 08861

Directive #9-1988

June 23, 1988

MEMORANDUM TO: All Municipal Court Judges

FROM: Chief Justice Robert N. Wilentz

SUBJECT: DIRECTIVE ON PLEA AGREEMENTS IN CERTAIN MUNICIPAL COURTS

The Supreme Court will permit a one-year limited test of regulated plea agreements in certain municipal courts effective for cases heard on and after September 1, 1988.

The experiment will be regulated by a monitoring and evaluating Committee. I will designate representatives of the public, county and municipal prosecutors, the Attorney General's office, the defense bar and judges to serve on that Committee. The Committee will design and implement methods of monitoring and evaluating the experiment and will report its results and recommendations, initially after six months and finally at the conclusion of the experiment. The six-month interim report will contain the opinion of the Committee as to whether the experiment should be terminated at that time or be allowed to continue for the full year.

For the purposes of the experiment, a plea agreement occurs when a prosecutor and the defense agree as to a guilty plea on condition that other charges will be dropped or that a specific sentence will be recommended to the judge by the prosecutor.

Plea agreements will be permitted in certain municipal courts during the experimental period strictly subject to the following conditions:

June 23, 1988
Page 2

1. No plea agreements whatsoever will be allowed in drunken driving or certain drug offenses. Those offenses are:

   A. Driving while under the influence of liquor or drugs (N.J.S.A. 39:4-50) and refusal to provide a breath sample (N.J.S.A. 39:4-50.2) and,

   B. Possession of marijuana or hashish (N.J.S.A. 2C:35-10a(4)); being under the influence of a controlled dangerous substance or its analog (N.J.S.A. 2C:35-10b); and use, possession or intent to use or possess drug paraphernalia, etc. (N.J.S.A. 2C:36-2).

   The municipal court may, for certain other offenses subject to minimum mandatory penalties, refuse to accept a plea agreement unless the municipal prosecutor represents that the possibility of conviction is so remote that the interests of justice require the acceptance of a plea to a lesser offense.

2. Plea agreements will be allowed only in those municipal courts where there is a municipal prosecutor and only in those cases handled by the municipal prosecutor; provided, however, that plea agreements will be allowed in any municipal court in cases handled by the Office of the Attorney General or the County Prosecutor.

3. No plea agreement will be allowed unless the defendant is either represented by counsel or makes a knowing waiver on the record of the right to be so represented.

June 23, 1988
Page 3

    4. In all plea agreement matters, before the plea is entered the prosecutor must represent to the court that the complainant has been informed of the agreement.

    5. Plea agreements will be allowed only in matters within the jurisdiction of the municipal court; in particular, plea agreements shall not be allowed to downgrade or dispose of indictable complaints without the consent of the county prosecutor, which consent shall be noted on the record. Municipal court judges are reminded not to dispose of nonindictable complaints that are related to indictable offenses without the consent of the county prosecutor.

    6. When a plea agreement is reached, the terms shall be set forth fully on the record in open court, along with the reasons and justification for the plea and the factual basis that supports it.

    7. There shall be no participation whatsoever on the part of the municipal court judge in the plea agreement process, with the exception of the decision in open court to accept or reject the proffered plea. If the judge determines that the interests of justice would not be served by accepting the agreement, the judge shall so state, and the defendant shall be informed of the right to withdraw the plea.

All judges and officers of municipal courts where the present prohibition against plea agreements will continue (i.e. where there is either no municipal prosecutor or the municipal prosecutor is not handling the case) must strictly enforce that prohibition and report any violations directly to me.

                                      R. N. W.

/rmy
28/648
c: Robert D. Lipscher
   Assignment Judges
   Presiding Judges-Municipal Courts
   Theodore J. Fetter
   Dennis L. Bliss
   Trial Court Administrators
   Municipal Court Liaisons
   Municipal Court Administrators and Clerks

INTERPRETERS

In those instances when the client does not speak English and requires an interpreter, the attorney should make the necessary arrangements for an interpreter and not assume that the court will provide one. The interpreter must also be administered an oath and be given explicit instructions not to editorialize or inject his or her personal feelings or biases into the interpretation, or responses to questions, but preferably to give a verbatim simultaneous translation. If the attorney is unable to locate a translator, he or she should give prior notice of the necessity of a translator to the court. The cost of the translator is sometimes borne by the defendant, but if prior notice is given to the court, the court will make arrangements, if possible, to obtain the appropriate translator. It should be noted that some Judges will not permit an interpreter other than one provided or previously approved by the court. It, therefore, is advisable, if you desire to provide and utilize your own translator, that you first obtain the permission of the court.

Recent legislation requires that all sign language interpreters be approved by the Administrative Office of the Courts as Certified Translators. A list of sign language interpreters may be obtained by writing to:

Interpreter Referral Service of the
State Division of the Deaf
Department of Labor
Trenton, New Jersey 08625-0058
609-984-7283   1-800-792-8339

JUVENILE WITNESSES

When a juvenile is a witness, many Municipal Court Judges will administer a special type of oath. The sole purpose of this oath is to question the juvenile witness to determine whether the juvenile has sufficient mental capacity to determine right from wrong and whether the juvenile will testify truthfully. It is, therefore, advisable to inform the Judge of a juvenile witness's age before the oath is administered. The practice of having a child testify against a parent is discouraged and should be used only when absolutely necessary.

TRIAL

The trial of a Municipal Court case is, in most respects, similar to the trial of any other non-jury matter. The standard of proof required in traffic and disorderly persons matters is the same as in any other criminal case, "beyond a reasonable doubt." As a matter of fact, traffic and disorderly persons offenses are often referred to as "quasi-criminal" in nature; however, a traffic or disorderly persons offense is not a "crime", as defined by the New Jersey Statutes.

Although most Municipal Court matters are heard on the return day of the summons, postponements are permitted for good cause. Failure to notify the court of a plea of not guilty at least three days prior to the hearing date, as indicated on traffic summonses, will most likely result in the case being postponed by the court to afford the prosecution the opportunity to subpoena its witnesses and prepare its case.

The Municipal Court is directed to hear cases in the following order:

1. Requests for postponements and appointment of attorney;
2. Guilty pleas to traffic offenses with an attorney;

3. Guilty pleas to traffic offenses without an attorney;

4. Guilty pleas to disorderly offenses with an attorney;

5. Guilty pleas to disorderly offenses without an attorney;

6. Not guilty pleas with an attorney;

7. Not guilty pleas without an attorney;

The rules of evidence and criminal procedure are applicable in the Municipal Courts with minor exceptions. If witnesses are to be subpoenaed, the attorney is responsible to issue the subpoena and furnish a copy to the Court. The attorney should also include the appropriate witness and mileage fee, if required.

Once a case is before the Municipal Court, the proceedings are usually conducted in the folloiwng manner:

1. Motions addressed to process and complaint;

2. Opening statements, if any;

3. State's testimony and evidence in support of the complaint and cross-examination;

4. Motion to dismiss the complaint at the close of the State's case for failure to prove prima facie case;

5. Evidence on behalf of the defendant and cross-examination thereto;

6. Rebuttal evidence and cross-examination;

7. Motions for judgment of acquittal;

8. Summations, if any;

9. Verdict;

10. Prosecutor and defendant or attorney's statement as to sentencing.

Due to the somewhat informal nature of Municipal Court proceedings, opening statements are unusual. However, if counsel chooses to make an opening statement, the court may welcome a brief summary of the evidence to be presented. The State must open first and if the defendant wishes to open he or she must do so immediately, or be precluded from doing so thereafter. The prosecution will then proceed to present its case by calling witnesses. Each witness called may be cross-examined by the defense. Once the prosecution has completed presentation of its case and rested, the defendant may move for a judgment of acquittal. The court will review the evidence presented, resolving all reasonable inferences most favorably to the State, and determine the sufficiency of the State's case. If the court finds that the State has not proved a prima facie case at this juncture, the motion shall be granted. If the motion is denied, the defendant may offer his or her evidence. Any witnesses called by the defense to testify are subject to cross-examination by the prosecution. After the defense has rested, the prosecution may offer witnesses in rebuttal, subject to cross-examination by the defense. If new evidence is received on rebuttal, the defense must be given an opportunity to contradict it on surrebuttal. At this point, if the evidence presented is insufficient to warrant a conviction, the court may, on motion of the defendant or its own, order the entry of the judgment of acquittal. If no acquittal is ordered, the defense and the prosecution may offer summations, though the court need not hear summations. The defense is required to present its summation first and the prosecution will follow. The time allowed to make summations is solely within the discretion of the court.

Once the summations have been concluded, the Judge is required to make a general finding of guilty or not guilty and he or she must find the facts of the case specially. This is generally done orally on the record, but the Judge may reduce his finding to writing and make them part of the judgment of the court. The Judge retains discretion to reserve decision for a reasonable period of time.

In the event the defense intends to have an expert witness testify, the defendant is responsible for all expert witness arrangements and fees. Of course, unless so stipulated, it is necessary for the attorney to qualify the witness as an expert and inquire as to whether the court acknowledges same. The qualification is accomplished in the same manner as would be done in the Superior Court.

OBJECTIONS

During the proceedings it may become necessary to raise objections as to hearsay testimony, relevancy, etc. When objecting, state the reasons and the basis of the objection. The Judge may or may not ask for a response from the adversary and then rule on the objection, unless he desires additional argument. Going "back and forth" with argument on an objection is discouraged. The attorney should be sufficiently alert to give reasons and anticipate the adversary's argument and, therefore, only one brief "speech" need be made. When the Judge rules on the objection, thank him or her for the ruling and cease argument.

Repeated objections of minimal value will most likely weaken the impact of more substantive and significant objections. It is, therefore, sometimes desirable to allow questions or answers which, although objectionable, are relatively unimportant so you can concentrate the Judge's attention on truly significant objectionable matters.

CONTEMPT

There are two classifications of contempt, direct and indirect. Direct contempts, or contempt in facie curiae, are those committed within the presence of the court and are constituted by any act or conduct which obstructs or tends to obstruct the administration of justice, including any interruption of the proceedings by disorderly behavior or insolent language. *State v. Jones,* 105 N.J. Super. 493 (Essex County Ct. 1969). For other acts which may constitute contempt in facie curiae, *see State v. Sax,* 139 N.J. Super. 157 (App. Div. 1976) (attorney's mode of attire); *In re Yengo,* 84 N.J. 111 (1980) (attorney's unexplained absence from court constitutes direct contempt). Direct contempts may be adjudicated summarily by the judge without notice or order to show cause. The order of contempt shall recite the facts and contain a certification by the Judge that he or she saw or heard the conduct which constituted the contempt. R. 1:10-1. Because the penalty for such offenses shall not exceed those for petty offenses, there is no right to trial by jury. Even when consecutive sentences are imposed for separate contempts and the total may exceed the maximum for petty offenses, there is no right to jury trial. *State v. Gonzales,* 134 N.J. Super. 472 (App. Div. 1975).

Indirect contempts are those which arise from matters not occurring in the presence of the court but which act to obstruct the administration of justice, such as the failure to obey an order of the court. Proceedings for such offenses shall be on notice and instituted only by the court on an Order for Arrest or an Order to Show Cause specifying the alleged acts or omissions. A person so charged shall be admitted to bail pending hearing. R. 1:10-2, 3. The proceedings shall not be heard by the Judge who brought the order except with the consent of the person charged. R. 1:10-4.

When the contempt consists of a failure to pay a fine or make restitution, the court may, upon motion of the person authorized to collect the fine, the prosecutor, or the county, recall him or her or issue a summons or warrant for his or her appearance. After a hearing, the fine may be suspended, reduced, the payment plan modified, or a term of imprisonment may be imposed. Any term of imprisonment "shall not exceed one day for each $20.00 of the fine nor forty days [for a] disorderly persons [offense,] or twenty-five days for a petty disorderly offense...." N.J.S.A. 2C:46-2a(2).

LEGAL ISSUES IN DRUNK DRIVING CASES
BY HONORABLE JOHN MCFEELEY, III, J.M.C.

INDEX

	Page
A. Probable Cause, Operation and Related Issues	81
B. Under the Influence and *Per Se* Offense	82
C. Refusal/Implied Consent	85
D. Constitutional Issues in Driving Under the Influence and Refusal Cases	86
E. Blood Testing	86
F. Sentencing Considerations	87
G. Miscellaneous Issues	90

Rev. 6/93

LEGAL ISSUES IN DRUNK DRIVING CASES
BY HONORABLE JOHN MCFEELEY, III, J.M.C.

A. Probable Cause, Operation and Related Issues

It is clear that the police may not randomly stop vehicles, without probable cause, or reasonble suspicion, to gather evidence as to violations of the motor vehicle laws. *Delaware v. Prouse,* 440 U.S. 468 (1979). In order to lawfully stop a motor vehicle the officer must have probable cause, or reasonable suspicion, in terms of an articulate and reasonable belief or particularized suspicion that there is a violation of the law. *State v. Coccomo,* 177 N.J. Super. 575 (Law Div. 1980), *State v. Kirk,* 202 N.J. Super. 28 (App. Div. 1985). A properly conducted police roadblock is an exception to the probable cause, or reasonable suspicion requirement. *Cf. State v. Coccomo, supra; State v. Egan,* 213 N.J. Super. 133 (App. Div. 1986); *Michigan v. Sitz,* 110 S.Ct. 2481 (1990).

There must be a rational basis for the site selection for the roadblock. *State v. Mazurek,* 237 N.J. Super. 231 (App. Div. 1989). Advance notice of the roadblock is not required and road signs posted prior to the roadblock and the presence of flashing lights and police cars is sufficient advance warning. *State v. DeCamera,* 237 N.J. Super. 300 (App. Div. 1989). A roadblock must balance legitimate law enforcement needs against the severity of the interference with individual fundamental liberties. A roadblock which is planned in a way which bears oppressively on motorists as a class is unconstitutional (Roadblock caused massive traffic jam) *State v. Barcia,* 235 N.J. Super. 311 (App. Div. 1989). In *State v. Moskal,* 246 N.J. Super. 12 (App. Div. 1991), the court upheld a D.W.I. roadblock based on the guidelines set forth in *State v. Kirk, supra.*

Generally, in a drinking and driving prosecution the probable cause for the stop is erratic driving, an equipment violation, an accident or some other violation of the motor vehicle law. *State v. Weber,* 220 N.J. Super. 420 (App. Div. 1987). Unusual or extraordinary circumstances, not amounting to a violation of the law may be enough to justify a motor vehicle stop. *State v. Goetaski,* 209 N.J. Super. 362 (App. Div. 1986) (vehicle operating on shoulder of 50 M.P.H. road with left turn signal on). *See also, State v. Martinez,* 260 N.J. Super. 75 (App. Div. 1992) (vehicle driven 10 M.P.H. in a 25 M.P.H. residential zone at 2:00 a.m.). In *State v. Martinez,* 260 N.J. Super. 75 (App. Div. 1992), the court found that it was objectively reasonable for the police to stop a vehicle traveling less than 10 mile per hour at 2:00 a.m. in a residential area. A motor vehicle stop may also be justified by the observations of a police officer who is stationed in a toll booth. *State v. Foley,* 218 N.J. Super. 210 (App. Div. 1987). Probable cause may not be based on the fact that a vehicle has tinted windows. *State v. Harrison,* 236 N.J. Super. 69 (Law Div. 1989). But see *State v. Oberlton,* 262 N.J. Super. 204 (Law Div. 1992). Improper placement of a license plate may, however, provide the basis for a valid stop. *State v. Murphy and Boyd,* 238 N.J. Super. 546 (App. Div. 1990).

An officer who observes a truck at night in a parking lot with lights on and engine running with defendant talking to a woman outside the cab in an area known for prostitution provides sufficient cause for the officer to question the defendant. *State v. George,* 257 N.J. Super. 493 (App. Div. 1992).

In handling a drunk driving case the facts in discovery and the client interview should be carefully evaluated to determine if there was probable cause for the initial stop of the defendant's vehicle. If the facts do not establish probable cause then a motion to suppress the evidence obtained from the unlawful search and seizure should be filed in the municipal court. *State v. Swiderski,* 94 N.J. Super. 14 (App. Div. 1967), (Rule 7:4-2). See also, *State v. Goetaski, supra,* 363 and 364. A motion to dismiss at the conclusion of the state's case can also be made if there was no probable cause or reasonable suspicion for the stop.

N.J.S.A. 39:4-50(a) prohibits *operation* of a motor vehicle by a person who is under the influence of intoxicating liquor or drugs *or* with a blood alcohol concentration of 0.10%

or above. Thus in any drinking driving prosecution it must be proven beyond a reasonable doubt that the defendant *operated* a motor vehicle. In most drunk driving prosecutions operation is proven by the observation of the arresting officer who actually saw the defendant operating the vehicle. It is now clear that the vehicle does not have to be in motion for a defendant to be found guilty of operating the vehicle, *State v. Mulcahy,* 107 N.J. 467 (1987) (defendant staggered out of a tavern, sat behind the steering wheel and attempted to put the key in the ignition at which point the officer took the keys and arrested the defendant). In *Mulcahy,* the court held that a person who is under the influence, who is in actual physical control of a motor vehicle and who attempts to operate the vehicle with the intent to drive is guilty of a violation even if the vehicle is not put in motion. See also, *State v. George,* 257 N.J. Super. 493 (App. Div. 1992) and *State v. Morris,* 262 N.J. Super. 413 (App. Div. 1992).

In *State v. Steine,* 203 N.J. Super. 275 (App. Div. 1985) the court held that "when a person in an intoxicated state places himself behind the wheel of a motor vehicle and not only intends to operate it in a public place, but actually attempts to do so (even though the attempt is unsuccessful) and there is a possibility of motion," he violates the statute. In *Steine,* the defendant's mother was attempting to push the defendant's vehicle and the court inferred that defendant was behind the wheel since the car could only be moved if the shift lever was held between park and reverse. Pursuant to both *Mulcahy* and *Steine* the defendant's intent to operate and physical control of the vehicle are sufficient to sustain a conviction. See also *State v. Sweeney,* 40 N.J. 359 (1963) and *State v. Daly,* 64 N.J. 122 (1973). In *State v. DiFrancisco,* 232 N.J. Super. 317 (Law Div. 1988) the defendant was found behind the wheel of his truck which was in a ditch and inoperable. The court held that there could be no intent to operate after the truck went into the ditch.

The statements made by the defendant to the investigating officer may also provide the element of operation. *State v. Dickens,* 130 N.J. Super. 73 (App. Div. 1974); *State v. Prociuk,* 145 N.J. Super. 570 (Cty. Ct. 1976). It should be noted that if defendant's statements are the product of custodial interrogation and not routine roadside questioning then the statements must be given in compliance with *Miranda. Berkemer v. McCarthy,* 468 U.S. 420 (1984), *State v. Weber,* 220 N.J. Super. 420 (App. Div. 1987), *State v. Nemesh,* 228 N.J. Super. 597 (App. Div. 1988).

The defendant's intent to operate can be inferred by the court based on all of the facts including defendant's statements, location of the vehicle and any other fact which would permit the inference that the defendant operated or intended to operate a vehicle. Presumable intent to operate can still be rebutted in the right factual setting. *State v. Daly,* 64 N.J. 122 (1973). Operation can also include coasting down an incline on a motorcycle with the engine off. *State v. Jeanette,* 172 N.J. Super. 587 (Law Div. 1980). N.J.S.A. 39:5-25 provides that the offense must be committed in the presence of the arresting officer. The term presence has been construed to mean the knowledge of facts which the officer acquires through the use of his senses. *State v. Macuk,* 57 N.J. 1 (1970); *State v. Mulcahy,* 107 N.J. 467 (1987); *State in the Interest of J.B., Jr.,* 131 N.J. Super. 6 (Cty. Ct. 1974); *State v. Dickens,* 130 N.J. Super. 73 (App. Div. 1974); *Bauer v. Cliffside Park,* 225 N.J. Super. 38 (App. Div. 1988). See also, *State v. Dannemiller,* 229 N.J. Super. 187 (App. Div. 1988).

A violation of N.J.S.A. 39:4-50 can occur whether the vehicle is operated on a public roadway or in a quasi-public or private area. *State v. McColley,* 157 N.J. Super. 525 (App. Div. 1978); *State v. Gillespie,* 100 N.J. Super. 71 (App. Div. 1968); *State v. Sisti,* 62 N.J. Super. 84 (App. Div. 1960). It should be noted that the implied consent statute, N.J.S.A. 39:4-50.2, is narrower than N.J.S.A. 39:4-50 in that it only applies to a vehicle operated on a public road, street or highway or quasi-public area, and not to vehicle operated on private property.

B. Under the Influence and Per Se Offense

N.J.S.A. 39:4-50(a), as amended effective April 7, 1983, provides for two distinctly different offenses. In addition to prohibiting operation of a motor vehicle while under the influence of alcohol, the statute also prohibits operating of a motor vehicle with a blood alcohol concentration of 0.10% or more. *State v. Kreyer*, 201 N.J. Super. 202 (App. Div. 1985); *State v. D'Agostino*, 203 N.J. Super. 69 (Law Div. 1984); *State v. O'Connor*, 220 N.J. Super. 104 (App. Div. 1984). Due to the addition of the 0.10% violation the statute is now referred to as a *per se* offense. *State v. Tischio*, 107 N.J. 504 (1987).

As a result of the statutory amendment it is no longer necessary for the state to prove that the defendant was under the influence. *State v. Tischio, supra*. The holding in *Tischio* provides that a defendant may be convicted when a properly administered breathalyzer test is administered within a reasonable time after the defendant was actually driving his vehicle and the result of the test is a blood alcohol level of at least 0.10%. The court in *Tischio* further held that the statute neither requires nor allows extrapolation evidence to demonstrate the defendant's blood alcohol level while actually driving. Under the holding in *Tischio* it is the blood alcohol level at the time of the breathalyzer test which is the essential element of the offense. The *per se* violation is established by a .10% reading regardless of any alleged tolerance in the machine, *State v. Lentini*, 240 N.J. Super. 330 (App. Div. 1990). In *State v. Oriole*, 243 N.J. Super. 638 (Law Div. 1990), the court held that extrapolation may be used in non *per se* violation cases.

The court in *Tischio* did not set forth what would be a reasonable time between the driving of a vehicle and the administration of the test. In *Tischio* the defendant was tested approximately one hour after he was stopped. The reasonableness of the time gap between driving of the vehicle and administration of the test will have to be dealt with on a case by case basis. *Cf. State v. Dannemiller*, 229 N.J. Super. 187 (App. Div. 1988). *State v. DiFrancisco*, 232 N.J. Super. 317 (Law Div. 1988), *State v. Samarel*, 231 N.J. Super. 134 (App. Div. 1989).

To establish a *per se* violation under the statute the state must prove that the breathalyzer test was administered by a qualified operator who administered the test in a proper manner using a machine which was in proper working order. The court in *Tischio* indicated that expert testimony attacking the reliability and accuracy of the breathalyzer has virtually no probative value in view of the court's holding in *Romano v. Kimmelman*, 96 N.J. 66 (1984) which reaffirmed the breathalyzer as a scientifically accurate device to measure a person's blood alcohol level. A challenge to the accuracy of breathalyzer results based on partition ratio variability was rejected in *State v. Downie*, 117 N.J. 450 (1990). In *Downie*, the court reaffirmed the accuracy of the breathalyzer as a scientific instrument and that breathalyzer results can be the subject of judicial notice. In *State v. Ghegan*, 213 N.J. Super. 383 (App. Div. 1986), however, the court held that the 0.10% reading was rebuttable.

In *Ghegan* the defendant produced an expert who testified that the defendant's behavior on the video tape was consistent with a 0.05% reading rather than the 0.25% as indicated by the breathalyzer. See also, *State v. Miller*, 220 N.J. Super. 106 (App. Div. 1985); but see, *State v. Manfredi*, 242 N.J. Super. 708 (Law Div. 1990).

The court in *State v. Allex*, 257 N.J. Super. 16 (App. Div. 1992) held that medical testimony based on videotape evidence of defendant's performance on physical tests cannot be used to countervail the readings of a properly administered breathalyzer test. The court in *Allex, supra*, held that *State v. Hammond* and *State v. Tischio* overruled *State v. Ghegan*. It is now clear that evidence as to defendant's sobriety cannot be used to attack the result of a properly administered breathalyzer test. *State v. Allex, supra*.

In *State v. Carey*, 263 N.J. Super. 418 (App. Div. 1993) the defendant was not permitted to introduce expert testimony or rely on the defense that occupational exposure to alcohol contributed to the breathalyzer reading. The court pointed out that voluntary intoxication is no defense to a DWI charge. The court also noted that contributing factors which render a defendant susceptible to alcohol are not a defense if alcohol contributed to the impairment of faculties.

In *State v. Nicastro*, 218 N.J. Super. 231 (Law Div. 1986) the court held that the police must have procedures to arrange for the defendant to have his own independent blood test.

In *State v. Weber*, 220 N.J. Super. 420 (App. Div. 1987), however, the court held that police have no duty to arrange for independent blood test. See also, *State v. Ettore*, 228 N.J. Super. 25 (App. Div. 1988) and *State v. Hicks*, 228 N.J. Super. 541 (App. Div. 1988).

In *State v. Dohme*, 223 N.J. Super. 485 (App. Div. 1988) the court held that upon timely objection by the defendant the state must produce the certificate which demonstrates that the ampoules used in the breathalyzers were randomly tested to show that they were properly constituted. The certificate referred to in *Dohme* is the assay report which the manufacturer of the ampoules obtains from an independent testing lab. The *Dohme* case has generated much discussion concerning the admissibility of the assay report. *Cf. State v. Cardone*, 146 N.J. Super. 23 (App. Div. 1976) and *Evidence Rule* 8. See also *State v. Ettore*, 228 N.J. Super. 25 (App. Div. 1988), *State v. Dohme (II)*, 229 N.J. Super. 49 (App. Div. 1988), *State v. Ernst*, 230 N.J. Super. 238 (App. Div. 1989). Spot checking of random ampoules, from the same batch used to test defendant, by the breathalyzer coordinator is sufficient prima facie proof that the ampoules used in testing defendant were properly constituted and mixed to proper proportions. *State v. Maure/Hobbs*, 240 N.J. Super. 269 (App. Div. 1990), aff'd 123 N.J. 457 (1991). Pursuant to *Maure/Hobbs* the coordinator's certificate can be admitted to prove this but the better practice is to also have the assay certificate. The defense may, of course, introduce evidence to demonstrate that the ampoules were not properly constituted.

Breathalyzer test ampoules need not be routinely produced in discovery without an adequate reasonable basis for believing that the test results were defective and that the production of the ampoule will actually assist the defense. *State v. Young*, 242 N.J. Super. 467 (App. Div. 1990).

A defendant may, of course, be convicted of operating under the influence without a breathalyzer reading. Such a conviction would be based on the defendant's operation of the vehicle, performance on balance tests, observations as to defendant's speech and behavior and the opinion of a qualified officer. *State v. Sisti*, 209 N.J. Super. 148 (App. Div. 1986); *State v. Buglione*, 233 N.J. Super. 110 (App. Div. 1989).

The Municipal Court Judge should make findings as to both bases so that the record is clear in the event of an appeal. *Sisti, supra*. In a case where the defendant refused to take a breathalyzer test such refusal is admissible in evidence. *State v. Stever*, 107 N.J. 543 (1987). The court in *Stever* held that taking the breath test is non-testimonial and therefore not subject to the privilege against self-incrimination.

To prove a violation for allowing another to operate a motor vehicle while under the influence the state must prove that the defendant knew or should have known that the operator was under the influence. *State v. Skillman*, 226 N.J. Super. 193 (App. Div. 1988). The offense of allowing is not a *per se* offense. In *State v. Samarel*, 231 N.J. Super. 134 (App. Div. 1989) the court held that the model 900 and 900A breathalyzer had been approved regardless of the name of the manufacturer. The court also held that a pre and post certificate of operability is preferred but if the pre test was within 30 days of arrest and there is no evidence of a malfunction a post test certificate is not required. See also, *State v. Laurick*, 231 N.J. Super. 464 (App. Div. 1989).

Involuntary intoxication is not a defense to a charge of driving while intoxicated and specific intent need not be proven for a DWI conviction. *State v. Hammond*, 118 N.J. 306 (1990). Violations of the motor vehicle laws are not offenses under the code of criminal justice and the code's provisions do not apply to motor vehicle offenses. *State v. Hammond, supra*.

The defense of entrapment, quasi-entrapment and duress are also not available to a defendant charged with DWI. *State v. Fogarty*, 128 N.J. 59 (1992). If the facts indicate police misconduct, such as police knowingly ordering a drunken defendant to drive, an entrapment based defense may be available. *Cf. State v. Fogarty, supra*.

The failure of the police officer to sign a traffic summons does not *per se* render the summons fatally defective but the court must look to all of the facts of the case to see if the defendant was prejudiced. *State v. Lattore*, 228 N.J. Super. 314 (App. Div. 1988). If, however, the complaint is not signed by the officer within the statute of limitations period for this offense the complaint should be dismissed. *State v. Brennan*, 229 N.J. Super. 342 (App. Div. 1990).

C. Refusal/Implied Consent

To secure a conviction under N.J.S.A. 39:4-50.4a the state must prove that the arresting officer had probable cause to believe that defendant had been operating a vehicle, or had control of a vehicle on a public road, street or highway or quasi-public area while under the influence of alcohol, that the defendant was arrested for driving while intoxicated and that defendant refused to submit to a breathalyzer test. Proof of actual operation of a motor vehicle is not required under the refusal statute and the defendant can in fact be acquitted of driving under the influence and still be found guilty of a violation of 39:4-50.4a. *State v. Wright*, 107 N.J. 488 (1987). The burden of proof for a violation of the refusal statute is by a preponderance of the evidence and not beyond a reasonable doubt.

It has been held that anything short of an unqualified, unequivocal assent to take the breathalyzer test is a refusal. *State v. Pandoli*, 109 N.J. Super. 1 (App. Div. 1970). It has also been held that a defendant cannot cure a refusal by changing his mind and deciding to take the test at a later time. *State v. Corrado*, 184 N.J. Super. 561 (App. Div. 1981). In *State v. Ginnetti*, 232 N.J. Super. 378 (Law Div. 1989) the court held that under the facts (defendant agreed to take test within 5 minutes of refusal) the refusal was cured. It is now clear that anything short of an unqualified, unequivocal assent to take the test constitutes a refusal and that the defendant cannot legally cure the refusal by later agreeing to take the test. *State v. Bernhart*, 245 N.J. Super. 210 (App. Div. 1991). Defendant's silence when asked to take the breathalyzer is sufficient for a refusal conviction and the police do not have to take defendant to the machine, hand him the hose and instruct him to blow into it. *State v. Sherwin*, 236 N.J. Super. 510 (App. Div. 1990).

In *State v. White*, 253 N.J. Super. 490 (Law Div. 1991) the court interpreted N.J.S.A. 39:4-50.2 to require that a defendant must provide more than one sample of breath if lawfully stopped for driving under the influence. The holding in *White* does not mean that the police may request an unlimited number of breath samples but only that the defendant must provide a sufficient number of samples to comply with *Romano v. Kimmelman*, 96 N.J. 66 (1984).

A defendant who is charged with both driving under the influence and refusal has no right to have separate trials for these offenses. In *State v. Grant*, 196 N.J. Super. 470 (App. Div. 1984) the court held that a joint trial of these offenses is not violative of the defendant's fifth amendment privilege.

It is clear that the prosecution need not prove that a qualified breathalyzer operator was present when the defendant refused to take the test. *In re Ferris*, 177 N.J. Super. 161 (App. Div. 1981). Presumably, under the holding in *Ferris* the state also would not have to prove that an operable breathalyzer machine was available.

If a defendant claims confusion due to the giving of both Miranda rights and refusal rights the defendant must bear the burden to convince the court that he had indeed been confused. *State v. Leavitt*, 107 N.J. 354 (1987). See also *State v. Sherwin*, 236 N.J. Super. 510 (App. Div. 1990) where defendant was read the refusal form twice and the court found defendant was not confused.

Upon conviction for a violation of N.J.S.A. 39:4-50.4a the municipal court shall revoke the defendant's driving privilege for six months which revocation shall be independent of any revocation for a violation of 39:4-50. The court shall also fine the defendant $250.00 to $500.00 and require that the defendant complete an alcohol rehabilitation program. For conviction of a subsequent violation the license revocation period is two years. A defendant with a prior 39:4-50 conviction but with no prior conviction for 39:4-50.4a is a second offender if convicted under the refusal statute. *In re Bergwall*, 85 N.J. 382 (1981). A conviction under the prior refusal statute N.J.S.A. 39:4-50.4 also subjects the defendant to the penalty for a second offense, upon conviction for a violation of N.J.S.A. 39:4-50.4a. *State v. Fahrer,* 212 N.J. Super. 571 (App. Div. 1986); *State v. Wilhalme,* 206 N.J. Super. 359 (App. Div. 1985). A prior conviction for refusal (N.J.S.A. 39:4-50.4a), however, cannot be used to impose an enhanced penalty for a subsequent DWI conviction. *State v. DiSomma,* 266 N.J. Super. 375 (App. Div. 1993).

D. Constitutional Issues in Driving Under the Influence and Refusal Cases

There is no Sixth Amendment right to counsel for the purpose of consultation prior to submitting to a breathalyzer test. *State v. DeLorenzo,* 210 N.J. Super. 100 (App. Div. 1986), *State v. Leavitt,* 107 N.J. 534 (1987). The taking of a breathalyzer test is considered to be non-testimonial and the Fifth Amendment privilege as to self-incrimination is not implicated. *State v. Stever,* 107 N.J. 543 (1987). Under the Fourth Amendment, of course, there must be probable cause to request that a person submit to a breathalyzer test. *State v. Wright,* 107 N.J. 488 (1987). See *State v. Dyal,* 97 N.J. 229 (1984) as to a blood sample.

Statements made by the defendant during routine roadside questioning are not subject to the Fifth Amendment privilege as they are not the product of custodial interrogation. *State v. Weber,* 220 N.J. Super. 420 (App. Div. 1987). Defendant's post-arrest statements in response to a police officer's request that he take a breathalyzer test were not the product of custodial interrogation and are therefore admissible. *State v. Stever,* 107 N.J. 543 (1987). Field sobriety testing of the defendant does not implicate the privilege against self-incrimination as such testing is non-testimonial in nature. *State v. Green,* 209 N.J. Super. 347 (App. Div. 1986).

The video taping of a defendant's sobriety tests during a drunk driving arrest also does not violate the Fifth Amendment. *State v. Nece,* 206 N.J. Super. 118 (Law Div. 1985); *State v. Bottomly,* 208 N.J. Super. 82 (Law Div. 1984). Both *Nece* and *Bottomly* rely on the non-testimonial nature of defendant's gestures and behavior and that they are relevant in a drunk driving prosecution. The court in *Nece* did hold that the defendant's non-*Mirandized* statements on the videotape had to be suppressed, however. Slurred nature of defendant's answers and answers to questions such as height, weight and date of birth are not testimonial. *Pennsylvania v. Muniz,* 110 S.Ct. 2638 (1990). Asking a defendant to calculate the date of his sixth birthday, however, is testimonial. *Muniz, supra.*

E. Blood Testing

A defendant who is arrested on probable cause for drunken driving has no constitutional right to prevent the involuntary taking of a blood sample provided that the sample is taken in a medically acceptable manner. *State v. Dyal,* 97 N.J. 229 (1984). In *Dyal* the court held that the patient-physician privilege does not bar the police from obtaining the results of a blood test from a hospital where the defendant was treated. The court in *Dyal* held that police should obtain a subpoena for the test results issued by a judge, in the municipality where the records are located, after a showing of probable cause. In *State v. Bodtman,* 239 N.J. Super. 33 (App. Div. 1990) the court held that a *Dyal* subpoena may issue if the police have a reasonable basis to believe that the operator of a motor vehicle was intoxicated and that probable cause is not required. The court should look at all facts known at the time of the event and those discovered within a reasonable time thereafter. *State v. Bodtman,* 239 N.J. Super. 33 (App. Div. 1990). See also *State v. Schreiber,* 240 N.J. Super. 507 (App. Div. 1990).

In *State v. Schreiber,* 122 N.J. 579 (1991) the court held that the patient-physician privilege is to be strictly construed and that it does not apply to a prosecution for violation of the motor vehicle laws. See also *State v. Bodtman,* 248 N.J. Super. 100 (Law Div. 1991). This does not mean that the police can cajole an unwilling doctor to violate the ethical duty to the patient. It does mean, however, that if medical personnel willingly provide facts as to the patient's intoxication to the police that the use of such facts is not barred by the privilege.

Pursuant to N.J.S.A. 2A:62A-10 and -11 a person who has taken a blood sample pursuant to a request from a law enforcement officer may prepare a notarized certificate that the sample was taken in a medically acceptable manner and such certificate shall be admissible in evidence. This statute also immunizes medical personnel for liability as the result of taking blood samples. The fact that a blood sample was taken in a hospital by qualified medical personnel is sufficient to establish that the sample was drawn in a medically acceptable manner without requiring the physician or hospital personnel to testify. *State v. Casale*, 198 N.J. Super. 462 (App. Div. 1985); *State v. Rypkema*, 191 N.J. Super. 388 (Law Div. 1983).

If the defendant resists the defendant can be restrained in a medically acceptable manner so that a blood sample can be taken. *State v. Woomer*, 196 N.J. Super. 583 (App. Div. 1984).

If a blood sample is taken from the defendant there is no requirement that the defendant be informed of his right to have his own blood test performed. *State v. Mercer*, 211 N.J. Super. 388 (App. Div. 1986). In *Mercer* the court also held that there is no requirement that the blood sample be saved so that defendant can have it examined and that the police are not required to inform the defendant of his right to have an independent blood test performed as is required if the defendant is given a breathalyzer test.

The laboratory report of a private hospital's blood alcohol content test is admissible without the testimony of a chemist pursuant to the business entries exception to the hearsay rule. *State v. Matulewicz*, 198 N.J. Super. 474 (App. Div. 1985), *mod.* 101 N.J. 27 (1985). The court in *State v. Flynn*, 202 N.J. Super. 215 (App. Div. 1985) followed the reasoning of the appellate division in *Matulewicz* and would not admit a state police laboratory report as to defendant's blood alcohol level. The court in *Flynn* would not allow the admission of the report either under *Evidence Rule* 63(13) or 63(15)(A). Subsequent to the decision in *Flynn* the Supreme Court remanded the *Matulewicz* case to permit the state to establish a record as to the availability of the hearsay exceptions to the chemists report. See 101 N.J. 27 (1985).

The *Flynn* case was also remanded for a factual hearing as in *Matulewicz*. In *State v. Weller*, 225 N.J. Super. 274 (Law Div. 1986) the court concluded that a blood alcohol test performed by a state police lab using a gas chromatograph is sufficiently reliable that the report may be admitted into evidence without the testimony of the chemist pursuant to evidence rules 63(13) or 63(15). The court in *Weller* also held that the state must make the charts from the gas chromatograph available to the defendant.

If a blood sample is obtained in another state it is the law of New Jersey not the law of the other jurisdiction which controls the admissibility of the evidence at trial. *State v. Konzelman*, 204 N.J. Super. 389 (Law Div. 1985).

Observations and opinions made by medical personnel as to a defendant's intoxication may not be barred by the physician-patient privilege. *State v. Phillips*, 213 N.J. Super. 534 (App. Div. 1986). Under the holding in *Phillips, supra,* only statements made with an expectation of confidentiality are to be excluded based on the physician-patient privilege. See also *State v. Schreiber, supra.*

F. Sentencing Considerations

The penalties which a defendant faces upon conviction for violating N.J.S.A. 39:4-50(a) and 39:4-50.4a are quite severe even if the minimum penalties are imposed. Additionally, the defendant is exposed to insurance surcharges totalling $3,000.00 over three years although the surcharges are not part of the court's sentence but instead are handled through the Division of Motor Vehicles. N.J.S.A. 17:29A-35b. Accordingly, the attorney who handles a drunk driving case should be fully aware of the possible sentences and available alternatives.

The attorney should be aware of the drunk driving victim's bill of rights N.J.S.A. 39:4-50.10, .11 and .12. Pursuant to that statute the victim has a right to be heard at sentencing. Pursuant to N.J.S.A. 39:4-51 a defendant who is sentenced to jail may be sentenced to a work release program and the attorney should make arrangements for same in the event of a conviction which will result in a jail sentence. The statute also provides that a defendant who is sentenced to an inpatient rehabilitation program may petition the court to serve the balance of the sentence in an outpatient program. This can be an important consideration in the case of a third offender. *State v. Rought,* 221 N.J. Super. 42 (Law Div. 1987). The court may in its discretion give the defendant retroactive credit for time spent in an inpatient alcohol program. *State v. Fyffe,* 244 N.J. Super. 310 (App. Div. 1990). A defendant who is sentenced to an inpatient program to satisfy the custodial requirement of a DWI sentence must be sentenced to the full term in the inpatient program. The defendant may be released to an outpatient program only at the request of the treatment agency and at the discretion of the sentencing court. *State v. George,* 257 N.J. Super. 493 (App. Div. 1992).

Pursuant to N.J.S.A. 39:4-50(a)(3) a second offender may serve a jail sentence at an intoxicated driver resource center. This provision does not apply to third offenders. The mandatory 48 hour jail sentence of a second offender may not be suspended. *State v. Walsh,* 236 N.J. Super. 151 (Law Div. 1989).

In the event that the defendant has a prior diving under the influence conviction it should be determined whether the defendant was represented by counsel or knowingly waived counsel at the time of the prior conviction.

If the defendant was unrepresented at the prior hearing and did not make a knowing waiver of counsel an argument can be made that the prior uncounselled conviction should not be used to enhance the penalty. *Baldasar v. Illinois,* 446 U.S. 222 (1980); *State v. Sweeney,* 190 N.J. Super. 516 (App. Div. 1974). If such an argument is raised the defendant bears the burden of proof. *State v. Laurick,* 222 N.J. Super. 636 (Law Div. 1987). The transcript of the prior hearing, if available, the ticket from the prior case or court docket are still all source to obtain information as to representation at the prior hearing. However, if the defendant knowingly waived his right to counsel, *Baldasar* does not apply. *State v. Laurick,* 231 N.J. Super. 464 (App. Div. 1989); *State v. Carey,* 230 N.J. Super. 402 (App. Div. 1989).

If it is established that a prior DWI conviction was uncounselled and that there was no waiver of counsel the only constitutional limit is that a defendant may not suffer an increased period of incarceration as a result of the prior uncounselled conviction. *State v. Laurick,* 120 N.J. 1 (1990). In the case of a second offender, if the first offense was uncounselled the maximum period of incarceration which the court may impose is thirty days. All of the enhanced penalties may be imposed even if the prior conviction was uncounselled. To avoid the imposition of the other enhanced penalties the defendant must file an application for post conviction relief in the court where the prior conviction occurred to vacate that conviction. *State v. Laurick, supra.* Generally, any attack on a prior conviction should be made, pursuant to *Rule* 3:22-2, in the court where the conviction was entered unless the conviction is presumptively void. *State v. Marshall,* 244 N.J. Super. 60 (Law Div. 1990).

A petition for post conviction relief must be filed within five years of the judgment of conviction unless the petition alleges facts which demonstrate that delay was due to defendant's excusable neglect. *State v. Mitchell,* 126 N.J. 565 (1992). The court should relax the rule only under exceptional circumstances. *Mitchell, supra.* The court's failure to elicit a factual basis for a plea is not necessarily of constitutional dimension unless there are contemporaneous indicia such as a claim of innocence or other evidence that the plea was not knowing and voluntary. *Mitchell, supra.*

The use of prior out of state convictions under predecessor statutes should also be questioned if the defendant faces enhanced penalties. *State v. Regan,* 209 N.J. Super. 596 (App. Div. 1986). The court in *Regan, supra,* held that defendant's prior New York conviction for driving while impaired could be used to sentence defendant as a third offender. The court in *Regan* relied on the interstate driver license compact, N.J.S.A. 39:50-1 *et seq.* In *State v. Cromwell*, 194 N.J. Super. 519 (App. Div. 1984) the defendant, a New Jersey licensee, had been convicted of driving under the influence in New York and his license in New Jersey was revoked pursuant to the compact. He was subsequently arrested in New Jersey and charged with a violation of N.J.S.A. 39:3-40. The court in *Cromwell, supra,* held that he could be sentenced under the enhanced penalty for driving while revoked under a suspension issued pursuant to N.J.S.A. 39:4-50 even though the underlying driving while intoxicated conviction was from New York State. The court in *Cromwell* also questioned the holding in *State v. Davis*, 95 N.J. Super. 19 (Law Div. 1967). In *Davis* the court refused to recognize a prior Pennsylvania conviction and sentenced defendant as a first offender.

An out of state resident who holds a New Jersey license may also have his driving privileges revoked in New Jersey by the Director of the Division of Motor Vehicles based on an out of state driving while under the influence conviction. *Matter of Johnson*, 226 N.J. Super. 1 (App. Div. 1988).

A defendant who is arrested twice within a relatively short period of time for driving under the influence may be convicted for both offenses. *State v. Metcalf*, 166 N.J. Super. 46 (App. Div. 1979); *State v. Costello*, 224 N.J. Super. 157 (App. Div. 1988).

The drunk driving statute is primarily deterrent in nature. *State v. Hawks*, 114 N.J. Super. 359 (1989); *State v. Sturn*, 119 N.J. Super. 80, 82 (App. Div. 1972); *State v. Bowman*, 131 N.J. Super. 209 (Law Div. 1974). Accordingly, the enhanced penalties of N.J.S.A. 39:4-50 must be imposed at sentencing on entry of a second drunk driving conviction (within ten years) regardless of the order in which the violations occurred. *State v. Petrello*, 251 N.J. Super. 476 (App. Div. 1991); *State v. Guiendon*, 113 N.J. Super. 361 (App. Div. 1971). It is now clear that if a defendant is convicted for the first violation after the conviction for the second violation that the defendant must be convicted as a second offender for the first violation. *Petrello, supra.* Defendant is subject to the enhanced penalties regardless of whether the defendant was previously advised orally or in writing of the penalties for a subsequent violation. *Petrello, supra.*

A prior conviction for refusal (N.J.S.A. 39:4-50.4a) cannot be used to impose an enhanced penalty for a subsequent DWI conviction. *State v. DiSomma*, 266 N.J. Super. 375 (App. Div. 1993).

It is clear that a defendant has a right to be heard before a prior conviction is used to subject the defendant to an enhanced penalty. *State v. Lima*, 144 N.J. Super. 236 (App. Div. 1976).

If a defendant was erroneously sentenced as a first offender when he should have been sentenced as a second offender and he is again convicted he should in fairness be sentenced as a second offender for what should be his third offense. *State v. Decher*, 196 N.J. Super. 157 (Law Div. 1984). A conviction under any prior section of N.J.S.A. 39:4-50 can be used to sentence as a multiple offender subject to the ten year limitation. *State v. Culbertson*, 156 N.J. Super. 167 (App. Div. 1978); *State v. Gelock*, 237 N.J. Super. 503 (App. Div. 1989).

The date of the prior offense and not the date of the prior conviction is to be used to determine whether defendant is to be sentenced as a multiple offender. *State v. Bischoff*, 232 N.J. Super. 515 (App. Div. 1989). A computer printout of defendant's driving record may be used for sentencing purposes. *State v. Carey*, 232 N.J. Super. 523 (App. Div. 1989). The signature of a judge of court clerk is not required, however, for the issuing of a traffic summons. *State v. Gonzalez*, 114 N.J. 592 (1989).

The attorney is encouraged to be innovative and resourceful in representing the drunk driving defendant. For this reason, various articles are printed herein in an effort to provide the attorney with a basis of understanding the complexity of this issue. Perhaps the single most useful resource for drunk driving defenses is: "Defense of Drunk Driving Cases," Richard E. Erwin, Matthew Bender Co. 1977 (two volumes with annual supplements). It is a must for municipal court attorney's library.

G. Miscellaneous Issues

A request for discovery in a DWI case should generally be limited to the scope of *Rule* 3:13-3. More particularized discovery demands which seek to enlarge the language of the rule are not permitted without leave of the court. If the defense believes the state has not supplied all relevant materials reasonably required for a defense the defense should move for an order compelling discovery prior to trial. *State v. Ford,* 240 N.J. Super. 44 (App. Div. 1990). See also *State v. Laurick,* 231 N.J. Super. 464 (App. Div. 1989). The *Ford* case limits the broad range of discovery permitted in *State v. Tull,* 234 N.J. Super. 486 (Law Div. 1989).

In *State v. Holup,* 253 N.J. Super. 320 (App. Div. 1992) the court recommended that each municipality provide a locked mail box for the municipal prosecutor and that all discovery requests be placed in the mail box. The court in *Holup* also reaffirmed that if discovery is not provided that defense counsel should move prior to trial for an order fixing a date by which discovery should be provided. Any sanction which is imposed on the prosecutor for failure to provide discovery, must be paid personally by the prosecutor and not the municipality. *State v. Holup, supra.*

DWI cases should not be dismissed due to the failure of a witness to appear on a peremptory trial date but the court should consider the imposition of costs. *State v. Prickett,* 240 N.J. Super. 139 (App. Div. 1990). See also *State v. Gallegan,* 117 N.J. 345 (1989) concerning the granting of adjournments as alternative to dismissal.

Failure of the police to videotape a DWI arrestee does not violate due process rights in absence of showing of prejudice. *State v. Gordon,* 261 N.J. Super. 462 (App. Div. 1993); see also *State v. Colasurdo,* 214 N.J. Super. 185 (App. Div. 1986) as to loss of video tape.

An indigent defendant may be entitled to an expert witness at state expense if the defendant can show that the expert is necessary for the defendant to prove that he was not intoxicated. *State v. Ryan,* 133 N.J. Super. 1 (Law Div. 1990). See also *State v. Manning,* 234 N.J. Super. 147 (App. Div. 1990).

For a defendant who is charged with DWI while operating a non-motorized pedal type bicycle see *State v. Machuzak,* 227 N.J. Super. 279 (Law Div. 1988); *State v. Johnson,* 203 N.J. Super. 436 (Law Div. 1985); *State v. Tehan,* 190 N.J. Super. 348 (Law Div. 1982), N.J.S.A. 39:4-14.3g, however, provides that a person who is operating a moped is subject to the provisions of N.J.S.A. 39:4-50.

It is now clear that a defendant who is charged with driving under the influence is not entitled to a jury trial for either a first, second or third offense. *State v. Ellis,* 121 N.J. 131 (1990); *State v. Graff,* 121 N.J. 131 (1990); *State v. Hamm,* 121 N.J. 109 (1990). If a defendant is charged with two or more factually related petty offenses, e.g. third offense DWI and third offense driving while revoked, and the cases are tried together without a jury the jail sentences imposed must not total more than six months. *State v. Linnehan,* 197 N.J. Super. 41 (App. Div. 1984).

HOW TO LOSE YOUR MUNICIPAL COURT CASE
By Frederick C. Schneider, III
Judge, Municipal Court of East Brunswick

You have just been retained to represent an individual charged with a serious traffic or disorderly persons offense scheduled for trial in two weeks. You have been paid a fee of approximately $500 for handling this case. The following is a partial list of ways in which you may lose this case.

1. ASK FOR AN ADJOURNMENT RIGHT AWAY—EVEN IF YOU DON'T NEED IT. YOUR CLIENT WILL BE IMPRESSED THAT IT IS GOING TO TAKE YOU ANOTHER THREE WEEKS TO PREPARE HIS CASE.

In actual fact, your best chance of winning your case in some courts may be to enter your appearance at least three days before trial, specify your not guilty plea, and indicate that you will be ready to proceed on the trial date. Under these circumstances you are in a strong position to oppose a State request for an adjournment. The State may be required to proceed with whatever witnesses and evidence it may have available at that time. In other courts, it may be the Judge's policy to always grant the State one adjournment. The severity of the charge may be a factor in his determination. Don't fail to remind the Judge that your client is paying a substantial fee for your appearance and that you have done all you are required to do to notify the court of your request for a trial. Fundamental fairness is on your side. Advance familiarity with court policy on this issue is obviously very helpful.

2. DON'T BOTHER TO INTERVIEW YOUR CLIENT AND HIS WITNESSES BEFORE TAKING THE CASE. LET AN ASSOCIATE HANDLE THE INITIAL INTERVIEW AND HAVE YOUR CLIENT INFORMED THAT YOU'LL MEET HIM AT COURT.

Nothing can be less impressive to observers than the attorney appearing for trial who has to ask a Judge, court attendant or Court Clerk to "page" his own client. Another problem frequently occurs when the client who has retained a particular attorney to represent him is surprised to find that an associate has been assigned to the case without prior notification and consent. Both situations raise serious questions in the mind of the client as to whether he is actually getting the quality of representation for which he has paid. All too frequently, the concerns of such a client are borne out by what actually occurs in the courtroom.

3. RELY ON YOUR CLIENT TO OBTAIN NEEDED DOCUMENTS AND TELL HIM TO BRING THEM TO COURT WITH HIM.

This is one of the most common reasons why a case is lost which could have been won, especially in bad check, uninsured motorists and revoked list cases. You are probably better equipped to obtain much of this information, particularly from banks, insurance agents, and the Division of Motor Vehicles. You know precisely what is required and you should know how to obtain it. It takes a little more work but after all your client is paying for this service. If your client was able to resolve his problem without expert assistance, he wouldn't have retained a lawyer. Even where your client has been asked to retrieve some of these essential documents himself, you should at least review them in your office for adequacy—at a time when an adjournment can still be obtained without having to appear personally in court to request it.

4. DON'T BOTHER TO DOUBLE-CHECK YOUR STATUTE BOOK BEFORE GOING TO COURT—AFTER ALL, IT'S A SIMPLE CASE AND YOU'VE HANDLED MANY LIKE IT BEFORE.

The law does change and even very active and experienced trial attorneys can overlook these changes when they occur. Unfortunately, we have seen lawyers proceed with a case totally unaware of serious mandatory penalties if their client is convicted, e.g. six month loss of license for leaving the scene of an accident with personal injury; two years loss of license for a second offense of driving an uninsured vehicle; thirty days minimum jail sentence for third offender shoplifters; 90 days in jail and $500.00 fine for a second offense of leaving the scene with personal injury.

Another problem area for defense attorneys is that of statutory presumptions working against his client, e.g. the presumption arising from concealment of unpurchased merchandise in shoplifting cases; that arising from non-payment within ten days of notice in bad check cases; presumption of knowledge in certain "leaving the scene" cases. Similarly, a lawyer representing a drunk driving defendant may not be familiar with a permissible adverse inference arising from a breathalyzer test refusal. *State v. Tabisz,* 129 N.J. Super 80 (App. Div. 1974).

Finally, an awareness of the elements of a particular offense is critical. For instance, the state must prove a uniquely worded element of knowledge on a charge of operating an uninsured vehicle belonging to someone else. In drunk driving cases, a total familiarity with the important cases dealing with the element of "operation" is essential.

Don't underestimate the complexity of the legal and factual issues which may decide your municipal court cases—it's all-important to your client!

5. HAVE SEVERAL DRINKS TO RELAX BEFORE GOING TO COURT.

I wish I didn't have to include this one but for a very few attorneys who regularly appear in municipal court, it's a much greater problem than they could possibly realize. These attorneys, who probably wouldn't consider appearing before a Superior Court Judge after drinking, mistakenly feel that they will function better after a full day in upper court by drinking during the two or three hours before night court. Not only is their public image and reputation in jeopardy but their client is being badly cheated. These few attorneys should hear themselves on tape—it would be a rude awakening. Needless to say, this admonition against drinking before going to court applies also to your client and his witnesses.

6. CROSS-EXAMINE ALL ASPECTS OF THE TESTIMONY OF ALL STATE WITNESSES.

The frequent result of a comprehensive cross-examination is to put the State's case in a second time, often strengthening the testimony of State witnesses in the eyes of the Judge. It is not uncommon for defense counsel to inadvertently supply a missing element of the alleged offense through cross-examination. One example is providing the speed zone in a speeding case where it has been left out by the prosecuting attorney. Another is inviting identification of the defendant by the complaining witness when the prosecutor has neglected to ask the witness to do so. Cross-examination should be limited to those areas where something can really be accomplished.

7. CALL ALL OF YOUR CLIENT'S AVAILABLE WITNESSES—THE MORE THE BETTER.

Unfortunately, the third, fourth or fifth witnesses are quite capable of crating [sic] a serious discrepancy on the defense side of the case. Unless their testimony is clearly going to bolster the testimony of earlier witnesses on a critical point and unless you are supremely confident of what their answers to important questions will be, the use of numerous corroborative witnesses can be very risky. Obviously, any witness should be interviewed before being called to the witness stand.

8. **SUBMIT AT THE END OF THE CASE WHEN GIVEN THE OPPORTUNITY TO MAKE A STATEMENT IN SUMMATION.**

If you feel that you have a shot at winning your case, take a minute or two to identify for the Judge those elements where you feel that State's case is weakest. Those weak areas are where you have your best opportunity of prevailing and those aspects should be argued briefly but aggressively on summation. A failure to do so may be misintepreted as a concession.

It would be easy for one reading these comments to conclude that the quality of legal representation before the Municipal Courts is generally poor. Such a conclusion would be erroneous but certainly many individual attorneys can improve their own case preparation and courtroom performance considerably. Your client is undergoing a substantial financial burden in retaining you to represent him. Is he getting his money's worth? Are you really earning your fee in Municipal Court?

STATEMENT IN DEFENSE OR MITIGATION

Pursuant to R. 7:6-6 the court may allow the defendant to present his or her defense or the court may allow a statement in mitigation of penalty in traffic cases by affidavit if an appearance in court would cause a hardship. This rule applies to all traffic offenses, except those which involve indictable offenses, accidents resulting in personal injury, operation of a motor vehicle while under the influence of alcohol or narcotics, permitting another who is under such influence to operate a vehicle in the defendant's control, reckless driving, or leaving the scene of an accident. A sample affidavit is provided in **Exhibit 24.**

When such a defense is permitted, the state's testimony is heard in the usual manner and thereafter the affidavit is read into the record. The subsequent judgment shall be sent by ordinary mail and if there is a finding of guilt, the defendant will be notified of the sentence imposed and directed to promptly comply with same.

Whether to allow the use of the statement in defense is at the discretion of the Municipal Court Judge.

EXHIBIT 24

STATE OF NEW JERSEY

Municipal Court of _____   County of: _____

_____   Traffic Ticket No. _____
(Court Address)

                                               Docket Nos. _____

_____
_____   **Statement In Defense Or**
            v.   **Mitigation of Penalty**

_____   (For use in traffic cases
            Defendant   pursuant to R. 7:6-6)

Charge(s): _____   _____
              (Statute Nos.)   (Description of Offense(s))

State of _____)
                                 ss.
County of _____)

I, _____, the defendant in the above case, residing at _____, being duly sworn upon my oath depose and say:

It would be an undue hardship for me to appear in person for trial. I understand my right to a reasonable postponement and waive my right to be present at the trial. I understand that if I plead NOT GUILTY, the Judge will hear the testimony of the complainant or other witnesses. If I plead GUILTY, the Judge may hear such testimony. I agree to abide by the judgment of the court. I understand that if convicted, for other than a parking offense, a record of same will be sent to the Division of Motor Vehicles which issued my license.

( ) I plead **GUILTY** to the above charge(s).
( ) I plead **NOT GUILTY** to the above charge(s).

Following are the facts which I present by way of defense or mitigation of the offense with which I am charged: _____

_____

_____

_____

_____

_____

EXHIBIT 24 (Continued)

I understand that the judgment of the Court, together with notice of all penalties which may be imposed, will be forwarded to me by mail at the above address and that I am bound by said judgment unless appealed to the County Court within 10 days after entry of the judgment.

Sworn and subscribed before me
this _____ day of _____ 19_____.   _____
                                                                                               Defendant

_____ Title_____
(Must be sworn to before person
authorized to administer oath.)

(Additional sheets may be attached but each must be signed by the defendant or you may use the back of this form.)

SENTENCING

In a Municipal Court proceeding involving an ordinance, petty disorderly, disorderly or traffic violation, it is not uncommon for the Judge to impose sentence immediately subsequent to the plea or finding of guilt. Of course, as specifically mentioned herein, certain motor vehicle offenses require specified minimum penalties, such as driving while under the influence, or driving while revoked or with no insurance. In those instances where there is a specified minimum penalty, the Judge must impose at least the minimum. Likewise, there are maximum penalties which cannot be exceeded. The attorney should always familiarize himself or herself with the minimum and maximum penalties involved, not only to advise the client, but also to insure that a penalty in excess of the maximum is not mistakenly imposed. *State v. Sweeney,* 190 N.J. Super. 516 (App. Div. 1983), provides that if the penalty imposed is less than the minimum mandatory, it must be corrected by the sentencing Judge.

N.J.S.A. 2C:44-6 provides that a Judge may postpone sentencing for the purpose of ordering that a presentence report be completed by the probation department. When the presentence report is received, the defendant and his or her attorney are afforded the opportunity to review it prior to sentencing and to state any corrections or objections on the record.

For disorderly and petty disorderly offenses occurring after September 1, 1979, a $25.00 Violent Crimes Compensation Board penalty must be imposed. See N.J.S.A. 2C:43-3.1a(2)(a). The penalty was increased to $50.00 per count for offenses occurring after December 23, 1991.

Fines and restitution for disorderly and petty disorderly offenses are governed by N.J.S.A. 2C:43-3. The statute provides that the maximum fine for a disorderly persons offense is $1,000.00 and for a petty disorderly persons offense, $500.00. Further, the court may impose an amount which is twice the defendant's pecuniary gain or the victim's loss, or such other higher amount specifically ordered by statute. Restriction of an actual amount determined by the court may also be imposed in addition to any other fine.

Maximum sentences of imprisonment for disorderly persons offenses shall not exceed six months, or thirty days for petty disorderly persons offenses pursuant to N.J.S.A. 2C:43-8. The idea of community service has also become increasingly popular and may be imposed in addition to, or in lieu of, a fine or period of incarceration. The community service imposed may be supervised locally or through the probation department. (**Exhibit 25**). See N.J.S.A. 2A:8-31.1.

It is not uncommon for a Judge at his own discretion, or upon the request of defense counsel, to impose a period of incarceration to be served on weekends only; however, this provision is applicable only for sentences of three months or less. This is particularly useful when a minimum mandatory period of incarceration resulting from driving while revoked must be imposed. See N.J.S.A. 2A:8-30.1.

Before a sentence is imposed, the attorney should make a statement indicating the defendant's status as to: 1) age; 2) marital status; 3) whether the defendant has any dependents; 4) with whom the defendant resides; 5) employment status; 6) prior convictions; 7) health problems; 8) weekly earnings; and 9) any other mitigating factors including the defendant's role in the offense.

Too frequently young attorneys feel that their task has been concluded once a verdict is announced. Nothing could be further from the truth and the attorney should be prepared to make the appropriate representations regarding the defendant for the purpose of sentencing.

Once the sentence has been announced, the attorney may have to intervene in making arrangements for partial payment of fines over a period of time. The attorney should also advise the client as to what is required in order to comply with the court's sentence and the possible consequences of non-compliance.

In the event a defendant receives a suspended sentence or probation he or she may be required to do one or more of the following as a condition of sentence:

1. Support his dependents and meet his family responsibilities;
2. Find and continue in gainful employment;
3. Undergo available medical or psychiatric treatment and enter and remain in a specified institution;
4. Pursue a prescribed course of study or vocational training;
5. Attend or reside in a facility established for the instruction, recreation and residence of persons on probation;
6. Refrain from frequenting unlawful or disreputable places or consorting with disreputable persons;
7. Not have in his possession any firearm or other dangerous weapon unless granted permission;
8. Make restitution for the fruits of his offense, in an amount he can afford to pay, for the loss or damage caused thereby;
9. Remain within the jurisdiction of the court and to notify the court or his or her probation officer of any change in his or her address or employment;
10. Report as directed to the court or his or her probation officer, to permit the officer to visit his or her home, and to answer all reasonable inquiries by the probation officer; and
11. Satisfy any other conditions reasonably related to rehabilitating the defendant and not unduly restricting his or her liberty or incompatible with his or her freedom of conscience.

Aside from the general conditions (**Exhibit 26**), the court may impose specific conditions as may be necessary. For example, in the case of a shoplifting offense, the defendant may be forbidden from entering the store in which the offense was committed.

EXHIBIT 25

PROGRAM BACKGROUND

Community Service is a concept rapidly gaining support throughout the United States. Each month thousands of offenders convicted of a variety of crimes are given "Community Service Orders"—legal commands to somehow pay back society for breaking its rules.

Community Service orders not only make the offender pay for breaking the law, but also, in many cases, keep the offender out of jail. This not only spares the offender the complex entanglements of incarceration, but also saves the taxpayer the immense cost of keeping the offender behind bars.

In his year-end report dated December 28, 1980, Chief Justice Warren Burger endorsed the community service trend. Mr. Burger stated that programs requiring offenders to do uncompensated work for public or charitable organizations as a condition of probation seemed to serve as an effective deterrent.

Community Service began in Camden County with the Juvenile Restitution Program. Since then it has expanded to the Pre-Trial Diversion Program and Adult Probation. Thousands of hours of useful work have been provided to needy agencies by community service workers.

ORGANIZATIONS SERVED BY COMMUNITY SERVED REFERRALS

Many types of agencies use community service referrals in varied kinds of work assignments. Participants are placed according to their job skills, transportation and geographic location.

Participating agencies are local municipalities, non-profit or charitable organizations that need the services provided by the program participants.

Probationers are required to make every effort to produce quality work wherever they are assigned. Each agency keeps in close contact with Community Service Staff. Progress in assignment, and problems encountered with attendance, behavior and job performance are regularly reported and acted upon.

PROBATIONER'S RESPONSIBILITY

Offenders ordered to do community service work are obligated to perform a specified number of hours during a specific time period. In addition all probationers must:

1. Work regularly and report at the assigned time.

2. Be cooperative and reliable at the worksite.

3. Be responsible for transportation to assigned worksite.

4. Wear proper clothing for the type of work assigned.

5. Maintain a record of community service hours completed.

6. Respond promptly to directives from community service staff.

7. Notify community service staff immediately of any changes such as change of job, address, telephone number, sickness, etc.

8. Document any absence for sickness by Doctor's note.

Failure to adhere to the conditions of the Community Service Program could result in Violation of Probation, and incarceration.

EXHIBIT 25 (Continued)

PARTICIPANT ELIGIBILITY AND EXCLUSION CRITERIA

Except as otherwise noted below, eligible candidates will include all persons receiving a sentence of probation as a result of guilty plea or conviction in a Superior or Municipal Court.

Those persons who have been found guilty of an offense as to which there is a mandatory penalty provided by statute are ineligible. Other types of offenders that should normally be excluded are:

1. Sex offenders;
2. Habitual violent offenders;
3. Offenders with an ongoing history of mental or physical illness;
4. Offenders who are associated with organized crime;
5. Drug dependent offenders.

It must be noted that "physical illness" as described in Exclusion #3 is not intended to exclude persons with physical handicaps. Persons with such conditions will be placed in community service areas developed to best suit their capabilities.

All rejections of probationers for acceptance into the Adult Community Service Program must be appealed to the sentencing court in accordance with the Rules of the Supreme Court.

The court will retain the right to establish the amount of service to be performed as a condition of probation, at sentencing or may in its discretion permit the Program Administrator or his subordinates to set the hours of service in accordance with the "Time Guidelines" set forth below.

EXHIBIT 25 (Continued)

COUNTY OF GLOUCESTER
STATE OF NEW JERSEY
PROBATION DEPARTMENT
P.O. BOX 638
WOODBURY, NEW JERSEY 08096

COMMUNITY SERVICE TIME GUIDELINES

The following time guidelines are established as a framework for uniform sentencing to the community service order. As previously noted, judicial discretion and/or special circumstances may warrant departure from the ranges outlined below. The guidelines were developed to enable the length of the community service order to be determined by: (1) the seriousness of the offense at conviction as defined by the N.J. Criminal Justice Code; (2) the assessment by the sentencing Judge as to appropriate sentence based upon consideration of all relevant factors; (3) practical consideration of the availability of community service placements.

A. Time Guidelines

Offense Category	Hours of Community Service		
	Min.	Med.	Max.
Disorderly persons offenses	40	70	100
Crimes—4th degree	60	130	200
Crimes—3rd degree	80	190	300
Crimes—1st & 2nd degree	100	250	400

B. Length of Probation Term

Hours of Comm. Service	Estimated Time to complete	Probation Term
40-100	2-5 months	1 year
101-200	5-10 months	2 years
201-400	10-20 months	3 years

The time guidelines are based upon the estimate that a participant will complete an average of 20 hours per month, per placement. Probation terms cited represent the minimum term that should accompany the corresponding community service order.

Exemplary performance may result in a recommendation to the court for a reduction in the number of hours set forth as a condition of probation, or by adjustment by the Project Director, if assigned hours have not been set forth in the order of probation.

102/Municipal Court

EXHIBIT 26

A-34   GLOUCESTER COUNTY PROBATION DEPARTMENT

STANDARD CONDITIONS FOR ADULT CRIMINALS ON PROBATION

Statement to be made by Probation Officer receiving
ADULT CRIMINALS ON PROBATION

"The execution (or imposition) of your sentence has been suspended by the Court and you have been placed on probation for a period of _____ years. This action is subject to your agreeing to comply and your compliance with the following standard conditions of probation which have been adopted by the Court and which I now hand you and also with any special conditions of probation which may be ordered by the Court now or in the future. If you fail to observe the conditions of probation you may be returned to Court and required to serve your sentence in an institution."

1. You will obey the laws of the United States, the laws of any and all States in which you may be and the ordinances of any and all municipalities in which you may be.

2. You will report to your Probation Officer at such times and places as he may direct.

3. You will answer promptly, truthfully and completely all inquiries made by your Probation Officer.

4. You will permit your Probation Officer to visit your residence at any time and to make any inquiries about you of any person who may have information concerning you.

5. You will promptly notify your Probation Officer whenever you change your place of residence.

6. You will not leave the State of New Jersey for a period of more than 24 hours without first securing the permission of your Probation Officer.

7. You will make sincere and vigorous efforts to obtain and keep regular and lawful employment and will notify your Probation Officer promptly if you change your place of employment or find yourself out of work.

8. You will cooperate in any physical and mental examination or tests, treatment and counselling your Probation Officer recommends to maintain a satisfactory standard of health and conduct.

9. You will pay through the Probation Department any and all monies ordered to be paid by the Court in strict accord with terms fixed by the Court.

10. You will comply with any additional special conditions of Probation specially imposed by the Court and communicated to you by your Probation Officer. In your case, the following (or no) special conditions are imposed at this time. (List any).

Read and explained to me: Signed:_____
                                              Probation Officer

_____
Signature of Probationer

Date:_____   Date:_____

MOTIONS CONCERNING SENTENCING

Rule 3:21-10(b) allows motions to be made at any time for:

1. Changing the custodial sentence to allow the defendant's entry into a custodial or non-custodial treatment or rehabilitation program for drug or alcohol abuse;

2. Permitting the defendant's release due to illness or infirmity;

3. Upon joint application of the defendant and the prosecuting attorney for good cause;

4. Changing the sentence as authorized by the Code of Criminal Justice;

5. Changing a custodial sentence to permit entry into the Intensive Supervision Program. (See Rule 3:21-10(e) for procedure to be followed for admittance into the Intensive Supervision Program). This provision is generally not applicable to municipal court offenses unless there are companion indictable offenses.

MOTION TO REDUCE OR CHANGE SENTENCE OR FOR NEW TRIAL

A motion to reduce or change a custodial sentence or for a new trial may be filed with the court of original jurisdiction pursuant to R.3:21-10 and R.7:4-7 respectively, within the time limits prescribed. Although this practice is not normally followed in the Municipal Court, the rule still applies. Such motions should be made in writing, upon notice to the prosecutor and with the appropriate affidavits and/or brief attached. These motions will be considered by the Municipal Court.

APPEALS

Appeals from Municipal Court determinations shall be brought within ten days of sentencing, unless for good cause shown. See R.7:8-1, R.1:3-4, R.3:23, R.3:24 and R.2:2-3(b).

If a case is appealed to the Superior Court, the Municipal Court no longer has any authority to grant a new trial or reconsideration. *State v. Hanemann*, 180 N.J. Super. 544 (App. Div. 1981). Further, constitutional and jurisdictional questions may be raised initially in the appellate court even if not argued in the Municipal Court. *State v. Celmar*, 175 N.J. Super. 242 (App. Div. 1978), *rev'd on other grounds* 80 N.J. 405 (1979). Interestingly, pursuant to *State v. Abbondanzo*, 201 N.J. Super. 181 (App. Div. 1985), if a defendant is improperly deprived of the right to an attorney at the Municipal Court level, the defect is not cured by an assignment of counsel on an appeal *de novo*.

A Notice of Appeal shall be filed and served within five days of filing upon the County Prosecutor and County Clerk along with the filing fee and Affidavit of Timely Filing. A copy of the Notice of Appeal and Certification of Timely Filing, serving as notification shall also be sent to the Municipal Court Prosecutor and the Municipal Court Clerk. See **Exhibits 27 through 32**. Failure to comply with these requirements shall cause the appeal to be dismissed without further notice or hearing and the record shall be remanded to the Municipal Court for execution of the Judgment. R.3:23-7. R.3:23-3 states that the Notice of Appeal shall set forth:

1. The title of action;

2. The name and address of the appellant and his or her attorney;

3. A general statement concerning the nature of the offense;

4. The date the Judgment was entered;

5. The sentence which was imposed;

6. Whether the defendant is in custody;

7. Whether a fine was imposed and whether it was paid or suspended;

8. The name of the court from which the appeal is taken;

9. A statement as to whether a stenographic record or sound recording was made in the Court from which the appeal is taken;

10. Where a verbatim record was taken, the attorney's certification that he or she has requested and made deposit for the transcript pursuant to R.2:5-3(a) and R.2:5-3(d) or has filed and served a motion for abbreviation of the transcript pursuant to R.2:5-3(c).

If the appellant is indigent, the County Court shall order that the transcript of the proceedings be furnished at the expense of the county, if the appeal is for a violation of a statute; or at the expense of the municipality if the violation involves an ordinance. R.3:23-8(a).

Once the Notice of Appeal has been filed, the Clerk of the Municipal Court shall forward to the Clerk of the County Court the original Complaint, Judgment of Conviction, exhibits retained by the Clerk and a transcript of the entire docket in the action and the same shall be delivered to the prosecuting attorney upon request. R.3:23-4(a). Upon the filing of a copy of the Notice of Appeal, the affidavits and the filing fees with the County Clerk, the County Clerk shall docket the appeal, fix a date for the hearing and mail written notice thereof to the prosecuting attorney and the appellant, or if represented, his or her attorney. R.3:23-4(b).

Where a verbatim record was made in the lower court, the original transcript shall be certified as correct and filed by the Clerk of the Municipal Court with the Clerk of the County Court. A certified copy of the transcript shall be served upon the prosecuting attorney within twenty days after filing the Notice of Appeal or within such time as the Court allows. In such cases, the appeal shall be heard *de novo* on the record, unless the record is so unintelligible as to prejudice the rights of any party. If the rights of the defendant were prejudiced below, the Superior Court will hold a plenary trial *de novo* without a jury. R.3:23-8(a). *See also, State v. Higgins,* 132 N.J. Super. 67 (App. Div. 1975). The court may also supplement the testimony whenever the Municipal Court erred in excluding evidence offered by the defendant, the state offers rebuttable evidence to discredit any supplemental evidence admitted hereunder, or the record being reviewed is partially unintelligible or defective. R.3:23-8(a).

However, an appeal *de novo* does not provide an opportunity to the prosecutor to present proofs which were not presented in the Municipal Court in an effort to sustain a conviction. *State v. Musgrave,* 171 N.J. Super. 477 (App. Div. 1979). If no record was made in the Municipal Court, the appeal shall be heard as a plenary trial *de novo* without a jury.

The Superior Court may limit argument on the record where the court has previously reviewed the transcript. *State v. Williamson,* 125 N.J. Super. 218 (App. Div. 1973). It has also been held that the Superior Court must give "due, although not necessarily controlling, regard to the opportunity of the magistrate (sic) to judge the credibility of the witnesses."

Briefs are required only when questions of law are involved on the appeal or if ordered by the court and shall be filed and served prior to the date fixed for the hearing or such date as the court may fix. R.3:23-8(b).

An appeal waives all defects in the record and acts as consent to amend the complaint by making the charge more specific, definite or certain, or in any other manner. If the appeal is from a conviction of an indictable offense, it shall not act as consent to amend the complaint to an indictable offense unless the defendant agrees to such amendment. R. 3:23-8(c).

A defendant may seek relief pending appeal pursuant to R.3:23-5. A sentence of probation shall be stayed and a sentence to pay a fine, costs, or a forfeiture may be stayed by the Municipal Court or the Superior Court upon such terms as the court deems appropriate. R.7:8-2. (See **Exhibit 33**). If a custodial sentence has been imposed, the defendant shall be admitted to bail, in accordance with the provisions of R.7:5-4, for a period not to exceed ten days, with sufficient surety conditioned for appearance. During the ten days, the defendant shall enter into a recognizance subject to the approval of the Superior Court. Thereupon, the trial court shall discharge him from custody. If the recognizance is not submitted within ten days, or is submitted and not approved, the bail may be revoked.

If, after the hearing on appeal, the defendant is convicted, the court shall impose sentence as provided by law, R.3:23-8(e), but such sentence shall not exceed that which was imposed by the lower court. *State v. DeBonis*, 58 N.J. 182 (1971). A more severe penalty, however, could be imposed on the *de novo* conviction when the Municipal Court sentence was predicated on the defendant's deliberate falsification. *State v. Pomo*, 95 N.J. 13 (1983). If the defendant is acquitted on appeal, the court shall order the defendant discharged, the conviction in the Municipal Court set aside and the return of all fines and costs paid by the defendant. R.3:23-8(e). The appropriate judgment will be entered and a copy shall be transmitted to the Municipal Court. R.7:8-3. Even if the defendant prevails on appeal, there is no provision that his transcript costs or the costs of appeal can be recovered from the Municipality. *State v. Kuhns*, 121 N.J. Super. 284 (App. Div. 1972).

EXHIBIT 27

WILLIAM J. HAYES, ESQ.
31 Black Horse Pike
Collings Lakes, N.J. 08094
(609) 561-3888
Attorney for Defendant

STATE OF NEW JERSEY	:	Municipal Court
	:	Township of Winslow
	:	County of Camden
v.		
	:	Summons No. E6810/E6811/E6812
JOHN A. DOE	:	NOTICE OF APPEAL

TO: JOHN JONES, ESQ., Prosecutor, Camden Co.
    Hall of Justice, 5th & Mickle
    Camden, N.J.

Take notice that John A. Doe, residing at 123 Main Street, Hometown, New Jersey, hereby appeals to the Superior Court of Camden County from the Judgment of the Municipal Court of the Township of Winslow, entered April 7, 1988, adjudging said defendant guilty of N.J.S.A. 39:4-50, driving under the influence, N.J.S.A. 39:4-98, speeding, and N.J.S.A. 39:4-88, failure to keep right, on which said Court imposed fines of $500.00, $70.00 and $60.00 and $15.00, $15.00 and $15.00 costs plus two years loss of license and 30 days of community service.

The defendant is not in custody. All fines, costs, loss of license and community service were stayed pending appeal.

A sound recording was made in the Winslow Township Municipal Court at time of trial pursuant to R. 7:4-5.

I certify that I have requested the transcript in accordance with R.2:5-3(a), and I have also made a sufficient deposit for the transcript in accordance with R.2:5-3(d).

Dated:
                                                          WILLIAM J. HAYES, ESQ.
                                                          Attorney for Defendant

EXHIBIT 28

WILLIAM J. HAYES, ESQ.
31 Black Horse Pike
Collings Lakes, N.J. 08094
(609) 561-3888
Attorney for Defendant

STATE OF NEW JERSEY	: Municipal Court : Township of Winslow : County of Camden
v.	
	: Summons No. E6810/E6811/E6812
JOHN A. DOE	: AFFIDAVIT OF FILING

1. I am the attorney for John A. Doe, defendant in this matter against whom judgment of conviction was entered in the Township of Winslow Municipal Court on April 7, 1988.

2. A notice of appeal was filed with the Clerk of the Township of Winslow Municipal Court on April 14, 1988 which is within 10 days of the entry of judgment of conviction.

3. On April 14, 1988, which is within 5 days of the date of which I filed the Notice of Appeal, I served a copy of the Notice of Appeal by certified mail, return receipt requested upon John Jones, Prosecutor of Camden County at the Hall of Justice, Camden, New Jersey.

4. I certify that the foregoing statements made by me are true. I am aware that if any of the foregoing statements made by me are willfully false, I am subject to punishment.

Dated: _____

_____
WILLIAM J. HAYES, ESQ.
Attorney for Defendant

EXHIBIT 29

WILLIAM J. HAYES
Attorney-at-Law
31 Black Horse Pike
Collings Lakes, N.J. 08094

Member N.J. & Pa. Bar Associations

April 14, 1988

Clerk, Municipal Court
Township of Winslow
Rt. 73
Braddock, N.J. 08037

RE: STATE v. JOHN DOE

TO WHOM IT MAY CONCERN:

Enclosed please find two copies of the Notice of Appeal and Certification of Timely Filing concerning the above captioned matter. I would appreciate it if you would file same with your office and return one conformed copy in the enclosed envelope.

Also, please find my check in the amount of $100.00 which represents the deposit on the transcript of the trial heard on April 7, 1988.

Thank you for your courtesy in this matter.

Sincerely yours,

William J. Hayes, Esq.

WJH:slm
CC: Clerk, Camden County
    Prosecutor, Winslow Twp.
    John Jones, Camden Co. Prosecutor

EXHIBIT 30

WILLIAM J. HAYES
Attorney-at-Law
31 Black Horse Pike
Collings Lakes, N.J. 08094

Member N.J. & Pa. Bar Associations

(609) 561-3888

April 14, 1988

Prosecutor, Municipal Court
Township of Winslow
Rt. 73
Braddock, N.J. 08037

RE: STATE v. JOHN DOE

Dear Sir:

Enclosed please find a copy of the Notice of Appeal and Certification of Timely Filing concerning the above captioned matter.

Thank you for your courtesy in this matter.

Sincerely yours,

William J. Hayes, Esq.

WJH:slm
CC: Clerk, Camden County
     Municipal Court, Winslow Twp.
     John Jones, Camden Co. Prosecutor

EXHIBIT 31

WILLIAM J. HAYES
Attorney-at-Law
31 Black Horse Pike
Collings Lakes, N.J. 08094

Member N.J. & Pa. Bar Associations

(609) 561-3888

April 14, 1988

Clerk, Camden County
Hall of Justice
5th and Mickle
Camden, N.J.

RE: STATE v. JOHN DOE

Dear Sir:

Enclosed please find the original and two copies of the Notice of Appeal and Certification of Timely Filing concerning the above captioned matter.

Also please find my check in the amount of $30.00 to cover costs of filing same.

Thank you for your courtesy in this matter.

Sincerely yours,

William J. Hayes, Esq.

WJH:slm
CC: Prosecutor, Winslow Twp.
     Municipal Court, Winslow Twp.
     John Jones, Camden Co. Prosecutor

EXHIBIT 32

WILLIAM J. HAYES
Attorney-at-Law
31 Black Horse Pike
Collings Lakes, N.J. 08094

Member N.J. & Pa. Bar Associations

(609) 561-3888

April 14, 1988

John Jones, Esq.
Prosecutor, Camden Co.
Hall of Justice, 5th & Mickle
Camden, N.J.

RE: STATE v. JOHN DOE

Dear Mr. Jones:

Enclosed please find a copy of the Notice of Appeal and Certification of Timely Filing concerning the above captioned matter.

Thank you for your courtesy in this matter.

Sincerely yours,

William J. Hayes, Esq.

WJH:slm
CC: Prosecutor, Winslow Twp.
    Municipal Court, Winslow Twp.
    Clerk, Camden County

EXHIBIT 33

WILLIAM J. HAYES, ESQ.
31 Black Horse Pike
Collings Lakes, N.J. 08094
(609) 561-3888
Attorney for Defendant

STATE OF NEW JERSEY	: Municipal Court
	: Township of Winslow
	: County of Camden
v.	:
	: Summons No. E6810/E6811/E6812
JOHN A. DOE	: ORDER STAYING SENTENCE

This matter being opened to the Court by William J. Hayes, Esq., attorney for defendant, John Doe, and it appearing that timely Notice of Appeal has been filed from the Winslow Township Municipal Court to the Superior Court of Camden County and good cause being shown;

It is on this _____ day of _____, 1988, ORDERED that the Court imposed fines of $500.00, $70.00 and $60.00 and $15.00, $15.00 and $15.00 costs plus two years loss of license and 30 days of community service be stayed pending hearing on the Appeal before the Superior Court of Camden County.

_____
Judge

INTERLOCUTORY APPEAL

Either the prosecutor or the defendant may seek leave from the Superior Court, Law Division to appeal from an Interlocutory Order of the Municipal Court and the prosecutor may appeal a pre- or post-trial judgment dismissing a complaint.

Although interlocutory appeals from Municipal Court determinations are relatively infrequent, there may be instances where the interests of the client and the interests of justice are best served by utilization of this procedure. An example of the use of an interlocutory appeal include review of a critical evidentiary ruling, as in *State v. Lanahan,* 110 N.J. Super. 578 (Cty. Ct. 1970). Another likely instance is where an appeal is taken from a Municipal Court's pretrial denial of an indigent defendant's motion for appointment at public expense of an expert relative to a drunk driving charge. In *State v. Zoppi,* 196 N.J. Super. 596 (Law Div. 1984), an interlocutory appeal was permitted to determine the issue as to whether a third time drunk driving offender has a right to a jury trial.

Appeals shall be taken within ten days after entry of the order by filing, with the Superior Court, Law Division, a Notice of Motion for Leave to Appeal. Time may not be enlarged for filing interlocutory appeals. R. 1:3-4(c). A copy of the Notice shall be filed with the clerk of the Municipal Court and a copy shall be served on the prosecuting attorney or on the defendant or his or her attorney at least ten days prior to the return date fixed therein. The original and all copies shall have annexed thereto copies of all papers of record and any affidavits essential to the determination thereof and shall be accompanied by a brief. The respondent shall file and serve his or her answering brief at least three days before the hearing. A copy of any Order entered by the Superior Court shall be promptly transmitted to the Clerk of the Municipal Court. R. 3:24(c).

EXPUNGEMENT

General Comments

Expungement, as defined by N.J.S.A. 2C:52-1(a), is the "extraction and isolation of all records on file within any court, detention or correctional facility, law enforcement or criminal justice agency concerning a person's detection, apprehension, arrest, detention, trial or disposition of an offense within the criminal justice system." The expungement of records shall include "complaints, warrants, arrests, commitments, processing records, fingerprints, photographs, index cards, 'rap sheets' and judicial docket records." N.J.S.A. 2C:52-1(b). The purpose of expungement is to provide relief to the one-time offender, but does not allow a periodic violator of the law a regular means of expunging police and criminal records. N.J.S.A. 2C:52-32. However, *State v. A.N.J.,* 192 N.J. Super. 350 (1983), *aff'd* 98 N.J. 421 (1985), provides that N.J.S.A. 2C:52-1 to 2C:52-32 allows expungement of more than one disorderly persons offenses.

N.J.S.A. 2C:52-2(a), dealing with indictable offenses, provides that in all cases where an individual is convicted of a crime, and has no prior or subsequent convictions and has not been adjudged a disorderly or petty disorderly person on more than two occasions, he or she may petition the Superior Court of the county in which the conviction was entered to expunge his or her record after ten years pass from the date of conviction, payment of fine, completion of probation or parole, or release from incarceration, whichever is later. When the validity of a prior conviction is at issue, proof of conviction is satisfied by introduction of a certified judgment of conviction. The burden then shifts to the petitioner to prove the invalidity of the conviction. The State may still attempt to rebut the petitioner's evidence by production of further evidence. *State v. H.G.G.,* 202 N.J. Super. 267 (App. Div. 1985).

Pursuant to N.J.S.A. 2C:52-2(b), records of conviction of the crimes of murder, manslaughter, treason, anarchy, kidnapping, rape, forcible sodomy, arson, perjury, false swearing, robbery, embracery, or a conspiracy or attempt to commit any of the foregoing and the Title 2C counterparts, or aiding, assisting or concealing any person accused of the foregoing, are not subject to expungement. Expungement shall also be denied in the case of a conviction for the sale or distribution of a CDS or possession thereof with intent to sell except when the CDS was 25 grams or less of marijuana or 5 grams or less of hashish. N.J.S.A. 2C:52-2(c).

N.J.S.A. 2C:52-3, dealing with disorderly and petty disorderly offenses, provides that "[a]ny person convicted of a disorderly ... or petty disorderly persons offense [who has no previous or subsequent conviction of a crime] or of another three disorderly ... or petty disorderly offenses may" petition for expungement after five years from the date of conviction, payment of fine, completion of probation or release from incarceration, whichever is later, in the Superior Court of the county in which the conviction was entered. *See also, State v. A.N.J.*, 98 N.J. 421 (1985).

N.J.S.A. 2C:52-4, dealing with ordinance violations, provides that "a person found guilty of violation of a municipal ordinance [who has no prior or subsequent conviction of a crime] and who has not been adjudged a disorderly ... or petty disorderly person on two or more occasions, may" file a petition with the Superior Court after two years from the date of conviction, payment of fine, completion of probation or release from incarceration, whichever is later.

N.J.S.A. 2C:52-4.1(a), dealing with juvenile delinquents, provides that for the purposes of expungement, any act which resulted in adjudication as a deliquent shall be classified as if that act were committed by an adult and such adjudications may be expunged pursuant to N.J.S.A. 2C:52-2, N.J.S.A. 2C:52-3, or N.J.S.A. 2C:52-4.

Pursuant to N.J.S.A. 2C:4.1(b), any juvenile deliquent may have his record expunged if:

1. Five years has elapsed since the final discharge of that person from legal custody or supervision or five years has elapsed after the entry of any other court order not involving custody or supervision;

2. He has not been convicted of a crime, or disorderly or petty disorderly offense, or adjudged a deliquent ... during the five years prior to the filing of a petition [for expungement], and no proceeding or complaint is pending seeking such a conviction or adjudication;

3. He was never adjudged a juvenile deliquent on the basis of an act which if committed by an adult would constitute a crime not subject to expungement;

4. He has never had an adult conviction expunged;

5. He has never had adult criminal charges dismissed following completion of supervisory treatment program or other diversionary program.

N.J.S.A. 2C:52-5 provides that any person convicted of an offense under Title 24 (now Chapters 35 & 36 of Title 2C) of the New Jersey Statutes where the CDS was 25 grams or less of marijuana or 5 grams or less of hashish and was twenty-one years of age or younger at the time of the offense may file a petition for expungement of such conviction and all records pertaining thereto after one year has elapsed from the date of the conviction, termination of parole or probation, or discharge from custody, whichever is later, provided that such person has not violated the conditions of his probation or parole and has no prior or subsequent convictions of a crime, no prior or subsequent violations of Title 24 or has not had any prior or subsequent criminal matters dismissed because of acceptance into a supervisory treatment program.

N.J.S.A. 2C:52-6 provides that pursuant to N.J.S.A. 2C:52-6(a), in all cases wherein a person was arrested for a crime, disorderly or petty disorderly offense or violation of a municipal ordinance and against whom the proceedings were dismissed, who was acquitted or who was discharged without a conviction or finding of guilt, may at any time after the disposition of the proceedings, present a petition for expungement of such records. Where the charges were dismissed following completion of a supervisory treatment program, such person shall be barred from relief until six months after the entry of the Order of Dismissal. N.J.S.A. 2C:52-6(b). Where the discharge, dismissal or acquittal, resulted from a determination that the person was insane or lacked the mental capacity to commit the crime charged, he shall be barred from relief. N.J.S.A. 2C:52-6(c).

N.J.S.A. 2C:52-7. Petition for Expungement

Every position for expungement filed pursuant to this chapter shall be verified and include:

a) Petitioner's date of birth.

b) Petitioner's date of arrest.

c) The statute or statutes and offense or offenses for which petitioner was arrested and of which petitioner was convicted.

d) The original indictment, summons or complaint number.

e) Petitioner's date of conviction, or date of disposition of the matter if no conviction resulted.

f) The court's disposition of the matter and the punishment imposed, if any.

Pursuant to N.J.S.A. 2C:52-8, a statement shall accompany such a petition with an affidavit or verification:

a. That there are no disorderly or petty disorderly persons or criminal charges pending at the time of filing; and

b. That petitioners have never been granted an expungement in this or any state in those instances where expungement of a criminal conviction is sought;

c. Setting forth the nature of the original charge, the court of disposition and the date of disposition in those instances where a person has received a dismissal of a criminal charge because of acceptance into a supervisory program.

However, an individual seeking expungement of disorderly persons offense does not need to establish that he or she has ever been granted expungement of another disorderly person conviction. *State v. A.N.J.*, 192 N.J. Super. 350 (1983).

Upon the filing of a petition, the court shall, by order, fix a time not less than thirty-five nor more than sixty days thereafter for hearing of the matter. N.J.S.A. 2C:52-9. A copy of each petition, together with a copy of all supporting documents shall be served upon those persons enumerated in N.J.S.A. 2C:52-10 within five days from the date of the order setting the date for the hearing.

The court may order the expungement without a hearing pursuant to N.J.S.A. 2C:52-11 if there are no objections from the persons or agencies notified and if there are no reasons as provided by N.J.S.A. 2C:52-14 for denial of relief. The court shall deny relief for any reason given by N.J.S.A. 2C:52-14 although no objections have been raised by those notified.

Pursuant to N.J.S.A. 2C:52-15, if an order for expungement is granted by the court, all records specified in said order shall be removed from the files of the agencies which have been notified and shall be placed in the control of a person designated by each agency. This person shall insure that the records are not released for any reason or utilized or referred to for any purpose. Expunged records, however, may be used by the agency to ascertain whether a person has had a prior conviction expunged when the agency is notified of a pending petition for expungement, pursuant to N.J.S.A. 2C:52-17, or be supplied to the Violent Crimes Compensation Board when any claim had been filed (N.J.S.A. 2C:52-18). Expunged records may also be used in determing whether to grant or deny a person's application for acceptance into a supervisory treatment program for subsequent charges, N.J.S.A. 2C:52-20. Expunged records shall be provided, when requested, for use in conjunction with a bail hearing or for purposes of sentencing, N.J.S.A. 2C:52-21, *State v. Stackhouse*, 194 N.J. Super. 371 (1985), or for determining whether parole should be granted, N.J.S.A. 2C:52-22, and shall also be provided to the Department of Corrections for use in classifying, evaluating and assigning persons placed in its custody to correctional and penal institutions.

Nothing contained in N.J.S.A. 2C:52 *et seq.* shall apply to arrest for motor vehicle offenses contained in Title 39, N.J.S.A. 2C:52-28, nor to records contained in the CDS Registry (which has been recently abolished). In any event, records contained in the Registry created by the Administrative Office of the Court shall not be expunged, N.J.S.A. 2C:52-31.

Forms regarding expungement procedures follow **(Exhibits 34 through 37).**

EXHIBIT 34

MITNICK, VOGELSON, JOSSELSON & DEPERSIA
35 KINGS HIGHWAY EAST
HADDONFIELD, N.J. 08033
(609) 795-2050
ATTORNEYS FOR Defendant

SUPERIOR COURT OF NEW JERSEY
CRIMINAL DIVISION
CAMDEN COUNTY

Plaintiff

STATE OF NEW JERSEY

vs.

Defendant

Docket No. 54024

CIVIL ACTION

VERIFIED PETITION FOR EXPUNGEMENT

TO: Superior Court Clerk
Camden County, New Jersey

The Petition of the defendant, an individual residing at City of Camden, County of Camden, New Jersey, respectfully shows that:

1. He is the defendant in the above-captioned matter. His date of birth is June 1, 1924.

2. That on or about October 25, 1985, the defendant was arrested in the City of Camden for alleged violations of N.J.S. 2C:12-1(A).

3. That on or about January 22, 1986, and in the Municipal Court of the City of Camden, the aforementioned charges against the defendant were dismissed.

4. That concerning the above-noted arrest of October 25, 1985 and under N.J.S. 2C:52-6A, wherein a person has been arrested or held to answer for a crime, disorderly persons offense, petty disorderly persons offense or municipal ordinance violation under the laws of this State or of any governmental entity thereof and against whom proceedings were dismissed or who was acquitted or who was discharged without a conviction or finding of guilt, may at any time following the disposition of

EXHIBIT 34 (Continued)

proceedings, present a duly verified petition, as provided in Section 2C:52-7, praying that records of such arrest and all records and information pertaining thereto be expunged.

WHEREFORE, your petitioner   prays that an Order may be entered directing the Clerk of the Court and the parties upon whom notice was served, to expunge from their arrest records, all evidence of the arrests and conviction of said defendant,

including any evidence of detention relating thereto, with such Order specifying those records to be expunged; and

Your Petitioner further prays that all such records to above be removed from their files and placed in the control of such person or persons designated by the Court to retain control over expunged records and that such persons shall insure that such records and the information contained therein shall not be released for any reason in accordance with the provisions of N.J.S.A. 2C:52-1.

                                    MITNICK, VOGELSON, JOSSELSON & DePERSIA

                                    BY_____
                                            Rocco A. DePersia

DATED: February 4, 1986

STATEMENT TO ACCOMPANY PETITION

There are no disorderly persons, petty disorderly persons or criminal charges pending against me at this time of the filing of this petition for expungement.

EXHIBIT 34 (Continued)

CERTIFICATION

I hereby certify that the foregoing statements are true according to the best of my knowledge, information and belief. I am aware that if any of the foregoing statements are willfully false, I am subject to punishment for contempt of court.

_____

EXHIBIT 35

MITNICK, VOGELSON, JOSSELSON & DEPERSIA
35 KINGS HIGHWAY EAST
HADDONFIELD, N.J. 08033
(609) 795-2050
ATTORNEYS FOR Defendant

SUPERIOR COURT OF NEW JERSEY
CRIMINAL DIVISION
CAMDEN COUNTY

Plaintiff

STATE OF NEW JERSEY

vs.

Defendant

Docket No. 54024

CIVIL ACTION

AFFIDAVIT OF SERVICE

STATE OF NEW JERSEY :
COUNTY OF CAMDEN :

I, ROCCO A. DE PERSIA, of full age, being duly sworn according to law, upon my oath, deposes and says:

1. I am an attorney at law of the State of New Jersey and a partner of the firm of Mitnick, Vogelson, Josselson & DePersia, attorneys for the defendant.

2. On Tuesday, March 25, 1986, my secretary mailed copies of the Order to Show Cause and Verified Petition for Expungement, by certified mail, return receipt requested, to the following people:

1. Colonel Pagano—Superintendent of State Police;

2. Irwin I. Kimmelman—Attorney General;

3. Samuel Asbell—Prosecutor of Camden County;

EXHIBIT 35 (Continued)

4. Chief of Police—Camden Police Department;

5. Clerk—Camden Municipal Court;

6. F.B.I.

_____

Sworn to and Subscribed to

before me this   day of

            , 1986.

_____
ROBERTA MARKOWITZ
A Notary Public of New Jersey
My Commission Expires Feb. 21, 1987

EXHIBIT 36

MITNICK, VOGELSON, JOSSELSON & DEPERSIA
35 KINGS HIGHWAY EAST
HADDONFIELD, N.J. 08033
(609) 795-2050
ATTORNEYS FOR Petitioner

SUPERIOR COURT OF NEW JERSEY
CRIMINAL DIVISION
CAMDEN COUNTY

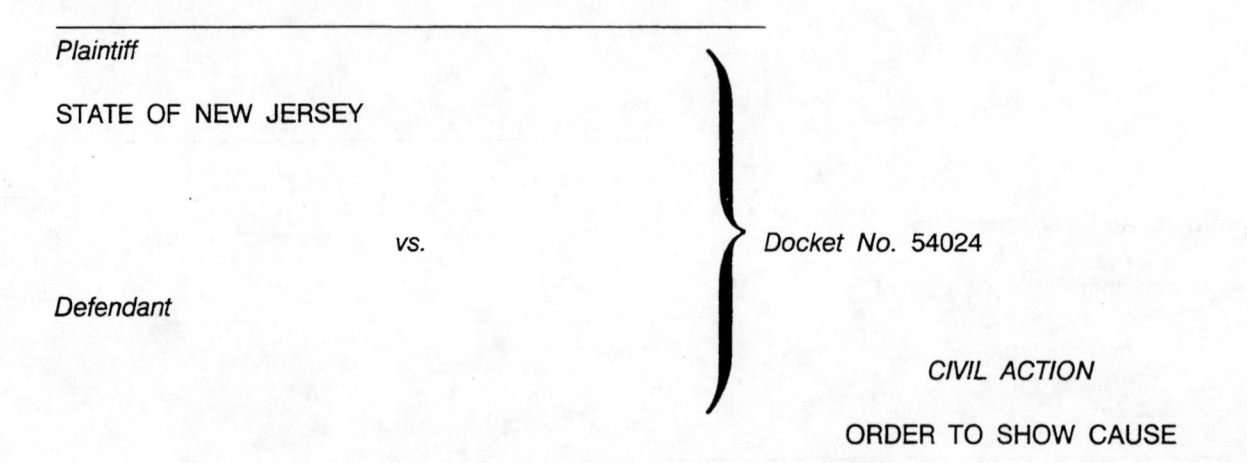

Plaintiff

STATE OF NEW JERSEY

vs.

Defendant

Docket No. 54024

CIVIL ACTION

ORDER TO SHOW CAUSE

This matter being opened to the Court by Rocco A. DePersia, Esquire, of the law firm of Mitnick, Vogelson, Josselson & DePersia, attorneys for the defendant, and it appearing to the Court upon a duly verified petition that good and sufficient reason exists for the issuance and entrance of the herein Orders:

NOW THEREFORE, it is on this day of , 1986, ORDERED as follows:

That the plaintiff herein, The State of New Jersey, show cause before this Court in the Camden County Hall of Justice, Camden, New Jersey on the day of , 1986, at o'clock in the noon, in Room why an Order should not be entered directing the Clerk of the Court and the parties upon whom notice is served to expunge from their records all evidence of the arrests and conviction of the defendant, including evidence of detention related thereto, with such Order specifying those records to be expunged all in accordance with the Order sought in the Verified Petition filed with the Court.

IT IS FURTHER ORDERED that true but uncertified copies of this Order and of the Verified Petition be served upon the plaintiff within five (5) days from the date hereof.

J.S.C.

EXHIBIT 37

MITNICK, VOGELSON, JOSSELSON & DEPERSIA
35 KINGS HIGHWAY EAST
HADDONFIELD, N.J. 08033
(609) 795-2050
ATTORNEYS FOR Defendant

SUPERIOR COURT OF NEW JERSEY
CRIMINAL DIVISION
CAMDEN COUNTY

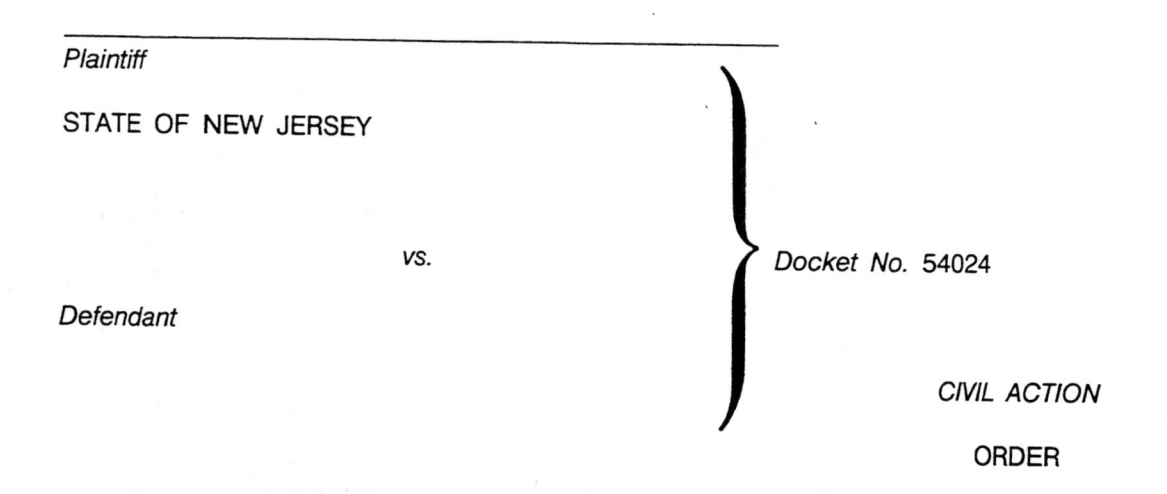

Plaintiff

STATE OF NEW JERSEY

vs.

Defendant

Docket No. 54024

CIVIL ACTION

ORDER

This matter being opened to the Court by Rocco A. DePersia, Esquire of the law firm of Mitnick, Vogelson, Josselson & DePersia, Esquires, attorneys for the defendant, , and it appearing that there has been no opposition to the Petition for Expungement as previously submitted to the Court;

It is, therefore, on this day of , 1986, ORDERED as follows:

That the plaintiff herein, the State of New Jersey, enter an Order directing the Clerk of the Court and the parties upon whom notice is served to expunge from their records all evidence of the arrest of the petitioner, including any evidence of detention related thereto, occurring October 25, 1985 in the City and County of Camden, State of New Jersey arising out of alleged violations of N.J.S.A. 2C:12-1(A) of Camden, Camden County, New Jersey, Case No. 54024, such Order specifying those records to be expunged, all in accordance with the Order sought in the verified petition filed with the Court.

EXHIBIT 37 (Continued)

It is further ORDERED that all such records are to be removed from their files and placed in control of such person or persons designated by the Court to retain control over expunged records and that such persons shall insure that such records and the information contained therein shall not be released for any reason except as provided under the provisions of N.J.S.A. 2C:52-1.

_____

RUDOLPH J. ROSSETTI, J.S.C.

TRAFFIC

General Comments

The Municipal Court has jurisdiction over all violations of Title 39 regarding the operation and the use of motor vehicles. The complaint and summons in such violations shall be in the form of a uniform traffic ticket (see **Exhibit 38**), and these complaints should contain the citation of the statute or ordinance number which was violated, a brief factual description of the violation, the street and municipality where the offense took place, and the name of the defendant or, if not available, the license number of the vehicle. However, the omission of such information does not necessarily invalidate the complaint. The complaint may be signed by anyone, but the summons must be signed by an officer, Judge or Court Clerk.

All traffic complaints are considered quasi-criminal but the defendant has no right to a jury trial provided the maximum fine which may be imposed does not exceed $1,000.00 or six months in prison. The defendant must be informed of his or her right to retain counsel at his or her own expense and must be granted a postponement if he or she wishes to do so. If there is a possibility of imprisonment or substantial loss of driving privilege, an indigent defendant must be informed of his or her right to have counsel assigned.

The trial date must be set at least five days from the date of the violation, unless the defendant waives this right. R. 7:6-4. Before accepting a guilty plea on a non-parking violation, the court must inform the defendant that a record of any conviction will be forwarded to the Division of Motor Vehicles to become a part of his or her driving record. R. 7:6-7.

In addition to any penalty prescribed for violations of Chapters 1 through 5c of Title 39, the Municipal Court may revoke the driver's license or registration certificate of the person convicted, if the violation is willful. This suspension shall be for a specified amount of time and not "indefinite".

When representing a client in a matter which may also be the subject of a subsequent civil case, the attorney should keep in mind that a guilty plea in Municipal Court may be used in the civil trial. A plea of not guilty, however, may not be used even if the defendant is found guilty. The defendant may enter a plea of guilty with reservation that it not be admissible in a subsequent civil proceeding. R. 7:4-2(b).

If the matter involves a violation in any way related to traffic controls, the attorney should contact the State Department of Transportation and/or the County Engineer to obtain the legal authority establishing the traffic light, stop sign or other form of traffic control in question. Although the authority is split as to whether the invalidity of a traffic control device is sufficient to defeat the state's case, the theory is that if a traffic control device has not been approved, it is invalid, and, therefore, there is no offense. The state must also prove that the offense occurred within the jurisdictional limits of the court.

There is no excuse for not rereading the statute involved to insure that the state is held to its proofs.

The section herein concerning trial preparation is applicable in traffic cases.

Miscellaneous traffic forms, including Accident Investigation Report (**Exhibit 39**), Accident Report Code Explanation (**Exhibit 40**), Order for Payment of Fines and Costs (**Exhibit 41**), Failure to Appear Notice (**Exhibit 42**), follow.

EXHIBIT 38

MUNICIPAL COURT
BOROUGH OF RUNNEMEDE
413 N. Black Horse Pike
Runnemede, New Jersey

N° 3441

COMPLAINT

YOU ARE HEREBY SUMMONED TO APPEAR BEFORE THIS COURT TO ANSWER THIS COMPLAINT CHARGING YOU WITH THE OFFENSE LISTED:

THE UNDERSIGNED CERTIFIES THAT (Please Print)

| DRIVER'S LICENSE NUMBER | | EXP DATE | STATE | ☐ Commercial License |

Name	First	Initial	Last
Address			
City		State	Zip Code	Telephone
Birth Date	Eyes	Sex	Weight	Height	Restrictions
Make of Vehicle	Year	Body Type	Color	☐ Commercial Vehicle
Lic Plate No	State	Exp Date	☐ Hazardous Material
OFFENSE DATE	Month	Day	Year	Time Hour	AM PM
LOCATION OF OFFENSE	Municipality RUNNEMEDE	County CAMDEN	Mun Code (Offense)
Describe Location		

DID UNLAWFULLY (PARK) (OPERATE) A

AND DID THEN AND THERE COMMIT THE FOLLOWING OFFENSE (ONE CHARGE PER COMPLAINT)

TRAFFIC OFFENSES - TITLE 39: (circle one)

(1) 3-4 Unregistered Vehicle ☐ (7) 4-85 Improper passing ☐
(2) 3-29 Failure to exhibit documents ☐ (8) 4-97 Careless Driving ☐
☐ D.L. or ☐ REG or ☐ INS (9) 4-124 Failure to turn ☐
(3) 3-33 Unclear Plates ☐ (10) 4-144 Failure to stop or yield ☐
(4) 3-66 Maintenance of lamps ☐ (11) 8-1 Failure to inspect ☐
(5) 3-76.2f Failure to wear seatbelt ☐ (12) 8-4 Failure to make repairs ☐
(6) 4-81 Failure to observe signal ☐
(13) 4-98 Speeding MPH in a _____ MPH zone
☐ 01-15 MPH ☐ 16-20 MPH ☐ 21-25 MPH ☐ 26-30 MPH ☐ 31-35 MPH ☐ 36-40 MPH

PENALTY SCHEDULE ON REVERSE

☐ Overtime Meter No. _____ ☐ Prohibited Area ☐ Double
PARKING OFFENSE

OTHER TRAFFIC/PARKING OFFENSE (Describe)

Statue No _____ Ordinance/Code No _____

THE UNDERSIGNED FURTHER STATES THAT THERE ARE JUST AND REASONABLE GROUNDS TO BELIEVE THAT YOU COMMITTED THE ABOVE OFFENSE AND WILL FILE THIS COMPLAINT IN THIS COURT CHARGING YOU WITH THAT OFFENSE.

Signature of Complainant _____

NOTICE TO APPEAR

| ☐ COURT APPEARANCE REQUIRED | COURT DATE | Month | Day | Year | Officer's ID No |

CONDITIONS

☐ Truck	☐ Accident	☐ Personal Injury	☐ Property Damage
AREA	☐ Business	☐ School	☐ Residential	☐ Rural
ROAD	☐ Dry	☐ Wet	☐ Snow	☐ Ice
TRAFFIC	☐ Light	☐ Medium	☐ Heavy	
VISIBILITY	☐ Clear	☐ Rain	☐ Snow	☐ Fog

| Equipment | ☐ Helicopter | ☐ Pace | ☐ VASCAR | ☐ Radar | ☐ Breathalyzer |
| Equipment Operator's Name | | Operator ID No | Unit Code |

SUMMONS/COMPLAINT   CP0171 (12/92)

COURT ACTION

BAIL FIXED		VIOLATIONS BUREAU
DATE		DATE
AMOUNT $		FINE $
		COSTS $
SIGNATURE PERSON SETTING BAIL		LATE CHARGES $
		AS OF (MO. DY)
		☐

BAIL AMOUNT $	WARRANT DATE
☐ FORFEITURE ☐ RETURNED	DATE RETURNED
(DATE)	(SIGNATURE OF JUDGE)

FTA DATE		
RODRIGUEZ NOTICE GIVEN	DATE	JUDGE
COUNSEL WAIVED		
COUNSEL ASSIGNED		
COUNSEL NAME		
COMPLAINT AMENDED TO		
OPERATION STIPULATED ☐ YES ☐ NO		
PLEA _____ FINDING _____

SENTENCE

FINE $ _____ JAIL _____ DAYS
COSTS $ _____ DL REVOKED _____
(S1) ATS $ _____ DL REVOCATION DATE _____
(S50) DWI $ _____ COMM SERV _____ DAYS
(S100) DWI $ _____ IDRC _____
(S50 SO. ENF.) $ _____ OTHER _____
CONTEMPT $ _____

OTHERS $ _____

_____
(SIGNATURE OF JUDGE DATE)

(WITNESSES, TESTIMONY, JUDGE'S NOTES, ETC.)

EXHIBIT 38 (Continued)

128/Municipal Court

EXHIBIT 38 (Continued)

EXHIBIT 38 (Continued)

EXHIBIT 39

EXHIBIT 39 (Continued)

SECTION A

Report of Accidents. The driver of a vehicle involved in an accident resulting in injury to or death of any person, or damage to property of any one person in excess of five hundred dollars ($500.00) shall within ten days after such accident forward a written report of such accident TO: MOTOR VEHICLE SERVICES, ACCIDENT REPORTING AND EVALUATION, CN 050, TRENTON, NEW JERSEY 08666-0050. Failure to report will result in the suspension of both driving and registration privileges. Under Chapter 4 of Title 39 these reports are not available for public information nor are they admissable in evidence for any other purpose in a proceeding or action arising out of the accident. They are solely for the use of the Department of Law and Public Safety in developing information useful in the prevention of accidents and for compliance with the Motor Vehicle Security Responsibility and Compulsory Insurance Laws. "A written report of an accident shall not be required if a law enforcement officer submits a written report of the accident to the division pursuant to R.S. 39:4-131."

INSTRUCTIONS
PLEASE PRINT OR TYPE
ALL INFORMATION
USE BLACK OR DARK BLUE INK

Begin by folding along this line ➡
Follow the instructions at the top of Section B.
Numbered arrows should point to
boxes on reverse side after folding.

1. Give exact date of accident.
2. If a vehicle is unoccupied, enter all available information. Be sure to enter the correct vehicle plate number.
3. Driver information must be entered exactly as it appears on each driver's license.
4. Owner information must be entered exactly as it appears on the registration certificate of each vehicle involved in the accident.
5. If you were involved in an accident in which there were more than two vehicles, an additional one of these report forms must be filled out. On that form, place the information for the third vehicle in the space marked "Your Vehicle No. 1" and mark it No. 3. Use the space marked "Other Vehicle No. 2" for the fourth vehicle, and mark it No. 4 and so on.
6. The location of the accident is very important and you should describe it as accurately as possible in the space provided.
7. For each person injured complete boxes 67,68,69,70, 71 and list names and addresses.
8. If there are more than two persons injured, another one of these report forms is needed. In the injury section of that report, record the required information for all additional injured persons.
9. Attach any additional report forms to page one. Each page of the report must be numbered in the upper right corner, dated and SIGNED on the bottom line.
10. Answer all questions to the best of your knowledge.
11. Send all reports to: Motor Vehicle Services
    Accident Reporting and Evaluation
    CN 050
    Trenton, New Jersey 08666-0050

SECTION B

REPORT OF MOTOR VEHICLE ACCIDENT

Be sure form is folded along this line before answering the questions below.
Numbered arrows should point to boxes on reverse side after folding.
Fill in the 13 boxes to the right by entering the number of the item which best describes the circumstances of the accident.
If a question does not apply enter a dash (—).
If an answer is unknown enter a "U".

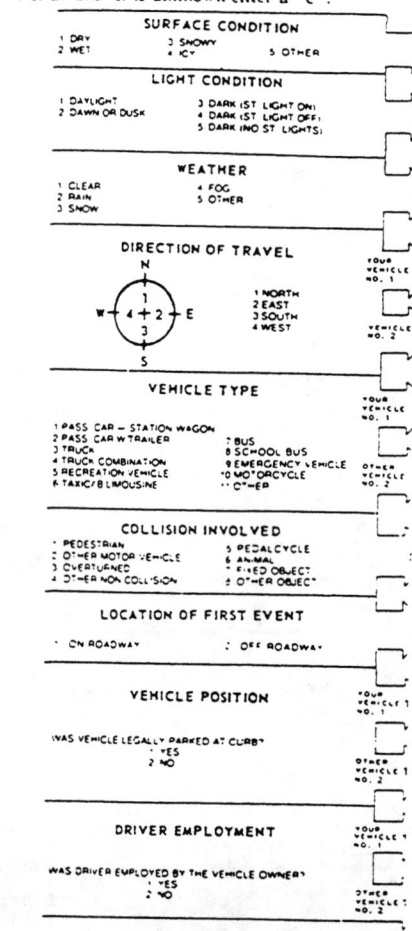

SURFACE CONDITION
1 DRY 3 SNOWY
2 WET 4 ICY 5 OTHER

LIGHT CONDITION
1 DAYLIGHT 3 DARK (ST LIGHT ON)
2 DAWN OR DUSK 4 DARK (ST LIGHT OFF)
5 DARK (NO ST LIGHTS)

WEATHER
1 CLEAR 4 FOG
2 RAIN   5 OTHER
3 SNOW

DIRECTION OF TRAVEL
1 NORTH
2 EAST
3 SOUTH
4 WEST

YOUR VEHICLE NO. 1
OTHER VEHICLE NO. 2

VEHICLE TYPE
1 PASS CAR — STATION WAGON
2 PASS CAR w TRAILER
3 TRUCK   7 BUS
4 TRUCK COMBINATION   8 SCHOOL BUS
5 RECREATION VEHICLE   9 EMERGENCY VEHICLE
6 TAXI/CAB LIMOUSINE   10 MOTORCYCLE
                         11 OTHER

COLLISION INVOLVED
1 PEDESTRIAN   5 PEDALCYCLE
2 OTHER MOTOR VEHICLE 6 ANIMAL
3 OVERTURNED   7 FIXED OBJECT
4 OTHER NON COLLISION 8 OTHER OBJECT

LOCATION OF FIRST EVENT
1 ON ROADWAY   2 OFF ROADWAY

VEHICLE POSITION
WAS VEHICLE LEGALLY PARKED AT CURB?
1 YES
2 NO

DRIVER EMPLOYMENT
WAS DRIVER EMPLOYED BY THE VEHICLE OWNER?
1 YES
2 NO

Please Read Instructions 1 Through 11 On Other Side of Fold Before Completing The Inside of Report.

DO NOT FILL IN

FOR USE OF INSURANCE COMPANY ONLY
Instructions for Insurance Company

With regard to an automobile liability insurance policy for the policyholder named on the reverse side hereof, the undersigned insurance company advises you in accordance with the items checked below:
☐ 1. No policy was in effect on the date of the accident.
☐ 2. Our policy for the named policyholder applies to him as the operator but it does not apply to the owner of the vehicle involved in the accident.
☐ 3. Our policy applies to the owner of the vehicle, but does not apply to the operator of the vehicle involved in the accident.
☐ 4. Other; explain.

MOTOR VEHICLE SERVICES
ACCIDENT REPORTING AND EVALUATION
CN 050
TRENTON, NEW JERSEY 08666-0050

Name of Insurance Company
MUST be signed by Authorized Representative

EXHIBIT 40

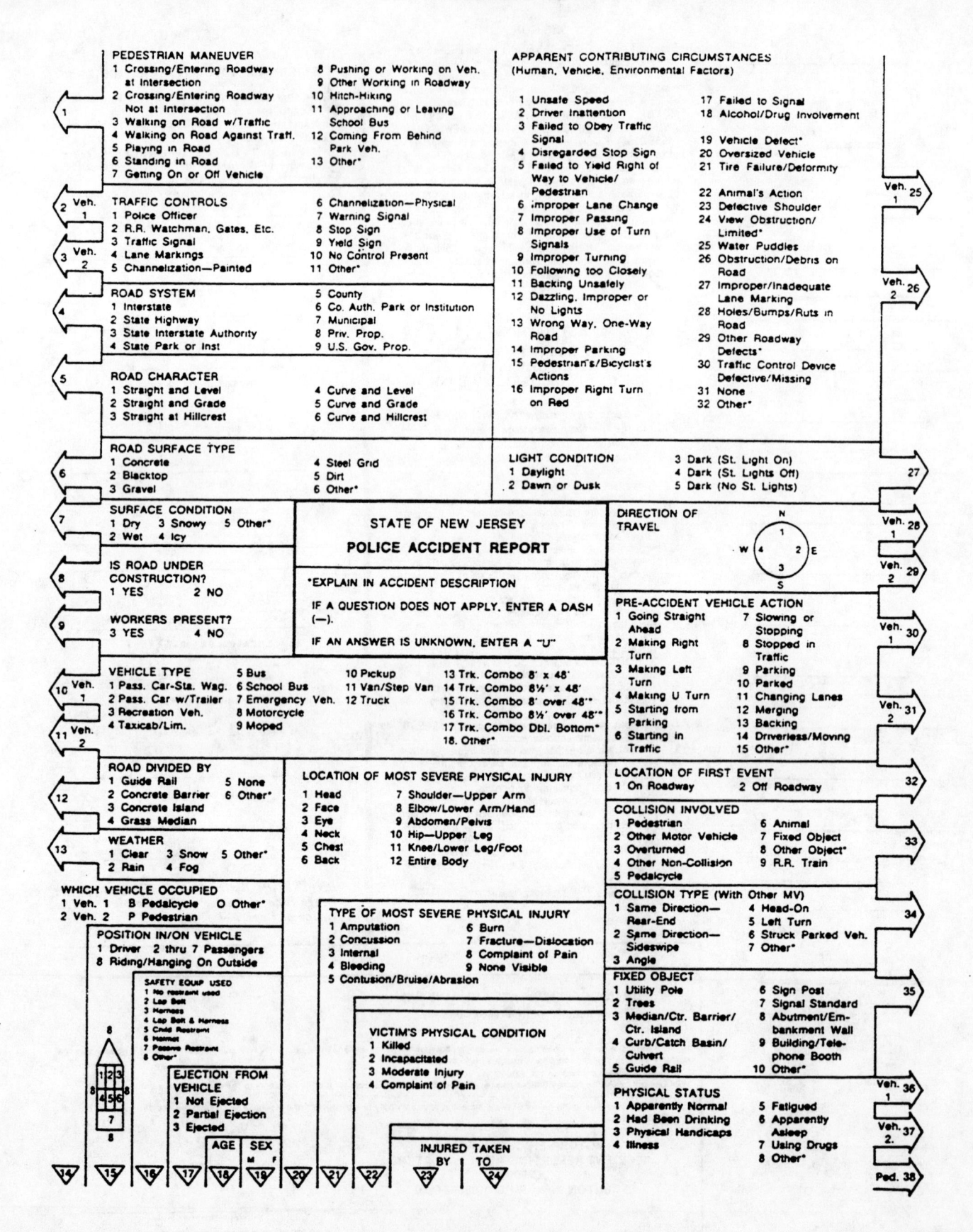

STATE OF NEW JERSEY
POLICE ACCIDENT REPORT

*Explain in accident description

IF A QUESTION DOES NOT APPLY, ENTER A DASH (—).

IF AN ANSWER IS UNKNOWN, ENTER A "U".

PEDESTRIAN MANEUVER
1. Crossing/Entering Roadway at Intersection
2. Crossing/Entering Roadway Not at Intersection
3. Walking on Road w/Traffic
4. Walking on Road Against Traffic
5. Playing in Road
6. Standing in Road
7. Getting On or Off Vehicle
8. Pushing or Working on Veh.
9. Other Working in Roadway
10. Hitch-Hiking
11. Approaching or Leaving School Bus
12. Coming From Behind Park Veh.
13. Other*

TRAFFIC CONTROLS
1. Police Officer
2. R.R. Watchman, Gates, Etc.
3. Traffic Signal
4. Lane Markings
5. Channelization—Painted
6. Channelization—Physical
7. Warning Signal
8. Stop Sign
9. Yield Sign
10. No Control Present
11. Other*

ROAD SYSTEM
1. Interstate
2. State Highway
3. State Interstate Authority
4. State Park or Inst
5. County
6. Co. Auth. Park or Institution
7. Municipal
8. Priv. Prop.
9. U.S. Gov. Prop.

ROAD CHARACTER
1. Straight and Level
2. Straight and Grade
3. Straight at Hillcrest
4. Curve and Level
5. Curve and Grade
6. Curve and Hillcrest

ROAD SURFACE TYPE
1. Concrete
2. Blacktop
3. Gravel
4. Steel Grid
5. Dirt
6. Other*

SURFACE CONDITION
1. Dry   3. Snowy   5. Other*
2. Wet   4. Icy

IS ROAD UNDER CONSTRUCTION?
1. YES   2. NO

WORKERS PRESENT?
3. YES   4. NO

VEHICLE TYPE
1. Pass. Car-Sta. Wag.
2. Pass. Car w/Trailer
3. Recreation Veh.
4. Taxicab/Lim.
5. Bus
6. School Bus
7. Emergency Veh.
8. Motorcycle
9. Moped
10. Pickup
11. Van/Step Van
12. Truck
13. Trk. Combo 8' x 48'
14. Trk. Combo 8½' x 48'
15. Trk. Combo 8' over 48"
16. Trk. Combo 8½' over 48"
17. Trk. Combo Dbl. Bottom*
18. Other*

ROAD DIVIDED BY
1. Guide Rail
2. Concrete Barrier
3. Concrete Island
4. Grass Median
5. None
6. Other*

WEATHER
1. Clear   3. Snow   5. Other*
2. Rain   4. Fog

WHICH VEHICLE OCCUPIED
1. Veh. 1   B. Pedalcycle   O. Other*
2. Veh. 2   P. Pedestrian

POSITION IN/ON VEHICLE
1. Driver   2 thru 7 Passengers
8. Riding/Hanging On Outside

SAFETY EQUIP USED
1. No restraint used
2. Lap Belt
3. Harness
4. Lap Belt & Harness
5. Child Restraint
6. Helmet
7. Passive Restraint
8. Other*

EJECTION FROM VEHICLE
1. Not Ejected
2. Partial Ejection
3. Ejected

LOCATION OF MOST SEVERE PHYSICAL INJURY
1. Head
2. Face
3. Eye
4. Neck
5. Chest
6. Back
7. Shoulder—Upper Arm
8. Elbow/Lower Arm/Hand
9. Abdomen/Pelvis
10. Hip—Upper Leg
11. Knee/Lower Leg/Foot
12. Entire Body

TYPE OF MOST SEVERE PHYSICAL INJURY
1. Amputation
2. Concussion
3. Internal
4. Bleeding
5. Contusion/Bruise/Abrasion
6. Burn
7. Fracture—Dislocation
8. Complaint of Pain
9. None Visible

VICTIM'S PHYSICAL CONDITION
1. Killed
2. Incapacitated
3. Moderate Injury
4. Complaint of Pain

INJURED TAKEN BY __ TO __

APPARENT CONTRIBUTING CIRCUMSTANCES
(Human, Vehicle, Environmental Factors)
1. Unsafe Speed
2. Driver Inattention
3. Failed to Obey Traffic Signal
4. Disregarded Stop Sign
5. Failed to Yield Right of Way to Vehicle/Pedestrian
6. Improper Lane Change
7. Improper Passing
8. Improper Use of Turn Signals
9. Improper Turning
10. Following too Closely
11. Backing Unsafely
12. Dazzling, Improper or No Lights
13. Wrong Way, One-Way Road
14. Improper Parking
15. Pedestrian's/Bicyclist's Actions
16. Improper Right Turn on Red
17. Failed to Signal
18. Alcohol/Drug Involvement
19. Vehicle Defect*
20. Oversized Vehicle
21. Tire Failure/Deformity
22. Animal's Action
23. Defective Shoulder
24. View Obstruction/Limited*
25. Water Puddles
26. Obstruction/Debris on Road
27. Improper/Inadequate Lane Marking
28. Holes/Bumps/Ruts in Road
29. Other Roadway Defects*
30. Traffic Control Device Defective/Missing
31. None
32. Other*

LIGHT CONDITION
1. Daylight
2. Dawn or Dusk
3. Dark (St. Light On)
4. Dark (St. Lights Off)
5. Dark (No St. Lights)

DIRECTION OF TRAVEL
N(1) E(2) S(3) W(4)

PRE-ACCIDENT VEHICLE ACTION
1. Going Straight Ahead
2. Making Right Turn
3. Making Left Turn
4. Making U Turn
5. Starting from Parking
6. Starting in Traffic
7. Slowing or Stopping
8. Stopped in Traffic
9. Parking
10. Parked
11. Changing Lanes
12. Merging
13. Backing
14. Driverless/Moving
15. Other*

LOCATION OF FIRST EVENT
1. On Roadway   2. Off Roadway

COLLISION INVOLVED
1. Pedestrian
2. Other Motor Vehicle
3. Overturned
4. Other Non-Collision
5. Pedalcycle
6. Animal
7. Fixed Object
8. Other Object*
9. R.R. Train

COLLISION TYPE (With Other MV)
1. Same Direction—Rear-End
2. Same Direction—Sideswipe
3. Angle
4. Head-On
5. Left Turn
6. Struck Parked Veh.
7. Other*

FIXED OBJECT
1. Utility Pole
2. Trees
3. Median/Ctr. Barrier/Ctr. Island
4. Curb/Catch Basin/Culvert
5. Guide Rail
6. Sign Post
7. Signal Standard
8. Abutment/Embankment Wall
9. Building/Telephone Booth
10. Other*

PHYSICAL STATUS
1. Apparently Normal
2. Had Been Drinking
3. Physical Handicaps
4. Illness
5. Fatigued
6. Apparently Asleep
7. Using Drugs
8. Other*

EXHIBIT 41

Municipal Court of _____   Docket No. _____

County of _____   Ticket No. _____

_____
(address)

_____
(Zip)

State of New Jersey

v.

_____
Defendant

ORDER

PAYMENT OF FINES AND COSTS
under N.J.S.A. 39:4-203.1 et seq.

    The defendant _____, more fully described below, having been charged with a violation of N.J.S.A. 39: _____, a non-parking traffic offense, on _____, 19____, and having been convicted on _____, 19____ and sentenced to pay a fine of $_____ and $_____ costs and it appearing that the defendant presently is unable to pay the fine and costs in full.

    It is ORDERED that the defendant pay $_____ (weekly) (monthly) commencing _____, 19____ (or in accordance with the following schedule:
_____
_____
_____ on account of said fine and costs and in any event to complete payment no later than _____, 19____.

    Payment shall be made in cash to the clerk of the court or by mailing check or money order made payable to this COURT **properly identified with the Docket number and Ticket number thereon as shown above.**

    If subsequent to the entry of ORDER, the defendant is unable to make payment as ORDERED, the defendant shall immediately advise the COURT why payment cannot be made on time.

    For failure to comply with this ORDER, a warrant may be issued for the arrest of the defendant charging the defendant with contempt of court **N.J.S.A. 2A:10-1C) AND DEFENDANT'S DRIVER'S LICENSE MAY BE SUSPENDED BY THIS COURT (N.J.S.A. 39:4-203-1 et seq.)**

    FURTHER ORDERED that defendant notify this COURT in writing within three (3) days of any change of address.

Date: _____   _____
                                                                                                                        Judge

EXHIBIT 41 (Continued)

I certify the following information is correct and acknowledge receipt of a copy of and understand this ORDER. I also understand that if my driver's license is suspended for failure to make payments, I must pay the Division of Motor Vehicles a $20 restoration fee.

_____
Defendant

_____   _____   _____
(address)   Drivers License No.   State

_____   _____   _____
                           (zip)   Date of Birth   Eye Code   Sex

Tele. No. (   ) _____

NOTE: Defendant should be given a copy of this ORDER. The COURT should keep the original.

EXHIBIT 42

(White)
DEFENDANT'S COPY

MUNICIPAL COURT OF _____

ADDRESS: _____

_____

Date: _____

TO:

COURT CODE	
DOCKET NO.	
SUMMONS NO.	
D.L. NO. & STATE	
REG. NO. & STATE	
REG. EXP. DATE	
DATE OF BIRTH	EYE CODE / SEX
VIOLATION(S) SECTION:	
VIOLATION DATE & TIME	

The records of this court indicate that

a complaint charging you with _____ was filed in this Court on
(Violation)
the Violation Date shown above and a summons was issued for your appearance in this Court on
_____. Since you failed to appear in Court and have not paid the prescribed fine,
(Date)

YOU ARE ORDERED to appear in this Court on _____ at _____. *If you wish to plead not guilty, you must notify this Court at least 3 days prior to the new court date.* If you wish to plead guilty, you must pay a total penalty of $_____ before your new court date. You must sign the back of the summons and return summons with your payment.

EXHIBIT 42 (Continued)

IF YOU FAIL TO APPEAR OR PAY THE PRESCRIBED PENALTY:

RESIDENTS OF NEW JERSEY: (1) A warrant will be issued for your arrest; (2) you may be subject to contempt of court and additional penalties, and (3) you may be subject to possible revocation of your driving privilege by the Director of the Division of Motor Vehicles.

NON-RESIDENT MOTORISTS: (1) Your driving privilege in New Jersey may be revoked, (2) your own Commissioner of Motor Vehicles requested to take action against you, and (3) a warrant may be issued for your arrest should you be found in this State.

PARKING OFFENDERS—RESIDENTS AND NON-RESIDENTS: In addition to the consequences listed above, a civil judgment may be entered against you.

BY ORDER OF THE JUDGE

_____
(Judge or Court Clerk)

Office Hours:_____

Telephone:_____

Drivers' Licenses

There are now three variations of a driver's license in circulation: without photograph, the photo driver's license, and the new form without photo. **Exhibit 43** is a memorandum explaining the codes on the photo license. A sample enlarged photo driver's license is **Exhibit 44**. The 8th, 9th, and 10th digits at the bottom of the license are described as the "Day of Year Numerically," which is the Julian Calendar date. The Julian Calendar is **Exhibit 45**. On the example, the license was issued on the 177th day of 1984 which is according to the Julian Calendar, June 26, 1984. For a leap year, the number differs by one after February 28.

138/Municipal Court

EXHIBIT 43

State of New Jersey

DEPARTMENT OF LAW AND PUBLIC SAFETY
DIVISION OF MOTOR VEHICLES
25 SOUTH MONTGOMERY STREET
TRENTON, NEW JERSEY 08666

IRWIN I. KIMMELMAN
ATTORNEY GENERAL

CLIFFORD W. SNEDEKER
DIRECTOR

August 15, 1985

Judge David A. Keyko, J.M.C.
Post Office Box 126
Woodbury Heights, New Jersey 08097

Dear Judge Keyko:

Director Snedeker has asked me to reply to your letter of August 7, 1984 concerning the date of issue appearing on photo driver licenses.

The date of issue is contained in the validation number in the lower right hand corner of the photo license. A sample validation would be HH842280123 ^ 17.50. The validation number is broken down as follows:

HH - These two letters are the initials of the agency issuing the document. HH would be the Haddon Heights Motor Vehicle Agency.

84 - These two numbers indicate the year the document was issued.

228 - These three numbers are the Julian Date, which is August 15th.

0123 - These four numbers are sequential numbers assigned by the computer.

^ - This character is called a "hat" and appears on all documents validated at a computerized agency.

17.50 - The numbers after the "hat" indicate the fee paid for the document.

Please accept my sincere apology for any confusion you may have experienced. If I can be of assistance to you in the future, please feel free to contact my office.

Respectfully,

R. L. Torlini
Assistant Director

New Jersey Is An Equal Opportunity Employer

Municipal Court/139

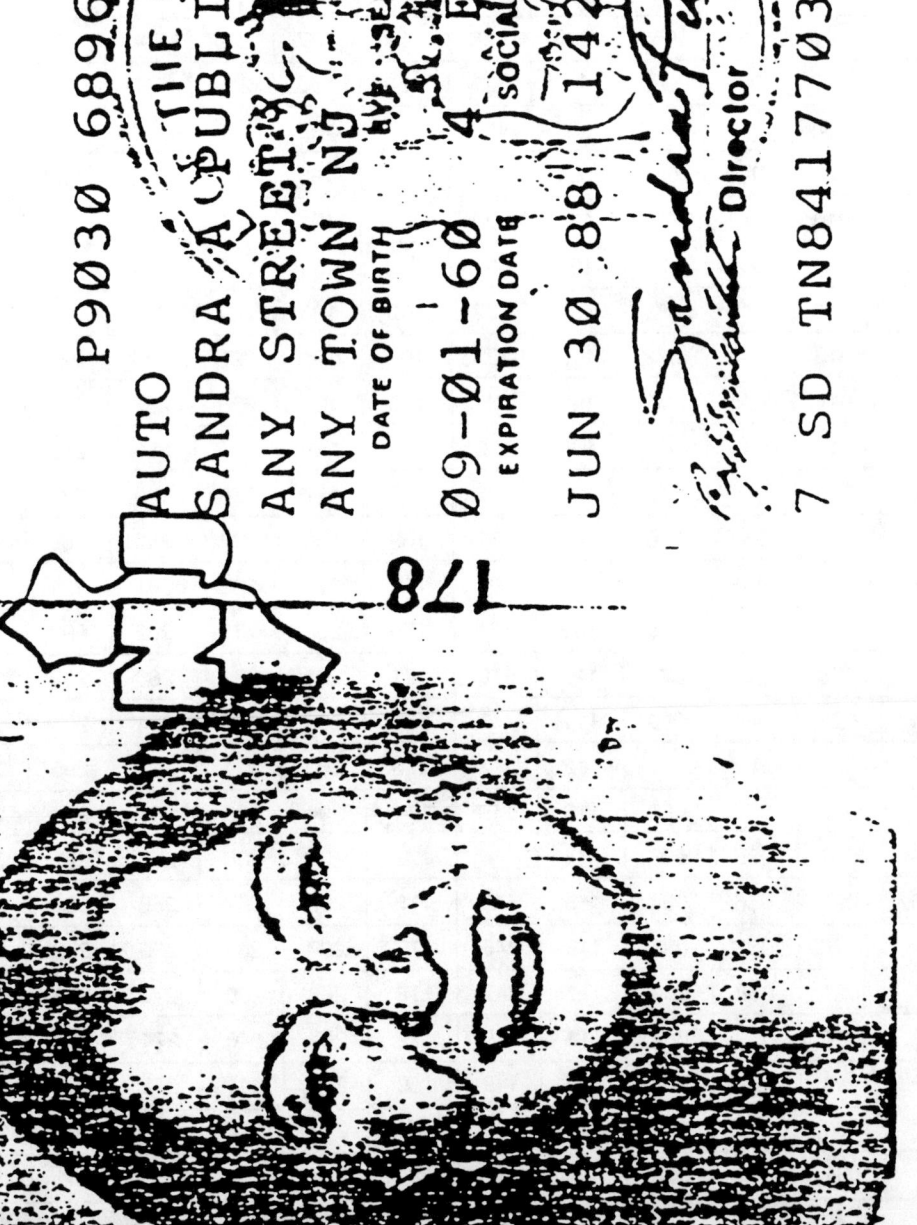

EXHIBIT 44

NEW JERSEY
DIVISION OF MOTOR VEHICLES DRIVER LICENSE

P9030 68961 59604

AUTO
SANDRA A. PUBLIC
ANY STREET
ANY TOWN NJ

DATE OF BIRTH
09-01-60

EXPIRATION DATE
JUN 30 88

HEIGHT RESTR

4 E 075-02 D0

SOCIAL SECURITY NUMBER
142-26-5856

Sandra Public
Director

7 SD TN8417703780   17.50

EXHIBIT 45

JULIAN DATE CALENDAR

Day	Jan	Feb	Mar	Apr	May	June	July	Aug	Sep	Oct	Nov	Dec	Day
1	001	032	060	091	121	152	182	213	244	274	305	335	1
2	002	033	061	092	122	153	183	214	245	275	306	336	2
3	003	034	062	093	123	154	184	215	246	276	307	337	3
4	004	035	063	094	124	155	185	216	247	277	308	338	4
5	005	036	064	095	125	156	186	217	248	278	309	339	5
6	006	037	065	096	126	157	187	218	249	279	310	340	6
7	007	038	066	097	127	158	188	219	250	280	311	341	7
8	008	039	067	098	128	159	189	220	251	281	312	342	8
9	009	040	068	099	129	160	190	221	252	282	313	343	9
10	010	041	069	100	130	161	191	222	253	283	314	344	10
11	011	042	070	101	131	162	192	223	254	284	315	345	11
12	012	043	071	102	132	163	193	224	255	285	316	346	12
13	013	044	072	103	133	164	194	225	256	286	317	347	13
14	014	045	073	104	134	165	195	226	257	287	318	348	14
15	015	046	074	105	135	166	196	227	258	288	319	349	15
16	016	047	075	106	136	167	197	228	259	289	320	350	16
17	017	048	076	107	137	168	198	229	260	290	321	351	17
18	018	049	077	108	138	169	199	230	261	291	322	352	18
19	019	050	078	109	139	170	200	231	262	292	323	353	19
20	020	051	079	110	140	171	201	232	263	293	324	354	20
21	021	052	080	111	141	172	202	233	264	294	325	355	21
22	022	053	081	112	142	173	203	234	265	295	326	356	22
23	023	054	082	113	143	174	204	235	266	296	327	357	23
24	024	055	083	114	144	175	205	236	267	297	328	358	24
25	025	056	084	115	145	176	206	237	268	298	329	359	25
26	026	057	085	116	146	177	207	238	269	299	330	360	26
27	027	058	086	117	147	178	208	239	270	300	331	361	27
28	028	059	087	118	148	179	209	240	271	301	332	362	28
29	029		088	119	149	180	210	241	272	302	333	363	29
30	030		089	120	150	181	211	242	273	303	334	364	30
31	031		090		151		212	243		304		365	31

Municipal Court/141

EXHIBIT 45 (Continued)

JULIAN DATE CALENDAR

FOR LEAP YEARS ONLY

Day	Jan	Feb	Mar	Apr	May	June	July	Aug	Sep	Oct	Nov	Dec	Day
1	001	032	061	092	122	153	183	214	245	275	306	336	1
2	002	033	062	093	123	154	184	215	246	276	307	337	2
3	003	034	063	094	124	155	185	216	247	277	308	338	3
4	004	035	064	095	125	156	186	217	248	278	309	339	4
5	005	036	065	096	126	157	187	218	249	279	310	340	5
6	006	037	066	097	127	158	188	219	250	280	311	341	6
7	007	038	067	098	128	159	189	220	251	281	312	342	7
8	008	039	068	099	129	160	190	221	252	282	313	343	8
9	009	040	069	100	130	161	191	222	253	283	314	344	9
10	010	041	070	101	131	162	192	223	254	284	315	345	10
11	011	042	071	102	132	163	193	224	255	285	316	346	11
12	012	043	072	103	133	164	194	225	256	286	317	347	12
13	013	044	073	104	134	165	195	226	257	287	318	348	13
14	014	045	074	105	135	166	196	227	258	288	319	349	14
15	015	046	075	106	136	167	197	228	259	289	320	350	15
16	016	047	076	107	137	168	198	229	260	290	321	351	16
17	017	048	077	108	138	169	199	230	261	291	322	352	17
18	018	049	078	109	139	170	200	231	262	292	323	353	18
19	019	050	079	110	140	171	201	232	263	293	324	354	19
20	020	051	080	111	141	172	202	233	264	294	325	355	20
21	021	052	081	112	142	173	203	234	265	295	326	356	21
22	022	053	082	113	143	174	204	235	266	296	327	357	22
23	023	054	083	114	144	175	205	236	267	297	328	358	23
24	024	055	084	115	145	176	206	237	268	298	329	359	24
25	025	056	085	116	146	177	207	238	269	299	330	360	25
26	026	057	086	117	147	178	208	239	270	300	331	361	26
27	027	058	087	118	148	179	209	240	271	301	332	362	27
28	028	059	088	119	149	180	210	241	272	302	333	363	28
29	029	060	089	120	150	181	211	242	273	303	334	364	29
30	030		090	121	151	182	212	243	274	304	335	365	30
31	031		091		152		213	244		305		366	31

(USE IN 1980, 1984, 1988, 1992)

Point System

Points are assessed against a defendant's driving record for moving violations, in accordance with N.J.S.A. 39:5-30.6, as a result of conviction in the Municipal Court. **Exhibit 46** is a listing of points to be assessed for moving violations. If a driver accumulates twelve or more points within two years or less, his or her license will be suspended for thirty days. If fifteen or more points are accumulated in a period greater than two years, there also shall be a thirty day suspension. However, if the driver accumulates at least twelve, but fewer than fifteen points in a period greater than two years, his or her license shall be suspended for thirty days unless the driver sends notice to the Division of Motor Vehicles within ten days of the date of mailing the proposed suspension indicating that he or she intends to attend an approved Driver Improvement Course.

Suspensions are effective fifteen days from the date of mailing of the notice by the Division of Motor Vehicles. In the event the driver fails to appear at any scheduled hearing or fails to attend class, his or her driver's license will be suspended for thirty days or such time as is contained in the proposed notice of suspension, whichever is greater.

If a driver successfully completes a Driver's Improvement Course, his or her license shall remain valid. However, if the driver receives one moving violation within the first year after completing the course, there will be a forty-five day suspension. If a second offense is committed within one year of completion, the suspension shall be for ninety days.

Hearings concerning contested points or other discrepancies concerning a driver's record are conducted by Administrative Law Judges.

It is always advisable to review your client's abstract to ascertain his or her point status as a conviction for a relatively minor offense may well result in a proposed or actual suspension of your client's license. If a suspension is possible, the driver may afford himself or herself an opportunity for a pre-conference hearing with an employee of the Division of Motor Vehicles. If an agreement is reached at the pre-conference hearing, the results will be binding. If no agreement is reached, a hearing before the Administrative Law Judge will be held. The Administrative Law Judge shall prepare an Initial Decision which is forwarded to the licensee and to the Division of Motor Vehicles. If the licensee disagrees with the Initial Decision, he or she may file an exception thereto with the Director. The Director of the Division of Motor Vehicles shall have forty-five days from the date of the Initial Decision to affirm, modify, or reverse the Administrative Law Judge's determination. If the licensee disagrees with the Director's determination, he or she may appeal, within forty-five days of the date of the Memorandum Decision, to the Appellate Division of the Superior Court.

EXHIBIT 46

MOTOR VEHICLE POINT SYSTEM

Editor's Note: For inquiries regarding the records of a particular driver, contact the Division of Motor Vehicles at (609) 588-7373.

13:19-10.1 Point Assessment

Any person who is convicted of any of the following offenses, including offenses committed while operating a motorized bicycle, shall be assessed points for each conviction in accordance with the following schedule:

N.J.S.A. Statutory	Violation Description	Points
27:23-29	Moving against traffic—N.J. Tpke., Garden State Pkwy. and Atlantic City Expressway	2
27:23-29	Improper passing—N.J. Tpke., Garden State Pkwy. and Atlantic City Expy.	4
27:23-29	Unlawful use of median strip—N.J. Tpke., Garden State Pkwy. and Atlantic City Expressway	2
39:3-20	Operating Constructor vehicle in excess of 30 mph	3
39:3-76.7, 39:4-14.3q	Operating motorcycle and/or motorized bicycle without helmet	2
39:4-14.3	Operating motorized bicycle on restricted highway	2
39:4-14.3d	More than 1 person on a motorized bicycle	2
39:4-35	Failure to yield to pedestrian in crosswalk	2
39:4-36	Failure to yield to pedestrian or passing a vehicle yielding to pedestrian in a crosswalk	2
39:4-41	Driving through safety zone	2
39:4-52, 39:5C-1	Racing on highway	5
39:4-55	Improper action or omission on grades and curves	2
39:4-57	Failure to observe directions of officer	2
39:4-66	Failure to stop before crossing sidewalk	2
39:4-66.1	Failure to yield to pedestrians or vehicles while entering or leaving highway	2
39:4-71	Improper driving on sidewalk	2
39:4-80	Failure to obey directions of officer	2
39:4-81	Failure to observe traffic signal	2
39:4-82	Failure to keep right	2
39:4-82.1	Improper operating of vehicle on divided highway or divider	2
39:4-83	Failure to keep right at intersection	2
39:4-84	Failure to pass right of vehicle proceeding in opposite direction	5
39:4-85	Improper passing on right or off roadway	4
39:4-85.1	Wrong way on one-way street	2
39:4-86	Improper passing, in "No Passing" zone	4
39:4-87	Failure to yield to overtaking vehicle	2
39:4-88	Failure to observe marked lanes	2
39:4-89	Tailgating	5
39:4-90	Failure to yield at intersection	2
39:4-90.1	Failure to use proper entrances to limited access highway	2
39:4-91, 39:4-92	Failure to yield to emergency vehicle	2
39:4-96	Reckless driving	5
39:4-97	Careless driving	2
39:4-97a	Destruction of agricultural or recreational property	2
39:4-97.1	Slow speed blocking traffic	2
39:4-98,	Speeding up to 14 mph above limit	2
39:4-99	Speeding 15-29 mph above limit	4
	Speeding 30 mph or more above limit	5
39:4-105	Failure to stop at traffic light	2
39:4-115	Improper turn at traffic light	3
39:4-119	Failure to stop at flashing red signal	2
39:4-122	Failure to stop for police whistle	2
39:4-123	Improper right or left turn	3
39:4-124	Improper turn: from approved turning course	3
39:4-125	Improper "U" turn	3
39:4-126	Failure to give proper signal	2
39:4-127	Improper backing or turning in street	2
39:4-127.1	Improper crossing of railroad grade crossing	2
39:4-127.2	Improper crossing of bridge	2
39:4-128	Improper crossing of railroad grade crossing by certain vehicles	2

EXHIBIT 46 (Continued)

39:4-128.1	Improper passing of school bus	5
39:4-128.4	Improper passing of frozen dessert truck	4
39:4-129	Leaving scene of accident—No injuries	2
39:4-129	Personal Injury	8
39:4-144	Failure to observe of stop or yield signs	2
39:5D-4	Moving violation out-of-state	2

13:19-10.2 Point Accumulation; period of suspension

(a) The Director shall, except for good cause, suspend a person's license to operate a motor vehicle and/or motorized bicycle in accordance with the following schedule:

POINTS ACCUMULATED	PERIOD OF SUSPENSION
12 to 15 points in a period of two years or less	30 days
16 to 18 points in a period of two years or less	60 days
19 to 21 points in a period of two years or less	90 days
22 to 24 points in a period of two years or less	120 days
25 to 27 points in a period of two years or less	150 days
28 or more points in a period of two years or less	not less than 180 days
15 to 18 points in a period greater than two years	30 days
19 to 22 points in a period greater than two years	60 days
23 to 26 points in a period greater than two years	90 days
27 to 30 points in a period greater than two years	120 days
31 to 35 points in a period greater than two years	150 days
36 or more points in a period greater than two years	not less than 180 days
12 to 14 points in a period greater than two years	30 days

(b) For good cause shown, the Director may in his discretion permit a person to attend a driver improvement course of the Division of Motor Vehicles in total or partial satisfaction of a period of suspension imposed under (a) above. In exercising his discretion, the Director shall consider the person's driving record, prior warnings or driver improvement school attendance, maturity and any other aggravating or mitigating factor.

13:19-10.3 Driver improvement program attendance

(a) A person who is permitted to attend a driver improvement program of the Division of Motor Vehicles in total or partial satisfaction of suspension or revocation shall agree to attend each session of the assigned driver improvement program and to comply with all rules governing attendance, conduct, instruction and examinations. A person who fails to comply with the foregoing requirements or who otherwise fails to successfully complete the assigned driver improvement program shall be subject to a driver license suspension for the period contained in the notice of proposed suspension. A person who successfully completes the assigned driver improvement program shall be officially warned with respect to future driving.

(b) A person whose driver license has been suspended pursuant to N.J.A.C. 13:19-10.2 may be required to attend and successfully complete a driver improvement program of the Division of Motor Vehicles as a condition for restoration of the driver license.

(c) The fee for attendance at a Division of Motor Vehicles Driver Improvement Program shall be $40.00.

(d) The Director is authorized to exercise discretionary authority to require any person who is licensed on a probationary basis in accordance with N.J.S.A. 39:3-10b to attend a Probationary Driver Program whenever said person accumulates two or more violations of the motor vehicle law which result in the assessment of four or more points under N.J.A.C. 13:19-10.1.

(e) A person who is required to attend a Probationary Driver Program shall agree to attend each session of the program and to comply with all rules governing attendance, conduct, instruction, and examinations. A person who fails to comply with the foregoing requirements or who otherwise fails to successfully complete the Probationary Driver Program shall be subject to a driver license suspension for the period contained in the notice of proposed suspension. A person who successfully completes the Probationary Driver Program shall be officially warned with respect to future driving.

(f) The fee for attendance at a Division of Motor Vehicles Probationary Driver Program shall be $40.00.

13:19-10.4 Advisory notice

(a) Whenever a person accumulates 6 or more

EXHIBIT 46 (Continued)

points, the Division shall send an official notice advising the motorist of such status.

(b) Whenever a person who is licensed on a probationary basis in accordance with N.J.S.A. 39:3-10b is first convicted of a motor vehicle violation requiring the assessment of points against the individual's driving record under N.J.A.C. 13:19-10.1 the Division shall send an official notice advising the motorist of the status of the driving record.

13:19-10.5 Reductions of point accumulation

Points recorded against the licensee shall be reduced in accordance with the provisions of N.J.S.A. 39:5-30.9.

13:19-10.6 Restoration, official warning, completion of Driver Improvement or Probationary Driver Program

(a) Persons whose licenses are restored after a suspension imposed under N.J.A.C. 13:19-10.2, persons who are officially warned after an administrative hearing and persons who successfully complete a Division Driver Improvement Program or a Probationary Driver Program may retain their licenses upon the express condition and understanding that any subsequent violation of the Motor Vehicle Laws of the State of New Jersey committed within a period of one year of the restoration, official warning or warning following successful completion of a Driver Improvement or Probationary Driver Program shall, except for good cause, result in suspension of driving privileges for the following periods.

1. When the subsequent violation occurs within six months of the date of the restoration, official warning or warning following completion of a Driver Improvement or Probationary Driver Program—90 days.

2. When the subsequent violation occurs more than six months but less than nine months after the restoration, official warning or warning following completion of a Driver Improvement or Probationary Driver Program—60 days.

3. When the subsequent violation occurs more than nine months but less than one year after the restoration, official warning or warning following completion of a Driver Improvement or Probationary Driver Program—45 days.

(b) A second violation of the Motor Vehicle Laws committed within one year of the restoration, official warning or warning following completion of a Driver Improvement or Probationary Driver Program shall, except for good cause, result in suspension of driving privileges for the following periods:

1. When the second violation occurs within six months of the date of restoration, official warning or warning following completion of a Driver Improvement or Probationary Driver Program—180 days.

2. When the second violation occurs more than six months but less than nine months after the restoration, official warning or warning following completion of a Driver Improvement or Probationary Driver Program—120 days.

3. When the second violation occurs more than nine months but less than one year after the restoration, official warning or warning following completion of a Driver Improvement or Probationary Driver Program—90 days.

(c) Persons, licensed on a probationary basis in accordance with N.J.S.A. 39:3-10b, who have been subject to a license suspension action under (a) or (b) above may be required to successfully complete additional programs of driver rehabilitation within the discretion of the Director.

13:19-10.7 Court ruling

The provisions of this subchapter shall not be affected by any revocation or suspension judicially imposed except that no lesser period of revocation or suspension shall be imposed than that directed by the court.

39:19-10.8 Driving during period of suspension

(a) Whenever the driving privileges of an individual have been suspended or revoked for any reason, either judicially or administratively:

1. Operation of a motor vehicle by the individual during the period of suspension or revocation shall be cause for extending the period of revocation or suspension for an additional six months, or for some other period determined by the Director.

2. Should information be received by the Division after restoration of an individual's driving privileges that the individual operated a motor vehicle during the period of revocation or suspension, the Director may revoke or suspend the individual's driving privileges for a period of six months, or for some other period which the Director determines.

3. In addition to the revocation or suspension of an individual's driving privileges as provided

EXHIBIT 46 (Continued)

for in paragraphs 1 an 2 above, the Director may determine to suspend the motor vehicle registration privileges of an owner-operator who operates a motor vehicle during a period of revocation or suspension of driving privileges. Such period of suspension of registration privileges shall coincide with the period of suspension of the individual's driving privileges, or for some other period to be determined by the Director.

Driver's Abstract

It is advisable to obtain the client's driving record before appearing in the Municipal Court for two reasons: to ascertain 1) if the client has a point problem, and 2) whether the defendant has been previously convicted of an offense which requires an enhanced penalty for a subsequent offense. The attorney should request a ten year abstract from the Division of Motor Vehicles; otherwise he or she will receive only a three year abstract. In circumstances where a defendant is charged with Revoked Driving (N.J.S.A. 39:3-40); Unlicensed (39:3-10); Uninsured (39:6B-2) and Driving While Under the Influence (39:4-50); the prosecutor, police or the court may already have in its files a copy of the client's abstract. When the attorney has obtained the client's abstract, the attorney should compare the abstract in the possession of the State with the defense's copy. It is not unusual for the two to differ since errors are sometimes made in transposing driver's license numbers from the ticket to the request form, and as little as one digit being off results in an improper or misleading abstract. Therefore, always check the State's version against the abstract the defense has obtained and more especially, double check the client's driver's license number against that appearing on all abstracts.

The ability to decipher an abstract is most important in those instances where the client is charged with a violation of N.J.S.A. 39:3-40 (Driving While Driver's License or Registration is Suspended or Revoked) and N.J.S.A. 39:3-10 (Unlicensed Driver); however, it is also significant to determine points or the applicability of enhanced penalties. Interpreting an abstract is not easily accomplished since the Division of Motor Vehicles installed their new computer. Each municipal court should have a fair sized booklet which includes all the codes utilized on the abstract. A brief synopsis of these codes appears on the reverse side of the certified abstract; however, they are woefully incomplete. See **Exhibit 47**. **Exhibit 48** is a complete listing of Municipal Court codes which, when listed under the "Event Responsibility" column, will disclose the name of the Municipal Court in which the "Event Description" took place. Counsel should also note that "M99" does not mean a Middlesex County Municipal or other court, it means "Miscellaneous Court Reported Action."

It should be noted that generally municipal courts will accept a certified abstract under the business exception rule, local rule, or Supreme Court directive. A computer printout, however, is unacceptable as proof because it is not certified.

In order to better understand and learn to read a certified abstract, refer to **Exhibit 49** which is a sample abstract.

Item #1 is the driver's license number wherein the first letter is the first letter of the driver's last name. Sometimes there is a discrepancy because the driver is a woman who has changed her last name as a result of a marriage. Not all entries would be necessarily transferred under the new first letter.

Item #2 is eye code. Eye Codes are as follows:

1—Black

2—Brown

3—Gray

4—Blue

5—Hazel

6—Green

7, 8 & 9—Sp. code

Item #3 is Date of Birth.

The Manual of Abbreviations used on Driver's Abstracts is **Exhibit 50.**

EXHIBIT 47

NEW JERSEY DIVISION OF MOTOR VEHICLES

EXPLANATION OF EVENT CODES ON ABSTRACT OF DRIVER HISTORY RECORD

EVENT RESPONSIBILITY CODES (COURT)
(Column 2)

A	ATLANTIC	J	HUDSON	S	SALEM	01-94	MUNICIPAL COURT
B	BERGEN	K	HUNTERDON	T	SOMERSET	95	COUNTY DISTRICT COURT
C	BURLINGTON	L	MERCER	V	SUSSEX	96	COUNTY COURT
D	CAMDEN	M	MIDDLESEX	W	UNION	97	JUVENILE COURT
E	CAPE MAY	N	MONMOUTH	Y	WARREN	M-99	MISCELLANEOUS COURT REPORTED ACTION
F	CUMBERLAND	P	MORRIS	Z	FOREIGN STATE	CRT	MISCELLANEOUS COURT REPORTED ACTION
G	ESSEX	Q	OCEAN	X	U.S. COMM. COURT		
H	GLOUCESTER	R	PASSAIC				

EVENT RESPONSIBILITY CODES (DIVISION)
(Column 2)

ACP	ALCOHOL COUNTERMEASURES (HEALTH DEPT.)
CIS	COMPULSORY INSURANCE/ACCIDENT REPORTING
COO	CERTIFICATE OF OWNERSHIP
CON	CONFERENCE UNIT
DIP	DRIVER IMPROVEMENT PROGRAM
DMV	DIVISION DIRECTOR
DRT	DRIVER TESTING
DVR	DRIVER
FAR	FATAL ACCIDENT REVIEW
FRJ	FINANCIAL RESPONSIBILITY/JUDGMENT
ISS	INSURANCE SURCHARGE
MFR	MEDICAL FITNESS REVIEW
OAL	OFFICE OF ADMINISTRATIVE LAW LIAISON
PDP	PROBATIONARY DRIVER PROGRAM
RES	RESTORATION AUTHORIZATION
RSU	REEXAMINATION SCHEDULING
SEC	SECURITY RESPONSIBILITY
SUS	SUSPENSION AUTHORIZATION
UCJ	UNSATISFIED CLAIMS AND JUDGMENTS

EVENT TYPE CODES
(Column 3)

A	ACCIDENT
C	CONFERENCE
D	FEE DUE
E	REEXAMINATION ACTIVITY
F	FEE PAYMENT
J	REFERRAL
K	REFERRAL WITH INTERVAL REPORTING
M	MEMO ENTRY
N	ADVISORY NOTICE
O	SUSPENSION ORDER
P	PROGRAM ACTIVITY
R	RESTORATION
S	SCHEDULED SUSPENSION
V	VIOLATION
W	WARNING NOTICE
X	CANCELLATION OF SCHEDULED SUSPENSION
Z	POINT CREDIT

EVENT RESPONSIBILITY CODES identify the Court or Division of Motor Vehicles unit responsible for the event and/or action taken.

EVENT TYPE CODES identify the major types of events and/or actions taken.

EVENT IDENTIFIER CODES uniquely identify each event and/or action taken. These codes are followed by a complete description of the event and/or action.

Municipal Court/149

EXHIBIT 48

CODE LISTING OF NEW JERSEY COURTS BY COUNTY

STATE OF NEW JERSEY
DEPARTMENT OF LAW AND PUBLIC SAFETY
DIVISION OF MOTOR VEHICLES
25 SOUTH MONTGOMERY STREET
TRENTON, NEW JERSEY 08666

ATLANTIC COUNTY

CODE A

Code	Locations
A02	Absecon City
A03	Atlantic City
A04	Brigantine City
A05	Buena Boro
A06	Buena Vista Twp.
A08	Egg Harbor City
A09	Egg Harbor Twp.
A11	Folsom Boro
A12	Galloway Twp.
A13	Hamilton Twp.
A14	Hammonton Town
A15	Linwood City
A16	Longport Boro
A17	Margate City
A19	Mullica Twp.
A20	Northfield City
A21	Pleasantville City
A23	Somers Point City
A24	Ventnor City
A81	Joint Court of Corbin City Estelle Manor Weymouth Twp.
A95	Atlantic Co. Dist. Ct.
A96	Atlantic Co. Ct.

BERGEN COUNTY

CODE B

Code	Locations
B02	Allendale Boro
B03	Alpine Boro
B04	Bergenfield Boro
B05	Bogota Boro
B06	Carlstadt Boro
B07	Cliffside Park Boro
B08	Closter Boro
B09	Cresskill Boro
B10	Demarest Boro
B11	Dumont Boro
B12	Elmwood Park
B13	East Rutherford Boro
B14	Edgewater Boro
B15	Emerson Boro
B16	Englewood City
B17	Englewood Cliffs Boro
B18	Fair Lawn Boro
B19	Fairview Boro
B20	Fort Lee Boro
B21	Franklin Lakes Boro
B22	Garfield City
B23	Glen Rock Boro
B24	Hackensack City
B25	Harrington Park Boro
B26	Hasbrouck Hgts. Boro
B27	Haworth Boro
B28	Hillsdale Boro
B29	Ho-Ho-Kus Boro
B30	Leonia Boro
B31	Little Ferry Boro
B32	Lodi Boro
B33	Lyndhurst Twp.
B34	Mahwah Twp.
B35	Maywood Boro
B36	Midland Park Boro
B37	Montvale Boro
B38	Moonachie Boro
B39	New Milford Boro
B40	North Arlington Boro
B41	Northvale Boro
B42	Norwood Boro
B43	Oakland Boro
B44	Old Tappan Boro
B45	Oradell Boro
B46	Palisades Interstate Pl.
B47	Palisades Park Boro
B48	Paramus Boro
B49	Park Ridge Boro
B50	Ramsey Boro
B51	Ridgefield Boro
B52	Ridgefield Park Twp.
B53	Ridgewood Twp.
B54	River Edge Boro
B55	River Vale Twp.
B56	Rochelle Park Twp.
B57	Rockleigh Boro
B58	Rutherford Boro
B59	Saddle Brook Twp.
B60	Saddle River Boro
B61	South Hackensack Twp.
B62	Teaneck Twp.
B63	Tenafly Boro
B64	Teterboro Boro
B65	Upper Saddle River Boro
B66	Waldwick Boro
B67	Wallington Boro
B68	Washington Twp.
B69	Westwood Boro
B70	Woodcliff Lake Boro
B71	Wood-Ridge Boro
B72	Wyckoff Twp.
B95	Bergen Co. Dist. Ct.
B96	Bergen Co. Ct.

BURLINGTON COUNTY

CODE C

Code	Locations
C03	Beverly City
C04	Bordentown City
C05	Bordentown Twp.
C06	Burlington City
C07	Burlington Twp.
C08	Chesterfield Twp.
C09	Cinnaminson Twp.

EXHIBIT 48 (Continued)

Code	Locations
C10	Delanco Twp.
C11	Delran Twp.
C12	Eastampton Twp.
C13	Edgewater Park Twp.
C14	Evesham Twp.
C15	Fieldsboro Boro
C16	Florence Twp.
C17	Hainesport Twp.
C18	Willingboro Twp.
C19	Lumberton Twp.
C20	Mansfield Twp.
C21	Maple Shade Twp.
C22	Medford Twp.
C23	Medford Lakes Boro
C24	Moorestown Twp.
C25	Mount Holly Twp.
C26	Mount Laurel Twp.
C28	North Hanover Twp.
C29	Palmyra Boro
C30	Pemberton Boro
C31	Pemberton Twp.
C32	Riverside Twp.
C33	Riverton Boro
C34	Shamong Twp.
C35	Southampton Twp.
C36	Springfield Twp.
C37	Tabernacle Twp.
C39	Westampton Twp.
C40	Woodland Twp.
C82	Joint Court of Bass River Twp. Washington Twp.
C83	Joint Court of New Hanover Twp. Wrightstown Boro
C95	Burlington Co. Dist. Ct.
C96	Burlington Co. Ct.
C82	Court sits in New Gretna

CAMDEN COUNTY

CODE D

Code	Locations
D02	Audubon Boro
D03	Audubon Park Boro
D04	Barrington Boro
D05	Bellmawr Boro
D06	Berlin Boro
D07	Berlin Twp.
D08	Brooklawn Boro
D09	Camden City
D10	Cherry Hill Twp.
D11	Chesilhurst Boro
D12	Clementon Boro
D13	Collingwood Boro
D15	Gibbsboro Boro
D16	Gloucester City
D17	Gloucester Twp.
D18	Haddon Twp.
D19	Haddonfield Boro
D20	Haddon Heights Boro
D21	Hi-Nella Boro
D22	Laurel Springs Boro
D23	Lawnside Boro
D24	Lindenwold Boro
D25	Magnolia Boro
D26	Merchantville Boro
D27	Mount Ephraim Boro
D28	Oaklyn Boro
D29	Pennsauken Twp.
D30	Pine Hill Boro
D31	Pine Valley Boro
D32	Runnemede Boro
D33	Somerdale Boro
D34	Stratford Boro
D36	Voorhees Twp.
D37	Waterford Twp.
D38	Winslow Twp.
D39	Woodlynne Boro
D95	Camden Co. Dist. Ct.
D96	Camden Co. Ct.

CAPE MAY COUNTY

CODE E

Code	Locations
E02	Avalon Boro
E03	Cape May City
E05	Cape May Point Boro
E06	Dennis Twp.
E07	Lower Twp.
E08	Middle Twp.
E09	North Wildwood City
E10	Ocean City
E11	Sea Isle City
E12	Stone Harbor Boro
E13	Upper Twp.
E15	West Cape May Boro
E16	West Wildwood Boro
E17	Wildwood City
E18	Wildwood Crest Boro
E19	Woodbine Boro
E95	Cape May Co. Dist. Ct.
E96	Cape May Co. Ct.

CUMBERLAND COUNTY

CODE F

Code	Locations
F02	Bridgeton City
F04	Commercial Twp.
F05	Deerfield Twp.
F06	Downe Twp.
F07	Fairfield Twp.
F08	Greenwich Twp.
F09	Hopewell Twp.
F10	Lawrence Twp.
F11	Maurice River Twp.
F12	Milville City Shiloh Boro
F16	Stow Creek Twp.
F17	Upper Deerfield Twp.
F18	Vineland City
F95	Cumberland Co. Dist. Ct.
F96	Cumberland Co. Ct.

ESSEX COUNTY

CODE G

Code	Locations
G02	Belleville Town
G03	Bloomfield Town
G04	Caldwell Boro
G05	Fairfield Boro
G06	Cedar Grove Twp.
G07	East Orange City
G08	Essex Fells Boro
G09	Glen Ridge Boro
G10	Irvington Town
G11	Livingston Town
G12	Maplewood Twp.
G13	Milburn Twp.
G14	Montclair Town
G21	Newark City
G23	North Caldwell Boro
G24	Nutley Town
G25	Orange City
G26	Roseland Boro
G27	South Orange Village
G28	Verona Boro
G29	West Caldwell Boro
G30	West Orange Town
G95	Essex Co. Dist. Ct.
G96	Essex Co. Ct.

GLOUCESTER COUNTY

CODE H

Code	Locations
H02	Clayton Boro
H03	Deptford Twp.
H04	East Greenwich Twp.
H05	Elk Twp.
H06	Franklin Twp.
H08	Glassboro Boro
H09	Greenwich Twp.
H11	Logan Twp.
H12	Mantua Twp.
H13	Monroe Twp.
H14	National Park Boro
H15	Newfield Boro
H16	Paulsboro Boro
H17	Pitman Boro
H20	Washington Twp.
H21	Wenonah Boro
H22	West Deptford Twp.
H23	Westville Boro
H25	Woodbury City
H26	Woodbury Hgts. Boro
H27	Swedesboro Boro
H28	Woolwich Twp.
H82	Joint Court of Harrison Twp. So. Harrison Twp.
H95	Gloucester Co. Dist. Ct.
H96	Gloucester Co. Ct.

HUDSON COUNTY

CODE J

Code	Locations
J02	Bayonne City
J03	East Newark Boro
J04	Guttenberg Town
J05	Harrison Town
J06	Hoboken City

EXHIBIT 48 (Continued)

J09 Jersey City
J12 Kearny Town
J13 North Bergen Twp.
J14 Secaucus Town
J15 Union City
J16 Weehawken Twp.
J17 West New York Town
J95 Hudson Co. Dist. Ct.
J96 Hudson Co. Ct.

HUNTERDON COUNTY

CODE K

Code	Locations
K03	Bethlehem Twp.
K10	Flemington Boro Mun.
K15	High Bridge Boro
K17	Kingwood Twp.
K18	Lambertville City
K22	Raritan Twp.
K23	Readington Twp.
K24	Stockton Boro
K26	Union Twp.
K81	Joint Court of
	Alexandria Twp.
	Frenchtown Boro
	Holland Twp.
	Milford Boro
K82	Joint Court of
	Delaware Twp.
	East Amwell Twp.
	West Amwell Twp.
K84	No. Hunterdon Ct. for
	Bloomsbury Boro
	Califon Boro
	Clinton Town
	Clinton Twp.
	Franklin Twp.
	Glen Gardner Twp.
	Hampton Boro
	Lebanon Boro
	Lebanon Twp.
	Tewksbury Twp.
K95	Hunterdon Co. Dist. Ct.
K96	Hunterdon Co. Ct.
K81	Ct. sits in Milford Boro
K82	Court sits in Ringoes
K84	Court sits in Annandale

MERCER COUNTY

CODE L

Code	Locations
L02	East Windsor Twp.
L03	Ewing Twp.
L04	Hamilton Twp.
L05	Hightstown Boro
L06	Hopewell Boro
L07	Hopewell Twp.
L08	Lawrence Twp.
L10	Pennington Boro
L11	Princeton Boro
L12	Princeton Twp.
L13	Trenton City
L14	Washington Twp.

L15 West Windsor Twp.
L95 Mercer Co. Dist. Ct.
L96 Mercer Co. Ct.

MIDDLESEX COUNTY

CODE M

Code	Locations
M02	Carteret Boro
M04	Cranbury Twp.
M05	Dunellen Boro
M06	East Brunswick Twp.
M07	Edison Twp.
M08	Helmetta Boro
M09	Highland Park Boro
M10	Jamesburg Boro
M11	Oldbridge Twp.
M12	Metuchen Mun.
M13	Middlesex Boro
M14	Milltown Boro
M15	Monroe Twp.
M16	New Brunswick City
M17	North Brunswick Twp.
M18	Perth Amboy City
M19	Piscataway Twp.
M20	Plainsboro Twp.
M21	Sayreville Boro
M22	South Amboy City
M23	South Brunswick Twp.
M24	South Plainfield Boro
M25	South River Boro
M26	Spotswood Boro
M27	Woodbridge Twp.
M95	Middlesex Co. Dist. Ct.
M96	Middlesex Co. Ct.
X01	N.J. Supreme Ct.
X02	N.J. Superior Ct.
X03	U.S. Commissioners
X04	U.S. Federal Institutions

MONMOUTH COUNTY

CODE N

Code	Locations
N02	Allenhurst Boro
N04	Asbury Park City
N05	Colt's Neck
N06	Atlantic Highlands Boro
N07	Avon-By-The-Sea Boro
N08	Belmar Boro
N10	Bradley Beach Boro
N11	Brielle Boro
N12	Deal Boro
N13	Eatontown Boro
N14	Englishtown Boro
N15	Fair Haven Boro
N16	Farmingdale Boro
N17	Freehold Boro
N18	Freehold Twp.
N19	Highlands Boro
N20	Holmdel Twp.
N21	Howell Twp.
N22	Interlaken Boro

N23 Keansburg Boro
N24 Keyport Boro
N25 Little Silver Boro
N26 Loch Arbour Village
N27 Long Branch City
N28 Manalapan Twp.
N29 Manasquan Boro
N30 Marlboro Twp.
N31 Matawan Boro
N32 Aberdeen Twp.
N33 Middletown Twp.
N34 Millstone Twp.
N35 Monmouth Beach Boro
N36 Neptune City Boro
N37 Neptune Twp.
N38 Tinton Falls Boro
N40 Ocean Twp.
N41 Ocean Grove
N42 Oceanport Boro
N43 Hazlet Mun.
N44 Red Bank Boro
N45 Roosevelt Boro
N46 Rumson Boro
N47 Sea Bright Boro
N48 Sea Girt Boro
N49 Shrewsbury Boro
N50 Shrewsbury Twp.
N51 South Belmar Boro
N52 Spring Lake Boro
N53 Spring Lake Heights Boro
N54 Union Beach Boro
N56 Wall Twp.
N59 West Long Branch Boro
N81 Joint Court of
 Allentown Boro
 Upper Freehold Twp.
N95 Monmouth Co. Dist. Ct.
N96 Monmouth Co. Ct.
N81 Court sits in Allentown

MORRIS COUNTY

CODE P

Code	Locations
P02	Boonton Town
P03	Boonton Twp.
P05	Butler Boro
P06	Chatham Boro
P07	Chatham Twp.
P08	Chester Boro
P09	Chester Twp.
P10	Denville Twp.
P11	Dover Town
P12	East Hanover Twp.
P14	Florham Park Boro
P15	Hanover Twp.
P16	Harding Twp.
P17	Jefferson Twp.
P18	Kinnelon Boro
P19	Lincoln Park Boro
P21	Madison Boro
P22	Mendham Boro
P23	Mendham Twp.
P25	Mine Hill Twp.
P26	Montville Twp.
P27	Morris Twp.
P28	Morris Plains Boro
P29	Morristown Town
P30	Mountain Lakes Boro

EXHIBIT 48 (Continued)

P31	Mount Arlington Boro
P33	Mount Olive Twp.
P34	Mount Tabor
P35	Netcong Boro
P36	Parsippany-Troy Hills Twp.
P37	Passaic Twp.
P38	Pequannock Twp.
P39	Randolph Twp.
P40	Riverdale Boro
P41	Rockaway Boro
P42	Rockaway Twp.
P43	Roxbury Twp.
P46	Victory Gardens Boro
P47	Washington Twp.
P48	Wharton Boro
P95	Morris Co. Dist. Ct.
P96	Morris Co. Ct.

OCEAN COUNTY

CODE Q

Code	Locations
Q01	Barnegat Twp.
Q02	Barnegat Light Boro
Q03	Bay Head Boro
Q04	Beach Haven Boro
Q05	Beachwood Boro
Q06	Berkeley Twp.
Q08	Brick Twp.
Q10	Dover Twp.
Q11	Eagleswood Twp.
Q13	Harvey Cedars Boro
Q14	Island Heights Boro
Q15	Jackson Twp.
Q16	Lacey Twp.
Q17	Lakehurst Boro
Q19	Lakewood Twp.
Q20	Lavlette Boro
Q22	Long Beach Twp.
Q23	Manchester Twp.
Q24	Mantoloking Boro
Q27	Ocean Gate Boro
Q28	Pine Beach Boro
Q29	Plumsted Twp.
Q30	Point Pleasant Boro
Q31	Pt. Pleasant Beach Boro
Q32	Seaside Heights Boro
Q33	Seaside Park Boro
Q34	Ship Bottom Boro
Q35	South Toms River Boro
Q36	Stafford Twp.
Q37	Surf City Boro
Q39	Tuckerton Boro
Q40	Little Egg Harbor Twp.
Q41	Ocean Twp.
Q95	Ocean Co. Dist. Ct.
Q96	Ocean Co. Ct.

PASSAIC COUNTY

CODE R

Code	Locations
R02	Bloomingdale Boro
R03	Clifton City
R04	Haledon Boro
R05	Hawthorne Boro
R06	Little Falls Twp.
R07	North Haledon Boro
R08	Passaic City
R09	Paterson City
R10	Pompton Lakes Boro
R11	Prospect Park Boro
R12	Ringwood Boro
R13	Totowa Boro
R14	Wanaque Boro
R15	Wayne Twp.
R16	West Milford Twp.
R17	West Paterson Boro
R95	Passaic Co. Dist. Ct.
R96	Passaic Co. Ct.

SALEM COUNTY

CODE S

Code	Locations
S02	Alloway Twp.
S03	Elmer Boro
S04	Elsinboro Twp.
S05	Lwr. Alloways Crk. Twp.
S06	Pennsville Twp.
S07	Mannington Twp.
S08	Oldmans Twp.
S09	Penns Grove Boro
S10	Pilesgrove Twp.
S11	Pittsgrove Twp.
S12	Quinton Twp.
S13	Salem City
S14	Upper Penns Neck Twp.
S15	Upper Pittsgrove Twp.
S16	Woodstown Boro
S95	Salem Co. Dist. Ct.
S96	Salem Co. Ct.

SOMERSET COUNTY

CODE T

Code	Locations
T03	Bedminster Twp.
T04	Bernards Twp.
T05	Bernardsville Boro
T06	Bound Brook Boro
T08	Branchburg Twp.
T09	Bridgewater Twp.
T10	Far Hills Boro
T11	Franklin Twp.
T12	Green Brook Twp.
T13	Hillsborough Twp.
T14	Manville Boro
T15	Millstone Boro
T16	Montgomery Twp.
T17	North Plainfield Boro
T18	Peapack-Gladstone Boro
T19	Raritan Boro
T20	Rocky Hill Boro
T21	Somerville Boro
T22	So. Bound Brook Boro
T23	Warren Twp.
T24	Watchung Boro
T95	Somerset Co. Dist. Ct.
T96	Somerset Co. Ct.

SUSSEX COUNTY

CODE V

Code	Locations
V02	Andover Twp.
V04	Branchville Boro
V05	Byram Twp.
V13	Hopatcong Boro
V15	Montague Twp.
V17	Newton Town
V18	Ogdensburg Boro
V19	Sandyston Twp.
V20	Sparta Twp.
V21	Stanhope Boro
V23	Sussex Boro
V24	Vernon Twp.
V26	Wantage Twp.
V81	Joint Court of Franklin Boro Hamburg Boro Hardyston Twp.
V82	Joint Court of Andover Boro Green Twp.
V83	Joint Court of Frankford Twp. Lafayette Twp.
V84	Joint Court of Fredon Twp. Hampton Twp. Stillwater Twp.
V95	Sussex Co. Dist. Ct. Walpack Twp.
V96	Sussex Co. Ct.
V81	Ct. sits in Franklin Boro
V82	Ct. sits in Andover Boro

UNION COUNTY

CODE W

Code	Locations
W02	Berkeley Heights Twp.
W03	Clark Twp.
W04	Cranford Twp.
W05	Elizabeth City
W06	Fanwood Boro
W07	Garwood Boro
W08	Hillside Twp.
W09	Kenilworth Boro
W10	Linden City
W11	Mountainside Boro
W12	New Providence Boro
W14	Plainfield City
W15	Rahway City
W16	Rodelle Boro
W17	Roselle Park Boro
W18	Scotch Plains Twp.
W19	Springfield Twp.
W20	Summit City

EXHIBIT 48 (Continued)

Code	Location
W21	Union Twp.
W22	Westfield Town
W23	Winfield Twp.
W95	Union Co. Dist. Ct.
W96	Union Co. Ct.

WARREN COUNTY

CODE Y

Code	Locations
Y02	Allamuchy Twp.
Y03	Alpha Boro
Y04	Belvidere Town
Y08	Greenwich Twp.
Y09	Hackettstown Town
Y15	Independence Twp.
Y17	Knowlton Twp.
Y18	Lopatcong Twp.
Y20	Oxford Twp.
Y22	Philipsburg Town
Y23	Pohatcong Twp.
Y24	Washington Boro
Y26	White Twp.
Y27	Mansfield Twp.
Y81	Cent. Warren Jt. Ct.
	Franklin Twp.
	Washington Twp.
Y82	No. Warren Ct.
	Blairstown Twp.
	Hardwick Twp.
	Hope Twp.
Y95	Warren Co. Dist. Ct.
	Frelinghuysen Twp.
	Harmony Twp.
	Liberty Twp.
	Pahaquarry Twp.
Y96	Warren Co. Ct.
Y81	Ct. sits in Washington

154/Municipal Court

EXHIBIT 49

STATE OF NEW JERSEY
DIVISION OF MOTOR VEHICLES
ABSTRACT OF DRIVER HISTORY RECORD

CERTIFIED - COMPLETE

DRIVER LICENSE NUMBER   FIRST NAME   M.I.   LAST NAME

STREET   CITY   STATE   ZIPCODE
                                           NJ   08093-1970

WEST DEPTFORD MUN CT   CLASS: D   ENDORSEMENTS:
CROWN POINT RD AND GROVE AV   RESTRICTIONS: 1
THOROFARE   NJ   08086   EXPIRATION: 10 31 1992

REQ. REF. NO.   UNIT NUMBER   ABSTRACT DATE   TYPE
                 9049   05 13 92   H

EVENT DATE MO. DAY YR.	EVENT RESPONSI-BILITY	EVENT TYPE	EVENT IDENTIFIER	EVENT DESCRIPTION	LIC	COM	CMV	HZM	FTL	PTS.	POSTING DATE MMDDYY
03 14 80	CIS	A	POLC	INVOLVED IN ACCIDENT-POLICE REPORTED							031885
03 14 80	H14	V	0496	RECKLESS DRIVING						5	071180
12 17 80	PDP	W	0001	WARNING AFTER PDP CLASS							021883
03 14 81	DMV	Z	PC03	POINT CREDIT-ANNUAL SAFE DRIVING						-3	030485
06 81	CIS	A	POLC	INVOLVED IN ACCIDENT-POLICE REPORTED							031885
06 02 81	H22	V	0450	OPERATE UNDER INFLUENCE LIQ/DRUGS							081383
07 02 81	H14	V	0310	UNLICENSED DRIVER							100983
07 21 81	M99	O	0450	OPERATE UNDER INFLUENCE LIQ/DRUGS	X	X					082483
12 24 81	CIS	O	FVIT	FAIL TO VERIFY INSURANCE-TERMINATE	X	X					020282
03 10 82	RES	R	LROC	RESTORE BASIC DRIV & REGIS PRIVS							031182
04 20 82	CIS	A	POLC	INVOLVED IN ACCIDENT-POLICE REPORTED							031885
04 20 82	H25	V	4144	DISREGARD OF STOP SIGN REGULATIONS						2	080582
12 15 82	H22	V	0310	UNLICENSED DRIVER							032583
04 20 83	DMV	Z	PC03	POINT CREDIT-ANNUAL SAFE DRIVING						-3	030485
04 20 84	DMV	Z	PC01	POINT CREDIT-ANNUAL SAFE DRIVING						-1	030485

I CERTIFY THAT ACCORDING TO THE RECORDS OF THIS DIVISION THIS LISTING IS A TRUE ABSTRACT OF THE DRIVER HISTORY RECORD OF THE INDIVIDUAL WHOSE DRIVER LICENSE NUMBER IS PRINTED OR TYPED ABOVE. THE RECORD INCLUDES ACCIDENTS, SUSPENSIONS AND CONVICTIONS FOR MOVING VIOLATIONS.

JUN 11 1992

DATE   SKIP LEE
                                       DIRECTOR

Municipal Court/155

EXHIBIT 49 (Continued)
STATE OF NEW JERSEY
DIVISION OF MOTOR VEHICLES
ABSTRACT OF DRIVER HISTORY RECORD

CERTIFIED - COMPLETE

DRIVER LICENSE NUMBER   FIRST NAME   M.I.   LAST NAME

STREET   CITY   STATE   ZIPCODE
    NJ   08093-1970

WEST DEPTFORD MUN CT   CLASS: D   ENDORSEMENTS:
CROWN POINT RD AND GROVE AV   RESTRICTIONS: 1
THOROFARE   NJ   08086   EXPIRATION: 10 31 1992

REQ. REF. NO.   UNIT NUMBER 9049   ABSTRACT DATE 05 13 92   TYPE H

EVENT DATE MO. DAY YR.	EVENT RESPONSI-BILITY	EVENT TYPE	EVENT IDENTI-FIER	EVENT DESCRIPTION	LIC	COM	CMV	HZM	FTL	PTS.	POSTING DATE MMDDY
				CONTINUED							
8 22 84	H22	V	4144	DISREGARD OF STOP SIGN REGULATIONS						2	06168
8 22 85	DMV	Z	PC02	POINT CREDIT-ANNUAL SAFE DRIVING						-2	09188
1 09 86	H14	O	VCCB	NO PAYMENT-VCCB PENALTY ASSESSMENT	X	X					10078
8 86	C11	S	FSFA	FAILURE TO APPEAR	X	X					11068
0 22 86	C11	O	FSFA	FAILURE TO APPEAR	X	X					10078
0 07 87	DVR	M	PAMV	PERSNL APPEAR UNSCHED-RSC TRENTON							10078
0 07 87	RES	F	REST	RESTORATION FEE PAID							10078
0 07 87	RES	R	LOBO	BASIC, BUS/COMMERCIAL PRIVILEGES							10078
2 20 88	CIS	A	POLC	INVOLVED IN ACCIDENT-POLICE REPORTED							05138
2 20 88	D08	V	0485	IMPROPER PASSING						4	04218
2 20 88	D08	V	0497	CARELESS DRIVING						2	04218
2 20 88	D29	V	129A	LEAVE SCENE ACCDNT-PERSONAL INJURY						8	11309
21 88	DIP	N	PTPS	POINT SYSTEM ADVISORY NOTICE DIP							04218
20 89	DMV	Z	PC03	POINT CREDIT-ANNUAL SAFE DRIVING						-3	11309

I CERTIFY THAT ACCORDING TO THE RECORDS OF THIS DIVISION THIS LISTING IS A TRUE ABSTRACT OF THE DRIVER HISTORY RECORD OF THE INDIVIDUAL WHOSE DRIVER LICENSE NUMBER IS PRINTED OR TYPED ABOVE. THE RECORD INCLUDES ACCIDENTS, SUSPENSIONS AND CONVICTIONS FOR MOVING VIOLATIONS.

JUN 11 1992
DATE

SKIP LEE
DIRECTOR

156/*Municipal Court*

EXHIBIT 49 (Continued)
STATE OF NEW JERSEY
DIVISION OF MOTOR VEHICLES
ABSTRACT OF DRIVER HISTORY RECORD

CERTIFIED - COMPLETE

DRIVER LICENSE NUMBER   FIRST NAME   M.I.   LAST NAME

STREET   CITY   STATE NJ   ZIPCODE 08093-1970

WEST DEPTFORD MUN CT
CROWN POINT RD AND GROVE AV
THOROFARE   NJ 08086

CLASS: D   ENDORSEMENTS:
RESTRICTIONS: 1
EXPIRATION: 10 31 1992

REQ. REF. NO.   UNIT NUMBER 9049   ABSTRACT DATE 05 13 92   TYPE H

EVENT DATE MO. DAY YR.	EVENT RESPONSI-BILITY	EVENT TYPE	EVENT IDENTI-FIER	EVENT DESCRIPTION	LIC	COM	CMV	HZM	FTL	PTS.	POSTING DATE MMDDYY
				CONTINUED							
03 05 89	Z46	V	4982	SPEEDING - 39 MPH IN 25 MPH ZONE						2	061989
03 19 89	ISS	M	SURC	DRIVER SURCHARGED							03198
05 14 89	ISS	O	ISNP	NON PAYMENT OF INSURANCE SURCHARGE	X	X					05238
05 89	DVR	M	PADE	PERSNL APPEAR UNSCHED-RSC DEPTFORD							052389
05 23 89	RES	F	REST	RESTORATION FEE PAID							05238
05 23 89	RES	R	LOBO	BASIC, BUS/COMMERCIAL PRIVILEGES							05238
09 02 89	H27	V	0497	CARELESS DRIVING						2	12268
09 02 89	H27	V	4504	REFUSAL TO SUBMIT TO CHEMICAL TEST							01309C
09 15 89	D29	S	FSFA	FAILURE TO APPEAR	X	X					11298
11 14 89	D29	O	FSFA	FAILURE TO APPEAR	X	X					12049
12 27 89	DIP	N	PTPS	POINT SYSTEM ADVISORY NOTICE DIP							122789
01 18 90	H27	O	4504	REFUSAL TO SUBMIT TO CHEMICAL TEST	X	X					01309C
04 01 90	ISS	M	SURC	DRIVER SURCHARGED							03199C
05 13 90	ISS	O	ISNP	NON PAYMENT OF INSURANCE SURCHARGE	X	X					05139C

I CERTIFY THAT ACCORDING TO THE RECORDS OF THIS DIVISION THIS LISTING IS A TRUE ABSTRACT OF THE DRIVER HISTORY RECORD OF THE INDIVIDUAL WHOSE DRIVER LICENSE NUMBER IS PRINTED OR TYPED ABOVE. THE RECORD INCLUDES ACCIDENTS, SUSPENSIONS AND CONVICTIONS FOR MOVING VIOLATIONS.

JUN 11 1992

DATE   DIRECTOR   SKIP LEE

Municipal Court/157

EXHIBIT 49 (Continued)
STATE OF NEW JERSEY
DIVISION OF MOTOR VEHICLES
ABSTRACT OF DRIVER HISTORY RECORD

CERTIFIED - COMPLETE

DRIVER LICENSE NUMBER　　　FIRST NAME　　M.I.　　LAST NAME

STREET　　　　　　　　　　CITY　　　　　　STATE　　ZIPCODE
　　　　　　　　　　　　　　　　　　　　　　NJ　　　08093-1970

WEST DEPTFORD MUN CT　　　　CLASS: D　　ENDORSEMENTS:
CROWN POINT RD AND GROVE AV　　　　　　RESTRICTIONS: 1
THOROFARE　　　NJ 08086　　　　　　　　EXPIRATION: 10 31 1992

REQ. REF. NO.　　UNIT NUMBER　　ABSTRACT DATE　　TYPE
　　　　　　　　9049　　　　　　05 13 92　　　　H

EVENT DATE MO. DAY YR.	EVENT RESPONSI-BILITY	EVENT TYPE	EVENT IDENTI-FIER	EVENT DESCRIPTION	LIC	COM	CMV	HZM	FTL	PTS.	POSTING DATE MMDDYY
				CONTINUED							
11 20 90	D29	O	129A	LEAVE SCENE ACCDNT-PERSONAL INJURY	X	X					113090
11 30 90	SUS	S	PTPB	POINT SYSTEM	X	X					010491
12 25 90	SUS	O	PTPB	POINT SYSTEM	X	X					010491
04　 91	ISS	M	SURC	DRIVER SURCHARGED							031791
05 19 91	ISS	O	ISNP	NON PAYMENT OF INSURANCE SURCHARGE	X	X					051991
09 13 91	H22	O	VCCB	NO PAYMENT-VCCB PENALTY ASSESSMENT	X	X					100491
02 14 92	H14	V	0450	OPERATE UNDER INFLUENCE LIQ/DRUGS							040192
03 23 92	H14	O	0450	OPERATE UNDER INFLUENCE LIQ/DRUGS	X	X					040192
04 01 92	ISS	M	SURC	DRIVER SURCHARGED							031592
04 01 92	SUS	S	0340	OPERATE DURING SUSPENSION PERIOD	X	X					050792
04 26 92	SUS	O	0340	OPERATE DURING SUSPENSION PERIOD	X	X					050792
				STATUS: SUSPENDED							

I CERTIFY THAT ACCORDING TO THE RECORDS OF THIS DIVISION THIS LISTING IS A TRUE ABSTRACT OF THE DRIVER HISTORY RECORD OF THE INDIVIDUAL WHOSE DRIVER LICENSE NUMBER IS PRINTED OR TYPED ABOVE. THE RECORD INCLUDES ACCIDENTS, SUSPENSIONS AND CONVICTIONS FOR MOVING VIOLATIONS.

JUN 11 1992

DATE　　　　　　　　　　　　　　　　　　　SKIP LEE
　　　　　　　　　　　　　　　　　　　　　DIRECTOR

EXHIBIT 49 (Continued)

EXPLANATION FOR ABSTRACT OF DRIVER HISTORY RECORD

DRIVER LICENSE INFORMATION

CLASS CODE

- A Commercial Vehicle
- B Commercial Vehicle
- C Commercial Vehicle
- D Auto
- E Motorcycle
- F Moped
- G Agricultural
- I Identification

ENDORSEMENT CODE

- T Double & Triple Trailer
- P Passenger
- N Tank Vehicle
- H Hazardous Materials
- M Motorcycle
- F Moped

RESTRICTION CODES

- 1 Corrective Lenses Required
- 2 Prosthetic Device
- 3 Mechanical Device
- 4 Hearing Impaired
- 5 Attached Restrictions
- L Except Vehicles with Air Brakes
- M Except Class A Passenger Vehicles
- N Except Class A & B Passenger Vehicles
- O Except Tractor-Trailer (Tow Trucks)
- P Pass End: School Bus Capacity 15-Only
- Q Except Passenger Vehicles Capacity 16+
- R Bus Mechanics—No Passengers
- S Except School Age Passengers
- U Class I Owner Only (was ID3)
- V Class I Violator Only (was ID5)
- W Class I Misc (was ID2, ID4, IDx)

DRIVER HISTORY INFORMATION

EVENT TYPE CODES

- A Accident
- C Conference
- D Fee Due
- E Reexamination Activity
- F Fee Payment
- J Referral
- K Referral with Interval Reporting
- M Memo Entry
- N Advisory Notice
- O Suspension Order
- P Program Activity
- R Restoration
- S Scheduled Suspension
- V Violation
- W Warning Notice
- X Cancellation of Scheduled Suspension
- Z Point Credit

EVENT RESPONSIBILITY CODES (DIVISION)

- ACP Alcohol Countermeasures (Health Dept.)
- CIS Compulsory Insurance/Accident Reporting
- COO Certificate of Ownership
- CON Conference Unit
- DIP Driver Improvement Program
- DMV Division Director
- DRT Driver Testing
- DVR Driver
- FAR Fatal Accident Review
- FRJ Financial Responsibility/Judgment
- ISS Insurance Surcharge
- MFR Medical Fitness Review
- OAL Office of Administrative Law Liaison
- PDP Probationary Driver Program
- RES Restoration Authorization
- RSU Reexamination Scheduling
- SEC Security Responsibility
- SUS Suspension Authorization
- UCJ Unsatisfied Claims and Judgments

EVENT DATE Date violation, accident or event occurred.

EVENT RESPONSIBILITY CODES Identify the Court or Division of Motor Vehicles unit responsible for the event and/or action taken.

EVENT TYPE CODES Identify the major kinds of events and/or actions taken.

EVENT DESCRIPTION A complete description of the event and/or action.

LIC "X" Basic driving privilege suspended ("O" Events).

COM "X" Commercial driving privilege suspended ("O" Events).

CMV "X" Violation committed in a commercial vehicle.

EXHIBIT 49 (Continued)

HZM "X" Violation committed while carrying hazardous materials.

FTL "X" Violation resulted in a fatality.

PTS Points assessed or credited if applicable.

POSTING DATE Date DMV recorded the violation, accident or event.

EXHIBIT 50

EXPLANATION OF NEW JERSEY
ABSTRACT OF DRIVER HISTORY

Event Date

This is the date that an event occurred or that action was imposed or taken. (e.g. For a moving violation, it is the date the violation occurred; for a suspension it is the date the suspension was imposed.)

Event Responsibility

Identifies the court or Division of Motor Vehicles unit responsible for the event and/or action taken.

Event Type

Identifies the major types of events and/or actions taken.

Event Identifier

Uniquely identifies each event and/or action taken.

Event Description

Provides a brief explanation of the event.

[Abstract Example Attached]

EXHIBIT 50 (Continued)

BASIC MOVING VIOLATIONS THAT APPEAR ON DRIVING RECORD

Column 4 Event Identifiers	Description
A011	Operating at Slow Speed Blocking Traffic
A222	Illegal Backing or Turning in Street
A223	Improper Passing
A224	"U" Turn Prohibited
A225	Illegal Use of Medial Strip
A227	Failure to Use Proper Entrances or Exits
333K	Vehicle in Hazardous Condition
A112 (2 pts.)	Speeding
A114 (4 pts.)	Speeding
A115 (5 pts.)	Speeding
9813	Retarding Traffic
9815	Improper Passing
2950	"U" Turn Prohibited
2920	Illegal Use of Medial Strip
9819	Vehicle in Hazardous Condition
9814	Moving Against Traffic
815A	Failure to Keep Right
815B	Improper Passing
9816	"U" Turn Prohibited
9817	Illegal Use of Medial Strip
9831	Refuse to Pay/Evade Toll Payment
9122 (2 pts.)	Speeding
9124 (4 pts.)	Speeding
9125 (5 pts.)	Speeding
12A2	Speeding
12B2	Speeding
9913	Fail To Obey Signs
914A	Moving Against Traffic
914B	Use Improper Lane
9915	"U" Turn Prohibited
9917	Illegal Use of Medial Strip
MVLO	Moving/Nonmoving Local Court Actions
0200	Criminal
0414	Juvenile
0541	Possession or Consumption of Alcoholic Beverage by a Minor
C115	Vehicular Homicide
3315	Consuming Alcohol: Vehicle or Public Place
19a1	Possession Controlled Dangerous Substance With Intent to Distribute
120A	Possession of Narcotic Drugs
120B	Under Influence of Narcotic Drugs

EXHIBIT 50 (Continued)

BASIC MOVING VIOLATIONS THAT APPEAR ON DRIVING RECORD (Continued)

Column 4
Event
Identifiers   **Description**

Identifier	Description
3261	Operating Under Influence of Liquor or Drugs
3262	Careless Driving
2962	Speeding
8122 (2 pts.)	Speeding
8124 (4 pts.)	Speeding
8125 (5 pts.)	Speeding
2930	Vehicle in Hazardous Condition
2940	Use of Improper Lane
2910	Moving Against Traffic
AB33	Purchase Alcoholic Beverage—Underage
3C20	No Liability Insurance—Snowmobile
0304	Unregistered Vehicle
0310	Unlicensed Driver (New Jersey Resident)
3101	Special Bus Driver License (Non-Compliance)
3111	Improper Use of Agricultural Driver License
3115	Improper Use of Driver License by Military
0312	Illegal Securing of Driver License
3132	Special Learner Permit (Non-Compliance)
0317	Fail To Comply With Non-Resident Duties
3191	Transporting Passengers for Hire Without Omnibus Registration
0320	Constructor Registered Vehicle Exceeding 30 MPH
0330	Improper Transfer or Destruction of Motor Vehicle
0332	Defaced Plates
0333	Improper Display of License Plates, Display of Fictitious Plates
0334	Applying for Driver License or Registration During Suspension or Revocation
0335	Lending or Using Registration or Plates on Other Vehicles
0337	False Information on Application
0338	Use of Counterfeit Plate or Plates Other Than Issued
3381	Altering, Counterfeiting Driver License or Registration Certificate
339A	Loaning Driver License
339b	Allowing Unlicensed Driver to Operate Vehicle
339c	Borrowing Driver License
0340	Operating While Suspended or Revoked
3767	Operate/Ride Motorcycle—No Helmet
0380	Improperly or Not Equipped With Approved Tires
4143	Improper Use of Motorized Bicycle
143d	Motorized Bike—Only One Passenger
143e	No Insurance Motorized Bicycle
143g	Operating Motorized Bicycle While Under the Influence of Intoxicating Liquor
143i	Motorized Bike—Not Registered

EXHIBIT 50 (Continued)
BASIC MOVING VIOLATIONS THAT APPEAR ON DRIVING RECORD (Continued)

Column 4 Event Identifiers	Description
143k	No License Plate on Motorized Bike
143q	Motorized Bike—No Approved Helmet
0435	Failure to Give Pedestrian Right to Complete Crossing
0436	Failure to Yield Right of Way to Pedestrian
4371	Failure to Yield to Blind Person
0440	Improper Passing of Street Car
0441	Driving Through Safety Zones Prohibited
0448	Using Motor Vehicle Without Consent of Owner
0449	Tampering With Vehicle
4491	Operating Motor Vehicle While in Possession of Narcotic Drugs. State Police Warning.
0450	Operating Under Influence of Liquor or Drugs
4504	Refuse Alcohol Breath Test
451A	Consuming Alcohol While Operating/Riding
0452	Racing on Highway
0455	Improper Action on Steep Grade or Curbs
0456	Delaying Traffic
4561	Willfully Disabling or Abandoning Vehicle on any Public Facility
4565	Abandonment of Vehicle on Public Highway
0457	Failure to Comply With Instructions of Police Officer
0458	Driving Vehicle With View to Sides and Rear Obstructed
0463	Placing Injurious Substance on Highway
0464	Throwing Objects From Motor Vehicle
0465	Improper Letting Off or Taking on Passengers
0466	Improper Emerging From Driveway, Alley, or Garage
4661	Improper Entering or Leaving Highway
0467	Obstructing Passage of Other Vehicles
0468	Operating Street Cars or Buses With Doors Open
0471	Improper Driving on Sidewalk
0480	Disregard of Officer Directing Traffic
0481	Failure to Observe Traffic Control Device
0482	Failure to Keep Right
4821	Improper Use of Divided Highway
0483	Failure to Keep Right at Intersection
0484	Failure to Pass to Right When Proceeding in Opposite Direction
0485	Improper Passing
4851	Wrong Way on One-Way Street
0486	Improper Passing, Crossing "No Passing" line
0487	Failure to Give Way to Overtaking Vehicle
0488	Improper Operation on Highway With Marked Lanes
0489	Following too Closely

EXHIBIT 50 (Continued)

BASIC MOVING VIOLATIONS THAT APPEAR ON DRIVING RECORD (Continued)

**Column 4
Event
Identifiers**   **Description**

Identifier	Description
0490	Failure to Yield Right of Way
4901	Failure to Use Proper Entrances or Exits
0491	Failure to Yield Right of Way to Emergency Vehicles
0492	Failure to Stop and Yield to Emergency Vehicle
0493	Failure to Yield to Procession
0496	Reckless Driving
0497	Careless Driving
497a	Destruction of Agricultural or Recreational Property
4971	Operating at Slow Speed Blocking Traffic
4982 (2 pts.)	Speeding
4984 (4 pts.)	Speeding
4985 (5 pts.)	Speeding
4100	Speeding Across Sidewalk
1284	No Stopping, Improper Passing of a Dessert Truck
4105	Improper Operation at Intersections Controlled by Traffic Signals
4115	Improper Turn at Traffic Control Signal
4116	Improper Turn at Green Arrow Traffic Control Signal
4117	Failure to Observe Pedestrian Interval at Traffic Control
4119	Failure to Stop at Flashing Red Signal
4122	Failure to Stop for Police (Whistle)
4123	Improper Right and Left Turns
4124	Improper Turn Marked Course
4125	"U" Turn Prohibited
4126	Failure to Give Proper Signal
4127	Illegal Backing or Turning in Street
1271	Improper Crossing of Railroad Grade Crossing
1272	Failure to Comply With Signals on Bridge
4128	Failure to Stop at Railroad Crossing
1281	Passing School Bus
129A	Leaving the Scene of Accident, Personal Injury
129B	Leaving Scene of Accident, Property Damage
129C	Failure to Show License and/or Registration
4144	Disregard of Stop Sign Regulation
4145	Failure to Yield Right of Way to Line of Vehicles Entering Through Street
4215	Failure to Obey Directional Signal or Sign
0535	Failure to Surrender Suspended License Certificates
05C1	Racing on Highway
0422	Striking an Animal With a Car
655b	Failure to Return License or Registration
6A15	Penalty for False or Fraudulent Representation of Insurance Coverage
06B2	No Liability Insurance on Motor Vehicle

EXHIBIT 50 (Continued)
MOTOR VEHICLE DIVISION ACTION/NON-ACTION IDENTIFIERS BY RELATED MOTOR VEHICLE BUREAUS

INSURANCE SURCHARGE RELATED IDENTIFIERS

Column 4 Event Identifiers	Description
ISNP	Nonpayment of Insurance Surcharge
ISCA	Failure to Change Insurance Surcharge
DCIS	Dishonored Check—Insurance Surcharge

UNSATISFIED CLAIMS AND JUDGMENTS RELATED IDENTIFIERS

Column 4 Event Identifiers	Description
SDDL	Failure to Deposit Security—Driver License
SFDL	Failure to Deposit Security—Out-of-State Accident—Driver License
PBDL	Failure to Repay Personal Injury Protection Benefits—Driver
FFDL	Failure to File Financial Statement—Driver
SADL	Settlement Agreement Default—Driver
SDRG	Failure to Deposit Security—Registration
SFRG	Failure to Deposit Security—Out-of-State Accident—Registration
PBRG	Failure to Repay Personal Injury Protection Benefits—Owner
FFRG	Failure to File Financial Statement—Owner
SARG	Settlement Agreement Default—Owner
SDLR	Failure to Deposit Security—Driver License/Registration
SFLR	Failure to Deposit Security—Out-of-State Accident—License/Registration
PBLR	Failure to Repay Personal Injury Protection Benefits—Driver/Owner
FFLR	Failure to File Financial Statement—Driver/Owner
SALR	Settlement Agreement Default—Driver/Owner

DRIVER CONTROL RELATED IDENTIFIERS

Column 4 Event Identifiers	Description
530B	Habitual Offender
BS0A	Bus License—Basic Driver License Suspension
BS01	Bus License—Driving Record Disqualification
BS02	Bus License—12 or More Points
BS03	Bus License—Accident
BS04	Bus License—Fail to Report Motor Vehicle Conviction to Employer
BS05	Bus License—Misstatement on Application
BS06	Bus License—Fail to Prove Fit, Character and Experience
BS07	Bus License—Fail to Report Medical Condition
BS08	Bus License—Fail Driving Test
BS09	Bus License—Fail Written Examination

166/Municipal Court

EXHIBIT 50 (Continued)

DRIVER CONTROL RELATED IDENTIFIERS (Continued)

Column 4 Event Identifiers	Description
BS10	Bus License—Fail to Submit Renewal Application
BS11	Bus License—Not Medically/Physically Qualified
BS12	Bus License—Criminal Record Qualification
BS13	Bus License—Not Proper Person
OSBT	Breath Test Refusal in Foreign State
PVPS	Persistent Violator
MDAP	Recommendation of the Medical Advisory Panel
CONV	Physically Unqualified—Convulsive
CARD	Physically Unqualified—Cardiovascular
BLKO	Physically Unqualified—Blackouts
SENL	Physically Unqualified—Senility
EYES	Physically Unqualified—Vision Deficiency
HOSP	Physically/Mentally Unqualified—State Hospital Report
MNTL	Physically Unqualified—Mental/Nervous Disability
FARX	Failure to Appear for Driver Reexamination
DCDL	Dishonored Check—Driver License
DCRG	Dishonored Check—Registration
DCLR	Dishonored Check—Driver License/Registration
DCDL	Dishonored Check—Driver License
DCRG	Dishonored Check—Registration
MSOS	Misstatement on Application—By Investigation—Suspended
0337	Misstatement of Fact on Application
MSNJ	Misstatement on Application—By New Jersey Investigation—Suspended
I312	Illegally Secured Driver License—Investigation
C312	Illegally Secured Driver License—Court Reported
FVIA	Failure to Verify Insurance—Accident
FVIT	Failure to Verify Insurance—Termination
OSDS	Secured New Jersey Driver License—Suspension Compact State
PREH	Prehearing Conference
OTBH	Opportunity Conference
INTR	Mandatory Interview Probationary Driver Program
PROG	Program Fee Due
EYES	Vision
PHYS	Physical Qualification
CTMV	Driver Reexamination—Court/Division of Motor Vehicle Record
PTPS	Driver Reexamination—Points
2ACC	Driver Reexamination—Two Accidents Within Six Months with Points
VOUL	Driver Reexamination—Voluntary
REST	Restoration Fee Paid
PRHR	Preliminary Hearing Referral
PLHR	Penalty Hearing Referral
ARIR	Alcohol Referral With Interval Reports

EXHIBIT 50 (Continued)

DRIVER CONTROL RELATED IDENTIFIERS (Continued)

Column 4 Event Identifiers	Description
MIRA	Medical Interval Report Agreement
DEAD	Driver Deceased
PROB	Probationary Driver Starts
MVOS	Probationary Driver Moved Out-of-State
HREQ	Hearing Request
HRWD	Hearing Request—Withdrawal
CRWD	Conference Request—Withdrawal
RREQ	Reschedule Request
CREQ	Conference Request—OTBH
PAMV	Personal Appearance at Division of Motor Vehicle—Unscheduled
CONV	Physically Unqualified—Convulsive No Action
MDAP	Medical Advisory—PNL Record—No Action
MDRP	Failed to Submit Medical Report—No Action
MNTL	Physically Unqualified Mental/Nerves—No Action
CARD	Cardiovascular—No Action
BLKO	Physically Unqualified—Blackouts—No Action
SENL	Physically Unqualified—Senility—No Action
BUSL	New Jersey Bus Driver License Denial—No Action
ISNP	Nonpayment of Insurance Surcharge—No Action
ISCA	Failed to Change Address ISS—No Action
OSBT	Breath Test Refusal Out-of-State—No Action
PTPS	Point System—No Action
PVPS	Persistent Violator—No Action
HOSP	Physically Unqualified—State Hospital Report—No Action
OSDD	Driving Under Influence—Foreign State—No Action
FPRX	Failed to Pass New Jersey Driver Reexamination—No Action
FARX	Failed to Appear—Driver Reexamination—No Action
EXAM	Failed to Pass Driver Reexamination—No Action
MSNJ	Misstatement Application by Investigation New Jersey—No Action
MSOS	Misstatement Application by Investigation Out-of-State—No Action
DIRG	Registration Suspension—Driver Improvement
OOBO	Bus Driving Privileges Only
LROW	Basic Driving and Registration Privileges With Warning
LROO	Basic Driving and Registration Privileges
LRBW	Basic Driving, Bus and Registration Privileges With Warning
LRBO	Basic Driving, Bus and Registration Privileges
LOOW	Basic Driving Privileges With Warning
LOOO	Basic Driving Privileges Only
LOBW	Basic Driving and Bus Privileges With Warning
LOBO	Basic and Bus Privileges
OROO	Registration Privileges Only

EXHIBIT 50 (Continued)

ACCIDENT RELATED IDENTIFIERS

Column 4 Event Identifiers	Description
FATL	Driver Reexamination—Fatal Accident
EFTL	Fatal Accident, Emergent
NFTL	Fatal Accident, Non-Emergent
POLC	Involved in Accident—Police Reported
DRVR	Involved in Accident—Driver Reported
OWNR	Involved in Accident—Owner Reported

VIOLATION RECORDS RELATED IDENTIFIERS

Column 4 Event Identifiers	Description
OSDD	Driving Under the Influence—Foreign State
PFDC	Dishonored Check—Court Fine Payment
FCIO	Failure to Comply With Installment Order
FSSC	Failure to Appear—Scofflaw
FSFA	Failure to Appear
PC01	One Point Credit—Annual Safe Driving
PC02	Two Point Credit—Annual Safe Driving
PC03	Three Point Credit—Annual Safe Driving

PROBATIONARY DRIVER RELATED IDENTIFIERS

Column 4 Event Identifiers	Description
PVPD	Persistent Violator—Probationary Driver Program
PTPD	Point System—Probationary Driver Program
0001	Warning After Probationary Driver Program Class
0002	Warning in Person
0003	Warning in Writing
PC03	Point Credit After Probationary Driver Program Class Completed
FCPD	Failure to Repeat Probationary Driver Program
FAPD	Failure to Accept Probationary Driver Program

Unlicensed Driver

N.J.S.A. 39:3-10 provides, in part, "No person shall drive a motor vehicle on a public highway in this State unless licensed to do so in accordance with this article ..."

Further the statute provides:

> A person violating this section shall be subject to a fine not exceeding $500.00 or imprisonment in the county jail for not more than 60 days, but if that person has never been licensed to drive in this State or any other jurisdiction, he shall be subject to a fine of not less than $200.00 and, in addition, the court shall issue an order to the Director of the Division of Motor Vehicles requiring the director to refuse to issue a license to operate a motor vehicle to the person for a period of not less than 180 days. The penalties provided for by this paragraph shall not be applicable in cases where failure to have actual possession of the operator's license is due to an administrative or technical error by the Division of Motor Vehicles.

The question then arises, "Whose responsibility is it to prove that the defendant was never licensed in New Jersey or any other state?" Is it not the responsibility of the state to prove this fact for purpose of sentence? In order for the state to prove this without an admission by the defendant, wouldn't it be necessary to write to every state Division of Motor Vehicles to search their records? One can easily recognize how cumbersome and unrealistic this approach would be. Just because a defendant is charged with being unlicensed and is unable to produce a license, expired or otherwise, does not mean that the defendant has never been licensed. The statute does not contain a presumption which would elevate N.J.S.A. 39:3-29 or 39:3-17 to N.J.S.A. 39:3-10 requiring the enhanced minimum penalty.

Further, the failure of the defendant to produce a driver's license does not automatically prove or even create a presumption that the defendant is unlicensed. Even if a New Jersey certified driving abstract shows that the defendant is not licensed in New Jersey, it does not mean that the defendant is not licensed in another state, even if the defendant is a resident of this state. Would it also not be necessary to obtain certified abstracts from each state to prove that the defendant was unlicensed? Of course, if the defendant admits to the officer that he or she is unlicensed or has never been licensed, this testimony may be presented at trial.

N.J.S.A. 39:3-29 provides:

> The driver's license, the registration certificate of a motor vehicle and an insurance identification card shall be in the possession of the driver or operator at all times when he is in charge of a motor vehicle on the highways of this State.

> The driver or operator shall exhibit his driver's license and an insurance identification card, and the holder of a registration certificate or the operator or driver of a motor vehicle for which a registration certificate has been issued, whether or not the holder, driver or operator is a resident of this State, shall also exhibit the registration certificate, when requested to do so by a police officer or judge, while in the performance of the duties of his office, and shall write his name in the presence of the officer, so that the officer may thereby determine the identity of the licensee and at the same time determine the correctness of the registration certificate, as it relates to the registration number and number plates of the motor vehicle for which it was issued; and the correctness of the evidence of a policy of insurance, as it relates to the coverage of the motor vehicle for which it was issued.

> Any person violating this section shall be subject to a fine not exceeding $100.00.

If a person charged with a violation of this section can exhibit his driver's license, insurance identification card and registration certificate, which were valid on the day he was charged, to the judge of the municipal court before whom he is summoned to answer to the charge, such judge may dismiss the charge. However, the judge may impose court costs.

Failure to present a valid driver's license does not give rise to a presumption that the defendant is unlicensed. However, it appears that a Municipal Court Judge may request a defendant to present a driver's license in court. (When else would a Judge want to see a defendant's driver's license?) Does the Judge have the authority to request a license which would have been in effect at the time of the alleged offense, or at the time of court? Such a request for a driver's license would not be subject to challenge under constitutional self incrimination standards, as it is non-testimonial evidence. But even if the defendant fails or refuses to display a driver's license to the Judge, he or she has still only violated N.J.S.A. 39:3-29, an offense which may be paid through the Violations Bureau thereby avoiding an increased penalty, unless it is construed as contemptuous conduct on the part of the defendant.

Therefore, if the standards set forth in this and the previous section are applied, it is extremely difficult, absent an admission by the defendant, or a guilty plea, to prove: 1) that the defendant was unlicensed and 2) that the defendant has never been licensed in this or any other state.

Driving While License or Registration is Suspended or Revoked

One of the more frequently cited traffic offenses which require the imposition of substantial penalties is violation of N.J.S.A. 39:3-40, which provides:

> No person to whom a driver's license has been refused or whose driver's license or reciprocity privileges have been suspended or revoked, or who has been prohibited from obtaining a driver's license, shall personally operate a motor vehicle during the period of refusal, suspension, revocation or prohibition. Also, no person whose motor vehicle registration has been revoked shall operate or permit the operation of such motor vehicle during the period of revocation. A person violating any of the provisions of this section shall be subject to the following penalties:
>
> a. First offense—a fine of $500.00;
>
> b. Second offense—a fine of $750.00 and imprisonment of not more than five days;
>
> c. Third offense—a fine of $1,000.00 and imprisonment of not less than ten days;
>
> d. Impose or extend a period of suspension not to exceed six months;
>
> e. When involved in an accident resulting in personal injury, imprisonment for not less than forty-five days;
>
> f. When under suspension for a violation of N.J.S.A. 39:4-50, a fine of $500.00, additional suspension for a period of not less than one year nor more than two years, and may be imprisoned in the county jail for not more than ninety days.

No person whose license or registration certificate has been revoked shall apply for the same during the period of revocation. Any violation of this section shall result in a fine of not more than $500.00, imprisonment for not more than three months or both at the discretion of the court. N.J.S.A. 39:3-34.

N.J.S.A. 39:3-40 also applies to an out-of-state licensed driver whose New Jersey privileges have been suspended and also if the out-of-state defendant's privileges were suspended in a reciprocal sister state.

As to sentencing, it is arguable that "imprisonment in the county jail for not more than 5 days" for a second offender does not mandate any jail time, as zero days is also "not more than five days." The same may also be said as to, "Upon conviction, the court should impose or extend a period of suspension not to exceed six months." The provision is self-contradictory. It purports to require imposition of an additional suspension, by use of the word "shall," but negates the imperative by saying "not to exceed six months." One day does not exceed six months, nor do ten days, and likewise zero days suspension does not exceed six months.

An individual's driver's license or registration certificate may be revoked administratively through the Division of Motor Vehicles for failure to maintain liability insurance, an excess accumulation of points, being involved in an accident resulting in death, misrepresentation on application for license or registration or other violation of Title 39.

Essentially there are two types of revocation: an administrative revocation and a court imposed revocation. The two should not be confused. Administrative revocations may result from: 1) failure to maintain liability insurance; 2) accumulation of points; 3) failure to appear in response to a traffic summons; 4) failure to pay fines and costs; or 5) such other violation of Title 39, as provided in N.J.S.A. 39:3-50. Court imposed suspensions most frequently result from: 1) driving while under the influence of alcohol or drugs; 2) driving without liability insurance; 3) driving during period of revocation; 4) reckless driving; 5) excessive speeding; 6) leaving the scene of an accident involving injury; or 7) other egregious moving violations. The difference between a court imposed suspension and an administrative suspension is substantial. If a defendant's driver's license is suspended in court, it is not necessary for the State to demonstrate that notice was received by the defendant. However, most administrative suspensions require notice be given to the defendant and are evidenced by a certified abstract **(Exhibit 49)**, a copy of the notice of suspension, and a copy of the mailing list (see **Exhibits 51 & 52**). As can be seen, such suspensions may be further extended by the Division of Motor Vehicles or the court. **(Exhibits 53 & 54)**. Further, in order to have a license restored, a restoration fee must be paid. If the defendant never surrendered the license or paid the restoration fee, or failed to attend the alcohol countermeasures program (where applicable), the defendant technically remains suspended until he complies with this provision.

The attorney should ascertain whether only the defendant's registration privileges were suspended, or both registration and license privileges. If the defendant drives a vehicle belonging to and registered by another, and only the defendant's registration privleges were suspended, then it is unlikely that the State can prevail on the summons.

In any event, no trial as to suspension or revocation should be attempted without a thorough study of the two leading cases. *State v. Wenof,* 102 N.J. Super. 370 (Law Div. 1968) and *State v. Hammon,* 116 N.J. Super. 244 (Camden County Ct. 1971).

If your client's driving privilege is suspended for a specified period of time, such as for excessive speed for 90 days, and the period of suspension has expired prior to the issuance of a summons for N.J.S.A. 39:3-40, one can argue that the suspension was served and once served, if the defendant drove, he or she is merely unlicensed, and not revoked. However, some statutes, such as N.J.S.A. 39:6B-2 specify a period of suspension and that the suspension remains effective until such time as the driver applies for restoration, which may then be permitted at the discretion of the Director of the Division of Motor Vehicles.

A ticket for N.J.S.A. 39:3-40, especially if it is an administrative suspension, is easily beatable by requiring the State to provide its proofs, such as a certified mailing list, certified abstract, written notice, and an innovative, thoughtful approach by counsel. Given the large number of summonses issued for this violation, most particularly those founded upon an administrative suspension, all such cases should be carefully and thoroughly reviewed prior to trial.

172/Municipal Court

EXHIBIT 51

STATE OF NEW JERSEY
AUTOMOBILE INSURANCE SURCHARGE AND COLLECTION

Driver License Number

Billing Number

INSURANCE SURCHARGE BILL

Billing Date
MAY 15, 1992

TOTAL ANNUAL ASSESSMENT FOR THIS BILLING NO. $ 100.00
TOTAL PAYMENTS/ADJUSTMENTS AS OF 04/26/92 * $ 51.00
SURCHARGE BALANCE FOR THIS BILL $ 49.00

30 days to pay from this date

* ANY PAYMENTS PROCESSED AFTER THIS DATE WILL BE REFLECTED ON YOUR NEXT BILL.

JOSHUA   **SAMPLE: INITIAL BILL**

PAYMENT DUE: JUN 14, 1992
THE PAYMENT DUE DATE DOES NOT APPLY TO THE "PAST DUE AMOUNT".

INSTALLMENT AMOUNT $ 17.00
PAST DUE AMOUNT $ 0.00
PLEASE PAY THIS AMOUNT $ 17.00

NOTICE OF PROPOSED SUSPENSION

Pursuant to N.J.S.A. 17:29A-33 ET. SEQ., N.J.A.C. 13:19-13.1 ET. SEQ., and N.J.S.A. 39:5-30, this bill is a NOTICE OF PROPOSED SUSPENSION of your driving privilege. If you do not make sufficient payment by the required payment date, your driving privilege will be suspended on 06/28/92. If your driving privilege is suspended, you will also have to pay a $30 restoration fee.

allows for payment processing time

VIOLATION DATE MO. DAY YR.	REPORTED BY DMV / COURT	VIOLATION CODE	DESCRIPTION OF SURCHARGEABLE EVENTS	PTS.	AMOUNT
07 28 89	FRANKLIN LAKES	V4982	SPEEDING	2	
10 22 89	KENILWORTH BORO	V4984	SPEEDING	4	
			TOTAL	6	$ 100.00

- - - - - - - - - - ► DETACH AND RETURN THIS PORTION OF YOUR BILL WITH PAYMENT ◄ - - - - - - - - - -

MAKE CHECK PAYABLE TO "STATE OF NJ-AISC"
DO NOT SEND CASH
PLEASE PAY BY MAIL

Driver License Number

AMOUNT ENCLOSED $

JOSHUA

Billing Date
MAY 15, 1992

Billing Number

Surcharge Balance $ 49.00
Installment Amount $ 17.00

Pay This Amount
$ 17.00

52S70304118305725199104731440 4SPECHJT000490000017009206261

Municipal Court/173

EXHIBIT 51 (Continued)
STATE OF NEW JERSEY
AUTOMOBILE INSURANCE SURCHARGE AND COLLECTION

INSURANCE SURCHARGE BILL

Driver License Number

Billing Number

Billing Date
JUL 01, 1991

30 days to pay from this date

NEW JERSEY LAW REQUIRES THAT YOU PAY AN INSURANCE SURCHARGE BASED ON CERTAIN MOTOR VEHICLE VIOLATIONS AND/OR SUSPENSIONS.

PLEASE SEE THE ENCLOSED INSURANCE SURCHARGE FACTS PAMPHLET FOR MORE INFORMATION.

PEDRO

SAMPLE: INSTALLMENT BILL

PLEASE NOTE:
ANNUAL POINT CREDITS DO NOT APPLY TO INSURANCE SURCHARGES.

TOTAL ANNUAL ASSESSMENT FOR THIS BILL $ 1,375.00 *

PAYMENT DUE BY 07/31/91

* A MONTHLY PAYMENT PLAN IS AVAILABLE FOR INDIGENTS. PLEASE SEE THE REVERSE SIDE OF THIS BILL. IF YOU QUALIFY FOR INDIGENT STATUS, YOU MAY PAY THE SURCHARGE IN 6 MONTHLY INSTALLMENTS. THE FIRST INSTALLMENT OF $ 234.00 IS DUE NO LATER THAN 07/31/91. THE REMAINING BALANCE WILL BE BILLED IN 5 MONTHLY INSTALLMENTS. PLEASE PAY BY MAIL.

NOTICE OF PROPOSED SUSPENSION

Pursuant to N.J.S.A. 17:29A-33 ET. SEQ., N.J.A.C.13:19-13.1 ET.SEQ., and N.J.S.A. 39:5-30, this bill is a NOTICE OF PROPOSED SUSPENSION of your driving privilege. If you do not make sufficient payment by the required payment date, your driving privilege will be suspended on 08/18/91. If your driving privilege is suspended, you will also have to pay a $30 restoration fee.
YOU MAY REQUEST A HEARING. SEE REVERSE SIDE.

VIOLATION DATE MO DAY YR	REPORTED BY DMV COURT	VIOLATION CODE	DESCRIPTION OF SURCHARGEABLE EVENTS	PTS.	AMOUNT
08 06 89	LINDEN CITY	V4985	SPEEDING	5	
08 12 89	ELIZABETH CITY	V0481	FAIL TO OBSERVE TRAFF CNTRL DEVICE	2	
12 02 89	LINDEN CITY	V0497	CARELESS DRIVING	2	
2 02 89	LINDEN CITY	V129B	LEAVE SCENE ACCDNT-PROPERTY DAMAGE	2	
9 25 90	ELIZABETH CITY	V0488	IMPROPER OPER-HWYS W/MARKED LANES	2	
			TOTAL POINT SURCHARGE	13	$ 275.00
08 06 89	LINDEN CITY	V0310	UNLICENSED DRIVER N.J. RESIDENT		$ 100.00
08 06 89	LINDEN CITY	V06B2	NO LIABILITY INS. ON MOTOR VEH		$ 250.00
05 02 90	DMV SUSPENSION	00340	DRIVING DURING PERIOD OF SUSP		$ 250.00
09 25 90	ELIZABETH CITY	V0340	OPERATING WHILE SUSPENDED		$ 250.00
12 02 89	LINDEN CITY	V0340	OPERATING WHILE SUSPENDED		$ 250.00

allows for payment processing time

TOTAL $ 1,375.00

▶ DETACH AND RETURN THIS PORTION OF YOUR BILL WITH PAYMENT ◀

MAKE CHECK PAYABLE TO "STATE OF NJ-AISC"
DO NOT SEND CASH

Driver License Number

PLEASE PAY BY MAIL

AMOUNT ENCLOSED $

PEDRO

Billing Date
JUL 01, 1991

Billing Number

Surcharge Balance
$ 1,375.00

Installment Amount
$ 234.00

Pay This Amount
$ 1,375.00

20A1001621710762219910236252201ABADOPJ013750000234009108129

174/Municipal Court

EXHIBIT 52

```
                                                                    PAGE    3
                     STATE OF NEW JERSEY
                  DIVISION OF MOTOR VEHICLES                   REPORT ID: AVN05OR3
                  CERTIFICATION OF MAILING LIST
                       ORDERS OF SUSPENSION

EVENT CODE   AUTOPIC   NAME OF ADDRESSEE   STREET        CITY           ST   ZIP         CNTY
SUS D 0340   R6018     JANET                              VILLAS         NJ   082513120   E
SUS D 0340   R6022     ANTHONY                            PLAINFIELD     NJ   070602920   W
SUS D 0340   R6686     LUIS                               PERTH AMBOY    NJ   088614035
SUS D 0340   R9023     EARL                               VINELAND       NJ   083604901   F
SUS D 0340   R9122     FRANCISCO                          NEWARK         NJ   071041653   G
SUS D 0340   S0490     JOSE                               JERSEY CITY    NJ   073051519   R
SUS D 0340   S1085     FRANK                              CLIFTON        NJ   070121805   R
SUS D 0340   S2460     SHEILA                             RINGWOOD       NJ   074560133   P
SUS D 0340   S3451     LEONID                             E BRUNSWICK    NJ   088162711   M
SUS D 0340   S4192     RUBEN                              BORDENTOWN     NJ   085052750   C
SUS D 0340   S6291     SCOTT                              MONMOUTH BCH   NJ   077501053   N
SUS D 0340   S7084     WILLIE                             PLAINFIELD     NJ   070602036   W
SUS D 0340   S8173     JOHN                               VILLAS         NJ   082512538   E
SUS D 0340   S8201     LOUIS                              OAK RIDGE      NJ   074388949   P
SUS D 0340   S9596     PATRICIA                           SECAUCUS       NJ   070943405   J
SUS D 0340   T3264     SCOTT                              COLONIA        NJ   070671904   X
SUS D 0340   T3392     STEVEN                             SEWELL         NJ   080802902   H
SUS D 0340   T3601     SYLVESTER                          MILLVILLE      NJ   083329719   F
SUS D 0340   T7605     JAMES                              KEASBEY        NJ   088321106   M
SUS D 0340   T9318     DONALD                             LINCROFT       NJ   077381325   N
SUS D 0340   T9500     LEROY                              TINTON FALLS   NJ   077242633
SUS D 0340   W0663     JOSEPHINE                          PLAINFIELD     NJ   07060       W
SUS D 0340   W0668     KENNETH                            SALISBURY      MD   21801       Z
SUS D 0340   W2178     JACQUELIN                          TRENTON        NJ   08618       L
SUS D 0340   W4365     ENNISE                             TRENTON        NJ   086306753
SUS D 0340   W4365     PAMELA                             ATLANTIC CITY  NJ   069013905   A
SUS D 0340   W4365     ROBERT                             NEWARK         NJ   071082845
SUS D 0340   W6476     VINCENT                            HACKENSACK     NJ   076014106   B
SUS D 0340   Y0217     PATRICIA                           EDISON         NJ   08818
SUS D 0340   Z6291     PATRICIA                           EDISON         NJ   08818
SUS D 0340   M2513     MELISSA                            BRADLEY BCH    NJ   07720
SUS D 3381             JUAN                               FORDS          NJ   088631444   N
```

Municipal Court/175

EXHIBIT 53

SUS O PTPB

Motor Vehicle Services
ORDER OF SUSPENSION

DATE PREPARED: 03/29/92

STATE OF NEW JERSEY
DIVISION OF MOTOR VEHICLES
25 SOUTH MONTGOMERY STREET
TRENTON, NEW JERSEY 08666
(609) 588-7373

008864

PAUL

> date the suspension order was produced by the computer system (assume 7-10 days between preparation and mailing, with checking/reviewing/certifying during that time)

YOUR NEW JERSEY DRIVING PRIVILEGE IS SUSPENDED AS OF 03/17/92 FOR 120 DAYS

* THIS SUSPENSION IS IN ADDITION TO OTHER SUSPENSION(S) OUTSTANDING EFFECTIVE 05/27/86

BY AUTHORITY OF N.J.S.A. 39:5-30, 39:5-30.8, AND N.J.A.C. 13:19-10.1 ET SEQ., MOTOR VEHICLE SERVICES HAS SUSPENDED YOUR NEW JERSEY DRIVING PRIVILEGE BECAUSE YOU HAVE 12 OR MORE POINTS ON YOUR DRIVING RECORD. A COPY OF YOUR RECORD IS ON THE BACK OF THIS ORDER.

YOU MUST SURRENDER YOUR CURRENT NEW JERSEY DRIVER LICENSE TO MOTOR VEHICLE SERVICES IMMEDIATELY. YOU MAY NOT DRIVE UNTIL YOU RECEIVE WRITTEN NOTICE OF RESTORATION FROM THE DIRECTOR.

TO HAVE YOUR DRIVING PRIVILEGE RESTORED AT THE END OF YOUR SUSPENSION PERIOD, YOU MUST PAY A $30 RESTORATION FEE.

Skip Lee
Director

------------------------- Detach Here And Return This Part -------------------------

PAUL

RESTORATION FEE DUE: $30.00

RETURN THIS PART WITH YOUR CURRENT NEW JERSEY DRIVER LICENSE AND YOUR $30 RESTORATION FEE CHECK OR MONEY ORDER, MADE PAYABLE TO N.J. MOTOR VEHICLE SERVICES, USING THE ENCLOSED RETURN ENVELOPE.

VF/D91116197410665000300000030092077RESFRESTSUSOPTPB920880219364

Services

TRENTON, NEW JERSEY 08666

002601

To Whom It May Concern:

I do hereby certify that the original Order of Suspension certified herein was not returned undelivered by Postal Authorities

Director

To Whom It May Concern:

I hereby certify that this is a true and correct copy of the Order of Suspension directed to the subject shown above.

176/Municipal Court

EXHIBIT 54

INSERT
MUNICIPAL COURT NAME &
ADDRESS

STATE OF NEW JERSEY

V.

TO:

COURT CODE	DOCKET NO.
SUMMONS / COMPLAINT NO.	
D.L. NO.	STATE
DATE OF BIRTH	EYE CODE	SEX
VIOLATION (S) SECTION	
VIOLATION (Description)	
VIOLATION DATE	TIME

NOTICE OF PROPOSED SUSPENSION OF DRIVING PRIVILEGES
FOR FAILURE TO APPEAR (Ch. 240, Laws of 1991)

The records of this Court indicate that a Complaint was filed and a Summons issued for your appearance on the offense described above. Since you have neither appeared in Court nor paid the prescribed penalty, **YOU ARE ORDERED** to appear in this Court on _____ at _____ AM / PM at the address listed above. If you wish to plead NOT guilty, you must notify this Court at least three (3) days prior to the new court date. If you wish to plead guilty, you must pay a total penalty of $_____ before your new court date. You must sign the back of the summons and return the summons with your payment.

IF YOU FAIL TO APPEAR OR PAY THE PRESCRIBED PENALTY:

RESIDENTS OF NEW JERSEY: (1) A warrant will be issued for your arrest, (2) you may be subject to contempt of court and additional penalties, and (3) this Court may order the suspension of your driving privileges or prohibit you from receiving or obtaining driving privileges.

NON-RESIDENTS OF NEW JERSEY: (1) This Court may order the suspension of your driving privileges in New Jersey or prohibit you from receiving or obtaining driving privileges, (2) you may be subject to contempt of court and additional penalties, (3) your own Commissioner of Motor Vehicles may be requested to take action against you, and (4) a warrant may be issued for your arrest should you be found in this State.

If you have any questions about this notice, please call (insert Mun. Ct. tel. #) between the hours of (insert Mun. Ct. office hours) for information. *Bring this notice with you when you appear.*

BY ORDER OF THE JUDGE

_____   _____
DATE   (JUDGE or COURT ADMINISTRATOR)

NOTE: Please return this Notice and your Summons when making payment. A receipt will be sent to you only if your payment is accompanied by a self-addressed stamped envelope.

SUSPENSION ORDER

IT IS ON THIS _____ day of _____ 19___ ORDERED pursuant to the authority of Chapter 240, Laws of 1991 (check as applicable)

☐ Defendant's driving privileges in this State are suspended;

☐ Defendant is prohibited from receiving or obtaining driving privileges in this State until such time as the defendant appears in court and complies with the Order of the Court.

FURTHER ORDERED that the Court Administrator forthwith mail the original of this ORDER to the Director of the Division of Motor Vehicles and that said Director enter upon its records the terms of this suspension or prohibition ORDER, and it is

FURTHER ORDERED that the Court Administrator of the court give a copy of this ORDER to the defendant or mail it to the defendant by ordinary mail at the defendant's last known address.

_____   _____
DATE   JUDGE

Administrative Office of the Courts
4-PART CARBONLESS FORM: **2ND Copy: DIVISION OF MOTOR VEHICLES**   CP0191 (4/92)

Driving While Driver's License or Registration Privilege is Suspended or Revoked Pursuant to N.J.S.A. 39:3-40

Relevant Case Law

State v. Handy, 74 N.J. Super. 294 (Law Div. 1962)

State v. Wenof, 102 N.J. Super. 370 (Law Div. 1968)

State v. Hammond, 116 N.J. Super. 244 (Camden Co. Ct. 1971)

State v. Pickens, 124 N.J. Super. 193 (App. Div. 1973)

State v. Fearick, 69 N.J. 32 (1976)

State v. McColley, 157 N.J. Super. 525 (App. Div. 1978)

State v. Raupp, 160 N.J. Super. 315 (App. Div. 1978)

State v. Roberson, 156 N.J. Super. 551 (App. Div. 1978)

State v. Graney, 174 N.J. Super. 455 (App. Div. 1980)

State v. Profita, 183 N.J. Super. 425 (App. Div. 1982)

State v. Duva, 192 N.J. Super. 418 (Law Div. 1983)

State v. Kindler, 191 N.J. Super. 358 (Law Div. 1983)

State v. Cromwell, 194 N.J. Super. 519 (App. Div. 1984)

State v. Somma, 215 N.J. Super. 142 (Law Div. 1986)

State v. Zalta, 217 N.J. Super. 209 (App. Div. 1987)

State v. Wrotny, 221 N.J. Super. 226 (App. Div. 1987)

State v. Rought, 221 N.J. Super. 42 (Law Div. 1987)

State v. Cattafi, 226 N.J. Super. 409 (App. Div. 1988)

Failure to Maintain Liability Insurance

N.J.S.A. 39:6B-1 *et seq.* is the Compulsory Insurance law and the pertinent part, for our purposes, provides pursuant to N.J.S.A. 39:6B-2 as follows:

> Any owner or registrant of a motor vehicle registered or principally garaged in this State who operates or causes to be operated a motor vehicle upon any public road or highway in this State without motor vehicle liability insurance coverage required by this act, and any operator who operates or causes a motor vehicle to be operated and who knows or should know from the attendant circumstances that the motor vehicle is without motor vehicle liability insurance coverage required by this act shall be subject, for the first offense, to a fine of $300.00 and a period of community service to be determined by the court, and shall forthwith forfeit his right to operate a motor vehicle over the highways of this State for a period of one year from the date of conviction. Upon subsequent conviction, he shall be subject to a fine of $500.00 and shall be subject to imprisonment for a term of 14 days and shall be ordered by the court to perform community service for a period of 30 days, which shall be of such form and on such terms as the court shall deem appropriate under the circumstances, and shall forfeit his right to operate a motor vehicle for a period of two years from the date of his conviction, and, after the expiration of said period, he may make application to the Director of the Division of Motor Vehicles for a license to operate a motor vehicle, which application may be granted at the discretion of the director. The director's discretion shall be based upon assessment of the likelihood that the individual will operate or cause a motor vehicle to be operated in the future without the insurance coverage required by this act. A complaint for violation of this act may be made to a municipal court at any time within six months after the date of the alleged offense . . . .

The key words of the statute are: "owner or registrant," "of a motor vehicle," "registered or principally garaged," "who knew or should have known by the attendant circumstances." The most obvious defense is that the defendant, although the operator, was driving a motor vehicle owned by another and he had no reason to believe that the vehicle was uninsured. The prosecution would argue that a driver has an affirmative duty to examine the documents or insurance card to determine whether the car is insured. If the owner was a stranger, or the owner drives the car himself or herself on other occasions known to the defendant, was it reasonable for the defendant to believe under the circumstances testified to that the vehicle was insured? If the operator was also the owner, this argument would be ineffective. If the car was registered and principally garaged in a state other than New Jersey, there is no violation of this statute. *State v. Arslanowk,* 167 N.J. Super. 387 (App. Div. 1979).

In some instances the police officer will issue a summons for violation of N.J.S.A. 39:6B-2 when the defendant has failed to produce a valid insurance identification card. If the defendant produces a card which was valid at the time of the offense, either the court, the prosecutor or defense counsel may move to amend the charge to N.J.S.A. 39:3-29 (no card in possession).

In those instances where the defendant has failed to produce an insurance card or policy at the time of trial, a rebuttable presumption is created that the person was uninsured when charged. (N.J.S.A. 39:6B-2).

Another defense to be alleged in those instances where the defendant was operating a moped, commercial truck or other type of vehicle is that these types of vehicles do not fall within the statutory definition of a "motor vehicle," and therefore, the statute does not apply. You may wish to cite the fact that failure to have insurance on a "motorized bicycle" is prohibited by a statute other than N.J.S.A. 39:6B-2, which provides for lesser penalties. *See* N.J.S.A. 39:4-14.3b (penalty), N.J.S.A. 39:4-14.3 (required coverage).

Another argument which may be put forth is that the vehicle driven by the defendant was covered by insurance on another vehicle in the same household, or as a "temporary replacement vehicle." In these instances it is advisable to obtain a letter indicating such coverage from the insurance agent or have the agent testify.

Instead of an insurance card (**Exhibit 55**), a defendant may attempt to produce the insurance "face sheet" and policy which may or may not be acceptable to the court.

In *State v. Kopp,* 176 N.J. Super. 528 (Law Div. 1980), the defendant contended that although he was not covered by any policy, he had sufficient reason to believe that he was in fact covered. Therefore, according to defendant's reasoning, he was not guilty of violating the statute. The court rejected this argument, instead establishing that knowledge of lack of insurance is not an essential element which must be proved in order to sustain a conviction under N.J.S.A. 39:6B-2. This decision was based on the legislative history of the statute, an examination of which reveals beyond doubt that to demand knowledge of lack of insurance to sustain a conviction is not within the legislative intent behind this law.

In the event a defendant's insurance coverage was cancelled by the insurance company, the state must prove that it was lawfully cancelled and that the defendant was sent or received notice of cancellation. *State v. Hochman,* 188 N.J. Super. 382 (App. Div. 1982). It follows that if the cancellation was not lawful, or if the defendant was not given written notice of the cancellation then a finding of not guilty must be entered.

It is not necessary to allege that the defendant is a subsequent offender to expose the defendant to enhanced penalties for a second offense. *State v. Lima,* 144 N.J. Super. 263 (App. Div. 1976). If the defendant's second offense occurred prior to adjudication of guilty of the first offense, it is still permissible to sentence the defendant as a second offender. *State v. Bowman,* 131 N.J. Super. 209 (Co. Ct. 1974) *aff'd* 135 N.J. Super. 210 (App. Div. 1975).

It has also been held that one who causes a vehicle in his or her control to be operated, although not the owner or operator, is liable to be punished in accordance with the statute. *State v. Schumm,* 146 N.J. Super. 30 (App. Div. 1977) *aff'd* 75 N.J. 199 (1977).

Given the substantial penalties which must be imposed upon a finding of guilty for both the first and subsequent offenses, it is incumbent upon the attorney to thoroughly analyze the statute, case law and facts in an effort to exculpate the defendant. There is only some decisional law to give guidance, however, and this fact allows the defense attorney to exercise originality and advocacy.

EXHIBIT 55

STATE OF NEW JERSEY INSURANCE IDENTIFICATION CARD

IV-1 (R4/77)
Company Code
☒ 003 THE ÆTNA CASUALTY AND SURETY COMPANY
☐ 325 THE STANDARD FIRE INSURANCE COMPANY
☐ 497 THE AUTOMOBILE INSURANCE COMPANY of Hartford, Connecticut

Ætna LIFE & CASUALTY

Office Issuing this Card:

Issued to: David A Keyko
             P.O. Box 126
             Woodbury Hts., N.J. 08097

Effective Date	Expiration Date	Policy Number
1-17-87	1-17-88	129SX21523749PAJ

Applicable with respect to the following Motor Vehicle:

Year	Make	Vehicle Identification Number	Authorized Representative
87	Lincoln	1LNBM91F1HY613239	William O. Bailey

(SEE IMPORTANT MESSAGE ON REVERSE SIDE.)

ANY ALTERATIONS WILL VOID THIS CARD

NON-TRAFFIC OFFENSES

Consumption of Alcohol While a Driver or Passenger in a Motor Vehicle

N.J.S.A. 39:4-51 a provides:

a. A person shall not consume an alcoholic beverage while operating a motor vehicle. A passenger in a motor vehicle shall not consume an alcoholic beverage while the motor vehicle is being operated. This subsection shall not apply to a passenger of a chartered or special bus operated as defined under R.S. 48:4-1 or an autcab, limousine or livery service.

b. A person shall be presumed to have consumed an alcoholic beverage in violation of this section if an unsealed container of an alcoholic beverage is located in the passenger compartment of the motor vehicle, the contents of the alcoholic beverage have been partially consumed and the physical appearance or conduct of the operator of the motor vehicle or a passenger may be associated with the consumption of an alcoholic beverage. For the purposes of this section, the term "unsealed" shall mean a container with its original seal broken or a container such as a glass or cup.

c. For the first offense, a person convicted of violating this section shall be fined $200.00 and shall be informed by the court of the penalties for a second or subsequent violation of this section. For a second or subsequent offense, a person convicted of violating this section shall be fined $250.00 or shall be ordered by the court to perform community service for a period of 10 days in such form and on such terms as the court shall deem appropriate under the circumstances.

In order for the state to prove its case under this statute, it must prove:

1) the defendant was the driver of or a passenger in a motor vehicle, and

2) that a motor vehicle was being operated, and

3) while the defendant was consuming an alcoholic beverage.

The statute further provides that an open and partially consumed alcoholic beverage in the possession of the defendant gives rise to a rebuttable presumption that the defendant was consuming the alcoholic beverage.

There is no state statute which proscribes simple possession of an alcoholic beverage in a motor vehicle. N.J.S.A 39:4-51a prohibits consumption, not possession. However, almost all municipalities have local ordinances which in some fashion prohibit simple possession of an alcoholic beverage in a motor vehicle or in a public place. These ordinances are distinctly separate violations usually requiring different and less exacting proofs than N.J.S.A. 39:4-51a.

N.J.S.A 39:4-51a may be proven by the defendant's admission, actual observation of consumption, or by a partially filled container along with other indicia of consumption or manifestation of same, such as the odor of alcoholic beverage on the breath of the defendant, etc.

Disorderly/Petty Disorderly and Local Ordinance Violations

Violations of the Disorderly Persons and Petty Disorderly Persons Ordinances are usually placed on summons forms similar to those used for indictable offenses (CDR-1), whereas local ordinance violations may be placed either on a CDR-1 form or a "ticket" form as appears as **Exhibit 56.** The rules applying to procedure, evidence and trial are the same as is usual in a non-jury criminal trial.

Local ordinance violations will also include zoning, rent control, possession of alcoholic beverages, parking, health, and other infractions. Most local ordinances are somewhat similar, but there may also be a substantial variance from town to town. It is, therefore, strongly recommended that defense counsel read the particular ordinance thoroughly prior to trial.

EXHIBIT 56

No. 219

MUNICIPAL COURT OF BOROUGH OF NATIONAL PARK
COUNTY OF GLOUCESTER

_____ v. _____ **COMPLAINT**
(NON-INDICTABLE OFFENSE)

DEFENDANT

STATE OF NEW JERSEY
COUNTY OF GLOUCESTER } ss.

THE UNDERSIGNED, BEING DULY SWORN, UPON HIS OATH DEPOSES AND SAYS:

NAME _____ (PLEASE PRINT)

STREET _____

CITY-STATE _____

ON THE _____ DAY OF _____ 19___ AT _____ M.

IN THE MUNICIPALITY OF _____

COUNTY OF _____ STATE OF NEW JERSEY

DID UNLAWFULLY VIOLATE THE PROVISIONS OF:

STATUTE: _____ REGULATION: _____

ORDINANCE: _____

BY COMMITTING THE FOLLOWING OFFENSE(S): _____

_____
_____
_____
_____
_____

THE UNDERSIGNED STATES THAT HE HAS JUST AND REASONABLE GROUNDS TO BELIEVE AND DOES BELIEVE THAT THE PERSON NAMED ABOVE COMMITTED THE OFFENSE(S) HEREIN SET FORTH CONTRARY TO LAW.

_____ _____
(DATE) (SIGNATURE AND IDENTIFICATION OF OFFICER)
(TO BE SIGNED WHEN ISSUING SUMMONS)

SUBSCRIBED AND SWORN TO

BEFORE ME THIS _____ DAY
OF _____ 19___ _____
(SIGNATURE OF COMPLAINANT - TO BE SIGNED WHEN TAKING OATH)

_____
(NAME AND TITLE OF PERSON ADMINISTERING OATH)

COURT APPEARANCE REQUIRED ☐

COURT APPEARANCE _____ DAY OF _____ 19___ AT _____ M.

ADDRESS OF COURT: 3 CLOYD AVENUE, NATIONAL PARK, N.J.

NON-DRIVING ALCOHOL OFFENSES

N.J.S.A. 33:1-77.   Sale to person under legal age; penalty; defenses

Anyone who sells any alcoholic beverage to a person under the legal age for purchasing alcoholic beverages is a disorderly person; provided, however, that the establishment of all of the following facts by a person making any such sale shall constitute a defense to any prosecution therefor: (a) that the purchaser falsely represented by producing a driver's license bearing a photograph of the licensee or by producing a photographic identification card issued pursuant to section 1 of P.L. 1968, c.313 (C. 33:1-81.2) or a similar card issued pursuant to the laws of another state or the federal government that he or she was of legal age to make the purchase, (b) that the appearance of the purchaser was such that an ordinary prudent person would believe him or her to be of legal age to make the purchase, and (c) that the sale was made in good faith relying upon such production of a driver's license bearing a photograph of the licensee or production of a photographic identification card issued pursuant to section 1 of P.L. 1968, c.313 (C. 33:1-81.2) or a similar card issued pursuant to the laws of another state or the federal government and appearance and in the reasonable belief that the purchaser was actually of legal age to make the purchase. (As amended, L. 1983, c.565, effective January 17, 1984.)

N.J.S.A. 33:1-81.   Unlawful acts by persons under legal age for purchase of alcoholic beverages; disorderly persons

It shall be unlawful for (a) a person under the legal age for purchasing alcoholic beverages to enter any premises licensed for the retail sale of alcoholic beverages for the purpose of purchasing, or having served or delivered to him or her, any alcoholic beverage; or

(b) A person under the legal age for purchasing alcoholic beverages to consume any alcoholic beverage on premises licensed for the retail sale of alcoholic beverages, or to purchase, attempt to purchase or have another purchase for him any alcoholic beverage; or

(c) Any person to misrepresent or misstate his age, or the age of any other person for the purpose of inducing any licensee or any employee of any licensee, to sell, serve or deliver any alcoholic beverage to a person under the legal age for purchasing alcoholic beverages; or

(d) Any person to enter any premises licensed for the retail sale of alcoholic beverages for the purpose of purchasing, or to purchase alcoholic beverages, for another person who does not because of his age have the right to purchase and consume alcoholic beverages.

Any person who shall violate any of the provisions of this section shall be deemed and adjudged to be a disorderly person, and upon conviction thereof, shall be punished by a fine of not less than $100.00. In addition, the court shall suspend the person's license to operate a motor vehicle for one year or prohibit the person from obtaining a license to operate a motor vehicle in this State for six months beginning on the date he becomes eligible to obtain a license or on the date of conviction, whichever is later. In addition to the general penalty prescribed for an offense, the court may require any person under the legal age to purchase alcoholic beverages who violates this act to participate in an alcohol education or treatment program authorized by the Department of Health for a period not to exceed the maximum period of confinement prescribed by law for the offense for which the individual has been convicted. (As amended, L. 1983, c.574, effective January 17, 1984.)

EXHIBIT 57

P.L. 1985, CHAPTER 113, *approved April 9, 1985*

1985 Senate No. 2679

An Act concerning alcoholic beverages, amending R.S. 33:1-81 and P.L. 1983, c.574 and supplementing Title 33 of the Revisted Statutes.

1   BE IT ENACTED *by the Senate and General Assembly of the State*
2 *of New Jersey:*

1   1. R.S. 33:1-81 is amended to read as follows:

2   33:1-81. It shall be unlawful for (a) a person under the legal age
3 for purchasing alcoholic beverages to enter any premises licensed for
4 the retail sale of alcoholic beverages for the purpose of purchasing,
5 or having served or delivered to him or her, any alcoholic beverage;
6 or
7   (b) A person under the legal age for purchasing alcoholic
8 beverages to consume any alcoholic beverage on premises licensed
9 for the retail sale of alcoholic beverages, or to purchase, attempt to
10 purchase or have another purchase for him any alcoholic beverage;
11 or
12   (c) Any person to misrepresent or misstate his age, or the age
13 of any other person for the purpose of inducing any licensee or any
14 employee of any licensee, to sell, serve or deliver any alcoholic
15 beverage to a person under the legal age for purchasing alcoholic
16 beverages; or
17   (d) Any person to enter any premises licensed for the retail sale
18 of alcoholic beverages for the purpose of purchasing, or to purchase
19 alcoholic beverages, for another person who does not because of his
20 age have the right to purchase and consume alcoholic beverages.
21   Any person who shall violate any of the provisions of this section
22 shall be deemed and adjudged to be a disorderly person, and upon

EXPLANATION—Matter enclosed in bold-faced brackets [thus] in the above bill is not enacted and is intended to be omitted in the law.
Matter printed in italics *thus* is new matter.

EXHIBIT 57 (Continued)

C113-2

23 conviction thereof, shall be punished by a fine of not less than $100.00.
24 In addition, the court shall suspend the person's license to operate
25 a motor vehicle for [one year] *six months* or prohibit the person from
26 obtaining a license to operate a motor vehicle in this State for [one
27 year] *six months* beginning on the date he becomes eligible to obtain
28 a license or on the date of conviction, whichever is later. In addition
29 to the general penalty prescribed for an offense, the court may require
30 any person under the legal age to purchase alcoholic beverages who
31 violates this act to participate in an alcohol education or treatment
32 program authorized by the Department of Health for a period not to
33 exceed the maximum period of confinement prescribed by law for the
34 offense for which the individual has been convicted.

1   2. Section 2 of P.L. 1983, c.574 is amended to read as follows:

2   2. This act shall take effect [immediately] *on July 1, 1985.*

1   3. (New section), Any person who was convicted of a violation
2 of R.S. 33:1-81 for an offense committed on or after January 17, 1984
3 through June 30, 1985 inclusive and who consequently had his motor
4 vehicle license suspended or postponed for one year may move to
5 have that penalty provision reviewed by the sentencing court. For good
6 cause shown, the court is authorized to reduce that penalty and the
7 person shall receive credit toward a new lesser period of suspension
8 or postponement for any time already under suspension or postpone-
9 ment.

1   4. This act shall take effect immediately and shall be retroactive
2 to January 17, 1984.

§2C:33-15. Possession and Consumption of Alcoholic Beverages by Minors.

1. a. Any person under the legal age to purchase alcoholic beverages who knowingly possesses without legal authority or who knowingly consumes any alcoholic beverage in any school, public conveyance, public place, or place of public assembly, or motor vehicle, is guilty of a disorderly persons offense, and shall be fined not less than $100.00.

b. Whenever this offense is committed in a motor vehicle, the court may in addition to the sentence authorized for the offense, suspend or postpone for up to 30 days the driving privilege of the defendant.

c. In addition to the general penalty prescribed for a disorderly persons offense, the court may require any person who violates this act to participate in an alcohol education or treatment program, authorized by the Department of Health, for a period not to exceed the maximum period of confinement prescribed by law for the offense for which the individual has been convicted.

d. Nothing in this act shall apply to possession of alcoholic beverages by any such person while actually engaged in the performance of employment pursuant to an employment permit issued by the Director of the Division of Alcoholic Beverage Control, or for a bona fide hotel or restaurant, in accordance with the provisions of *R.S.* 33:1-26.

2. This act shall take effect upon the effective date of Title 2C, the New Jersey Code of Criminal Justice (P.L. 1978, c.95).

§2C:33-16. Unauthorized Bringing of Alcoholic Beverages Onto School Premises.

Any person of legal age to purchase alcoholic beverages, who knowingly and without the express written permission of the school board, its delegated authority, or any school principal, brings or possesses any alcoholic beverages on any property used for school purposes which is owned by any school or school board, is guilty of a disorderly persons offense.

§2C:33-17. Offer or Serve Alcoholic Beverages to an Underage Person.

Anyone who purposely or knowingly offers or serves or makes available an alcoholic beverage to a person under the legal age for consuming alcoholic beverages or entices that person to drink an alcoholic beverage is a disorderly person. This section shall not apply to a guardian or to a first cousin or closer relative by blood, marriage or adoption of the person under legal age for consuming alcoholic beverages if the guardian or relative is of the legal age to consume alcoholic beverages or to a religious observance, ceremony or rite. This section shall also not apply to any person in his home who is of the legal age to consume alcoholic beverages who offers or serves or makes available an alcoholic beverage to a person under the legal age for consuming alcoholic beverages or entices that person to drink an alcoholic beverage in the presence of and with the permission of the guardian or first cousin or closer relative by blood, marriage or adoption of the person under the legal age for consuming alcoholic beverages if the guardian or relative is of the legal age to consume alcoholic beverages.

(Eff. 8/28/85, Ch. 311, L.1985)

DRUG OFFENSES

General Comments

The Comprehensive Drug Reform Act of 1986 as amended effective June 28, 1989 essentially supplanted all prior provisions of Title 24. The offenses which come under the jurisdiction of the Municipal Court are as follows:

N.J.S.A. 2C:35-10(a)4 prohibits the possession of 50 grams or less of marijuana or five grams of hashish or less inclusive of dilutants.

N.J.S.A. 2C:35-10(b) prohibits the use or being under the influence of a controlled dangerous substance.

N.J.S.A. 2C:35-10(c) provides that any person who is knowingly in possession of a controlled dangerous substance or analog and who fails to voluntarily deliver the substance to the nearest law enforcement officer is guilty of a disorderly persons offense.

N.J.S.A. 2C:36-2 prohibits the possession of drug paraphernalia.

N.J.S.A. 2C:36-6 and 24:21-51 prohibit the sale, distribution and possession of a hypodermic syringe.

Violations of the above statutes constitute disorderly persons offenses for which the defendant may be fined up to $1,000 and/or incarcerated for up to six months, in addition to other mandatory penalties. As to N.J.S.A. 2C:35-10(a), in the event the offense was committed within 1,000 feet of a school, the court must impose 100 hours of community service. A $500 Drug Enforcement Reduction Penalty must be imposed for violations of all disorderly persons offenses (N.J.S.A. 2C:35-15(a)), as well as a lab fee of $50 per charge (N.J.S.A. 2C:35-20). In the event the defendant pleads guilty or is found guilty of a violation of Title 2C:35, the defendant's driving privileges shall be suspended for not less than six, nor more than 24 months. It should also be noted that the statute provides that the court, in its discretion, may suspend the defendant's driving privileges for a like period even if the defendant is granted a Conditional Discharge.

In order for the State to prove a drug violation, it must, of course, prove that the substance was, in fact, a drug. This is accomplished by transporting the evidence to the state police lab for examination. The state police lab will forward a written report of its findings to the local police and the report should be available at trial or prior to trial and it is, therefore, discoverable. It is not unusual for pills, in particular, to be found *not* to be a controlled dangerous substance, therefore giving rise to a motion to dismiss. The defense counsel should always carefully examine the lab report to determine whether or not the substance, in fact, is a drug as defined by statute. This is particularly relevant as oftentimes bogus drugs are sold while being represented to be something other than they are. In the event it is anticipated that the attorney will wish to cross-examine the state police lab technician, it is suggested that prior notice of such intention be transmitted to the court so as to avoid the necessity of postponement.

VICTIM-WITNESS RIGHTS IN NEW JERSEY

Introduction

For far too long the rights and needs of victims of criminal acts have been largely ignored. While the rights of the criminal have steadily been expanded by virtue of judicial interpretation of constitutional protections afforded to all citizens, it appears that these guarantees are most notably invoked where the defendant has committed a criminal act. It seems that the more heinous the offense, the greater the accused demands that the state observe his or her constitutional rights. Courts have increasingly required strict adherence to guaranteeing the rights of the accused at almost any and all costs, including dismissal of serious charges against blatant offenders. As this phenomenon became more obvious and apparent, inequities in the criminal justice system became the rule rather than the exception. It is no wonder that the public at large, constituted primarily of law abiding citizens, have become more vocal in their criticism of the courts and judges alike.

We have all, at one time or another, heard numerous horror stories involving serious crimes where the accused has been set free without punishment as a result of a technical violation of his or her "rights." It has come to the point where many, both from within and outside of the criminal justice system, have wondered aloud, "Was the Constitution designed to protect only the guilty?" "Can our system of justice operate fairly to serve its intended goal if the rights of the accused are so far out of balance with the rights of the victim and the interests of a law abiding society?" It may be asserted that the greater the scope and magnitude of the rights of the accused, there is necessarily an undesirable reduction in protection of the victim/public to be secure in their person and property. Why should victims, whose only offense is being in the wrong place at the wrong time, be punished more severely by the system than the perpetrator who has committed the offense?

It can readily be asserted that in our modern day society the balance between the rights of the accused and the protections of the victim has been tilted overwhelmingly in favor of the accused by constitutional guarantees of due process and other safeguards, while victims and witnesses continue to endure emotional suffering, physical pain, financial loss, humiliation, and inconvenience.[1]

Fortunately, the pendulum has begun to move slowly but certainly in the other direction. On the Federal level, in April of 1982, the President created a Task Force on Victims of Crime which resulted in the passage of the Victim and Witness Protection Act.[2] Congress has mandated that the United States Attorney General develop and implement guidelines for the vehicle of Justice which would promote and insure observance of victims' and witnesses' rights.

Further, a number of states, including New Jersey, have implemented Victims of Violent Crime Compensation Boards which provide for payment of medical expenses incurred by an innocent victim of crime. However, the Violent Crimes Compensation Board is purely an economic reimbursement mechanism and does little, if anything at all, to address the goal of sensitivity to the plight of the victim or witness.

The purpose of this discussion is to explore the necessary role by victims and witnesses in our criminal justice system and to review recently enacted legislation addressing this enlightened concept of victim/witness sensitivity and the goals to be achieved by judges and other official participants in a serious effort to attain "justice for all."

Statement of Problem

In 1985, the New Jersey Supreme Court Task Force on Municipal Court Improvement summarized the problem as follows:

> Historically, individual victims of crime have often complained that their victimization has often extended far beyond the immediate physical or emotional trauma

associated with the crime itself. In many cases they have felt mistreated and abused by investigating law enforcement agencies immediately after the incident and during case preparation. Victims and witnesses have felt particularly vulnerable to intimidation and threats of retaliation for their participation in the prosecution of defendants. They have complained about repeatedly being called on to give up time from work and family obligations to participate in the various stages of a criminal prosecution. They have frequently been dismayed at the number of delays and last-minute adjournments of their cases, sometimes with no consideration by authorities to their own personal inconvenience. Often they have received little or no information as to the status of the case in which they have played such a vital role. Victims have frequently not been consulted with regard to plea negotiations or the sentencing of defendants. Finally, they have not received restitution for the financial loss, property damage, or personal injury that they have sustained. Some of these victims of crime have stated that they felt victimized by the criminal justice system to a greater extent than by the offenders themselves.[3]

Case 1. A young mother of two children is assaulted, raped, and robbed in a shopping center parking lot. Almost two years later she is summoned to court to face her attackers who have remained free on bail. The painful prospect of reliving the terrifying experience is sheer agony. When testifying she is subjected to thinly veiled innuendos suggesting that she provoked the sexual attack. She must endure repeated questioning concerning her past and present sexual experiences. As she awaits the next round of questioning from defense counsel she is humiliated, tearful, and resentful of a system which allows such abuse of an innocent victim, and determines that it would have been much better if she had not reported this offense.

Case II. Jason Sawyer, an hourly blue collar employee, has struggled long and hard to repair and furnish his modest home of which he has been justly proud. Returning home after working a double shift he finds that his home has been ransacked and wrecked, and any item of value has been carried off. The culprits are apprehended and then the real nightmare begins. Not only is none of his property recovered, but he must then be subjected to repeated court appearances for further investigation, Grand Jury and the trial itself. After the case is postponed several times to allow the prosecutor or defense counsel time to prepare, the trial date finally arrives and after waiting six hours to testify on his own time without pay, he is advised that a plea bargain has been entered into which results in probation for the offenders. Sawyer walks from the courthouse shaking his head and wondering why he ever bothered to take the time to get involved in the case.

The foregoing are simple examples of the ordeal which a victim or witness in our system must undergo in an effort to bring offenders to justice. Little, if any, concern is exhibited toward the innocent victim as the emphasis is on the accused. It is easily understandable why victims and witnesses arrive at the conclusion that it is just not worth the effort. Accordingly, there are a substantial number of criminal prosecutions which are withdrawn because key witnesses fail to appear in court.[4] It has been demonstrated that the likelihood of conviction decreases as the number of postponements increases.[5] Without cooperation and participation of victims and witnesses in our system of criminal justice, the system must fail in its efforts to hold offenders responsible for their actions.

Crime in New Jersey

According to the 1985 New Jersey Uniform Crime Reports, there is one criminal offense committed in this state approximately every one and one-half minutes. On the average, during a twenty-four hour period there was one murder; seven rapes, eight arsons, fifty-two aggravated assaults, fifty-three robberies, 138 motor vehicle thefts, 219 burglaries, and 586 larcenies.[6] Such substantial numbers have one thing in common: whether a crime against the person or a crime against property, each of them involved victims, who will usually be called upon to cooperate and testify if the offender is apprehended. There is little doubt that the cooperation of victims and witnesses is essential; therefore, efforts must be made to acccommodate them.

Needs of Victims and Witnesses

In order to insure cooperation of victims and witnesses in the search for the truth, we must provide for the fulfillment of two needs: (a) relief from inconvenience attendant to court appearances, and (b) affording greater participation in a system designed to make the victim "whole."[7] According to the *Participant's Manual for Judges on the Rights of Victims and Witnesses,* the interests of victims and witnesses are best served by attempting to avoid administrative "runarounds," and loss of time and wages which results from delay, waiting and frequent postponements. Victims would also benefit from restitution, compensation, medical expenses, crisis intervention, protection from intimidation, explanation of court procedures, prompt return of property, improved scheduling, transportation, and more compassion from law enforcement officers and court personnel.[8]

Further, victims recommend that to improve the system it should provide that more attention be given to victim's opinions on case dispositions, and they be given the opportunity to attend trial and sentencing and participate in sentencing.[9] Victims desire greater consideration in scheduling court dates, better legal representation and notice of final outcome and sentence.[10] Essentially, the needs of victims and witnesses are not unreasonable nor unobtainable. They are no more than any reasonable person would desire should he or she be a victim or witness in a similar situation.

Positive Effects of Victim/Witness Sensitivity

The *Participant's Manual for Judges on the Rights of Victims and Witnesses* cites several reasons that criminal justice personnel should listen to what victims have to say about the system.

First, victim satisfaction with the judicial process is essential to its operation.[11] If a victim or witness lacks the desire to pursue the offender because he or she feels disillusioned with the criminal justice system, the offender is in essence allowed to "beat the system" and remains unpunished only to commit additional crimes.

Secondly, although the present criminal justice system serves to add to the loss which victims experience, establishing a victim's right to meaningful participation helps reduce emotional trauma and their sense of disorder, and demonstrates respect for their rights.[12]

Third, despite the fact that most attorneys feel that increased victim participation would result in harsher penalties, there is no evidence to support this assumption.[13] To the contrary, evidence exists that this would not be the end result, according to Deborah A. Kelly's article in the *Participant's Manual for Judges on the Rights of Victims and Witnesses*. For example, Ms. Kelly states that in Florida, pretrial settlement conferences which included victims were disposed of more quickly and victims did not demand harsher penalties, but usually agreed with official recommendations while at the same time, victims who participated felt a more positive attitude toward the court.[14]

Lastly, Kelly's article asserts that due process can be extended to victims without affecting the rights of the defendant.[15] California recently approved a Victims's Bill of Rights which insures due process and notice to victims thereby benefiting both victims and potential victims. This law is a clear public statement that there should be greater concern with the human side of crime rather than technical administrative procedures and preoccupation with defendant's rights to the exclusion of a just result.

Goals of Victim/Witness Sensitivity

Foremost in mind when dealing with victims and witnesses we should strive for the following goals which would serve to protect the financial and mental stability of those who have been threatened or brutalized by an offender. These goals are as follows:

1. To reduce victim's fears about participating in the prosecution of a case, which can be accomplished by treating them as fellow human beings and explaining court

procedures to them so that their appearance will not add to the anxiety which they already experience as a result of the crime.

2. To increase their willingness and ability to testify, as only with their help will the criminal justice system accomplish its purpose to convict and punish the offenders.

3. To help both victims and witnesses maintain positive attitudes toward the criminal justice system thereby fostering a cooperative attitude and encouraging them to work within the system in its efforts toward the efficient and effective administration of justice.

Victim/Witness Legislation in New Jersey

As usual, New Jersey is at the legislative forefront among states in the union in efforts to accommodate victim/witness sensitivity. Legislative efforts have evolved in three basic areas: victim's compensation law, restitution statutes, and the Victim's Bill of Rights and Drunk Driving Victim's Bill of Rights.

N.J.S.A. 52:4B-36 serves as a declaration of the rights to which crime victims and witnesses are entitled. They are as follows:

a. To be treated with dignity and compassion by the criminal justice system;

b. To be informed about the criminal justice process;

c. To be free from intimidation;

d. To have inconvenience associated with participation in the criminal justice process minimized to the fullest extent possible;

e. To make at least one telephone call provided the call is reasonable in both length and location called;

f. To medical assistance if, in the judgment of the law enforcement agency, medical assistance appears necessary;

g. To be notified if presence in court is not needed;

h. To be informed about available remedies, financial assistance and social services;

i. To be compensated for their loss whenever possible;

j. To be provided a secure, but not necessarily separate, waiting area during court proceedings;

k. To be advised of case progress and final disposition; and

l. To the prompt return of property when no longer needed as evidence.

In taking steps to further expand victim/witness assistance, New Jersey has also done the following:

1. Established the Office of Victim-Witness Assistance per N.J.S.A. 52:4B-40;

2. Authorized the Office of Victim-Witness Assistance to develop and coordinate a statewide victim-witness rights information program per N.J.S.A. 52:4B-41 the purposes of which are set forth in N.J.S.A. 52:4B-42 as follows:

   a. To provide victims or their representatives with information about available social and medical services, including emergency services, in the victim's immediate geographical area;

   b. To provide victims or their representatives with information about compensation available under the "Criminal Injuries Compensation Act of 1971" and the court's authority to order restitution;

c. To provide victims or their representatives with information about contacting the county office of victim-witness advocacy or county prosecutor's office;

d. To provide a twenty-four hour toll free telephone number which provides information regarding the act;

e. To provide victims and witnesses with a detailed description of their rights under the Crime Victim's Bill of Rights;

f. To gather information from across the country and make that information available to the Office of Victim-Witness Advocacy, police agencies, hospitals, prosecutors, courts and others who provide assistance to victims of crime; and

g. To sponsor conferences for personnel in the field of victim assistance and compensation to improve and expand services to victims.

3. Established the Office of Victim-Witness Advocacy under N.J.S.A. 52:4B-43;

4. Established standards to insure the rights of victims are enforced per N.J.S.A. 52:4B-44, which also sets forth the services the county prosecutor's office shall provide to victims and witnesses involved in the prosecution of a case;

5. To appoint a county victim-witness coordinator per N.J.S.A. 52:4B-45;

6. To provide for coordination between law enforcement agencies and the Office of Victim-Witness Advocacy per N.J.S.A. 52:4B-46;

7. To change the police training course curriculum to provide for training regarding victim and witness needs and assistance per N.J.S.A. 52:4B-47;

8. To provide for the Division of Criminal Justice to assist county prosecutors and law enforcement agencies regarding the act per N.J.S.A. 52:4B-48;

9. To provide for annual reports from the Office of Victim-Witness Advocacy and county prosecutors to the Attorney General per N.J.S.A. 52:4B-49 regarding the provision of services required by this act.

The foregoing is a relatively recently enacted law and it is much too early to tell whether or not it will have the desired significant impact on the attitude of the criminal justice systems. There is a tremendous need to impress upon those persons involved in the criminal justice system to familiarize themselves with the provisions of the new law and to give force and effect to its implementation in an effort to achieve its desired end.

Of perhaps greater significance because of the degree of public awareness of drunk driving laws is the Drunk Driving Victim's Bill of Rights embodied in N.J.S.A. 52:4B-50.9 *et seq.* The law provides at 39:4-50.11 that victims shall have the right to:

a. Make statements to law enforcement officers regarding the facts of the motor vehicle accident and to reasonable use of a telephone.

b. Receive medical assistance for injuries resulting from the accident.

c. Contact the investigating officer and see copies of the accident reports, and in the case of a surviving spouse, child or next of kin, the autopsy reports.

d. Be provided by the court adjudicating the offense, upon the request of the victim in writing with:

  1. Information about their role in the court process;

  2. Timely advance notice of the date, time and place of the defendant's initial appearance before a judicial officer, submission to the court of any plea agreement, the trial and sentencing;

  3. Timely notification of the case disposition, including trial and sentencing;

4. Prompt notification of any decision or action in the case which results in the defendant's provisional or final release from custody; and

5. Information about the status of the case at any time from the commission of the offense to final disposition or release of the defendant.

e. Receive, when requested from any law enforcement agency involved with the offense, assistance in obtaining employer cooperation in minimizing loss of pay and other benefits resulting from their participation in the court process;

f. A secure waiting area, after the motor vehicle accident, during investigations, and prior to a court appearance;

g. Submit to the court adjudicating the offense a written or oral statement to be considered in deciding upon sentencing and probation terms. This statement may include the nature and extent of any physical harm or psychological or emotional harm or trauma suffered by the victim, the extent of any loss of earnings, or ability to work suffered by the victim and effect of the offense upon the victim's family.

Victim/Witness Sensitivity in the Municipal Courts

Although no formalized victim/witness services presently exist at the local police department or Municipal Court level, counties are now beginning to institute programs as required by state statute. At present, N.J.S.A. 52:4B-22 requires municipal police departments to have available and post in a public place information, booklets, pamphlets, and other pertinent written information supplied by the Violent Crimes Compensation Board relating to the availability of crime victims' compensation, including all necessary applications to be filed with the board.

Despite this lack of institutionalized victim/witness assistance services, and without necessarily being conscious of it, many individual police officers, court clerks, municipal prosecutors, and judges on a daily basis regularly assist victims and witnesses by referring them to county or other private agencies, providing case information, explaining court procedures, giving directions, etc.

More specific recommendations which may easily be implemented in the Municipal Courts include:

1. Establishing an "on call" subpoena system for witnesses and victims wherein the victim or witness would be given a number to call on the court date, or furnish a number to be called where the victim or witness may be reached so that they could be summoned to court on short notice, if needed.[16] In the case of postponements or last minute rescheduling, this system would save unnecessary travel to and waiting at court thereby minimizing inconvenience. Such an "on call" system can easily be implemented by a notice on the subpoena form, scheduling notice, or correspondence routinely sent with instructions to either call the court on the day of the hearing or to supply the court with their telephone number so they may be notified.

2. Interpreters should be made available for the deaf or non-English speaking public at the expense of the court.

3. Separate waiting areas for victims or witnesses should be set aside so that they are not subject to pressure or threats from the defendants.

4. Every effort should be made to return property of the victim being held as evidence so as to minimize deprivation of its use by the rightful owner.[17] Use of photographs should be encouraged, especially in the instance of perishable items.

5. Transportation to and from court for victims and witnesses should be facilitated.[18]

6. Court Clerks should respect confidential information of victims including addresses, places of employment and telephone numbers.

7. Victims and witnesses should notified if defendants in custody are released.[19]

8. Cases which involve sensitive issues or sensitive victims should be scheduled for special session or at the end of the court session to minimize the traumatic effect. These would include youthful victims, lewdness, intra-family disputes, and similar matters.

9. The victims or witnesses should be given status reports as to the case.

10. Directions to court and instructions on where to park can be printed on scheduling notices.

11. Court clerks and judges should take the victim's schedule of availability into consideration when rescheduling cases.

12. Obtain a statement in writing from the victim for sentencing purposes which can convey to the judge what the victim or witness may not be able to properly articulate on the stand due to fear or other anxieties. N.J.S.A. 2C:44-6 provides for a victim's statement to be attached to the presentence report prepared by the probation department. In the absence of a presentence report, the judge may address the victim or witness from the bench as to the impact of the crime on his or her life.

13. Referral of victims or witnesses with special problems to the victim witness coordinator of the county.

In reviewing the above, it can easily be seen that with relatively minimal effort the needs of the victims and witnesses may be fulfilled, thereby improving the image of the court while at the same time incurring the cooperation of victims and witnesses.

The Role of the Judge

The central figure in the justice system is the judge as he or she is responsible for the proper conduct of the trial and to insure protection of the rights of all parties involved. There are certain minor steps which judges may take to insure victim and witness satisfaction, which are as follows:

1. Judges should use their judicial authority to protect victims and witnesses from harassment, threats, intimidation, and harm.

2. Judges may impose as a condition of bail that there shall be no access to the victim or witness by the defendant.[20] They can also require that as a further condition of bail, the defendant commit no new crimes while out on bail.[21]

3. Allow the victim's family to remain in the courtroom as long as it does not interfere with the right of the defendant to a fair trial.

4. Judges should outwardly demonstrate sensitivity to the needs of victims and witnesses.

5. Court should begin on time with infrequent recesses so as to proceed promptly to conclusion and minimize inconvenience to victims and witnesses.

6. Utilize restitution as a condition of sentencing to make victims whole.

7. Encourage that the victim receive full information concerning the proceedings.

8. Judges should treat all victims and witnesses with courtesy, respect, and fairness and explain pertinent procedural aspects to the parties.

Generally speaking, judges perform an essential role in preserving the rights of victims and insuring relief from anxiety and frustration. Judges can go a long way to reduce the hostility of victims and witnesses by appropriately admonishing a guilty party and fully explaining the effect of the defendant's conduct upon the victim and society in general.

Further, judges can also improve procedures such as in a situation where a witness is too upset to testify, a staff member from a victim-witness program, when available, can be called to help compose the witness so the case can proceed. A judge who allows victim and witness input can reduce hostility toward himself and the criminal justice system as a whole as people feel sentences are too lenient.[22]

By deliberately calling attention to the victim-witness movement, complementing it and supporting it, judges thus encourage cooperation from prosecutors and law enforcement officers. Beneficial visibility is also provided to the judge who promotes the program.

Summary

In conclusion, victims claim that decisions are made without their knowledge and seriously affect them, their families, their personal security and their property rights.[23] Lawmakers have heard the cries of victims and witnesses in the emergence of such organizations as the National Organization for Victim Assistance (NOVA), Mothers Against Drunk Driving (MADD), and the Crimes Victims Assistance Organization, to name a few, and have taken the initial steps toward greater equality of their treatment in the criminal justice system. This is evidenced by the enactment of the Crime Victim's Bill of Rights and Drunk Driving Bill of Rights, establishment of the Violent Crimes Compensation Board and offices for victim-witness assistance and advocacy, etc. Judges and court clerks familiar with the system fail to realize the confusion and fear of a citizen involuntarily placed in a role of the crime victim or essential witness to the prosecution, and unless court personnel and all participants in the criminal justice system are cognizant and responsive to the concerns of the people, the "people's court" cannot function in the manner in which it was intended. In the article by Deborah P. Kelly in the *Participant's Manual for Judges on the Rights of Victims and Witnesses,* she said that "victims do not ask to conduct or sing solo, they merely ask that their voices be allowed to join in the chorus."[24] This is a simple analogy that expresses the fact that the criminal justice system should and has begun looking at victims and witnesses with consideration, compassion, dignity, and respect.

1. Peter Finn, "Collaboration Between the Judiciary and Victim-Witness Assistance Programs," *Court Review,* Vol. 23, #2 (Spring, 1986), 17.

2. *Ibid.,* p. 7.

3. *Report of the Supreme Court Task Force on the Improvement of Municipal Courts* (Trenton: Administrative Office of the Courts, 6/28/85), p. 78.

4. Finn, *op. cit.,* p. 13.

5. *Ibid.*

6. *Uniform Crime Reports, State of New Jersey,* 1985 (Trenton: State of New Jersey, Division of State Police), p. 10.

7. *Participant's Manual for Judges on the Rights of Victims and Witnesses* (Nevada: National Judicial College, 1984), p. 9.

8. *Ibid.*

9. *Ibid.,* p. 11.

10. *Ibid.*

11. *Ibid.,* p. 12.

12. *Ibid.*

13. *Ibid.*

14. *Ibid.*

15. *Ibid.*
16. *Report of the Supreme Court Task Force, op. cit.,* p. 83.
17. *Ibid.,* p. 87.
18. *Ibid.*
19. *Ibid.,* p. 91.
20. *Participant's Manual for Judges, op. cit.,* p. 54.
21. *President's Task Force on Victims of Crime—Final Report, December, 1982,* (Washington, D.C.: U.S. Government Printing Office), p. 23.
22. Finn, *op. cit.,* p. 10.
23. *Report of the Supreme Court Task Force, op. cit.,* p. 89.
24. *Participant's Manual for Judges, op. cit.,* p. 12.

Bibliography

1. Finn, Peter. "Collaboration Between the Judiciary and Victim-Witness Assistance Programs," *Court Review,* Vol. 23, #2 (Spring, 1986), 7-15.
2. *Participant's Manual for Judges on the Rights of Victims and Witnesses.* Nevada: National Judicial College, 1984.
3. *President's Task Force on Victims of Crime—Final Report, December 1982.* Washington, D.C.: U.S. Government Printing Office.
4. *Report of the Supreme Court Task Force on the Improvement of Municipal Courts.* Trenton: Administrative Office of the Courts, 6/25/85. (Appendix A, Positions Papers, Committee on Accountability).
5. *Special Court News* (a publication for Judges by the ABA National Conference of Special Court Judges). Vol. 5, #2, January, 1984.
6. *Uniform Crime Reports, State of New Jersey, 1985.* Trenton: State of New Jersey, Division of State Police.

If you are a victim of a drunk driving accident involving injury or property loss to you ...

1. You have the right to make a statement to the police concerning the happening of the accident.
2. You have the right to reasonable use of a telephone.
3. You have the right to receive medical treatment for injuries caused by the accident.
4. You have a right to see copies of the accident reports.
5. You will be given, upon written request:
   a. Information about your role in the court process;
   b. Notice of the defendant's first appearance before the court, any plea agreement, the trial, and sentencing;
   c. Timely notice of the outcome of the case.

6. You have the right to receive the assistance of the police department in obtaining your employer's cooperation to minimize loss of pay or other benefits as a result of your appearance in court.

7. You have the right to a secure waiting area during investigations and before a court appearance.

8. You have the right to submit a written or oral statement to be considered in imposing sentence upon the defendant.

ALCOHOL TREATMENT REHABILITATION ACT

History

On February 9, 1976, Governor Byrne signed bill A-613 into public law. The Alcoholism Treatment and Rehabilitation Act (ATRA) decriminalized public drunkenness in New Jersey. The law was fully implemented in May, 1977, and (1) established a Division of Alcoholism and Advisory Council on Alcoholism, (2) provided for designation and licensing of intoxication treatment facilities, (3) prescribed procedures to be followed in the arrest of intoxicated persons, and (4) authorized the establishment of service forces to assist the police with their responsibilities under the law. The Division of Motor Vehicles is also responsible for cooperating with the Division of Alcoholism regarding tests for alcohol in the bodies of auto drivers and pedestrians who die as a result of a traffic accident or auto drivers who survive traffic accidents which are fatal to others.

Overview

The Alcohol Treatment Rehabilitation Act (ATRA) can be a most effective tool for the Municipal Court practitioner. The Act, found at N.J.S.A. 26:2B-1 *et seq.*, provides at N.J.S.A. 26:2B-15 that "any person who is intoxicated and who voluntarily applies for treatment or is brought to a facility by a police officer ... may be afforded treatment at an intoxication treatment center or other facility." Such person who is brought to the facility shall remain there until no longer incapacitated or intoxicated. These facilities are commonly referred to as "De-Tox" centers. Additionally, N.J.S.A. 26:2B-16 provides that a police officer may transport a person believed to be intoxicated to a "De-Tox" center without arrest. The subsequent section, N.J.S.A. 26:2B-17, provides that any person who is arrested for violation of a municipal ordinance, disorderly or petty disorderly persons offense and who is not also arrested for a misdemeanor can also be taken to the appropriate facility by the arresting officer. After detoxification, the Municipal Court Judge must inform the defendant of the existence of available alcohol treatment. If the defendant requests such treatment in writing, a physician shall be appointed to conduct the examination. Such a request by the defendant is not admissible against the defendant in any proceeding. The physician must report to the court no later than three days after the examination and if the defendant is in need of and requests further treatment, the Court may impose up to thirty days in-patient and/or sixty days out-patient treatment. The Municipal Court proceedings are suspended during this period. If the Judge does not feel that the defendant is in need of treatment, the Municipal Court proceedings are resumed. If the defendant, however, does undergo treatment and successfully completes it, the charges are dismissed.

After May 9, 1977, ATRA repeals existing ordinances, resolutions, by-laws, regulations and laws prescribing penalties for public intoxication and prohibits the enactment of any new ones outlawing drunkenness and equivalent offenses. See N.J.S.A. 26:2B-26 which reads as follows:

> No county, municipality, or other political subdivision of the State shall adopt any law, ordinance, bylaw, resolution or regulation having the force of law a. rendering public intoxication or being found in any place in an intoxicated condition an offense, a violation or the subject of criminal or civil penalties or sanctions of any kind; b. inconsistent with the provisions and policies of this act:

> Nothing herein contained shall affect any laws, ordinances, bylaws, resolutions or regulations against driving after drinking alcohol, driving under the influence of alcohol, or other similar offenses that involve the operation of motor vehicles, machinery or other hazardous equipment.

The advantages of this legislation are obvious. First, it affords the defendant who is charged with an offense which is alcohol related the opportunity to obtain the necessary treatment and secondly, it allows the defendant to dispose of the offense against him without the imposition of a fine or period of incarceration.

The option of treatment in lieu of prosecution does not apply to motor vehicle or indictable offenses.

Initially, clients may be disinclined to admit having an alcohol problem, but upon learning that the charges may be dismissed if treatment is received, the defendant may be become more amenable. Accordingly, the attorney should always be familiar with the existence of the program.

Purpose

The most important aspect of the law is that public drunkenness is no longer a crime but is recognized as a disease characterized by uncontrollable use of alcoholic beverages or use which substantially injures a person's health or substantially interferes with his or her social and economic functions. The purpose of ATRA is to afford intoxicated persons the opportunity to receive treatment rather than punishment when no crime has been committed or treatment in lieu of prosecution if they have committed a minor offense.

People can voluntarily submit to treatment and can be assisted to a treatment facility by a police officer. A person assisted to a facility by a police officer shall not be considered to be arrested and no entry or other record shall be made indicating an arrest.

Goals

The goals of ATRA can be summed up as follows:

1. To reduce the incalculable human and economic cost of alcoholism and problems related to alcohol.

2. To assist the recovery of those persons not at risk.

3. To substitute treatment by the health care community in place of prosecution by the criminal justice system.

4. To lessen the tremendous cost of intoxication and alcoholism to the criminal justice system.

5. To free bench time for more serious matters.

6. To allow criminal justice resources to be directed to more serious crimes and more severe correctional problems.

7. To provide an effective, humane, and inexpensive means of prevention and control of alcoholism and public intoxication.

8. To give law enforcement personnel effective alternatives and resources to handle intoxicated people.

9. To reduce the amount of intoxicated persons admitted to jails.

Definitions

An INTOXICATED PERSON is one whose mental or physical functioning is substantially impaired as a result of the use of alcoholic beverages.

INCAPACITATED means the condition of the person who is, as a result of alcohol, unconscious or has his or her judgment so impaired that he or she is incapable of realizing and making rational decisions regarding his or her need for treatment, is in need of substantial medical attention, or is likely to suffer substantial physical harm.

Involuntary Treatment vs. Voluntary Treatment

The Act expresses a clear preference for voluntary treatment over involuntary treatment. Involuntary treatment is permitted only in exceptional and very clearly prescribed circumstances. If a person has repeatedly come to the attention of the police for intoxicated incidents and related illegal behavior, and has been advised of the treatment opportunity but has chosen to be taken home, the police might tell the person that he or she has the choice of entering a program or being charged with an offense if there is related criminal behavior, such as disorderly conduct. If an intoxicated person refuses treatment at that point and is charged with an offense, the Court still has the discretion of ordering treatment in a diversionary program or as a part or probation. The arrest as described should be made as a means, after all other suggestions have failed, to force the alcoholic to recognize his or her need for treatment.

Role of the Police

As of May 9, 1977, police officers no longer have the option to arrest for being drunk in a public place; however, these provisions do not affect any laws or ordinances against driving while under the influence or other similar offenses that involve the operation of motor vehicles, machinery or other hazardous equipment. See N.J.S.A. 26:2B-26.

Police have the following choices for managing intoxicated persons:

A person who appears intoxicated, but not incapacitated, in a public place and appears to be in need of help, with the person's consent can be:

A. Transported or sent home;

B. Transported or sent to a licensed intoxication treatment facility designated in the annual list of the Division of Alcoholism; or

C. Transported or sent to a medical facility.

Without the intoxicated person's consent, no action should be taken unless it appears the person is incapacitated by alcohol. A person so intoxicated that he or she appears incapacitated by alcohol, and obviously cannot consent or decide for himself or herself if he or she needs treatment, should be taken into protective custody and transported to a designated intoxication treatment center or emergency medical facility depending upon the circumstances. Any person unconscious or injured should be taken to an emergency medical facility.

Persons arrested for only a disorderly persons or municipal offense and who the officer believes to be intoxicated may be taken by the officer directly to a detoxification treatment center or other appropriate facility or may first be processed on the criminal charges and then taken to the facility. The center can detain the arrested person until no longer intoxicated, but not for more than 48 hours. When a high misdemeanor or misdemeanor is committed by an intoxicated or incapacitated person, public drunkenness is not an issue and regular police procedures for apprehension apply. This also applies to any offense of driving while under the influence.

If a person who has been drinking is neither intoxicated nor incapacitated, he or she should be left alone unless criminal activity is observed or suspected.

Role of the Court

ATRA authorizes the Courts of New Jersey to grant a defendant's request for commitment to a designated intoxication treatment program in lieu of prosecution.

When a defendant charged with a violation of any municipal ordinance, petty disorderly persons offense or disorderly persons offense committed while intoxicated is first brought before the Court, the law requires that the Court advise the defendant that:

1. If he or she has not been admitted to an intoxication treatment facility or examined by a physician, he or she is entitled to make a request in writing for a medical examination to determine whether he or she is an alcoholic who will benefit by treatment. (Exhibits A and B).

2. If a defendant makes such a request, he or she must be admitted to a designated intoxication treatment center or other facility designated by the Court for examination by a physician. The cost of the examination is to be borne by the defendant, his or her third party insurance carrier, or the Court.

3. The defendant may be detained at the facility for the examination, after which he or she will be returned to custody for further proceedings in the case.

4. The proceedings will be stayed while the request for examination and treatment is under consideration. (Exhibit C).

If the defendant makes a written request for examination pursuant to the above, he or she may be placed under the supervision of the Probation Department. The physician is required to report his or her findings, the facts upon which the findngs are based and the reasons for the findings to the Court within three days of the examination. If the physician reports that the defendant is an alcoholic who would benefit by treatment, the Court must inform the defendant that:

1. He or she is entitled to make a request in writing for commitment to treat his or her alcoholism.

2. The Court must consider the examination report of the physician, nature of the offense charged, defendant's past criminal record, and any other relevant evidence in determining whether to grant defendant's request for commitment.

3. If the defendant is committed per his or her request, he or she must consent in writing to the terms of the commitment which may include in-patient treatment not to exceed 30 days, and out-patient treatment not to exceed 60 days. (Exhibit D).

4. The defendant will be discharged from the commitment at the expiration of the period specified in the court Order or when it is determined that treatment will no longer benefit him or her.

5. The proceedings for the offense are stayed for the term of the commitment if commitment is granted by the Court.

6. The Court will receive a report at the end of the commitment period stating whether the defendant successfully completed the program.

7. Upon successful completion, the Court will dismiss the charges against the defendant. (Exhibit F).

8. Upon failure to successfully complete the program, based upon the report and any other relevant evidence, the Court has the discretion to take such action as it deems appropriate, including dismissal of the charges or ordering an end to the stay of prosecution and proceeding with the trial on the criminal charges.

9. If the defendant is convicted and sentenced after failure to successfully complete the program, the Court will reduce the term of the sentence by the period during which the defendant was afforded treatment.

After giving the above advice and the defendant consents in writing to commitment for treatment, the Court must determine whether the defendant is an alcoholic who would benefit by treatment by applying the factors in paragraph 2. If the defendant is committed to a treatment program, he or she may be placed under the supervision of the Probation Department. See N.J.S.A. 26:2B-18.

If the Court does not order treatment in lieu of prosecution, then the stay of criminal proceedings must be vacated.

The law expressly provides that in no event shall a request for examination, any statement made by the defendant during the course of the examination or any finding of a physician pursuant to the provisions of the law be admissible against the defendant in any proceeding, which coincides with federal confidentiality regulations prohibiting the release of information concerning application and participation in such programs.

Suggestions for Types of Cases Judges Should Refer

Some types of cases which arise out of alcoholic related problems which Municipal Court Judges may want to refer through ATRA are:

1. Simple Assault;
2. Bar Fights;
3. Domestic Cases;
4. Abusive Language;
5. Harassment;
6. Loitering;
7. Trespass; and
8. Possession of Alcohol in Public.

Role of Probation

After the Municipal Court orders diversion pursuant to ATRA, the Probation Department will screen the individual and thereafter refer the person to the appropriate treatment program. The Probation Officer will follow the person's progress while in treatment and upon successful completion will notify the Court recommending the complaint(s) be dismissed. If the person does not successfully complete a treatment program or if the Probation Department determines the person is not a candidate for treatment under ATRA, the person will be sent back to the Court for further action. If the Municipal Court is unsure whether a person is appropriate for diversion, the Probation Department is always willing to arrange for an alcohol evaluation prior to further action.

Requirement to Effectively Implement Law

It is important to note that this law requires active cooperation to be effectively implemented and Municipal Court Judges should be aware of the benefits to the individual with an alcohol problem and to society as a whole since the law is designed to provide treatment for the problem and not punishment. Municipal Court Judges can equate ATRA to a Conditional Discharge for drug offenses, as both provide diversion for the defendant without having the person plead guilty to a disorderly persons offense. Municipal Court Judges should consider that the alcoholic has slowly acquired a complex set of behavior patterns over the years and revising the process and regaining self-control usually requires years and is often a life-long process. There are often many instances of contact with a detoxification facility, hospital, half-way house, Alcoholics Anonymous, the criminal justice system and other help providing sources. It is not uncommon for a police officer to find a person previously treated back on the street in an intoxicated state. These instances are common during recovery of most alcoholics and do not necessarily indicate a failure of any system. Most ATRA referrals are first and second offenders.

Exhibits G through K include sample forms for Notice of Motion, Order, and sample Defendant's certification which may be used by counsel on behalf of the defendant who is charged with an alcohol related offense in the Municipal Court.

EXHIBIT A

REQUEST BY DEFENDANT TO BE EXAMINED

I, _____ , have been apprised of my rights pursuant to N.J.S.A. 26:2B-7, *et seq.* I respectfully submit my request for a stay of the court proceedings in relation to the case Docket No. _____ in order that I may obtain the required examination. I understand that this initial diversion is not a guarantee of acceptance into the program. I also understand that if I fail to fully cooperate with all affiliated agents, I may jeopardize my chances of diversion.

Defendant's Name:

Address:

Telephone Number:

Social Security Number:

Municipal Court:

Docket Number:

Charge:

D.O.B.:

_____
Defendant's Signature

_____
Date

EXHIBIT B

COURT REFERRAL

The defendant, _____ , appeared before this court on charges that are alcohol related. Pursuant to N.J.S.A. 26:2B-7, *et seq.*, the defendant has been apprised of his rights which include an evaluation as to alcoholism by the Alcohol Diversion Program. With a formal request submitted by said defendant, this court referral is enacted.

_____
Signature of Judge

_____
Date

EXHIBIT C

STATE OF NEW JERSEY

MUNICIPAL COURT OF: COUNTY OF:

                                       DOCKET NO.

                vs.   **ORDER**
                                       Temporary Commitment
                                       and Stay of Proceedings
                     Defendant.

TO THE HONORABLE   , Judge;

Pursuant to the provisions of N.J.S.A. 26:2B-7, *et seq.*, application is hereby made for Stay of Proceedings and Temporary Commitment of the Defendant.

This Defendant has been charged with a violation of N.J.S.A.   , a disorderly person offense or a Municipal Ordinance, Section   and has been determined by the court to be an alcoholic in need of treatment.

It is thereby ORDERED that the Defendant be committed for not more than:

       _____ 30 days in-patient treatment,

       _____ 60 days out-patient treatment,

       _____ or both, not to exceed 90 days, and that
                proceedings be stayed for that period of time.

DATED: _____

                                                                                , Judge

By affixing his/her signature, the defendant agrees to the terms of commitment stated above.

                                                                   _____

                                                                              , Defendant

EXHIBIT D

CLIENT-PROBATION DEPARTMENT PARTICIPATION AGREEMENT

Under provisions of the Alcohol Treatment and Rehabilitation Act of 1976, (N.J.S.A. 26:2B-7, *et seq.*) any person who is arrested for violation of a municipal ordinance or for a disorderly persons offense may request an examination to determine if he/she has an alcohol problem. If, as a result of such examination, a problem is apparent, the defendant may request a stay of proceedings. The court may grant this request at which point the defendant is to obtain alcohol treatment. If progress toward rehabilitation is made during the period of treatment, the original charges may be dismissed.

1. I understand that in order to be considered for this treatment program, the Court may order me to obtain a complete physical examination by a Court appointed physician.

2. I understand that the Court may also order me to participate in an alcohol educational program.

3. I understand that upon completion of the medical examination and/or educational program, the court can order me to participate in a 30 day in-patient treatment program for alcoholism.

4. I also understand that the court can order me to participate in a 60 day out-patient treatment program.

5. I understand that the in-patient and out-patient treatment may take as long as 90 days, in addition to the medical examination and/or educational program.

6. I understand that I must participate in all meetings to which I am assigned. Also, I must show a desire to want to deal with my problems.

7. I understand that at any time I may leave the program. If I leave the program without the consent of the Court, my case will be returned for prosecution.

I have read the above and fully understand everything.

Signature: _____

Date: _____

Witness: _____

EXHIBIT E

PROBATION REFERRAL AGREEMENT
MARYVILLE OUTPATIENT

I, _____ consent to out-patient treatment at Maryville rather than face legal action.

I understand that at Maryville I will be given an alcohol evaluation, and if appropriate, retained for ongoing treatment. It is certainly within the realm of possibility, that an in-patient treatment program may be recommended in certain instances.

Treatment at Maryville will consist of the following minimal requirements, for a minimum of three (3) months:

1. Individual, couple, family therapy sessions at the discretion of the counselor but at least once a month.
2. Attendance at an AA or NA meeting once a week.
3. Educational Film/Lecture once a week.

Each client is responsible for his/her own fee which is based upon one's income and Maryville's sliding fee scale. A one time evaluation fee is $35.00. Failure to keep an appointment for an evaluation without calling ahead to cancel will result in a $10.00 surcharge for each broken appointment.

I understand that as a working person I can be afforded the convenience of an evening appointment (5 PM & later). I will forfeit that convenience if I make an evening appointment and fail to keep it without prior notification. Thereafter I will be expected to make day time appointments and arrange for that with my employer.

I understand that I will be *therapeutically discharged* from Maryville and returned to the probation authorities if I meet anyone of the following criteria:

1. Failure to comply with the treatment requirements recommended by my counselor. It is my responsibility to find my own means of transportation to comply with the program.
2. Demonstration of behavior that is determined to be inappropriate and counter-productive to one's own or another client's recovery, growth or safety.
3. Continued use of alcohol and/or other non-prescription drug substance, which is a direct violation of my treatment.

I agree to contact Maryville Outpatient for an appointment within one week. I understand that Maryville must make a monthly report to the Probation Department on my progress. I authorize Maryville to release to the Probation Department information relevant to all aspects of my treatment including my failure to make an initial appointment. I also authorize my probation officer to release to Maryville information relevant to all aspects of my treatment.

_____
Client's Signature

_____
Date

_____
Probation Officer

EXHIBIT F

STATE OF NEW JERSEY

Municipal Court of _____   County of _____

Docket No. _____

_____

v.

ORDER
Dismissal of Charges
(Alcoholism Treatment
and Rehabilitation Act
N.J.S.A. 26:2B-7 et seq.)

Defendant

_____

The defendant, _____, residing at _____
_____, having been charged with a violation of
N.J.S.A. _____, a disorderly persons offense or a Municipal
Ordinance, _____;

The defendant having successfully completed

_____ sessions of alcohol education

_____ days of in-patient treatment

_____ days of out-patient treatment

_____ total number of days

in accordance with the Order of Temporary Commitment and Stay of Proceedings entered by this court on _____, 19_____;

It is thereby ORDERED on this day, _____, 19_____, that the above charges against _____ be dismissed.

_____
Judge

Court Id. No. _____

210/Municipal Court

EXHIBIT G

TOMASELLO, DRISCOLL & ROZANSKI
Counsellors at Law
135 N. Broad Street
Woodbury, New Jersey 08096
(609) 848-1010
Attorneys for

___

STATE OF NEW JERSEY : MUNICIPAL COURT
:
        Plaintiff :
: Complaint No.
vs. :
:
: NOTICE OF MOTION
        Defendant :
:

___

To: , Prosecutor

PLEASE TAKE NOTICE that on the   day of   , 19   , the undersigned will apply to the above named Court, to be heard at the Municipal Court of   , at   for an Order for a stay of the proceedings and a medical examination under N.J.S.A. 26:2B-17.

                                                WILLIAM I. ROZANSKI
                                                Attorney for Defendant

Dated:

EXHIBIT H

TOMASELLO, DRISCOLL & ROZANSKI
Counsellors at Law
135 N. Broad Street
Woodbury, New Jersey 08096
(609) 848-1010
Attorneys for

_____

STATE OF NEW JERSEY

    Plaintiff

vs.

    Defendant

_____

: MUNICIPAL COURT
:
: Complaint No.
:
:
: ORDER
:

  THIS MATTER having come before the Court upon Motion of William I. Rozanski, Attorney for Defendant, _____, and Defendant having consented to the entry of this Order; and for good cause shown,

  IT IS This _____ day of _____, 19____:

  ORDERED that Defendant,_____, shall submit to a medical exam to determine if he is an alcoholic who would benefit from treatment under the provisions of N.J.S.A. 26:2B *et seq.*, which examination shall be arranged through the_____
_____ County Probation Department.

_____
             J.M.C.

EXHIBIT I

TOMASELLO, DRISCOLL & ROZANSKI
Counsellors at Law
135 N. Broad Street
Woodbury, New Jersey 08096
(609) 848-1010
Attorneys for

STATE OF NEW JERSEY :
: MUNICIPAL COURT
Plaintiff :
: Complaint No.
vs. :
:
: NOTICE OF MOTION
Defendant :
:

To: , Prosecutor

PLEASE TAKE NOTICE that on the   day of   , 19   , the undersigned will apply to the above named court, to be heard at the Municipal Court of   , for an Order for a stay of the proceedings and an Order permitting alcohol treatment pursuant to N.J.S.A. 26:2B-17.

WILLIAM I. ROZANSKI
Attorney for Defendant

Dated:

EXHIBIT J

TOMASELLO, DRISCOLL & ROZANSKI
Counsellors at Law
135 N. Broad Street
Woodbury, New Jersey 08096
(609) 848-1010
Attorneys for

_____

STATE OF NEW JERSEY	:	
Plaintiff	:	MUNICIPAL COURT
vs.	:	Complaint No.
	:	
	:	ORDER
Defendant	:	
	:	

_____

THIS MATTER having come before the court upon Motion of Defendant, _____, for a stay of the proceedings under the provisions of the Alcohol Treatment Rehabilitation Act, N.J.S.A. 26:2B-1 *et seq.* and it appearing from the medical examination that the Defendant is an alcoholic who would benefit from treatment and for good cause shown and the Defendant having consented to the entry of this Order;

IT IS This _____ day of _____, 19_____:

ORDERED that these proceeds are stayed until further Order of the court and the Defendant is ordered to undergo alcohol treatment through the Gloucester County Probation Department for a period not to exceed _____ days; and upon receipt of a report from the Probation Department indicating that the Defendant has successfully completed his period of alcoholic treatment and rehabilitation the above captioned matter will be dismissed.

_____
J.M.C.

I HEREBY CONSENT
TO THE FORM AND ENTRY
OF THE WITHIN ORDER.

_____
Defendant

EXHIBIT K

TOMASELLO, DRISCOLL & ROZANSKI
Counsellors at Law
135 N. Broad Street
Woodbury, New Jersey 08096
(609) 848-1010
Attorneys for

_____

STATE OF NEW JERSEY : MUNICIPAL COURT
        Plaintiff :
         : Complaint No.
vs. :
         : DEFENDANT'S CERTIFICATION
        Defendant :

_____

STATE OF NEW JERSEY :
    ss.
COUNTY OF GLOUCESTER :

1. I am the Defendant in the above-captioned matter.

2. On_____, I had 6-7 beers prior to coming home and being involved in an incident with my Wife that is the subject of this Complaint.

3. I have been attending alcohol rehabilitation through Maryville once a week since _____ and A.A. meetings three times per week since that time.

4. My Wife and I have separated and she will be filing for a Divorce.

5. I am an alcoholic and I believe that I would benefit by continuing with alcohol rehabilitation.

6. Attached is a note from my Doctor confirming my problems with alcohol.

The above statements made by me are true to the best of my knowledge and belief. I am aware that if any of them are willfully false, I am subject to punishment.

_____
                                                Defendant

APPENDIX A
APPLICABLE NEW JERSEY RULES OF COURT

216/Municipal Court

Part VII
RULES GOVERNING PRACTICE IN THE MUNICIPAL COURTS
TABLE OF CONTENTS

Rule 7:1.	Scope	218
Rule 7:2.	Indictable Offenses; Proceedings Under Uniform Fresh Pursuit Law	218
Rule 7:3.	Non-Indictable Offenses; Complaint, Summons, Warrant, Notice In Lieu Of Complaint	218
	7:3-1. Complaint; Warrant or Summons; Preliminary Hearing	218
	7:3-2. Mediation of Minor Disputes, Notice in Lieu of Complaint	219
	7:3-3. Form of Subpoena	219
Rule 7:4.	Trial Of Offenses By The Municipal Court Judge	219
	7:4-1. Applicability	219
	7:4-2. Proceedings Before Trial	219
	(a) Arraignment.	219
	(b) Pleas.	219
	(c) Adjournment.	220
	(d) Pretrial Procedure.	220
	(e) Motions.	220
	(f) Motions to Suppress.	220
	(g) Trial of Complaints Together.	220
	(h) Depositions and Discovery.	221
	(i) Dismissal.	221
	(j) Transfer to the Chancery Division, Family Part.	221
	7:4-3. Venue; On Disqualification of Judge	221
	(a) Generally.	221
	(b) On Disqualification of Judge.	221
	7:4-4. Appearances; Exclusion of Public; Opening Statement	222
	(a) Presence of Defendant.	222
	(b) Appearance of Prosecution.	222
	(c) Exclusion of Public.	222
	(d) Opening Statement.	222
	7:4-5. Record of Proceedings; Transcripts	222
	(a) Record.	222
	(b) Transcript.	222
	(c) Supervision.	222
	7:4-6. Sentence and Judgment	223
	(a) Sentence.	223
	(b) Judgment.	223
	(c) Reasons for Sentence.	223
	(d) Conviction of a Corporation.	223
	(e) Probation.	223
	(f) Credit for Confinement Pending Sentence.	223
	(g) Correction or Reduction of Sentence.	223
	(h) Identification Following Conviction.	223
	7:4-7. New Trial	223
	7:4-8. Plea Agreements	224
Rule 7:5.	Bail	225
	7:5-1. Applicability of Superior Court Rules	225
	7:5-2. Place of Deposit	225
	7:5-3. Authority to Admit to Bail	225
	7:5-4. Bail After Conviction	225

Rule 7:6.	**Traffic Offenses**		226
	7:6-1. Complaint and Summons		226
	(a) Form.		226
	(b) Issuance.		226
	(c) Records and Reports.		226
	7:6-2. Improper Disposition of Traffic Tickets; Contempt of Court		226
	7:6-3. Procedure on Failure to Appear		226
	(a) Residents—Parking Cases.		226
	(b) Residents—Non-Parking Cases.		227
	(c) Non-Residents—All Traffic Cases.		227
	7:6-4. Trial Date; Adjournment		227
	7:6-5. Calendar Parts; Sessions		227
	7:6-6. Statement in Mitigation or Defense by Affidavit; Judgment		228
	(a) Statement in Mitigation or Defense by Affidavit.		228
	(b) Judgment.		228
	7:6-7. Notice to Defendant on Guilty Plea		228
Rule 7:7.	**Violations Bureau**		228
	7:7-1. Designation; Functions		228
	7:7-2. Location		228
	7:7-3. Designated Offenses; Schedule of Penalties		229
	7:7-4. Plea and Payment of Fine and Costs		229
Rule 7:8.	**Appeals**		229
	7:8-1. Appeals		229
	7:8-2. Stay		230
	7:8-3. Reversal; Remission of Fine and Costs		230
Rule 7:9.	**Municipal Courts: Statutory Penalty Proceedings**		230
Rule 7:10.	**General Provisions; Administration**		230
	7:10-1. Local Rules		230
	7:10-2. Amendment of Process or Pleading		230
	7:10-3. Court Calendar; Attorneys		230
	(a) Calendar.		230
	(b) Appearances of Attorneys.		230
	7:10-4. Financial Control		231
	(a) Fines and Forfeitures.		231
	(b) Receipts and Disbursements.		231
	(c) Payment of Moneys Due.		231
	(d) Docket; Fiscal Forms and Procedure; Recordkeeping		231
	7:10-5. Oath of Municipal Court Judge		231

Part VII
RULES GOVERNING PRACTICE IN THE MUNICIPAL COURTS

RULE 7:1. SCOPE

The rules in Part VII, together with the rules in Part III, insofar as applicable and unless otherwise expressly provided by law or these rules, govern the practice and procedure in all criminal, quasi-criminal and penal actions in the municipal courts and all such actions transferred from a municipal court to the Superior Court, Chancery Division, Family Part pursuant to R. 5:1-2(c)(3) and R. 5:1-3(b)(2). Whenever approval is given for the exercise of such jurisdiction by the Special Civil Part in a particular county, the court may be divided by the Chief Justice into sections for separate hearing of civil and criminal matters.

Note: Source—R.R. 8:1-1, 8:12-1. Amended June 29, 1973 to be effective September 10, 1973; amended July 21, 1978 to be effective immediately; amended December 20, 1983 to be effective December 31, 1983; amended November 7, 1988 to be effective January 2, 1989.

RULE 7:2. INDICTABLE OFFENSES; PROCEEDINGS UNDER UNIFORM FRESH PURSUIT LAW

The provisions of R. 3:2 (complaint), R. 3:3 (warrant or summons upon complaint) and R. 3:4-1, 3:4-2, 3:4-3 and 3:4-5 (proceedings before the committing judge) are applicable to the municipal courts in respect of indictable offenses; the provisions of R. 3:4-4 are applicable to such courts in proceedings under the Uniform Fresh Pursuit Law.

Note: Source—R.R. 8:3-1(a) (first four sentences), 8:3-2(a)(1), 8:3-2(a)(2) (first, second, fifth, sixth sentences), 8:3-2(b)(1) (first, second, third sentences), 8:3-2(b)(2) (first, second sentences), 8:3-2(c)(1), 8:3-2(c)(3)(i)(ii)(iii) (first sentence, first clause), 8:3-2(c)(4), 8:3-2(d)(1)(2), 8:3-3; amended July 26, 1984 to be effective September 10, 1984.

RULE 7:3. NON-INDICTABLE OFFENSES; COMPLAINT, SUMMONS, WARRANT, NOTICE IN LIEU OF COMPLAINT

7:3-1. Complaint; Warrant or Summons; Preliminary Hearing

The provisions of R. 3:2 (complaint), R. 3:3 (warrant or summons upon complaint), R. 3:4-1 (appearance before committing judge) and R. 3:4-2 (procedure after filing of complaint) are applicable to municipal courts in respect of all non-indictable offenses, except as follows:

(a) A summons issued upon a complaint charging a non-indictable offense may be served either in accordance with R. 4:4-4 or by mailing it to the defendant's last known address.

(b) If the Administrative Director of the Courts has, pursuant to R. 1:32-3, prescribed the form of complaint and summons for non-indictable offenses, a law enforcement officer may make, sign and issue such complaint and summons, serving the summons upon the defendant and thereafter, without unnecessary delay, filing the complaint with the court named therein; except that in lieu of service on the defendant, the summons may, in cases involving non-moving traffic offenses, be served by affixing it to the vehicle involved in the violation and, in cases involving any violation of a statute or ordinance relating to motor vehicles, if the defendant is a corporation, partnership or unincorporated association, the summons may be served upon the operator of the vehicle.

(c) If a summons directed to a defendant which is a corporation, partnership or unincorporated association is returned "not served" and the court is satisfied that the summons could not be served, he shall order the defendant to cause its appearance and plea to be entered by a day certain. A copy of such order, together with a copy of the summons, shall, within 5 days after the entry thereof be served upon the defendant by mailing the same by registered or certified mail, return receipt requested, to the address where the defendant usually receives its mail, unless it appears by affidavit that such place is unknown and cannot be ascertained after inquiry.

(d) A summons may issue in lieu of a warrant if the person taking the complaint has reason to believe that the defendant will appear.

Note: Source—R.R. 8:3-1(a) (fifth and sixth sentences), 8:3-2(a)(2) (third and fourth sentences), 8:3-2(b)(1) (fourth and fifth sentences), 8:3-2(c)(3)(iii) (first sentence, second clause) (iv); amended July 26, 1984 to be effective September 10, 1984.

7:3-2. Mediation of Minor Disputes, Notice in Lieu of Complaint

If a person seeks to file a complaint or a complaint is filed charging an offense that may constitute a minor dispute, a notice may issue to the person making the charge and the person or persons charged, requesting their appearance before the court, or such person or program designated by the court and approved by the Assignment Judge to provide mediation under R. 1:40-7. If on the return date of a summons, it appears to the court that the offense charged may constitute a minor dispute, the court may order the persons involved to mediation in accordance with R. 1:40-7.

Note: Source—R.R. 8:3-1(b), amended July 29, 1977 to be effective September 6, 1977; amended November 1, 1985 to be effective January 2, 1986; amended July 14, 1992 to be effective September 1, 1992.

7:3-3. Form of Subpoena

In cases involving non-indictable offenses law enforcement officers may issue and serve subpoenas to testify in the form prescribed by the Administrative Director of the Courts. Courts having jurisdiction over such offenses, the Division of State Police, the Division of Motor Vehicles and any other agency so authorized by the Administrative Director of the Courts may supply subpoena forms to their law enforcement officers. After service of a subpoena the officer shall attach a copy of the subpoena to the appropriate complaint and promptly file them with the court.

Note: Source—R.R. 8:10-1A.

RULE 7:4. TRIAL OF OFFENSES BY THE MUNICIPAL COURT JUDGE

7:4-1. Applicability

Except as otherwise provided by R. 7:6 (Traffic Offenses) and 7:7 (Violations Bureau), the provisions of R. 7:4 apply to the trial by the court of all complaints charging offenses within its trial jurisdiction and all indictable offenses triable by it upon the defendant's waiver of indictment and trial by jury.

Note: Source—1969 revision.

7:4-2. Proceedings Before Trial

(a) Arraignment.

(1) Except as otherwise provide by paragraph (2) of this rule, arraignment shall be conducted in open court and shall consist of reading the complaint to the defendant or stating to him the substance of the charge, and calling on him, after he is given a copy of the complaint, to plead thereto. The defendant may waive the reading of the complaint.

(2) When a defendant is represented by an attorney and desires to plead not guilty, unless the court otherwise orders, such plea shall be entered by the filing, at or before the time fixed for arraignment, of a written statement, signed by the attorney, certifying that the defendant has received a copy of the complaint, has read it or the attorney has read it or explained it to him, understands the substance of the charge, and pleads not guilty to the charge.

(b) Pleas. A defendant may plead not guilty or guilty, but the court may in its discretion refuse to accept a plea of guilty, and shall not accept such plea without first addressing the defendant personally and determining by inquiry of the defendant and of others in the court's discretion that the plea is made voluntarily with understanding of the nature of the charge and the consequences of the plea and that there is a factual basis for the plea. Upon the request of the defendant the court may at the time of the acceptance of a plea of guilty order that such plea shall not be evidential in any civil proceeding. If a defendant refuses to plead or stands mute or if the court refuses to accept a plea of guilty, the court shall enter a plea of not guilty. If a plea of guilty is entered, the court may hear the witnesses in support of the complaint prior to judgment and sentence, and after such hearing may, in its discretion, refuse to accept the plea. A defendant, corporation, partnership, or unincorporated association may enter a plea by an agent pursuant to R. 7:7-4 and may appear by an officer or agent provided the appearance is consented to in writing by the named party defendant and the court finds that the interest of justice would not require the appearance of counsel. If the defendant is a corporation, partnership or unincorporated association and fails to respond to an order entered pursuant to R. 7:3-1(c), the court, if satisfied that service was duly made, shall enter an appearance and a plea of not guilty for the defendant and thereupon proceed to hear the complaint.

(c) Adjournment. On or before the return day of a warrant or summons, the court may adjourn the hearing for a period not exceeding 14 days, except that an adjournment for a longer period or additional adjournments may be granted if the court deems postponement of the hearing to be reasonably necessary. In contested matters the court, on granting an adjournment, shall specify a trial date. The court shall cause the complaining witness, all defendants and all other known witnesses to be notified of any adjournment, which together with the reasons therefore, shall be noted in the record.

(d) Pretrial Procedure. The pretrial procedure provided by R. 3:13-1 may be employed in the court's discretion upon its own or a party's motion.

(e) Motions. R. 3:10-1 (defenses and objections which may be raised), R. 3:10-2 (defenses and objections which must be raised before trial), R. 3:10-3 (defenses and objections which may be raised only before or after trial), and R. 3:10-4 (defense of lack of jurisdiction) are applicable to actions in the municipal court except that for purposes of this rule the reference in R. 3:10-2, to indictment or accusation shall be deemed to mean the complaint and R. 3:10-3 shall be deemed also to include the defense that an ordinance under which a complaint is made is unconstitutional. The court shall upon request provide an opportunity for the presentation of such motions before proceeding to trial. Motions may be made orally and informally, but affidavits or oral testimony may be presented thereon when required. A motion shall include all such defenses and objections then available to the defendant. The court or clerk shall briefly note in the record all defenses or objections raised by motion and the disposition thereof. Appeals from orders dismissing or refusing to dimiss a complaint may be taken to the Superior Court, Law Division pursuant to R. 3:24.

(f) Motions to Suppress. Except for cases involving a search pursuant to warrant, motions to suppress evidence in matters subject to trial within the municipal court may be filed and heard therein in any case in which the Attorney General, county prosecutor, or municipal prosecutor is prosecuting attorney on behalf of the State and on notice to said prosecutor. Briefs, if ordered by the court, shall be served and filed prior to the date fixed for hearing as directed by the court. When a motion to suppress evidence is granted, the order shall be entered forthwith and the clerk shall within ten days thereafter dispatch a copy thereof to all parties and to the county prosecutor. All further proceedings in the municipal court shall be stayed pending a timely appeal by the State pursuant to R. 3:24. Property the use of which is suppressed pursuant to an order entered under this rule, and which is not otherwise subject to lawful detention, shall be delivered to the person entitled thereto only after a decision on any appeal by the State. Denial of motion to suppress heard in the municipal court may be reviewed on appeal from a judgment of conviction pursuant to R. 3:23, notwithstanding that such judgment is entered following a guilty plea.

(g) Trial of Complaints Together. The court may order that 2 or more complaints be tried together if the offenses arose out of the same facts and circumstances, regardless of the number of defendants. In all other matters, with the consent of the persons charged, the court, for convenience, may consolidate complaints for trial.

(h) Depositions and Discovery. Depositions and discovery in any case in which the defendant may be subject to imprisonment or other consequence of magnitude if convicted shall be as provided by R. 3:13-2 and R. 3:13-3 provided that the municipality in which the case is to be tried has a municipal prosecutor. In all other cases the court may order depositions to be taken and discovery made in criminal actions as provided by R. 3:13-2 and R. 3:13-3.

(i) Dismissal. If the complaint is not moved on the return day, the court may direct that it be heard on a specified date and a notice thereof be served on the complaining witness, all defendants and all other known witnesses by subpoena. Upon failure of trial to be held on the day set, the court, after first notifying the county prosecutor if the offense charged is indictable, may order the complaint dismissed. A complaint may be dismissed by the court for good cause at any time on the motion of the state or municipality or on the motion of the defendant. Upon dismissal the warrant shall be recalled.

A complaint on file for more than 6 months may at the discretion of the court be transferred to an inactive list. A matter on the inactive list for more than one year may be dismissed by the court on its own motion upon notice to the prosecuting attorney. Upon dismissal a warrant if issued shall be recalled.

(j) Transfer to the Chancery Division, Family Part. An action pending in a municipal court may be transferred to the Superior Court, Chancery Division, Family Part pursuant to R. 5:1-2(c)(3) and R. 5:1-3(b)(2).

Note: Source—R.R. 8:3-2(c)(3)(iii) (second, third and sixth sentences), 8:4-2, 8:4-3, 8:4-4, 8:4-5, 8:4-6, 8:4-7, 8:4-8, 8:4-10, 8:10-4, 8:10-6(h). Paragraph (a) amended July 7, 1971 to be effective September 13, 1971; paragraph (e) amended July 14, 1972 to be effective September 5, 1972; paragraph (b) amended July 29, 1977 to be effective September 6, 1977; paragraph (g) amended July 24, 1978 to be effective September 11, 1978; paragraph (e) amended July 16, 1979 to be effective September 10, 1979; paragraph (i) adopted December 20, 1983 to be effective December 31, 1983; paragraph (h) amended November 2, 1987 to be effective January 1, 1988; new paragraph (f) added, former paragraphs (f), (g), (h), (i) redesignated as paragraphs (g), (h), (i), (j) respectively June 9, 1989 to be effective June 19, 1989.

7:4-3. Venue; On Disqualification of Judge

(a) Generally. Except as otherwise provided by law, the prosecution for an offense shall be had in the jurisdiction in which the offense was committed.

(b) On Disqualification of Judge. In the event of the disqualification or inability for any reason of a judge to hear any pending matter, and in addition to the provisions in R. 1:12-3(a), the judge may transfer the matter for trial to any municipality within the vicinage, provided that:

(1) the judge of the municipality has been designated as an acting judge of the court of origin by the Assignment Judge of the vicinage pursuant to R. 1:12-3(a); and

(2) the transferring judge has found that transfer of the matter will not substantially inconvenience any party and is with the consent of the defendant and the complainant; and

(3) upon completion of the trial the transferee court shall forthwith advise the original court of the disposition made and shall remit to it the complaint, judgment, and all records and any fines and costs collected; and

(4) upon any such transfer the original court shall retain jurisdiction and shall maintain all necessary records as though the matter had been tried in the original court which shall be responsible for effecting final disposition of the matter.

(5) the municipality of the court of origin shall bear the costs of prosecution of the matter.

Note: Source—R.R. 8:6; caption amended, paragraph (a) caption added and paragraph (b) adopted July 24, 1978 to be effective September 11, 1978; paragraph (b) amended November 1, 1985 to be effective January 2, 1986.

7:4-4. Appearances; Exclusion of Public; Opening Statement

(a) Presence of Defendant. Except as otherwise provided by R. 7:4-2(b) and 7:6-6, the defendant shall be present at every stage of the trial and at the imposition of sentence, but his voluntary absence after the trial has commenced in his presence shall not prevent continuing the trial to and including the entry of judgment. A corporation, partnership or unincorporated association shall appear by its attorney, except where pro se appearance has been allowed pursuant to R. 7:4-2(b). The defendant's presence is not, however, required at a reduction of sentence.

(b) Appearance of Prosecution. Whenever in his judgment the interests of justice so require, or upon the request of the court, the Attorney General, county prosecutor, municipal court prosecutor, or muncipal attorney, as the case may be, may appear in any court on behalf of the state, or of the municipality, and conduct the prosecution of any action, but if the Attorney General, county or municipal court prosecutor or municipal attorney does not appear, any attorney may appear on behalf of any complaining witness and prosecute the action for and on behalf of the state or the municipality.

(c) Exclusion of Public. The court, in its discretion and with the defendant's consent, may exclude from the courtroom during the trial or hearing of any matter involving domestic relations, bastardy cases, sex offenses, school truancy and parental neglect any person not directly interested in the matter being heard or tried.

(d) Opening Statement. An opening statement shall be given by the municipal court judge prior to the commencement of the court session concerning court procedures and rights of defendants. This statement shall not be a substitute for the judge advising an individual defendant of his or her rights prior to hearing.

Note: Source—R.R. 8:4-1, 8:5, 8:7-1 (first and second sentences); paragraph (a) amended July 29, 1977 to be effective September 6, 1977; paragraph (c) amended July 24, 1978 to be effective September 11, 1978; caption amended and paragraph (d) adopted November 5, 1986 to be effective January 1, 1987.

7:4-5. Record of Proceedings; Transcripts

(a) Record. When required by order of the Supreme Court, a court shall cause all proceedings to be recorded by sound recording equipment approved by the Administrative Office of the Courts. When not so required a court may at its expense cause proceedings to be recorded either by sound recording equipment or by a reporter. When sound recording equipment is used, in addition thereto, or when the proceedings are not otherwise to be recorded, at the request and expense of any party the court shall permit a record of the proceedings to be made by a certified shorthand reporter. Every sound recording and stenographic record of proceedings made pursuant to this rule shall be kept by the clerk of the court or by the reporter, as the case may be, for three years.

(b) Transcript. If the proceedings have been sound recorded, any person may order a transcript from the clerk of the court, and if proceedings have been recorded stenographically any person may order a transcript from the reporter. In either instance the charge therefore shall not exceed the transcript rates as provided by law. The person preparing a transcript shall certify to its accuracy.

(c) Supervision. The recording of proceedings and the preparation of transcripts thereof, whether by sound recording or stenographic reporters, shall be subject to the supervision and control of the Administrative Director of the Courts.

Note: Source—R.R. 8:7-5(a)(b)(c), 8:10-7. Deleted and new rule adopted July 7, 1971 to be effective September 13, 1971; paragraph (a) amended July 24, 1978 to be effective September 11, 1978.

7:4-6. Sentence and Judgment

(a) Sentence. If the defendant has been convicted or pleaded guilty to an indictable offense, the court may postpone imposition of a sentence for a period not exceeding 30 days in order to obtain a presentence investigation from the chief probation officer of the county. If the defendant has been convicted or pleaded guilty to a non-indictable offense, sentence shall be imposed immediately unless the court postpones sentencing for a period not exceeding 30 days in order to obtain a presentence report or for other good cause. Pending sentence the court may commit the defendant or continue or alter the bail. Before imposing sentence the court shall afford the defendant and his counsel an opportunity to make a statement on defendant's behalf and to present any information in mitigation of punishment. Where a sentence has been opened and vacated, the defendant shall be resentenced forthwith, except where a new trial is granted.

(b) Judgment. A judgment of conviction shall set forth the complaint, the plea, the findings, the adjudication and sentence. It shall contain the number of the section and the title or a reasonably short description of the statute or ordinance under which conviction was had, the names and addresses of the witnesses sworn and a list of exhibits produced at the trial. If the defendant is found not guilty or for any other reason is entitled to be discharged, the judgment shall be entered accordingly. The judgment shall be signed by the court and entered by the clerk. If at the time of hearing judgment is reserved, the court upon the entry of judgment of acquittal shall forthwith mail a copy thereof to the defendant by ordinary mail; otherwise, the defendant shall be notified to appear for entry of judgment and sentencing.

(c) Reasons for Sentence. The provisions of R. 3:21-4(f) shall apply to the municipal courts.

(d) Conviction of a Corporation. R. 3:21-6 is applicable in the event of a conviction of a corporation.

(e) Probation. A convicted defendant may be placed on probation in accordance with R. 3:21-7. The order of the court shall refer to the standard conditions filed with the Superior Court.

(f) Credit for Confinement Pending Sentence. R. 3:21-8 is applicable in the event a defendant has been in custody prior to the imposition of a custodial sentence.

(g) Correction or Reduction of Sentence. The provisions of R. 3:21-10 (change or reduction of sentence) shall apply to the municipal courts.

(h) Identification Following Conviction. The court may order a person convicted of a non-indictable offense to submit to the taking of fingerprints when the identity of the person is in question.

Note: Source—R.R. 8:7-8(a)(b)(c)(d), 8:7-11(a)(b). Paragraph (a) amended June 29, 1973 to be effective September 10, 1973. Paragraph (c) adopted and former paragraphs (c)(d)(e)(f) redesignated to (d)(e)(f)(g), respectively July 17, 1975 to be effective September 8, 1975; paragraph (h) adopted July 22, 1983 to be effective September 12, 1983; paragraph (e) amended July 26, 1984 to be effective September 10, 1984; paragraph (c) amended July 14, 1992 to be effective September 1, 1992.

7:4-7. New Trial

The court may, on defendant's motion, grant him a new trial if required in the interest of justice. The court may vacate the judgment if entered, take additional testimony and direct the entry of a new judgment. A motion for a new trial based on the ground of newly discovered evidence may be made only before, or within 2 years after, final judgment. A motion for a new trial based on other grounds shall be made within 10 days after the entry of judgment of conviction, or within such further time as the court fixes during the 10-day period. In no event shall this rule be construed to limit the right of a defendant to apply to the court for a new trial on the ground of fraud or lack of jurisdiction.

Note: Source—R.R. 8:7-10.

7:4-8. Plea Agreements

(a) Plea agreements shall be permitted in the municipal courts under Guidelines established by the Supreme Court.

(b) Plea agreements will be allowed only in those municipal courts where there is a municipal prosecutor and only in those cases handled by the municipal prosecutor; provided, however, that plea agreements will be allowed in any municipal court in cases handled by the Office of the Attorney General or the County Prosecutor.

(c) No plea agreement will be allowed unless the defendant is either represented by counsel or makes a knowing waiver on the record of the right to be so represented.

(d) In all plea agreement matters, before the plea is entered the prosecutor must represent to the court that the complainant and the victim, if the victim is present at the hearing, have been consulted about the agreement.

(e) Plea agreements will be allowed only in matters within the jurisdiction of the municipal court; in particular, plea agreements shall not be allowed to downgrade or dispose of indictable complaints without the consent of the County Prosecutor, which consent shall be noted on the record.

(f) When a plea agreement is reached, the terms and the factual basis that supports it shall be set forth fully on the record in open court.

(g) The Court shall not accept a plea agreement involving sentence recommendations that circumvent minimum sentences imposed by law for the offense(s).

(h) If the judge determines that the interest of justice would not be served by accepting the agreement, the judge shall so state, and the defendant shall be informed of the right to withdraw the plea.

Note: Adopted June 29, 1990, to be effective immediately.

GUIDELINES FOR OPERATION OF PLEA AGREEMENTS IN THE MUNICIPAL COURTS OF NEW JERSEY

GUIDELINE 1. Purpose. The purpose of these Guidelines is to allow for flexibility in the definitions and exclusions relating to the plea agreement process as that process evolves and certain offenses come to demand lesser or greater scrutiny.

GUIDELINE 2. Definitions. For the purpose of these Guidelines, a plea agreement occurs in a municipal court matter whenever the prosecutor and the defense agree as to the offense or offenses to which a defendant will plead guilty on condition that any or all of the following occur:

(a) the prosecutor will recommend to the court that another offense or offenses be dismissed,

(b) the prosecutor will recommend to the court that it accept a plea to a lesser or other offense (whether included or not) than that originally charged,

(c) the prosecutor will recommend a sentence(s), not to exceed the maximum permitted, to the court or remain silent at sentencing.

GUIDELINE 3. Prosecutor's Responsibilities. Nothing in these Guidelines should be construed to affect in any way the prosecutor's discretion in any case to move unilaterally for an amendment to the original charge or a dismissal of the charges pending against a defendant if the prosecutor determines and represents on the record the reasons in support of the motion.

GUIDELINE 4. Limitation. No plea agreements whatsoever will be allowed in drunken driving or certain drug offenses. Those offenses are:

A. Driving while under the influence of liquor or drugs (N.J.S.A. 39:4-50) and refusal to provide a breath sample (N.J.S.A. 39:4-50.2) and,

B. Possession of marijuana or hashish (N.J.S.A. 2C:35-10a(4)); being under the influence of a controlled dangerous substance or its analog (N.J.S.A. 2C:35-10b); and use, possession or intent to use or possess drug paraphernalia, etc. (N.J.S.A. 2C:36-2).

The municipal court may, for certain other offenses subject to minimum mandatory penalties, refuse to accept a plea ageement unless the municipal prosecutor represents that the possibility of conviction is so remote that the interests of justice require the acceptance of a plea to a lesser offense.

RULE 7:5. BAIL

7:5-1. Applicability of Superior Court Rules

Except as otherwise provided by R. 7:5-2 and 7:5-3, the provisions of R. 3:26-1(a) (bail before conviction), 3:26-2 (authority to admit to bail), 3:26-3 (bail for witness), 3:26-4 (deposit of bail), 3:26-5 (justification of sureties), 3:26-6 (forfeiture), and 3:26-7 (exoneration) apply to the municipal courts.

Note: Source—R.R. 8:9-1(a)(b), 8:9-3, 8:9-4 (first four sentences), 8:9-5, 8:9-6(a)(b)(c)(d), 8:9-7, 8:9-8; amended July 26, 1984 to be effective September 10, 1984.

7:5-2. Place of Deposit

Bail given in the municipal court shall be deposited with the clerk of the court. If the defendant is subsequently held for the action of the grand jury or waives a probable cause hearing or the complaint is referred to the county prosecutor, the clerk of the municipal court shall forward the bail to the clerk of the county in which the offense was committed. If the offense is subsequently downgraded and remanded, the county prosecutor shall forthwith so advise the county clerk who shall thereupon return the bail to the municipal court where the offense will be tried. At the surety's discretion bail may also be deposited with the person in charge of the place of confinement where the defendant is then in custody and such custodian shall then transmit the bail to the appropriate court clerk as is herein provided.

Note: Source—R.R. 8:9-4 (fifth and sixth sentences); amended July 17, 1975 to be effective September 8, 1975; amended July 24, 1978 to be effective September 11, 1978.

7:5-3. Authority to Admit to Bail

In any case in which the municipal court judge has fixed the amount of bail, he may designate the taking of the recognizance by the clerk or any other person authorized by law to take recognizances, other than the arresting officer. In the absence of the judge, a person arrested and charged with a nonindictable offense which may be tried by the judge, may, before his appearance before him, be admitted to bail by the clerk of the court; and in the absence of the judge and the clerk, may be admitted to bail by any other person authorized by law to admit persons to bail other than the arresting officer, designated for such purpose by the judge.

Note: Source—R.R. 8:9-2(a)(b).

7:5-4. Bail After Conviction

When a sentence has been imposed and an appeal from the judgment of conviction has been taken, the trial judge shall admit the appellant to bail for a period not exceeding 10 days during which time the appellant shall enter into a recognizance with sufficient surety conditioned for his appearance before the court to which the appeal has been taken and to abide the judgment thereof. Thereupon the trial court shall forthwith discharge him from custody. The recognizance shall be subject to the approval of the court to which the appeal is taken. If a recognizance is not submitted within the said 10 days or if submitted but is not approved, then in the court's discretion bail may be revoked. The judge or his clerk shall transmit to the county clerk any cash deposit and any recognizance so taken.

Note: Source—R.R. 8:9-9, 8:9-10.

RULE 7:6. TRAFFIC OFFENSES

7:6-1. Complaint and Summons

(a) Form. In cases involving violations of statutes or ordinances relating to the operation or use of motor vehicles, hereinafter designated as "traffic offenses", the complaint and summons shall be a uniform traffic ticket in the form prescribed by the Administrative Director of the Courts. On a complaint and summons for a non-moving traffic offense, in lieu of the name of the defendant it shall be sufficient to set forth the license number of the vehicle involved, and it shall be presumed that the owner of the vehicle is the defendant charged with the violation.

(b) Issuance. The complaint may be made and signed by a law enforcement officer, or by any other person, but the summons shall be signed and issued only by such officer, or the judge, clerk or deputy clerk of the court in which the complaint is, or is to be filed. R. 7:3 relating to warrants and summons in respect of nonindictable offenses generally, shall be applicable to cases involving a traffic offense, except as otherwise herein provided.

(c) Records and Reports. Each court shall be responsible for all uniform traffic tickets printed and distributed to law enforcement officers or others in his municipality, and for their proper disposition, and shall prepare or cause to be prepared such records and reports relating to such uniform traffic tickets as the Administrative Director of the Courts prescribes. The provisions of this paragraph shall also apply to the Director of the Division of Motor Vehicles and the Superintendent of State Police, in the Department of Law and Public Safety and to the responsible official of any other agency authorized by the Administrative Director of the Courts to print and distribute the uniform traffic ticket to its law enforcement personnel.

Note: Source—R.R. 8:10-1(a)(b)(c). Paragraph (c) amended July 26, 1984 to be effective September 10, 1984.

7:6-2. Improper Disposition of Traffic Ticket; Contempt of Court

The aid by any person in the disposition of a traffic ticket or summons in any manner other than that authorized by the court may constitute a contempt.

Note: Source—R.R. 8:10-2.

7:6-3. Procedure on Failure to Appear

(a) Residents—Parking Cases. If a defendant residing in this State fails to appear or answer a traffic summons for a parking offense, the court shall mail a notice to him on a form approved by the Administrative Director of the Courts. If the defendant fails to comply with the provisions of the notice, a warrant may be issued except if the notice is returned to the court by the post office marked to indicate that the defendant cannot be located. If the warrant is not executed within 30 days after issue or the notice is returned to the court by the post office, the court shall then mark the case as closed on its records. If bail has been posted and the defendant fails to appear or answer within 30 days after it was posted or on the date specified by the court, the court shall declare a forfeiture of the bail and the court shall mark the case as closed on its records. A copy of the notice and any envelope returned by the post office and a copy of any warrant issued shall be filed with the complaint. A case marked closed may be reopened and a bail forfeiture may be set aside if it appears that justice so requires.

(b) Residents—Non-Parking Cases. If a defendant residing in this State fails to appear or answer a traffic summons for a non-parking traffic offense, the court shall either issue a warrant for his arrest or mail a notice to him on a form approved by the Administrative Director of the Courts. If a notice is mailed to the defendant and he fails to comply with its provisions, a warrant shall be issued. If the warrant is not executed within 30 days after issue and no bail has been posted, the court shall promptly report the failure to appear or answer to the Division of Motor Vehicles on a form approved by the Administrative Director of the Courts and mark the case as closed on its records but if bail has been posted, the court shall declare a forfeiture of the bail and report the forfeiture to the Division of Motor Vehicles in accordance with the provisions of R.S. 39:5-42. A case marked closed may be reopened and a bail forfeiture may be set aside if it appears that justice so requires.

(c) Non-Residents—All Traffic Cases. If a defendant residing outside this State fails to appear or answer a traffic summons within 30 days of the return date of such summons and no bail has been posted, the court shall mail a notice to the defendant on a form approved by the Administrative Director of the Courts and file a copy with the complaint provided, however, that the mailing of such notice in parking cases shall be discretionary with the court. If the defendant fails to appear or otherwise answer within 30 days of the mailing of the notice in a non-parking traffic case, the court shall promptly mail a copy of the notice to the Division of Motor Vehicles and mark the case as closed on its records. If the defendant fails to comply with the provisions of the notice in a parking case or if no notice is mailed in such case within 60 days of the return date of the summons, the court shall mark the case as closed on its records. If a non-resident defendant fails to appear or answer a traffic summons within 30 days of the return date thereof, and he has posted bail, the court shall declare a forfeiture of the bail and in a parking case mark the case as closed on its records and in a non-parking traffic case report the forfeiture to the Division of Motor Vehicles in accordance with the provisions of R.S. 39:5-42. A case marked closed may be reopened and a bail forfeiture may be set aside if it appears that justice so requires.

Note: Source—R.R. 8:10-3(a)(b). Paragraph (a) amended November 5, 1986 to be effective January 1, 1987.

7:6-4. Trial Date; Adjournment

The date fixed for the trial of any traffic offense shall be at least 5 days from the date of its commission unless the defendant, having been informed of his right to such trial date, waives it and the court in its discretion fixes an earlier date. If a hearing is adjourned, the court may detain the defendant in safe custody unless he makes a cash deposit or gives a recognizance in accordance with R. 7:5 in an amount not exceeding $500, or himself qualifies and justifies in real estate security situated in this State in twice the amount fixed for the bail.

Note: Source—R.R. 8:10-5, 8:10-6(g).

7:6-5. Calendar Parts; Sessions

Insofar as practicable, traffic offenses shall be tried separate and apart from other offenses. If a court sits in part and one part sitting in daily session has been designated as a traffic court, traffic offenses shall be tried in such part only, or if a court has designated a particular session (which may be an evening session) as the traffic session, traffic offenses shall be tried only in such session, except for good cause shown. Otherwise the court shall designate the time for the trial of traffic offenses. The Administrative Division of the Courts may, where necessary, direct a court to hold more frequent traffic sessions, or to coordinate sessions held by him with those regularly scheduled by other municipal court judges in the county.

Note: Source—R.R. 8:10-6(a)(b)(c)(d)(f).

228/Municipal Court

7:6-6. Statement in Mitigation or Defense by Affidavit; Judgment

(a) Statement in Mitigation or Defense by Affidavit. In all traffic cases except those involving indictable offenses; accidents resulting in personal injury; operation of a motor vehicle while under the influence of intoxicating liquor or a narcotic or habit-producing drug or permitting another person who is under such influence to operate a motor vehicle owned by the defendant or in his custody or control; reckless driving; or leaving the scene of an accident, the court may permit the defendant to present his statement in defense or mitigation of penalty imposed upon conviction or enter a guilty plea by affidavit if the court determines that it would be an undue hardship on the defendant to require him to appear in person at the time and place set for trial; and the defendant, having been fully informed of his right to a reasonable postponement of the trial, waives in writing his right to be present at the trial.

(b) Judgment. If a defendant presents his statement in mitigation or defense by affidavit, the court shall send him a copy of the judgment by ordinary mail.

Note: Source—R.R. 8:10-8(a)(b). Paragraph (b) amended June 29, 1973 to be effective September 10, 1973. Paragraph (a) amended July 17, 1975 to be effective September 8, 1975; paragraph (a) amended July 29 to be effective September 6, 1977; paragraph (a) amended November 2, 1987 to be effective January 1, 1988.

7:6-7. Notice to Defendant on Guilty Plea

Before accepting a plea of guilty to a traffic offense other than a parking offense, the court shall inform the defendant that a record of the conviction will be sent to the Director of the Division of Motor Vehicles of this State or the Commissioner of Motor Vehicles of the state where defendant received his license to drive, to become a part of his driving record.

Note: Source—R.R. 8:10-9(a).

RULE 7:7. VIOLATIONS BUREAU

7:7-1. Designation; Functions

If the court determines that the efficient disposition of its business and the convenience of defendants so requires, it may establish a violations bureau and designate as the violations clerk the clerk or deputy clerk of the court or, with the prior approval of the Supreme Court pursuant to R. 1:17-1 any other appropriate official or employee (except an elected official or officer or employee of a police department) of the municipality in which the court is held, or if none is available, any other suitable and responsible person. The judge designated to preside over the Special Civil Part of the Superior Court may designate the clerk, deputy clerk or other employee of the court as violations clerk. The violations clerk shall accept appearances, waiver of trial, pleas of guilty and payments of fine and costs in non-indictable offenses, subject to the limitations hereinafter prescribed. The violations clerk shall serve under the direction and control of the court designating him.

Note: Source—R.R. 8:10-10(a). Amended November 7, 1988 to be effective January 2, 1989.

7:7-2. Location

Whenever practical the violations bureau shall be in a public building. The location shall be designated by the court subject to the approval of the Administrative Director of the Courts and the violations clerk shall take pleas and accept payment of fines and costs only at such location. An appropriate sign reading "Violations Bureau, _____ Municipal Court" shall be posted at the entrance to the violations bureau.

Note: Source—R.R. 8:10-10(e).

7:7-3. Designated Offenses; Schedule of Penalties

The court shall by order, which may from time to time be amended, supplemented or repealed, designate the non-indictable offenses within the authority of the violations clerk, provided that such offenses shall not include:

(1) non-parking traffic offenses requiring an increased penalty for a subsequent violation;

(2) offenses involving traffic accidents resulting in personal injury;

(3) operation of a motor vehicle while under the influence of intoxicating liquor or a narcotic or habit-producing drug or permitting another person who is under such influence to operate a motor vehicle owned by the defendant or in his custody or control;

(4) reckless driving;

(5) careless driving where there has been an accident resulting in personal injury;

(6) leaving the scene of an accident;

(7) driving while on the revoked list;

(8) driving without being licensed.

The court by published order, which shall be submitted to and approved by the Assignment Judge of the county in which the court is located, shall specify the amount of fines and costs to be imposed for each offense within the authority of the violations clerk, including, in the discretion of the court higher fines and costs for second and subsequent offenses, provided such fines and costs are within the limits declared by statute or ordinance. A schedule of such penalties shall be posted for public view at the violations bureau.

Note: Source—R.R. 8:10-10(b), 8:10A. Amended July 7, 1971 to be effective September 13, 1971. Subparagraphs (3) and (4) amended and new subparagraph (5) added July 29, 1977 to be effective September 6, 1977; subparagraphs (2), (5) and (8) amended and subparagraph (9) deleted July 22, 1983 to be effective September 12, 1983.

7:7-4. Plea and Payment of Fine and Costs

A person charged with an offense within the authority of the violations clerk may, upon signing the plea of guilty and waiver of trial on the back of the summons and upon ascertaining the fine and costs established for the offense charged, pay the same, either by mail or in person, to the violations clerk on or before the return date of the summons, provided that when the summons is marked to indicate that a court appearance is required, payment may not be made to the violations clerk even though the offense is on the schedule of penalties. If the defendant is a corporation, partnership or unincorporated association, the plea and waiver may be signed on its behalf by any of its agents or employees. The court in its discretion may authorize the violations clerk to accept such plea and payment after the return date of the summons.

Note: Source—R.R. 8:3-2(c)(3)(iii) (third sentence, second clause), 8:10-10(c).

RULE 7:8. APPEALS

7:8-1. Appeals

Appeals from judgments of conviction shall be taken in accordance with Rules 3:23 and 3:24, and in extraordinary cases and in the interests of justice, in accordance with R. 2:2-3(b). Appeals from judgments of conviction and interlocutory orders in municipal court actions heard in the Law Division, Special Civil Part pursuant to R. 6:1-2(a)(5) shall be taken to the Appellate Division pursuant to Rules 2:2-3(a)(1) and 2:2-4, respectively.

Note: Source—R.R. 8:11-1. Amended July 14, 1992 to be effective September 1, 1992.

7:8-2. Stay

A sentence to pay a fine, a fine and costs, a forfeiture, an order for probation, or a revocation of the license to operate a motor vehicle may be stayed by the court in which the conviction was had or to which the appeal is taken upon such terms as the court deems proper.

Note: Source—R.R. 8:11-2.

7:8-3. Reversal; Remission of Fine and Costs

A fine or a fine and costs paid pursuant to a judgment of conviction and disbursed by the court in accordance with R. 7:10-4(a) shall be remitted by the recipient thereof to the defendant or his attorney upon the service upon the recipient of a copy of the order of reversing the judgment.

Note: Source—R.R. 8:11-3.

RULE 7:9. MUNICIPAL COURTS: STATUTORY PENALTY PROCEEDINGS

The provisions of R. 4:70 govern the practice and procedure in the municipal court in summary proceedings for enforcement of statutory penalties and for confiscation or forfeiture of chattels.

Note: Source—R.R. 7:18-1, 7:18-2, 7:18-3, 7:18-4. Amended June 29, 1973 to be effective September 10, 1973; caption and text amended November 2, 1987 to be effective January 1, 1988.

RULE 7:10. GENERAL PROVISIONS; ADMINISTRATION

7:10-1. Local Rules

Any judge of a municipal court may, with the approval of the Administrative Director of the Courts, make rules for the orderly conduct of the proceedings of his court, not inconsistent with these rules.

Note: Source—R.R. 8:12-2.

7:10-2. Amendment of Process or Pleading

The court may amend any process or pleading for any omission or defect therein, or for any variance between the complaint and the evidence adduced at the trial but no such amendment shall be permitted which charges a different substantive offense (other than a lesser included offense). If the defendant is surprised as a result of such amendment, the court shall adjourn the hearing to some future day, upon appropriate terms.

Note: Source—R.R. 8:12-3.

7:10-3. Court Calendar; Attorneys

(a) Calendar. The court calendar shall follow as closely as possible, the following order: (1) applications for adjournment; (2) unlitigated motions; (3) arraignments; (4) guilty pleas; (5) litigated motions; (6) contested matters with an attorney; (7) other contested matters.

(b) Appearances of Attorneys. Appearances by attorneys shall be entered promptly with the court or clerk. Unless the appearance is entered, the attorney shall not receive priority on the trial list.

Note: Source—R.R. 8:13-8(a)(b).

7:10-4. Financial Control

(a) Fines and Forfeitures. Moneys received by a court as fines or forfeitures, together with the financial reports covering such funds, shall be forwarded by the court on or before the tenth day of each month as follows:

(1) To the custodian of the funds of the municipality where such moneys were received in the course of enforcing municipal ordinances or local regulations, if assessed and collected by the municipal court, or to the custodian of the funds of the municipality in which the violation occurred, if assessed and collected by a county district court.

(2) To the custodian of the funds of the municipality or of the county, or to such state agency or officer, as the case may be, where the moneys were collected in the course of enforcing state laws and regulations, as provided by law.

(b) Receipts and Disbursements. The court shall keep an accurate account of all fees, costs and moneys received, as well as of any moneys disbursed and to whom disbursed. Receipts shall be turned over to the appropriate municipal, county or state finance officer, or deposited as soon after receipt as practical, in a bank or banks authorized to do business in this State. No disbursement shall be made except by check drawn on such bank. The court shall issue or cause to be issued and shall obtain a receipt in the form and manner prescribed by the Administrative Director of the Courts in every instance where money is received or disbursed.

(c) Payment of Moneys Due. No moneys due the court, its employees, or any persons attending upon it, for salaries, fees, costs or other charges shall be deducted from receipts but shall be paid only on a voucher submitted by the court to the appropriate finance officer.

(d) Docket; Fiscal Forms and Procedures; Record-Keeping. The court shall maintain such separate dockets in such form as the Administrative Director of the Courts prescribes. All fiscal forms, procedures and record-keeping shall conform to the requirements of the Administrative Director of the Courts.

Note: Source—R.R. 8:13-9(a)(b)(c)(d), 8:13-10(a), paragraph (a) amended July 21, 1978 to be effective immediately.

7:10-5. Oath of Municipal Court Judge

The oath of office of a municipal court judge before entering upon the duties of his office shall be taken before a judge of the Superior Court. The original shall be filed with the clerk of the municipal court and a copy thereof filed with the Administrative Director of the Courts.

Note: Source—R.R. 8:13-3 (first sentence). Amended July 26, 1984 to be effective September 10, 1984.

Part I
RULES OF GENERAL APPLICATION

1:40-7. Mediation of Minor Disputes in Municipal Court Actions

(a) Referral. A mediation notice may issue pursuant to R. 7:3-2 requiring the parties to appear at a mediation session to determine whether mediation pursuant to these rules and guidelines is an appropriate method for resolving the minor dispute. No referral to mediation shall be made if the complaint involves (1) serious injury, (2) repeated acts of violence between the parties, (3) clearly demonstrated psychological or emotional disability of a party, (4) incidents involving the same persons who are already parties to a Superior Court action between them, or (5) matters arising under the Domestic Violence Act.

(b) Term of Service. A municipal court mediator shall be accorded a specific term by the Assignment Judge not to exceed two years, subject to reappointment. The Assignment

Judge may, sua sponte or on request of the municipal court judge, remove a mediator upon the determination that the individual is unable properly to perform the mediator's functions.

Note: Adopted July 14, 1992 to be effective September 1, 1992.

Part III
RULES GOVERNING CRIMINAL PRACTICE

3:1-6. Trial of Non-Indictables in Superior Court

(a) Generally. Proceedings involving charges constituting disorderly persons offense or a petty disorderly persons offense shall be heard in Superior Court when they are brought pursuant to N.J.S. 2C:34-2b, N.J.S. 2C:37-8, or as otherwise required by law, and shall be governed by the rules in Part III insofar as applicable.

(b) Transfer From the Municipal Court to the Superior Court, Chancery Division, Family Part. An offense or violation pending in municipal court may be transferred for trial and disposition to the Chancery Division, Family Part pursuant to R. 5:1-3.

Note: Source—Adopted August 28, 1979 to be effective September 1, 1979. Formerly designated as R. 3:1-5(a), redesignated and new paragraph (b) added December 20, 1983, to be effective December 31, 1983.

RULE 3:2. COMPLAINT: CONTENTS, SERVICE

The complaint shall be a written statement of the essential facts constituting the offense charged made upon oath before a judge or other person empowered by law to take complaints. Whenever practicable a copy thereof shall be served on the defendant at the time of service of the summons or execution of the warrant. The clerk or deputy clerk shall accept for filing any complaint made by any person.

Note: Source—R.R. 3:2-1(a)(b); amended July 26, 1984 to be effective September 10, 1984.

RULE 3:3. SUMMONS OR WARRANT UPON COMPLAINT

3:3-1. Issuance

(a) Summons or Warrant. A summons or arrest warrant shall be issued by a judge of a court having jurisdiction in the municipality in which the offense is alleged to have been committed or in which the defendant may be found, or by the clerk or a deputy clerk of that court, only if it appears to such judge, clerk or deputy clerk from the complaint, or from an affidavit or deposition taken under oath, that there is probable cause to believe that an offense has been committed and that the defendant has committed it. A summons may issue instead of a warrant, as provided in subsection (b), or if the defendant is a corporation. A warrant may issue to any officer authorized by law to execute it. Instead of detaining a person arrested without a warrant, the officer may give such person a summons as provided in Rule 3:4-1(b).

(b) Guidance on Issuance. Whenever application for a warrant or summons is made before a judge or clerk authorized to issue a warrant, either under this Rule upon the filing of a complaint or an indictment, or pursuant to R. 3:4-1 after an arrest without warrant, a summons shall issue rather than a warrant unless the judge or clerk finds that any of the following conditions exists:

(1) The accused is charged with murder, kidnapping, aggravated manslaughter, manslaughter, robbery, aggravated sexual assault, sexual assault, aggravated criminal sexual contact, criminal sexual contact, aggravated assault, aggravated arson, arson, burglary, violations of Chapter 35 of Title 2C that constitute first or second degree crimes, any crime involving the possession or use of a firearm, or conspiracies or attempts to commit such crimes;

(2) The accused has previously failed to respond to a summons;

(3) The judge or clerk has reason to believe that the accused is dangerous to himself, to others or to property;

(4) There are one or more outstanding arrest warrants for the accused;

(5) The whereabouts of the accused are unknown and an arrest warrant is necessary to subject him to the jurisdiction of the court; or

(6) The judge or clerk has reason to believe that the accused will not appear in response to a summons.

(c) Failure of Defendant to Appear After Summons. If a defendant who has been duly summoned fails to appear, or if there is reasonable cause to believe that he will fail to appear, an arrest warrant shall issue. If a defendant corporation fails to appear after having been duly summoned, a plea of not guilty shall be entered by the court if it is empowered to try the offense for which the summons was issued, and it may proceed to trial and judgment without further process; if the court is not so empowered it shall proceed as though the defendant had appeared.

(d) Additional Warrants or Summonses. More than one warrant or summons may issue on the same complaint.

(e) Identification Procedures Upon Issuance of Summons. In cases where a summons has issued in the lieu of warrant pursuant to this rule, the defendant shall undergo all post arrest identification procedures, which are required by law upon an arrest, on the return date of the summons. In the event that the defendant does not appear on the return date or refuses to submit to the post arrest identification procedures, the court may on its own, or at the request of the prosecutor, order the issuance of an arrest warrant.

(f) Procedure When No Warrant or Summons is Issued. When pursuant to subsection (a) of this rule, neither a warrant nor summons is issued on complaint, the judge shall, after notice to the defendant, complainant, and appropriate prosecuting agency, determine whether there is probable cause for the issuance of a summons or warrant. If no such probable cause is found, the complaint shall be dismissed.

Note: Source—R.R. 3:2-2(a)(1)(2)(3) and (4); paragraph (a) amended, new paragraph (b) adopted and former paragraphs (b) and (c) redesignated as (c) and (d) respectively July 21, 1980 to be effective September 8, 1980; paragraph (b) amended and paragraph (e) adopted July 16, 1981 to be effective September 14, 1981; paragraph (b) amended July 22, 1983 to be effective September 12, 1983; caption and paragraph (a) amended and paragraph (f) adopted July 26, 1984 to be effective September 10, 1984; paragraph (b) amended January 5, 1988 to be effective February 1, 1988.

3:3-2. Form and Contents of Warrants and Summons

The warrant or summons shall be signed by the committing judge or issued in his name and signed by the court clerk or deputy court clerk and shall describe the offense charged in the complaint. The warrant shall also contain the defendant's name, or if his name is unknown, any name or description which identifies him with reasonable certainty, and shall be directed to any officer authorized by law to execute the same, commanding that the defendant be arrested and brought before the court issuing the warrant. The summons shall be directed to the defendant named in the complaint, requiring him to appear before the court in which the complaint is made at the time and place stated therein and informing him that a warrant for his arrest will issue upon his failure to so appear.

Note: Source—R.R. 3:2-2(b).

3:3-3. Execution or Service; Return

(a) By Whom. The warrant shall be executed and the summons served by any officer authorized by law.

(b) Territorial Limits. The warrant may be executed and the summons served at any place within this State. An officer arresting a defendant in a county other than the one in which the warrant was issued shall take him, without unecessary delay, before the nearest available committing judge authorized to admit to bail in accordance with R.3:26-2, who may admit to bail conditioned on the defendant's appearance before the court issuing the warrant. Nothing in this rule shall affect the provisions of N.J.S. 2A:156-1 to 2A:156-4 (Uniform Act on Intrastate Fresh Pursuit).

(c) Execution of Warrant. The warrant shall be executed by the arrest of the defendant. The officer need not have the warrant in his possession at the time of the arrest, but upon request he shall show the warrant to the defendant as soon as possible. If the officer does not have the warrant in his possession at the time of the arrest, he shall inform the defendant of the offense charged and of the fact that a warrant has been issued.

(d) Service of Summons. The summons shall be served in accordance with R.4:4-4.

(e) Return. The officer executing a warrant shall make prompt return thereof to the court which issued the warrant. The officer serving a summons shall make return thereof to the court before whom the summons is returnable on or before the return day.

Note: Source—R.R. 3:2-2(c).

3:3-4. Defective Warrant or Summons

(a) Amendment. No person arrested under a warrant or appearing in response to a summons shall be discharged from custody or dismissed because of any technical insufficiency or irregularity in the warrant or summons, but the warrant or summons may be amended to remedy any such technical defect.

(b) Issuance of New Warrant or Summons. If prior to or during the hearing as to probable cause, it appears that the warrant executed or summons issued does not properly name or describe the defendant, or the offense with which he is charged, or that although not guilty of the offense specified in the warrant or summons there is reasonable ground to believe that he is guilty of some other offense, the court shall not discharge or dismiss the defendant but shall forthwith cause a new complaint to be filed and thereupon issue a new warrant or summons.

Note: Source—R.R. 3:2-2(d).

RULE 3:4. PROCEEDINGS BEFORE THE COMMITTING JUDGE; PRETRIAL RELEASE

3:4-1. Procedure After Arrest

(a) A person arrested under a warrant issued upon a complaint shall be taken, without unnecessary delay, before the court named in the warrant. A person arrested without a warrant for any offense shall be taken, without unnecessary delay, before the nearest available committing judge if the person demands to be taken before a judge.

(b) Whenever a law enforcement officer has effected an arrest without a warrant for murder, kidnapping, aggravated manslaughter, manslaughter, robbery, aggravated sexual assault, sexual assault, aggravated criminal sexual contact, criminal sexual contact, aggravated assault, aggravated arson, arson, burglary, violations of Chapter 35 of Title 2C that constitute first or second degree crimes, any crime involving the possession or use of a firearm, or conspiracies or attempts to commit such crimes, the arrested person shall be taken to the police station where a complaint-warrant shall be prepared forthwith. After the complaint-warrant is prepared, the person arrested shall be taken without unnecessary delay before the nearest available committing judge. If there is probable cause to believe that one of said crimes has been committed by the arrested person, the warrant shall be issued by the judge, court clerk or deputy clerk. The judge shall have the authority to issue a complaint-summons if the judge determines that the defendant will appear in response to a summons. The judge before whom the arrested person is taken shall advise such person of that person's rights in accordance with R. 3:4-2.

(c) Whenever a law enforcement officer has effected an arrest without a warrant for an offense other than an offense enumerated in paragraph (b) hereof, the arrested person shall be taken to a police station where the officer in charge shall, after completion of all post-arrest identification procedures required by law, prepare a complaint-summons, issue it to the person arrested and release that person in lieu of continued detention. However, the officer has the discretion not to prepare a complaint-summons if the officer determines that any of the conditions set forth in paragraph (d) exist. If the officer determines not to prepare a complaint summons, a complaint-warrant shall be prepared forthwith and the person arrested shall be taken without unnecessary delay before the nearest available committing judge. If there is probable cause to believe that the defendant committed the offense, the judge, court clerk, or deputy clerk shall issue the complaint-warrant unless it is determined that none of the conditions set forth in paragraph (d) hereof exist in which case a complaint-summons shall be prepared, issued, and the person arrested shall be released. The judge before whom the arrested person is taken shall advise such person of that person's rights in accordance with R. 3:4-2.

(d) An officer shall have the discretion not to issue a complaint-summons when any of the following conditions exists:

(1) The person has previously failed to respond to a summons;

(2) The officer has reason to believe that the person is dangerous to himself, to others or to property;

(3) There is one or more outstanding arrest warrants for the person;

(4) The prosecution of the offense or offenses for which the person is arrested or the prosecution of any other offense or offenses would be jeopardized by immediate release of the person;

(5) The person cannot provide satisfactory evidence of personal identification; or

(6) The officer has reason to believe the person will not appear in response to a summons.

Note: Source—R.R. 3:2-3(a), 8:3-3(a). Amended July 7, 1971 to be effective September 13, 1971; caption amended, former rule redesignated as paragraph (a) and paragraphs (b) and (c) adopted July 21, 1980 to be effective September 8, 1980; paragraph (b) amended July 16, 1981 to be effective September 14, 1981; paragraphs (a) and (b) amended, new paragraph (c) adopted and former paragraph (c) redesignated paragraph (d) and paragraph (d)(7) deleted November 5, 1986 to be effective January 1, 1987; paragraphs (b) and (c) amended April 10, 1987 to be effective immediately; paragraph (b) amended January 5, 1988 to be effective February 1, 1988.

3:4-2. Procedure After Filing of Complaint

At a defendant's first appearance before the court following the filing of a complaint, the judge thereof shall inform the defendant of the charge made against him and if a copy of the complaint has not previously been furnished to the defendant, shall furnish him with a copy thereof. The judge shall also inform the defendant of his right not to make a statement as to the charge against him and that any statement made by him may be used against him. In counties where a pretrial intervention program is approved by the Supreme Court for operation under R. 3:28, the judge shall also inform the defendant of the existence of such program, the name of the program director and the location at which application may be made for enrollment in such program. The judge shall also inform the defendant of his right to retain counsel or, if indigent and constitutionally or otherwise entitled by law to counsel, of his right to have counsel furnished without cost. If the defendant asserts he is indigent, unless he affirmatively and with understanding of his waiver of his right states his intention to proceed without counsel, the judge shall have him complete the appropriate form as prescribed by the Administrative Director of the Courts, if such form has not yet been completed. If the complaint charges the defendant with an indictable offense, the court shall refer him to the Office of the Public Defender. If the complaint charges the defendant with a nonindictable offense and the court is satisfied that he is indigent and that he is constitutionally or otherwise entitled by law to have counsel furnished, the court shall assign counsel to represent him in accordance with R. 3:27-2. The court shall allow the defendant a reasonable time and opportunity to consult counsel before proceeding further. If the complaint charges the defendant with an indictable offense, the court shall inform him of his right to have a hearing as to probable cause and of his right to indictment by the grand jury and trial by jury, and if the offense charged may be tried by the court upon waiver of indictment and trial by jury, the court shall so inform the defendant. All such waivers shall be in writing, signed by the defendant, and shall be filed and entered on the docket. If the complaint charges an indictable offense which cannot be tried by the court on waiver, it shall not ask for or accept a plea to the offense. The court shall admit the defendant to bail as provided in R. 3:26 and R. 7:5.

Note: Source—R.R. 3:2-3(b), 8:4-2 (second sentence). Amended July 7, 1971 effective September 13, 1971; amended April 1, 1974 effective immediately.

3:4-3. Hearing as to Probable Cause on Indictable Offenses

(a) If the defendant does not waive indictment and trial by jury but does waive a hearing as to probable cause, the court shall forthwith bind him over to await final determination of the cause. If the defendant does not waive a hearing as to probable cause and if before the hearing an indictment has not been returned against the defendant with respect to the offense charged after notice to the county prosecutor the court shall hear the evidence offered by the State within a reasonable time and the defendant may cross-examine witnesses against him. If, from the evidence, it appears to the court that there is probable cause to believe that an offense has been committed and the defendant has committed it, the court shall forthwith bind him over to await final determination of the cause; otherwise, the court shall discharge him from custody if he is detained. Notice to the county prosecutor may be oral or in writing. An entry shall be made on the docket as to when and how such notice was given. A probable cause hearing shall be prosecuted by the municipal prosecutor in the absence of a county prosecutor.

(b) After concluding the proceeding the court shall transmit, forthwith, to the county prosecutor all papers in the cause. Whether or not the court finds probable cause, it shall continue in effect any bail previously posted in accordance with R. 3:26 or any other condition of pretrial release not involving restraints on liberty; and any bail taken by the court shall be transmitted to the county clerk. If the defendant is discharged for lack of probable cause and an indictment is not returned within 120 days, the bail shall thereafter be returned and conditions of pretrial release, if any, terminated.

Note: Source—R.R. 3:2-3(c). Paragraph designations added and paragraphs (a) and (b) amended July 16, 1979 to be effective September 10, 1979.

3:4-4. Proceedings in Arrest Under Uniform Fresh Pursuit Law

If an arrest is made in this State by an officer of another state in accordance with the provisions of N.J.S. 2A:155-1 to N.J.S. 2A:155-7, inclusive (Uniform Law on Fresh Pursuit), he shall take the arrested person, without unnecessary delay, before the nearest available committing judge who shall conduct a hearing for the purpose of determining the lawfulness of the arrest. If he determines that the arrest was lawful, he shall commit the person to await, for a reasonable time, the issuance of an extradition warrant by the Governor of this State, or admit him to bail for such purpose. If the court determines that the arrest was unlawful it shall discharge the person arrested.

Note: Source—R.R. 3:2-3(d), 8:3-3(d).

3:4-5. Effect of Technical Insufficiency or Irregularity in the Proceedings

A defendant held in custody under a commitment after a hearing as to probable cause shall not be discharged nor shall such hearing be deemed invalid because of any technical insufficiency or irregularity in the commitment or prior proceedings not prejudicial to the defendant, or because the offense for which the defendant is held to answer is other than that stated in the complaint or arrest warrant.

Note: Source—R.R. 3:2-3(e), 8:3-3(e).

RULE 3:5. SEARCH WARRANTS

3:5-1. Authority to Issue

A search warrant may be issued by a judge of a court having jurisdiction in the municipality where the property sought is located.

Note: Source—R.R. 3:2A-1.

3:5-2. Grounds for Issuance

A search warrant may be issued to search for and seize any property, including documents, books, papers and any other tangible objects, obtained in violation of the penal laws of this State or any other state; or possessed, controlled, designed or intended for use or which has been used in connection with any such violation; or constituting evidence of or tending to show any such violation.

Note: Source—R.R. 3:2A-2, 3:2A-7.

RULE 3:10. PLEADINGS AND MOTIONS BEFORE TRIAL; DEFENSES AND OBJECTIONS

3:10-1. Pleadings and Motions

Pleadings in criminal actions shall consist only of the complaint, the indictment or accusation, and the plea. Any defense or objection capable of determination without trial of the general issue may be raised before trial by motion to dismiss or for other appropriate relief.

Note: Source—R.R. 3:5-5(a)(b)(1).

3:10-2. Defenses and Objections Which Must Be Raised Before Trial

The defense of double jeopardy and all other defenses and objections based on defects in the institution of the prosecution or in the indictment or accusation, except as otherwise provided by R. 3:10-3 (defenses which may be raised only before or after trial) and R. 3:10-4 (lack of jurisdiction), must be raised by motion before trial. Failure to so present any such defense constitutes a waiver thereof, but the court for good cause shown may grant relief from the waiver.

Note: Source—R.R. 3:5-5(b)(2) (second and fourth sentences).

3:10-3. Defenses and Objections Which May Only Be Raised Before or After Trial

The defense that the indictment or accusation fails to charge an offense and the defense that the charge is based on a statute or regulation promulgated pursuant to statute which is unconstitutional or invalid in whole or in part may only be raised by motion either before trial or within 10 days after a verdict of guilty or within such further time as the court may fix during such 10-day period, or on appeal. Such defenses shall not be considered during trial.

Note: Source—R.R. 3:5-5(b)(2) (first sentence).

238/Municipal Court

3:10-4. Lack of Jurisdiction

The court shall notice the defense of lack of jurisdiction in the court at any time during the pendency of the proceeding except during trial.

Note: Source—R.R. 3:5-5(b)(2)(fifth sentence).

RULE 3:13. PRETRIAL; DEPOSITIONS; DISCOVERY

3:13-1. Pretrial Procedure

(a) Pretrial Conferences. At any time after the filing of the indictment or accusation the court shall order one or more conferences to consider the results of negotiations between the parties relating to plea and other matters as will promote a fair and expeditious disposition or trial. At the conclusion of a conference the court shall prepare and file a memorandum of the matters agreed upon. A pretrial conference shall be conducted within 60 days of arraignment. No admissions made by the defendant or his attorney at the conference shall be used against the defendant unless the admissions are reduced to writing and signed by the defendant and his attorney.

(b) Pretrial Hearings. Hearings to resolve issues relating to the admissibility of statements by defendant, pretrial identifications of defendant and sound recordings may be held at any time prior to trial and, upon a showing of good cause, hearings as to admissibility of other evidence may also be so held.

Note: Source—R.R. 3:5-3(a)(b). Paragraph designations and paragraph (b) adopted July 16, 1979 to be effective September 10, 1979; paragraph (a) amended July 21, 1980 to be effective September 8, 1980; paragraph (b) amended July 15, 1982 to be effective September 13, 1982.

3:13-2. Depositions

(a) When Authorized. If it appears to the judge of the court in which a complaint, indictment or accusation is pending that a material witness is likely to be unable to testify at trial because of death or physical or mental incapacity, the court, upon motion and notice to the parties, and after a showing that such action is necessary to prevent manifest injustice, may order that a deposition of the testimony of such witness be taken and that any designated books, papers, documents or tangible objects, not privileged, be produced at the same time and place. If a witness is committed for failure to give bail to appear to testify at a trial or hearing, the court on written motion of the witness and upon notice to the parties may direct that his deposition be taken, and after the deposition has been subscribed the court may discharged the witness.

(b) Procedure. The deposition shall be videotaped unless the court orders otherwise. The deposition shall be taken before the judge at such location as will be convenient to all parties. If, because the deposition is to be taken outside of the State, the judge is unable to preside, the deposition shall be taken before a person designated by the judge to perform that function. All parties and counsel shall have a right to be present at the deposition. Examination, cross-examination and determination of admissibility of evidence, shall proceed in the same manner as at trial. Videotaping shall be done by a person independent of both prosecution and defense and chosen by the judge.

(c) Use. Depositions taken pursuant to this rule may be used at trial in lieu of live testimony of the witness in open court if the witness is unable to testify because of death or physical or mental incapability. In the case of a witness deposed to allow discharge from committment for failure to give bail as provided in paragraph (a) above, the deposition may be used, in addition, if the court finds that the party offering the deposition has been unable to procure the attendance of the witness by subpoena or otherwise. The deposition shall be admissible insofar as allowable under the Rules of Evidence applied as though the witness were then present and testifying. The deposition shall not be used unless the court finds that the circumstances surrounding its taking allowed full preparation and cross-examination by all parties. A record of the videotaped testimony, which shall be part of the official record of the court proceedings, shall be made in the same manner as if the witness were present and testifying, but, in addition, the videotape shall be retained by the court. If the court finds that use of the videotaped testimony would be unfairly prejudicial to a party, he may order that only the audiotape of the testimony be used or that the transcript of the witness's testimony be read to the jury if either of these limitations would prevent such prejudice.

(d) Jury Instruction. In any case where a deposition is used in any form, the court shall instruct the jury that this procedure is employed for the convenience of the witness and that the jury should draw no inference from its use.

Note: Source—R.R. 3:5-8(a) (b) (c) (d) (e). Text of former rule deleted and new rule adopted November 5, 1986 to be effective January 1, 1987.

3:13-3. Discovery and Inspection

(a) Discovery by the Defendant. Upon written request by the defendant, the prosecuting attorney shall permit defendant to inspect and copy or photograph any relevant.

(1) books, tangible objects, papers or documents obtained from or belonging to him;

(2) records of statements or confessions, signed or unsigned, by the defendant or copies thereof, and a summary of any admissions or declarations against penal interest made by the defendant that are known to the prosecution but not recorded;

(3) grand jury proceedings recorded pursuant to R. 3:6-6;

(4) results or reports of physical or mental examinations and of scientific tests or experiments made in connection with the matter or copies thereof, which are within the possession, custody or control of the prosecuting attorney;

(5) reports or records of prior convictions of the defendant;

(6) books, papers, documents, or copies thereof, or tangible objects, buildings or places which are within the possession, custody or control of the State;

(7) names and addresses of any persons whom the prosecuting attorney knows to have relevant evidence or information including a designation by the prosecuting attorney as to which of those persons he may call as witnesses;

(8) record of statements, signed or unsigned, by such persons or by co-defendants which are within the possession, custody or control of the prosecuting attorney and any relevant record of prior conviction of such persons;

(9) police reports which are within the possession, custody, or control of the prosecuting attorney;

(10) warrants, which have been completely executed, and the papers accompanying them including the affidavits, transcript or summary of any oral testimony, return or inventory;

(11) names and addresses of each person whom the prosecuting attorney expects to call to trial as an expert witness, his qualifications, the subject matter on which the expert is expected to testify, a copy of the report, if any, of such expert witness, or if no report is prepared, a statement of the facts and opinions to which the expert is expected to testify and a summary of the grounds for each opinion. If this information is requested and not furnished, the expert witness may, upon application by the defendant, be barred from testifying at trial.

(b) Discovery by the State. A defendant who seeks discovery shall permit the State to inspect and copy or photograph.

(1) results or reports of physical or mental examinations and of scientific tests or experiments made in connection with the matter or copies thereof, which are within the possession, custody or control of defense counsel;

(2) any relevant books, papers, documents or tangible objects, buildings or places or copies thereof, which are within the possession, custody or control of defense counsel;

(3) the names and addresses of those persons known to defendant whom he may call as witnesses at trial and their written statements, if any, including memoranda reporting or summarizing their oral statements;

(4) written statements, if any, including any memoranda reporting or summarizing the oral statements, made by any witnesses whom the State may call as a witness at trial;

(5) name and address of each person whom the defense expects to call to trial as an expert witness, his qualifications, the subject matter on which the expert is expected to testify, and a copy of the report, if any, of such expert witness, or if no report is prepared, a statement of the facts and opinions to which the expert is expected to testify and a summary of the grounds for each opinion. If this information is requested and not furnished the expert may, upon application by the prosecutor, be barred from testifying at trial.

(c) Documents Not Subject to Discovery. This rule does not require discovery of a party's work product consisting of internal reports, memoranda or documents made by that party or his attorney or agents, in connection with the investigation, prosecution or defense of the matter nor does it require discovery by the State of records or statements, signed or unsigned, of defendant made to defendant's attorney or agents.

(d) Protective Orders.

(1) Grounds. Upon motion and for good cause shown the court may at any time order that the discovery or inspection sought pursuant to this rule be denied, restricted, or deferred or make such other order as is appropriate. In determining the motion, the court may consider the following: protection of witnesses and others from physical harm, threats of harm, bribes, economic reprisals and other intimidation; maintenance of such secrecy regarding informants as is required for effective investigation of criminal activity; protection of confidential relationships and privileges recognized by law; any other relevant considerations.

(2) Procedure. The court may permit the showing of good cause to be made, in whole or in part, in the form of a written statement to be inspected by the court alone, and if the court thereafter enters a protective order, the entire text of the statement shall be sealed and preserved in the records of the court, to be made available only to the appellate court in the event of an appeal.

(e) Time. Defendant's request for discovery shall be made within 10 days of the entry of the plea and the prosecutor shall respond within 10 days of the receipt by him of the defendant's request. Defendant, without request therefor, shall provide the State discovery as provided in this rule within 20 days of compliance with the defendant's discovery request.

(f) Continuing Duty to Disclose: Failure to Comply. If subsequent to the compliance with a request by the prosecuting attorney or defense counsel or with an order issued pursuant to the within rule and prior to or during trial a party discovers additional material or witnesses previously requested or ordered subject to discovery or inspection, he shall promptly notify the other party or his attorney of the existence thereof. If at any time during the course of the proceedings it is brought to the attention of the court that a party has failed to comply with this rule or with an order issued pursuant to this rule, it may order such party to permit the discovery or inspection of materials not previously disclosed, grant a continuance, or prohibit the party from introducing in evidence the material not disclosed, or it may enter such other order as it deems appropriate.

Note: Source—R.R. 3:5-11(a) (b) (c) (d) (e) (f) (g) (h). Paragraphs (b) (c) (f) and (h) deleted; paragraph (a) amended and paragraphs (d) (e) (g) and (i) amended and redesignated June 29, 1973 to be effective September 10, 1973. Paragraph (b) amended July 17, 1975 to be effective September 8, 1975; paragraph (a) amended July 15, 1982 to be effective September 13, 1982; paragraphs (a) and (b) amended July 22, 1983 to be effective September 12, 1983.

3:21-4. Sentence

(a) **Imposition of Sentence; Bail.** Sentence shall be imposed without unreasonable delay. Pending sentence the court may commit the defendant or continue or alter the bail.

(b) **Presence of Defendant; Statement.** Sentence shall not be imposed unless the defendant is present or has filed a written waiver of the right to be present. Before imposing sentence the court shall address the defendant personally and ask him or her if he or she wishes to make a statement in his or her own behalf and to present any information in mitigation of punishment. The defendant may answer personally or by his or her attorney.

(c) **Sentence to Probation.** The court, at time of sentence, shall inform defendants sentenced to probation what penalties might be imposed on revocation should they not adhere to the conditions of their probation.

(d) **Extradition.** Nothing herein contained shall be construed as affecting the provisions of N.J.S. 2A:160-5 (relating to extradition) or the power of the court to resentence a defendant after reversal of the judgment by reason of error in the sentence.

(e) **Extended or Enhanced Term of Imprisonment; Sentence Pursuant to N.J.S.A. 24:21-29 or N.J.S.A. 2C:35-8.** A motion pursuant to N.J.S.A. 2C:44-3 or N.J.S.A. 2C:43-6f for the imposition of an extended term of imprisonment, or a motion for enhancement of a sentence pursuant to N.J.S.A. 24:21-29 or a motion for enhanced sentence pursuant to N.J.S.A. 2C:35-8, shall be filed with the court by the prosecuting attorney within 14 days of the entry of defendant's guilty plea or of the return of the verdict. Where the defendant is pleading guilty pursuant to a negotiated disposition, the prosecutor shall file the motion prior to the plea. A copy of the motion shall be served on the defendant and defendant's counsel. For good cause shown the court may extend the time for filing the motion. The sentence shall include a determination as to whether the defendant was convicted and sentenced to an extended term of imprisonment as provided in N.J.S.A. 2C:43-7, 2C:44-3 and 2C:44-6e, N.J.S.A. 2C:43-6f or whether the defendant was being sentenced pursuant to N.J.S.A. 24:21-29, or N.J.S.A. 2C:35-8, and the commitment or order of sentence which directs the defendant's confinement shall so specify.

(f) **Reasons for Sentence.** At the time sentence is imposed the judge shall state his reasons for imposing such sentence including his findings pursuant to the criteria for withholding or imposing imprisonment or fines under N.J.S.A. 2C:44-1 to 2C:44-3 and the factual basis supporting his finding of particular aggravating or mitigating factors affecting sentence.

(g) **Notification of Right to Appeal.** After imposing sentence, whether following the defendant's plea of guilty or a finding of guilty after trial, the court shall advise the defendant of his right to appeal and, if he is indigent, of his right to appeal as an indigent.

(h) **Sentence Imposed Pursuant to N.J.S.A. 2C:44-1(f)(2).** In the event the court imposes sentence pursuant to N.J.S.A. 2C:44-1(f)(2), such sentence shall not become final until 10 days after the date sentence was pronounced.

Note: Source—R.R. 3:7-10(d). Paragraph (f) amended September 13, 1971, paragraph (c) deleted and paragraphs (d), (e) and (f) redesignated (c), (d) and (e) July 14, 1972 to be effective September 5, 1972; paragraph (e) adopted and former paragraph (e) redesignated as (f) August 27, 1974 to be effective September 9, 1974; paragraph (b) amended July 17, 1975 to be effective September 8, 1975; paragraphs (d) and (e) amended August 28, 1979 to be effective September 1, 1979; paragraph (d) amended December 26, 1979 to be effective January 1, 1980; paragraph (g) adopted July 26, 1984 to be effective January 1, 1987; paragraph (d) amended November 2, 1987 to be effective January 1, 1988; paragraph (d) amended January 5, 1988 to be effective February 1, 1988; new paragraph (c) adopted and former paragraphs (c), (d), (e), (f), and (g) redesignated (d), (e), (f), (g), and (h) respectively June 29, 1990 to be effective September 4, 1990; paragraph (b) amended July 14, 1992 to be effective September 1, 1992.

3:21-5. Judgment

The judgment shall be signed by the judge and entered by the clerk. A judgment of conviction shall set forth the plea, the verdict or findings, the adjudication and sentence, a statement of the reasons for such sentence, and a statement of credits received pursuant to R. 3:21-8. If the defendant is found not guilty or for any other reason is entitled to be discharged judgment shall be entered accordingly. A copy of the judgment shall be forwarded to all parties and their counsel by the clerk forthwith upon entry.

Note: Source—R.R. 3:7-10(e); amended August 27, 1974 to be effective September 9, 1974; amended July 29, 1977 to be effective September 6, 1977; amended November 1, 1985 effective January 2, 1986.

3:21-6. Conviction of a Corporation

If a corporation is convicted of an offense the court shall give judgment thereon and shall cause such judgment to be enforced in the same manner as a judgment in a civil action.

Note: Source—R.R. 3:7-10(f).

3:21-7. Probation and Suspended Sentence

After conviction, unless otherwise provided by law, the court may suspend the imposition of a sentence or the defendant may be placed on probation.

(a) Conditions. The order shall require the defendant to comply with standard conditions adopted by the court and filed with the clerk thereof (except as otherwise ordered), as well as such special conditions, including a term of imprisonment pursuant to N.J.S.A. 2C:45-1c, as the court imposes. As a condition of probation the court may impose a term of community-related service to be performed by the defendant under such terms and conditions as the court may determine. A copy of the order, together with the standard and special conditions, shall be furnished the defendant, and read and explained to him by the probation officer, whereupon the defendant and the probation officer shall sign a joint statement, to be filed with the clerk of the court, as to the officer's compliance with such reading and explanation requirement. If the defendant refuses to sign such statement, he shall be resentenced.

(b) Detention. The court may, pursuant to N.J.S.A. 2C:45-3a(3), upon a showing of probable cause that he has committed another offense, detain without bail pending determination of the charge, a defendant who was sentenced to probation or whose sentence was suspended.

(c) Revocation. At any time before termination of the period of suspension or probation, the court may revoke a suspension or probation pursuant to N.J.S.A. 2C:45-3.

Note: Source—R.R. 3:7-10(g). Amended July 16, 1979 to be effective September 10, 1979; amended August 28, 1979 effective September 1, 1979.

3:21-8. Credit for Confinement Pending Sentence

The defendant shall receive credit on the term of a custodial sentence for any time he has served in custody in jail or in a state hospital between his arrest and the imposition of sentence.

Note: Source—R.R. 3:7-10(h)(first sentence).

3:21-10. Reduction or Change of Sentence

(a) Time. Except as provided in paragraph (b) hereof, a motion to reduce or change a sentence shall be filed not later than 60 days after the date of the judgment of conviction. The court may reduce or change a sentence, either on motion or on its own initiative, by order entered within 75 days from the date of the judgment of conviction and not thereafter.

(b) Exceptions. A motion may be filed and an order may be entered at any time (1) changing a custodial sentence to permit entry of the defendant into a custodial or non-custodial treatment or rehabilitation program for drug or alcohol abuse, or (2) amending a custodial sentence to permit the release of a defendant because of illness or infirmity of the defendant or (3) changing a sentence for good cause shown upon the joint application of the defendant and prosecuting attorney, or (4) changing a sentence as authorized by the Code of Criminal Justice, or (5) changing a custodial sentence to permit entry into the Intensive Supervision Program.

(c) Procedure. A motion filed pursuant to paragraph (b) hereof shall be accompanied by supporting affidavits and such other documents and papers as set forth the basis for the relief sought. A hearing need not be conducted on a motion filed under paragraph (b) hereof unless the court, after review of the material submitted with the motion papers, concludes that a hearing is required in the interest of justice. All changes of sentence shall be made in open court upon notice to the defendant and the prosecuting attorney. An appropriate order setting forth the revised sentence and specifying the change made and the reasons therefor shall be entered on the record.

(d) Consideration During Appeal. Notwithstanding R. 2:9-1(a), the trial court may reconsider a sentence pursuant to this Rule during the pendency of an appeal upon notice to the Appellate Division.

(e) Intensive Supervision. Motions for change of custodial sentence and entry into the Intensive Supervision Program, as provided for in paragraph (b) of this rule, shall be addressed entirely to the sound discretion of the three-judge panel assigned to hear them. Because of the nature of the program, there shall be no administrative or judicial review at the several levels of eligibility established under the program. No further appellate review of the panel's substantive decision shall be afforded. The three-judge panel shall have the authority to resentence offenders, in accordance with applicable statutes, in the event they fail to perform satisfactorily following entry into the program.

Note: Source—R.R. 3:7-13(a)(b); paragraph (b) amended and redesignated as (c) new paragraph (b) adopted July 17, 1975 to be effective September 8, 1975; paragraph (b) amended August 28, 1979, to be effective September 1, 1979; new paragraph (d) adopted July 16, 1981 to be effective September 14, 1981; paragraph (a) amended July 15, 1982 to be effective September 13, 1982; paragraph (b) amended and paragraph (e) adopted July 22, 1983 to be effective September 12, 1983.

CHAPTER V. APPEALS FROM COURTS OF LIMITED CRIMINAL JURISDICTION
RULE 3:23. APPEALS FROM JUDGMENTS OF CONVICTION IN COURTS OF LIMITED CRIMINAL JURISDICTION

3:23-1. Exclusive Method of Review

Except as provided by R. 2:2-3(b), review of a judgment of conviction in a criminal action or proceeding in a court of limited criminal jurisdiction shall be by appeal as provided by R. 3:23.

Note: Source—R.R. 3:10-1.

3:23-2. Appeal; How Taken; Time

The defendant, his legal representative or other person aggrieved by a judgment of conviction (including a judgment imposing a suspended sentence) entered by a court of limited jurisdiction shall appeal therefrom by filing a notice of appeal with the clerk of the court below within 20 days after the entry of judgment. Within 5 days after the filing of the notice of appeal, one copy thereof shall be served upon the prosecuting attorney, as hereinafter defined, and one copy thereof shall be filed with the county clerk together with the filing fee therefor and an affidavit of timely filing of said notice with the clerk of court below and service upon the prosecuting attorney (giving his name and address). On failure

244/Municipal Court

to comply with each of the foregoing requirements, the appeal shall be dismissed by the Superior Court, Law Division without further notice or hearing.

Note: Source—R.R. 1:3-1(c), 1:27B(d), 3:10-2, 3:10-5. Amended November 22, 1978 to be effective December 7, 1978; amended July 11, 1979 to be effective September 10, 1979; amended November 5, 1986 to be effective January 1, 1987.

3:23-3. Notice of Appeal; Contents

The notice of appeal shall set forth the title of the action; the name and the address of the appellant and his attorney, if any; a general statement of the nature of the offense; the date of the judgment; the sentence imposed; whether the defendant is in custody; and if a fine was imposed, whether it was paid or suspended; and the name of the court from which the appeal is taken. There shall be included in the notice of appeal a statement as to whether or not a stenographic record or sound recording was made pursuant to R. 7:4-5 in the court from which the appeal is taken. Where a verbatim record of the proceeding was taken, the notice of appeal shall also contain the attorney's certification that he has either complied with R. 2:5-3(a) (request for transcript) and R. 2:5-3(d) (deposit for transcript) or that he has filed and served a motion for abbreviation of transcript pursuant to R. 2:5-3(c).

Note: Source—R.R. 3:10-3. Amended July 7, 1971 to be effective September 13, 1971.

3:23-4. Duties of Clerks of the Trial Court and Superior Court, Law Division

(a) Preparation of Transcript. Upon the filing of the notice of appeal, the clerk of the court below shall forthwith deliver to the county clerk the complaint, the judgment of conviction, the exhibits retained by him, and a transcript of the entire docket in the action, and the county clerk shall deliver copies thereof to the prosecuting attorney on his request.

(b) Docketing; Hearing Date. Upon the filing of a copy of the notice of appeal, the affidavit and the payment of the filing fees, as provided by R. 3:23-2 the county clerk shall docket the appeal and shall thereafter fix a date for the hearing of the appeal and mail written notice thereof to the prosecuting attorney and the appellant, or, if he is represented, his attorney.

Note: Source—R.R. 3:10-4. Caption amended November 22, 1978 to be effective December 7, 1978.

3:23-5. Relief Pending Appeal

(a) Relief from Custodial Sentence. If a custodial sentence has been imposed, and an appeal from the judgment of conviction has been taken, the defendant shall be admitted to bail in accordance with the provisions of R. 7:5-4.

(b) Relief from Fine. A sentence to pay a fine, a fine and costs, or a forfeiture may be stayed by the court in which the conviction was had or to which the appeal is taken upon such terms as the court deems appropriate.

(c) Relief from Order for Probation. An order for probation may be stayed if an appeal is taken.

Note: Source—R.R. 3:10-6. Paragraph (c) amended July 24, 1978 to be effective September 11, 1978.

3:23-6. Transmittal of Recognizance or Cash Deposit

The judge of the court below or his clerk shall transmit to the county clerk any recognizance taken in accordance herewith or cash deposited in lieu of such recognizance.

Note: Source—R.R. 3:10-7.

3:23-7. Dismissal of Appeal

If the appeal shall be dismissed for failure to comply with the requirements of R. 3:23-2 or 3:23-8(a) or (b) or for failure to prosecute, the matter and the record therein shall forthwith be remanded to the court from which the appeal was taken for execution of the judgment therein.

Note: Source—R.R. 3:10-9.

3:23-8. Hearing on Appeal

(a) Plenary Hearing; Hearing on Record; Correction or Supplementation of Record; Transcript for Indigents. If a verbatim record or sound recording was made pursuant to R. 7:4-5 in the court from which the appeal is taken, the original transcript thereof duly certified as correct shall be filed by the clerk of the court below with the county clerk, and a certified copy served on the prosecuting attorney by the clerk of the court below within 20 days after the filing of the notice of appeal or within such extension of time as the court permits. In such cases the trial of the appeal shall be heard de novo on the record unless it shall appear that the rights of either party may be prejudiced by a substantially unintelligible record or that the rights of defendant were prejudiced below in which event the court to which the appeal has been taken may either reverse and remand for a new trial or conduct a plenary trial de novo without a jury. The Court shall provide the municipal court with reasons for the remand. The court may also supplement the record and admit additional testimony whenever (1) the municipal court erred in excluding evidence offered by the defendant, (2) the state offers rebuttal evidence to discredit supplementary evidence admitted hereunder, or (3) the record being reviewed is partially unintelligible or defective. If the appellant, upon application to the court appeal to, is found to be indigent, the court shall order the transcript of the proceedings below furnished at the county's expense if the appeal involves violation of statute and at the municipality's expense if the appeal involves violation of an ordinance. If no such record was made in the court from which the appeal is taken, the appeal shall operate as an application for a plenary trial de novo without a jury in the court to which the appeal is taken.

(b) Briefs. Briefs shall be required only if questions of law are involved on the appeal or if ordered by the court and shall be filed and served prior to the date fixed for hearing or such other date as the court fixes.

(c) Waiver; Exception. The appeal shall operate as a waiver of all defects in the record including any defect in, or the absence of, any process or charge laid in the complaint, and as a consent that the court may, during or before the hearing of the appeal, amend the complaint by making the charge more specific, definite or certain, or in any other manner, including the substitution of any charge growing out of the act or acts complained of or the surrounding circumstances of which the court from whose judgment or sentence the appeal is taken had jurisdiction, except that if the appeal is from a conviction for an indictable offense, the appeal shall not operate as a consent that the complaint may be amended so as to charge such an offense or a new or different indictable offense, unless the defendant agrees to such amendment.

(d) Defenses Which Must Be Raised Before Trial. The defenses of double jeopardy, lack of jurisdiction in the court, failure of the complaint to charge an offense, the unconstitutionality of the statute, regulation promulgated pursuant to statute or ordinance under which the complaint is made and all other defenses and objections based on defects in the institution of the prosecution or in the complaint must be raised by motion and determined in accordance with R. 3:10.

(e) Disposition by Superior Court, Law Division. If the defendant is convicted, the court shall impose sentence as provided by law. If the defendant is acquitted, the court shall order the defendant discharged, the conviction in the court below set aside, and the return of all fines and costs paid by the defendant. An appropriate judgment shall be entered and a copy thereof transmitted to the court below.

(f) Appearance by Prosecuting Attorney. The prosecuting attorney shall appear and act on behalf of the respondent at the hearing.

Note: Source—R.R. 3:10-13. Paragraph (b) amended by order of September 5, 1969 effective September 8, 1969; paragraph (a) amended June 29, 1973 to be effective September 10, 1973; paragraph (a) amended July 29, 1977 to be effective September 6, 1977; paragraphs (a), (b) and (e) amended November 22, 1978 to be effective December 7, 1978; paragraphs (a), (b) and (e) amended July 11, 1979 to be effective September 10, 1979; paragraph (a) amended February 17, 1983 to be effective immediately.

3:23-9. Prosecuting Attorney Defined

In all appeals under R. 3:23 the prosecuting attorney shall be:

(a) The Attorney General, where required by law.

(b) The municipal attorney, in a case involving a violation of a municipal ordinance.

(c) The county prosecutor, in all other cases.

(d) With the consent of the court, the attorney for a complaining witness or other person interested in the prosecution may be permitted to act for the prosecuting attorney.

Note: Source—R.R. 3:10-13. Paragraph (b) amended September 5, 1969 to be effective September 8, 1969; paragraph (d) amended November 22, 1978 to be effective December 7, 1978; paragraph (d) amended July 11, 1979 to be effective September 10, 1979.

RULE 3:24. APPEALS FROM ORDERS IN COURTS OF LIMITED CRIMINAL JURISDICTION

(a) Either the prosecuting attorney or the defendant may seek leave to appeal to the Superior Court, Law Division from an interlocutory order entered before trial by a court of limited criminal jurisdiction.

(b) The prosecuting attorney may appeal, as of right, a pre-trial or post-trial judgment dismissing a complaint and, notwithstanding the provisions of paragraph (a), an order suppressing evidence entered in a court of limited criminal jurisdiction.

(c) Appeals pursuant to this rule shall be taken within 10 days after the entry of such order by filing with the Superior Court, Law Division in the county of venue a notice of motion for leave to appeal under paragraph (a) or the notice of appeal under paragraph (b), except that an appeal from the grant of a motion to suppress shall be taken within 30 days after the entry of the order. A copy of the notice shall be filed with the clerk of the court below, and a copy thereof shall be served on the prosecuting attorney as defined by R. 3:23-9 or on the defendant or defendant's attorney, as appropriate, at least 10 days prior to the return date fixed therein. The original filed with the court and the copy served shall have annexed thereto copies of all papers of record and any affidavits essential to the determination of the motion and shall be accompanied by a brief. The respondent shall file and serve any answering brief and other papers in opposition at least 3 days before the hearing. With respect to interlocutory applications, the court may grant or deny leave to appeal on terms and may elect simultaneously to grant the motion and decide the appeal on the merits on the papers before it, or it may direct the filing of additional briefs or make such other order as it deems appropriate for the expeditious disposition of the matter. A copy of any order or judgment entered by it shall be promptly transmitted to the clerk of the court below.

(d) On appeal by the State from the grant of a motion to suppress the matter shall be tried de novo on the record. In cases in which the Attorney General or county prosecutor did not appear in the municipal court, the State shall be permitted to supplement the record and to present any evidence or testimony concerning the legality of the contested search and seizure. The defendant shall be permitted to offer related evidence in opposition to the supplementary evidence offered by the State.

Note: Adopted February 25, 1969 to be effective September 8, 1969. Caption amended, paragraph designations added, former rule amended and designated as paragraphs (a) and (c), and new paragraph (b) adopted July 16, 1979 to be effective September 10, 1979; paragraphs (b) and (c) amended, paragraph (d) added June 9, 1989 to be effective June 19, 1989.

3:26-2. Authority to Admit to Bail

A judge of the Superior Court in the county in which the offense was committed or the arrest made may admit to bail. Any other judge may admit to bail any person charged with any offense except murder, kidnapping, manslaughter, aggravated manslaughter, aggravated sexual assault, sexual assault, aggravated criminal sexual contact, or a person arrested in any extradition proceeding. When a person charged with an offense shall have been committed to jail after hearing by reason of bail having been denied, only a judge of the Superior Court may thereafter admit him to bail.

Note: Source—R.R. 3:9-3(a)(b)(c); amended July 24, 1978 to be effective September 11, 1978; amended May 21, 1979 to be effective June 1, 1979; amended August 28, 1979 to be effective September 1, 1979; amended July 26, 1984 to be effective September 10, 1984.

3:26-3. Bail for Witness

(a) Authority to Issue. A Superior Court judge may, on application, bind with sufficient surety all persons who can give testimony relevant to a prosecution for a crime.

(b) Application. The application shall be captioned in Superior Court and titled "In the Matter of (name of person alleged to be a material witness)". The application shall include a copy of the pending indictment, complaint, or accusation and an affidavit containing: (1) the name and address of the person alleged to be a material witness, (2) the grounds for belief that the person has material and necessary information concerning the pending criminal action, and (3) the reasons why the alleged material witness is unlikely to respond to a subpoena. If the application requests an arrest warrant, the affidavit shall set forth why immediate arrest is necessary.

(c) Order to Appear. If a preponderance of evidence supports issuance of a material-witness order against the person named in the application, the court may order the person to appear at a hearing to determine whether the person should be adjudged a material witness. The order and a copy of the application shall be served personally on the alleged material witness at least 48 hours before the hearing and shall advise the person of: (1) the time and place of the hearing, and (2) the right to be represented by an attorney and to have an attorney appointed if the person cannot afford one.

(d) Warrant for Immediate Detention. If there is clear and convincing evidence that the person will not be available as a witness unless immediately detained, the court may issue an order requiring that the person be brought before the court immediately. If the detention does not take place during regular court hours, the persons shall be brought to the emergency-duty Superior Court judge. The judge shall inform the person: (1) the reason for detention, (2) the time and place of the hearing to determine whether the person is a material witness, and (3) that the person has a right to an attorney and to have an attorney appointed if the person cannot afford one. The judge shall set conditions for release, or, if there is clear and convincing evidence that the person will not be available as a witness unless detention is continued, the judge may order the person held until the material-witness hearing, which shall take place on the next calendar day.

(e) Material Witness Hearing. At the material-witness hearing, the person shall have the rights: (1) to be represented by an attorney and to have an attorney appointed if the person cannot afford one, (2) to be heard and to present witnesses and evidence and unless otherwise sealed by the court for good cause, (3) to have all of the evidence in support of the application, and (4) to confront and cross-examine witnesses. If there is clear and convincing evidence that the person possesses information material to the prosecution of a pending criminal action and is unlikely to respond to subpoena, the judge shall: (1) set forth findings of facts on the record, and (2) set the conditions of release of the material witness.

(f) Conditions of Release or Detention. Conditions of release for a material-witness or for a person held on an application for a material-witness order shall be the least restrictive to effect the order of the court including but not limited to: (1) placing the witness in the custody of a designated person or organization agreeing to supervise the person; (2) restricting the travel, association, or place of abode of the person during the period of detention; or (3) setting bail. No person may be detained in the absence of posting bail when any other alternative will secure the appearance of the person. A person detained as a material witness or pending a material-witness hearing shall be lodged in appropriate quarters and shall not be held in a jail or prison.

(g) Deposition. The prosecutor, defendant, or material witness may apply to the Superior Court for an order directing that a deposition be taken to preserve the witness's testimony, for use at trial if the witness becomes unavailable, as provided by Rule 3:13-2. After a deposition has been taken, the judge shall vacate the material-witness order.

Note: Source—R.R. 3:9-4. First paragraph re-designated paragraph (a) and paragraphs (b), (c), (d), (e), (f) and (g) added July 14, 1992 to be effective September 1, 1992.

3:26-4. Form and Place of Deposit; Location of Real Estate; Record of Recognizances, Discharge and Forfeiture Thereof

(a) Deposit of Bail. A person admitted to bail shall, together with his sureties, sign and execute a recognizance before the person authorized to take bail or, if the defendant is in custody, the person in charge of the place of confinement. The recognizance shall contain the terms set forth in R. 1:13-3(b) and shall be conditioned upon the defendant's appearance at all stages of the proceedings until final determination of the matter, unless otherwise ordered by the court. One or more sureties may be required. Cash may be accepted, and in proper cases no security need be required. A corporate surety shall be one approved by the Commissioner of Insurance and shall execute the recognizance under its corporate seal, cause the same to be duly acknowledged and shall annex thereto proof of authority of the officers or agents executing the same and of corporate authority and qualifcation. Bail given in the Superior Court shall be deposited with the clerk of the county in which the offense was committed, provided that upon order of the court bail shall be transferred from the county of deposit to the county in which defendant is to be tried. Real estate offered as bail for indictable and non-indictable offenses shall be approved by and deposited with the clerk of the county in which the offense occurred and not with the Municipal Court clerk. In any county, with the approval of the Assignment Judge, a program may be instituted for the deposit in court of cash in the amount of 10 percent of the amount of bail fixed.

(b) Limitation on Individual Surety. Unless the court for good cause otherwise permits, no surety, other than an approved corporate surety, shall enter into a recognizance or undertaking for bail if there remains undischarged any previous recognizance or bail undertaken by him.

(c) Real Estate in Other Counties. Real estate owned by a surety located in a county other than the one in which the bail is taken may be accepted in which case the clerk of the court in which the bail is taken shall forthwith transmit a copy of the recognizance certified by him to the clerk of the county in which the real estate is situated, who shall record it in the same manner as if the recognizance had been taken in his county.

(d) Record of Recognizance. The clerk of every court, except the municipal court, before which any recognizance shall be entered into shall record immediately, in alphabetical order in a book kept for that purpose, the names of the persons entering into the recognizance, the amount thereof and the date of its acknowledgement. Such book shall be kept in the clerk's office of the county in which such court shall be held, and be open for public inspection. In municipal court proceedings the record of the recognizance shall be entered in the docket book maintained by the clerk.

(e) **Record of Discharge; Forfeiture.** When any recognizance shall be discharged by court order upon proof of compliance with the conditions thereof or by reason of the judgment in any matter, the clerk of the court shall enter the word "discharged" and the date of discharge at the end of the record of such recognizance. When any recognizance is forfeited, the clerk of the court shall enter the word "forfeited", and the date of forfeiture at the end of the record of such recognizance, and shall give notice of such forfeiture to the county counsel. When real estate of the surety located in a county other than the one in which the bail was taken is affected, the clerk of the court in which such recognizance is given shall forthwith send notice of the discharge or forfeiture and the date thereof to the clerk of the county where such real estate is situated, who shall make the appropriate entry at the end of the record of such recognizance.

(f) **Cash Deposit.** When a person other than the defendant deposits cash in lieu of bond, the person making the deposit shall file an affidavit concerning the lawful ownership thereof, and on discharge such cash may be returned to the owner named in the affidavit.

(g) **Ten Percent Cash Bail.** Whenever bail is set pursuant to Rule 3:26-1, unless the order setting bail specifies to the contrary, bail may be satisfied by the deposit in court of cash in the amount of ten percent of the amount of bail fixed and defendant's execution of a recognizance for the remaining ninety percent. No surety shall be required unless the court fixing bail specifically so orders. When cash equal to ten-percent of the bail fixed is deposited pursuant to this Rule, if the cash is owned by someone other than the defendant, the owner shall charge no fee for the deposit other than lawful interest and shall submit an affidavit with the deposit so stating and also listing the names of any other persons for whom the owner has deposited bail. The person making the deposit authorized by this subsection shall file an affidavit concerning the lawful ownership thereof, and on discharge such cash may be returned to the owner named in the affidavit.

Note: Source—R.R. 3:9-5(a)(b)(c)(d)(e)(f)(g). Paragraph (a) amended June 29, 1973 to be effective September 10, 1973; paragraph (a) amended July 16, 1979 to be effective September 10, 1979; paragraph (g) adopted November 5, 1986 to be effective January 1, 1987; paragraph (a) amended November 7, 1988 to be effective January 2, 1989; paragraphs (f) and (g) amended July 14, 1992 to be effective September 1, 1992.

3:26-5. Justification of Sureties

Every surety, except an approved corporate surety, shall justify by affidavit and be required to describe therein the property by which he proposes to justify and the encumbrances thereon, the number and amount of other recognizances and undertakings for bail entered into by him and remaining undischarged, if any, and all his other liabilities. No recognizance shall be approved unless the surety thereon shall be qualified.

Note: Source—R.R. 3:9-6.

3:26-6. Forfeiture

(a) **Declaration.** Upon breach of a condition of a recognizance, the prosecuting attorney shall move the court for a declaration of forfeiture of the bail, and the clerk of the court shall forthwith send notice of the forfeiture to the county counsel or the municipal attorney, as appropriate, who shall forthwith proceed to collect the forfeited amount.

(b) **Setting Aside.** The court may direct that a forfeiture be set aside if its enforcement is not required in the interest of justice upon such conditions as it imposes.

(c) **Enforcement; Remission.** When a forfeiture is not set aside, the court shall on motion enter a judgment of default and execution may issue thereon. After entry of such judgment, the court may remit it in whole or in part in the interest of justice.

Note: Source—R.R. 3:9-7(a)(b)(c)(first sentence)(d).

3:26-7. Exoneration

When the condition of the recognizance has been satisfied or the forfeiture thereof has been set aside or remitted, the court shall exonerate the obligors and release any bail. A surety may be exonerated by a deposit of cash in the amount of the recognizance or by a timely surrender of the defendant into custody.

Note: Source—R.R. 3:9-8.

RULE 4:70. SUMMARY PROCEEDINGS FOR COLLECTION OF STATUTORY PENALTIES

4:70-1. Applicability of Rule

(a) Any penalty imposed by any statute or ordinance which may be collected or enforced by a summary civil proceeding shall be collected and enforced pursuant to R. 4:70 in every court upon which jurisdiction is conferred by the statute imposing the penalty. This rule shall not, however, be applicable if a statute requires a civil penalty to be collected by a plenary action. Proceedings for the confiscation or forfeiture of chattels shall conform, insofar as possible, with the provisions of R. 4:70.

(b) A claim for the recovery of a penalty pursuant to R. 4:70 may include a count for injunctive or other relief provided that the claims are authorized by statute or ordinance and are founded upon a single transaction or series of transactions, and provided further that such action be commenced in a court having jurisdiction to grant the injunctive relief.

Note: Source—R.R. 4:89, 5:2-6(a)(c) (first sentence), 7:13-1, 7:14. Amended July 14, 1972 to be effective September 5, 1972; former rule redesignated paragraph (a) and paragraph (b) adopted July 24, 1978 to be effective September 11, 1978.

4:70-2. Complaint; Verification

The complaint, which shall be in writing and verified, shall specify (1) the person alleged to have violated the provision of statute for whose violation is imposed a penalty to be enforced in a summary manner; (2) the statute and provision thereof violated; and (3) the time, place and nature of such violation. If the proceeding is instituted by a governmental body or officer, the verification of the complaint may be made on information and belief by any person duly authorized to act on its or his behalf.

Note: Source—R.R. 7:13-2.

4:70-3. Process

(a) Issuance; Return; Warrant or Summons; Service. Upon the filing of a complaint, a summons specifying the provisions of the statute alleged to have been violated shall issue and shall be returnable in not less than 5, nor more than 15 days, except that if the statute so provides, a warrant may issue in lieu of a summons, without court order, and shall be returnable forthwith. The Administrative Director of the Courts may prescribe special forms of complaints and summonses for use in proceedings under R. 4:70, and a law enforcement officer may make and sign any such prescribed complaint and summons, serving the summons upon the defendant and thereafter filing the complaint promptly with the court therein named. Unless so served, process may be served and executed by any person authorized to serve and execute process in the court in which the proceedings are brought or by any other person designated for that purpose by the statute imposing the penalty.

(b) Arrest Without Warrant. If the statute imposing the penalty authorizes arrest without a warrant for a violation committed within the view of a law enforcement officer, for which a penalty is imposed enforceable in a summary manner, the officer shall upon making such arrest for such a violation without a warrant, bring the defendant before a court having jurisdiction of the proceedings and shall forthwith file a complaint. In such case no process for the defendant's appearance shall issue, but upon the filing of the complaint the matter shall proceed as though process had issued and had been there and then duly served and returned.

(c) Authority of Clerk as to Process. The clerk of the court in which the proceedings are instituted or the deputy clerk thereof may sign, seal and issue any process required to be issued under R. 4:70, except a warrant of commitment.

Note: Source—R.R. 7:13-3, 7:13-4, 7:13-5, 7:13-6, 7:13-17.

4:70-4. Penalties; Payment; Hearing

(a) Payment Upon Plea of Guilty. For violations where the statutory penalty does not exceed $50 for each offense, including where the minimum statutory penalty does not exceed $50 for each offense, the defendant at any time before the hearing date, upon presentation of a signed plea of guilty and waiver of trial endorsed on the summons, may pay the penalty and costs by appearing before the court or violations clerk or by mailing the same to the court or violations clerk subject to the limitations prescribed in R. 7:7.

(b) Summary Hearing; Judgment Without Filing of Pleadings. On the return of the process or at any time to which the trial has been adjourned, the court in which the proceedings were instituted shall summarily, without the filing of any pleadings except the complaint, hear the testimony and determine and give judgment in the matter, whether for the recovery of a money penalty or costs or both, or otherwise, or for the defendant. Unless otherwise provided in the statute imposing the penalty, such hearing shall be without a jury.

(c) Adjournment of Hearing: Defendant Detained; Bond for Release During Adjournment. If the court in which the proceedings were instituted, adjourns the hearing it shall, except where the first process was a summons, detain the defendant in custody, unless he makes deposit in cash, in the amount of the penalty claimed and costs, or enters into a bond with at least one sufficient surety in double the amount of the penalty claimed and costs, or if there is no money penalty, then in such sum, not exceeding $500 as the court fixes, conditioned for his appearance on the adjourned date, and from day to day thereafter until judgment is rendered and further conditioned, unless the court otherwise orders, to abide by the judgment of the court. If the plaintiff is a governmental body or officer, the bond shall run to it or him, and, if forfeited, may be prosecuted by the obligee. If the plaintiff is the State, the bond shall run to it and, if forfeited, may be prosecuted at the relation of a person authorized by law to prosecute the penalty proceeding.

Note: Source—R.R.7:13-6A, 7:13-7, 7:13-8, 7:13-9; paragraph (a) amended July 15, 1982 to be effective September 13, 1982; paragraph (a) amended July 22, 1983 to be effective September 12, 1983.

4:70-5. Judgment; Commitment

(a) Form of Judgment. The judgment of conviction in proceedings under R. 4:70 shall be signed by the judge or judicial officer rendering it and shall be in the form prescribed by the Administrative Director of the Courts, which form may be modified to include provision for injunctive or other relief in proceedings under R. 4:70-1(b).

(b) Commitment of Defendant Failing to Pay Judgment. If the statute imposing the penalty provides for commitment of the defendant upon his failure to pay forthwith the amount of any money judgment rendered against him, the court shall direct him to be committed to any institution and for such time as the statute authorizes, unless the judgment is sooner paid. The form of commitment shall be added beneath the signature to the judgment, signed in duplicate by the judge or other judicial officer, and in the form prescribed by the Administrative Director of the Courts. One of the duplicates shall serve the purpose of a warrant of commitment.

(c) Money Judgment; Execution, Property and Persons Subject to. If a money judgment is rendered against a defendant, execution may issue, in the form prescribed by the Administrative Director of the Courts, against the goods and chattels of the defendant; against defendant's real estate if the judgment is entered in the Civil Judgment and Order Docket; and against the body of an individual defendant provided the court in which the judgment is rendered shall by special order so direct and shall designate in said order the maximum number of days during which the defendant may be detained in custody under such body execution.

(d) Costs. The costs prescribed by the statute imposing the penalty in any proceeding under R. 4:70 shall be recovered by the plaintiff if the judgment is rendered against the defendant.

Note: Source—R.R. 7:13-10, 7:13-11, 7:13-12, 7:13-13, 7:13-14, 7:13-16; paragraph (a) amended July 24, 1978 to be effective September 11, 1978; paragraph (c) amended June 29, 1990 to be effective September 4, 1990.

Part V
CHANCERY DIVISION, FAMILY PART

5:1-2. Actions Cognizable

The following actions shall be cognizable in the Family Part:

(a) Civil Family Actions Generally. All civil actions in which the principal claim is unique to and arises out of a family or family-type relationship shall be brought in the Family Part. Such actions shall include all actions and proceedings provided for in Chapters II and III of Part V; all civil actions and proceedings formerly designated as matrimonial actions; all civil actions and proceedings formerly cognizable in the Juvenile and Domestic Relations Court; and all other civil actions and proceedings unique to and arising out of a family or a family-type relationship.

(b) Juvenile Delinquency Actions.

(c) Criminal and Quasi-Criminal Actions.

(1) Criminal actions brought pursuant to N.J.S. 2C:13-4a (interference with custody) and N.J.S. 2C:24-5 (willful nonsupport) shall be prosecuted in the Family Part subject to transfer to the Law Division pursuant to R. 3:1-5(b) in the event the defendant is entitled to and demands trial by jury.

(2) All other indictable offenses pending in the Law Division may be transferred to the Family Part for trial and disposition pursuant to R. 3:1-5 provided that (A) the gravamen of the offense charged arises out of a family or a family-type relationship between the defendant and a victim, (B) the defendant has waived trial by jury pursuant to R. 1:8-1, (C) the defendant and the prosecutor have both consented to such transfer.

(3) Any nonindictable offense or violation pending in the municipal court and any indictable offense within the trial jurisdiction of the municipal court may be transferred for trial and disposition to the Family Part pursuant to R. 5:1-3(b) provided that the gravamen of the offense or violation arises out of a family or family-type relationship between the defendant and a victim.

Note: Source—new. Adopted December 20, 1983, to be effective December 31, 1983.

5:1-3. Transfer of Actions To and From the Family Part

(a) Civil Actions. The transfer of civil family actions to or from the Family Part to or from any other trial division or part of a trial division of the Superior Court shall be governed by R. 4:3-1(b).

(b) Criminal and Quasi-Criminal Actions.

(1) The transfer of criminal actions between the Law Division and the Family Part shall be governed by R. 3:1-5.

(2) The transfer of proceedings pending in a municipal court shall be on motion made by the defendant, the complaining witness or the municipal prosecutor. If there is a pending Family Part matter the motion shall be made to the judge assigned to that case and if no judge has been assigned, then to the presiding judge of that vicinage. If there is no pending Family Part matter, then the motion should be made to the presiding judge of the Family Part where the municipal court is located.

(c) Juvenile Delinquency Actions. The transfer of juvenile delinquency actions between the Family Part and other courts shall be governed by R. 5:23. The referral of a juvenile delinquency action to the Law Division for prosecution as in the case of an adult shall be governed by R. 5:22.

Note: Source—new. Adopted December 20, 1983, to be effective December 31, 1983; paragraph (b)(2) amended November 1, 1985 to be effective January 2, 1986.

Part VI
LAW DIVISION, SPECIAL CIVIL PART

6:1-2. Cognizability

(a) Matters Cognizable in the Special Civil Part. The following matters shall be cognizable in the Special Civil Part:

(1) Civil actions seeking legal relief when the amount in controversy does not exceed $7,500;

(2) Small claims actions in those counties that heretofore have had small claims divisions, which are defined as all actions in contract and tort (exclusive of professional malpractice, probate, and matters cognizable in the Family Division or Tax Court) and actions between a landlord and tenant for rent, or money damages, or for the return of all or a part of a security deposit, when the amount in dispute, including any applicable penalties, does not exceed, exclusive of costs, the sum of $1,500. The Small Claims Section may provide such ancillary equitable relief as may be necessary to effect a complete remedy. Actions in lieu of prerogative writs and actions in which the primary relief sought is equitable in nature are excluded from the Small Claims Section;

(3) Summary landlord/tenant actions;

(4) Summary proceedings for the collection of statutory penalties;

(5) Municipal court actions, pursuant to R. 7:1, in the counties of Bergen, Hudson and Warren.

(b) Distinct Negligence Claims. An action for damages resulting from negligence composed of several distinct claims may be brought in the Special Civil Part if the amount recoverable on each claim is within the monetary limit even though the amount recoverable on all claims exceeds that limit.

(c) Waiver of Excess. Where the amount recoverable on a claim exceeds the monetary limit of the Special Civil Part or the Small Claims Section, the party asserting the claim may waive the excess over the applicable limit and recover a sum not exceeding the limit plus costs.

Note: Adopted November 7, 1988 to be effective January 2, 1989; caption added to paragraph (a) and paragraph (a) amended July 17, 1991 to be effective immediately; paragraphs (a)(1) and (2) amended July 14, 1992 to be effective September 1, 1992.

APPENDIX B

BREATHALYZER MANUAL

Municipal Court/255

BREATHALYZER

MODEL 900

INSTRUCTION MANUAL

National Draeger, Inc.
The Breathalyzer Division
P.O. Box 120
Pittsburgh, PA 15230
412—787-8383

Contents Copyright 1970 9-003-3277-00
1985 Edition

Reproduced with permission

FOR CLASS USE ONLY

NOTICE

This model instrument equipped with a mechanical lock on the galvanometer. When you receive the instrument it will be in the locked position and must be unlocked to operate.

TO UNLOCK: Turn small knurled metal knob located on top of galvanometer counter clockwise with fingers only, as far as it will turn, approximately 2½ turns.

TO LOCK: Turn lock screw clockwise as far as it will go, finger tight, only.

When moving the instrument it is advisable to lock the galvanometer to prevent mechanical damage.

Do not move balance wheel before removing shipping screw.

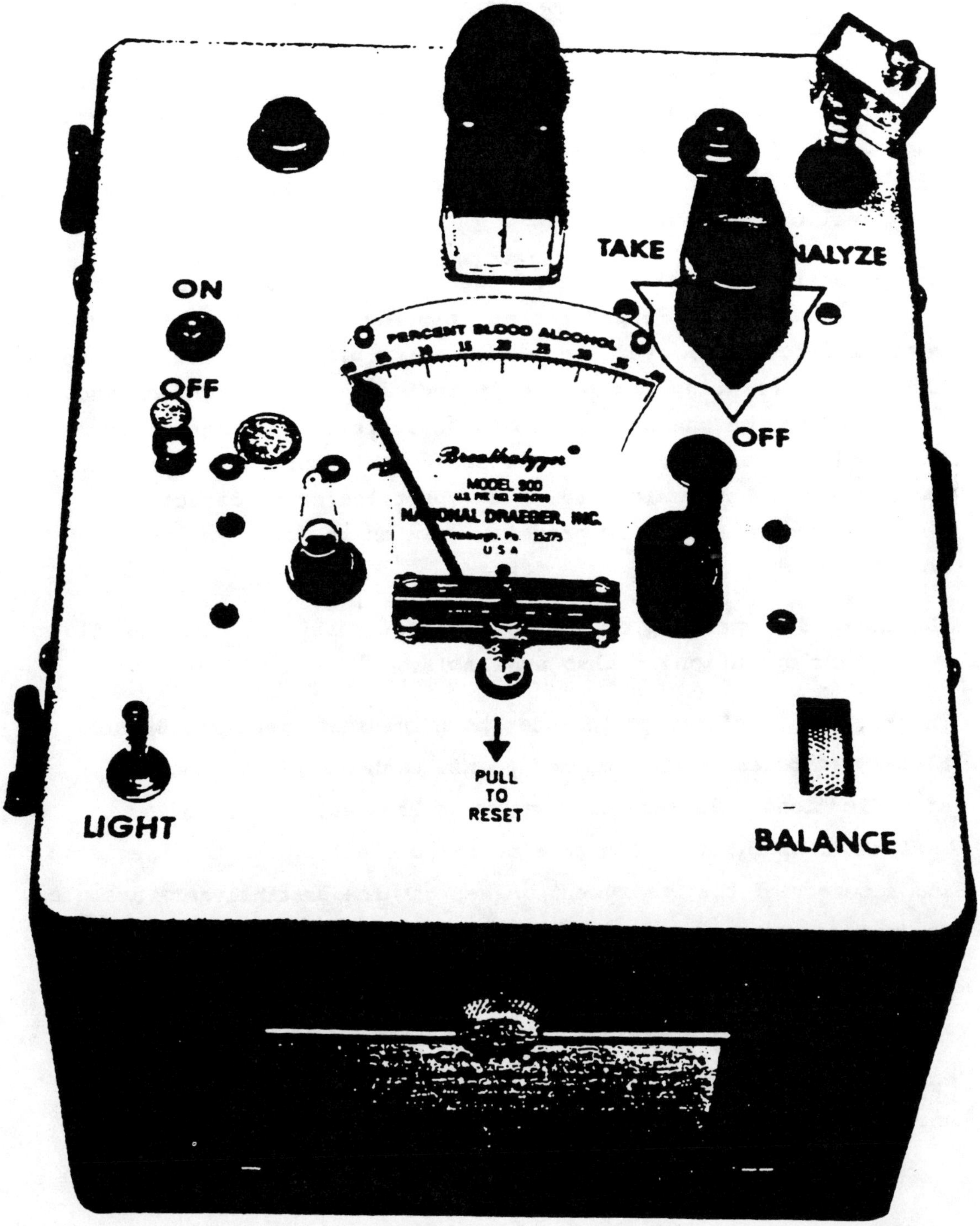
TAKE
ON
PERCENT BLOOD ALCOHOL
OFF
OFF
MODEL 900
LIGHT
PULL
TO
RESET
BALANCE

PREFACE

This manual is designed to familiarize you with the basic nomenclature and operating procedures of the Model 900 Breathalyzer®. The Model 900 is an evidential breath testing instrument. The test result is read directly on a linear scale located on the top panel of the instrument.

An optional permanent record of the test result can be obtained by inserting a test record ticket (provided with the Breathalyzer® certified test kit) over the two locating pins immediately above the scale. Printing ink (not supplied) is transferred from the ink reservoir on the left side of the scale to a rubber arrow attached to the underside of the scale indicator. After the test is completed, the scale reading may be transferred directly to the test record ticket by pressing down on the clear plastic shield assembly.

The Model 900 operates on 115 volt 60 Hz. Optional 12VDC or 220 volt 50 Hz operation is also available.

The Breathalyzer® system includes both the instrument and Breathalyzer® ampoules, each produced to NATIONAL DRAEGER'S exacting specifications. Be sure to always use Breathalyzer® ampoules. NATIONAL DRAEGER, INC. can take no responsibility for the precision and accuracy of the instrument unless genuine Breathalyzer® ampoules are used.

We trust your new instrument will provide many years of trouble-free service. Please contact NATIONAL DRAEGER, INC. or your authorized NATIONAL DRAEGER, INC. distributor should you have any further questions.

MODEL 900

TOP PANEL COMPONENTS

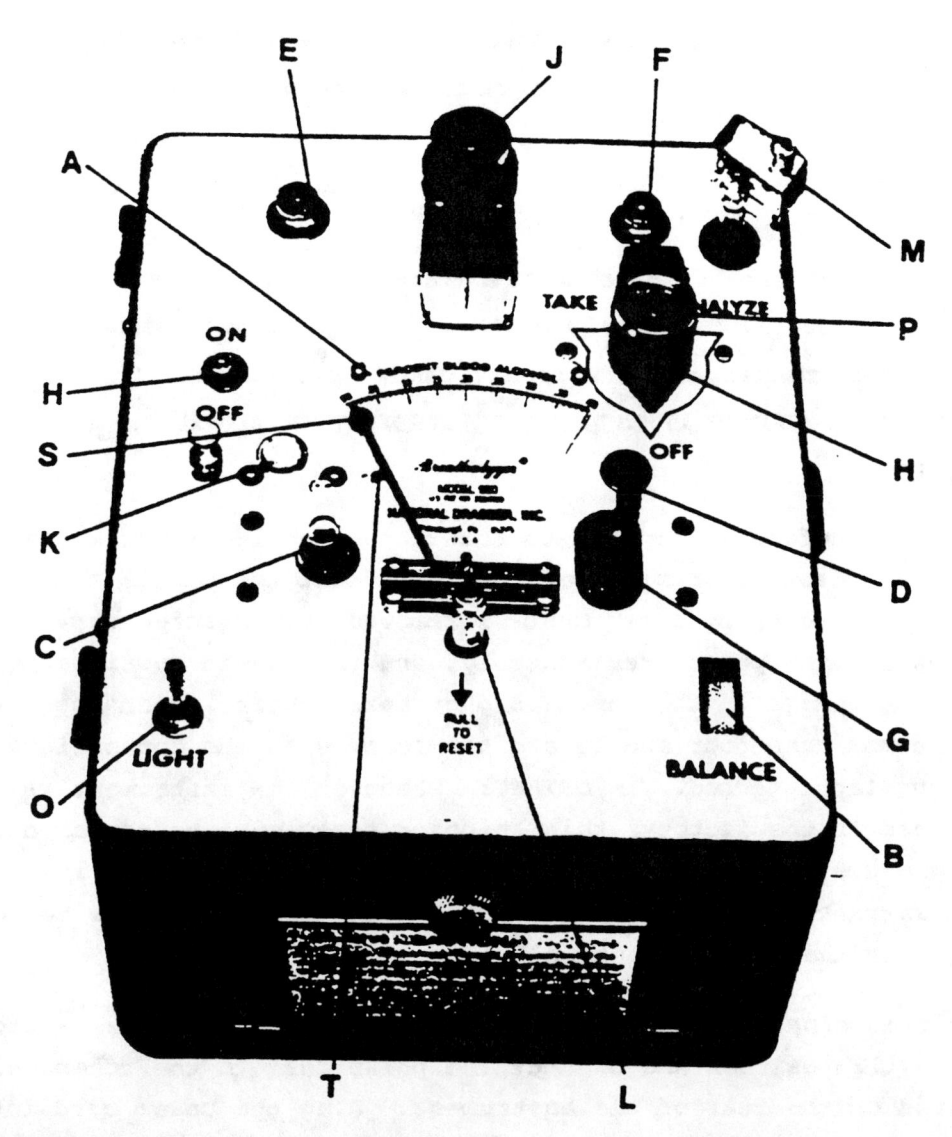

A. BLOOD ALCOHOL SCALE
B. LIGHT BALANCE ADJUSTMENT
C. REFERENCE AMPOULE
D. DELIVERY TUBE
E. CHAMBER EMPTY LIGHT (RED)
F. CHAMBER FULL LIGHT (GREEN)
G. TEST AMPOULE
H. CONTROL KNOB
J. GALVANOMETER
K. POINTER INK PAD
L. BLOOD ALCOHOL POINTER ADJUSTMENT
M. RETRACTABLE SAMPLE TUBE
N. POWER SWITCH
O. PHOTOMETER LAMP SWITCH
P. SAMPLE CHAMBER THERMOMETER
Q. READ LIGHT
R. AMPOULE LIFT
S. BAC POINTER
T. SCALE POINTER STOP

FIGURE 1

SETTING UP THE 900 BREATHALYZER®

At the time of shipment your new Model 900 has passed a series of final tests and quality inspections at the NATIONAL DRAEGER, Inc. factory. In the event the instrument shows evidence of shipping damage, you should file a claim immediately with the shipping company. NATIONAL DRAEGER, INC. is not responsible for shipping damage.

Included with the 900 Breathalyzer® are an AC power cord, ampoule guage, flushing bulb assembly, instructional manual, maintenance manual, and a warranty card. THE WARRANTY CARD SHOULD BE COMPLETED AT ONCE AND FORWARDED TO NATIONAL DRAEGER, INC.

Caution - Before attempting to rotate the knurled thumb wheel located on the lower right of the instrument top panel, the instrument shipping screw must be removed. This screw serves to immobilize the photometer assembly, and thus avoid possible shipping damage to the threaded photometer shaft. Open the instrument case door and locate the screw with the appropriate warning tag attached. IMPORTANT: Whenever the instrument is returned to the factory, this shipping screw must be replaced in the photometer assembly. Failure to do so will void the instrument warranty. It is recommended that the shipping screw be kept with the instrument at all times.

Once the shipping screw has been removed, place the power switch in the OFF position and connect the power cord to the receptacle located on the rear of the instrument. Plug the power cord into a suitable power source.

Next, check the mechanical centering of the galvanometer as follows:

If the galvanometer has a knob lock at its top, loosen this lock completely. With power switch in OFF position, turn knob at rear of galvanometer until the pointer is precisely aligned with

Setting Up the 900 Breathalyzer® - Continued

the center line of the galvanometer. Mechanical centering may only be necessary when the Breathalyzer® is first received, or subsequently moved.

OPERATING THE 900 BREATHALYZER®

The following description relates the sequence shown on the Breathalyzer® operational checklist.

PREPARATION:

Throw Power Switch to ON, Wait Until Thermometer Shows 50°C ± 3°C

The acceptable operating range for the Model 900 Breathalyzer® is 47° to 53°C. It will take approximately 30 minutes to arrive at this temperature from room temperature. It is permissible to leave the instrument in the ON position indefinitely, thus maintaining a proper operating temperature at all times and avoiding the 30 minute warm-up period. When the instrument is kept on for extended periods of time, such as four or five hours or more, the lid should be left off the instrument to avoid an excessive heat buildup.

Gauge Reference Ampoule, Then Insert Into Left-Hand Ampoule Holder

Using the go/no go gauge provided with the instrument, check the diameter of a certified Breathalyzer® ampoule with each end of the gauge. If the ampoule fits into both ends of the gauge, it should be discarded and another certified ampoule chosen. Once an ampoule properly fits the GO end of the gauge only, check the liquid level in the ampoule by sighting across the top edge of the gauge, to assure that the bottom of the meniscus formed by the liquid within the ampoule is aligned with or slightly above

Operating the 900 Breathalyzer® - Continued

the top edge of the gauge. Once the ampoule has passed these tests, it should be inserted in the left ampoule well of the instrument.

Gauge Test Ampoule, Open, Insert Bubbler, and Connect to Outlet

Using the go/no go gauge provided with the instrument, check the diameter of a certified Breathalyzer® ampoule with each end of the gauge. If the ampoule fits into both ends of the gauge, it should be discarded. An acceptable ampoule fits into the GO end of the gauge only. Check the liquid level in the ampoule by sighting across the top edge of the gauge, assuring that the bottom of the meniscus formed by the liquid within the ampoule is aligned with or slightly above the top edge of the gauge. With the ampoule still in the gauge, snap off the top of the ampoule by holding the gauge and grasping the top of the ampoule. Roll the hand holding the top of the ampoule away from the gauge. The small neck of the ampoule has been weakened so that breaking it off at this point is a simple matter.

Each certified test kit (NATIONAL DRAEGER, part number 003-0006-00) includes a plastic mouthpiece and glass bubbler tube in a common package. Remove the glass bubbler tube from this package by pushing the small end through the plastic, taking care to handle it at the elbow end. Remove the rubber sleeve from the metal delivery tube and attach it to the large diameter of the glass bubbler. Insert the small diameter (tapered end) of the bubbler into the ampoule. Remove the ampoule from the gauge and place it in the test ampoule well. Connect the open end of the rubber tube to the delivery tube. While other procedures are acceptable, this suggested method is easy and systematic.

Care should be taken when inserting and connecting the glass bubbler to the delivery tube. Excessive forcing of the glass bubbler against the side wall of the ampoule may cause the end of the bubbler to break off or the ampoule to fracture. If the

Operating the 900 Breathalyzer® - Continued

ampoule should break, immediately turn off the instrument power and disconnect the power cord. Flush the acid away wherever present with a mixture of water and baking soda or other suitable acid neutralizer.

PURGE:

Turn to TAKE, Flush Out (With Room Air), Turn to ANALYZE

With the instrument selector knob in the TAKE position, the flushing bulb assembly is connected to a breath tube and squeezed approximately 10 times. A green piston-up lamp on the top panel will come on. Next, turn the selector knob to ANALYZE. The room air sample will bubble through the ampoule.

When RED Empty Signal Appears, Wait 1½ Minutes, Turn on Light, BALANCE

A 90 second analyze time begins when the bubbling in the ampoule ends. Once the ANALYZE time is complete, depressing the photometer lamp switch will cause the photometer lamp to go on. With this lamp on, rotate the knurled balance wheel, observing the position of the galvanometer needle. Continue to rotate the balance wheel in one direction or the other until the galvanometer needle is precisely aligned with the center line of the galvanometer. With this accomplished, the photometer lamp switch should be released.

Set Scale Pointer on Start Line

The scale pointer can be moved by pulling the knurled knob at the base of the pointer toward the operator and rotating it. The scale pointer stop should be pushed, which in turn raises a stop for the pointer and thus facilitates positioning the pointer on the start line of the alcohol scale. The start line is slightly to the left of the .00% line.

Operating the 900 Breathalyzer® - Continued

ANALYSIS:

Turn to TAKE, Take Breath Sample, Turn to ANALYZE (Record Time)

Although the green piston-up light will illuminate when a sample of 52.5 cc's has been received from the accused, the subject should blow into the instrument as long as possible. The operator should encourage the subject to do this. If an inadequate sample is obtained, it is only necessary to try again. There is no need to reset the instrument. Once an acceptable sample has been received, the selector knob should be rotated clockwise to the ANALYZE position.

When RED Empty Signal Appears, Wait 1½ Minutes, Turn on Light, BALANCE

A 90 second analyze time begins when the bubbling in the ampoule ends. Once the ANALYZE time is complete, depressing the photometer lamp switch will cause the photometer lamp to light. With the photometer lamp on, rotate the knurled balance wheel, observing the position of the galvanometer needle. Continue to rotate the balance wheel until the needle is precisely aligned with the center line of the galvanometer. With this accomplished, the photometer lamp switch should be released.

* Record the Test Results.

* Disconnect the rubber sleeve from the metal distributor tube, lift the ampoule, bubbler, and rubber sleeve from the Breathalyzer® as a unit. Without removing bubbler from ampoule, remove rubber sleeve. Return rubber sleeve to outlet. Dispose of ampoule and bubbler.

* Return the Selector Knob to the OFF position. Selector Knob should remain in the OFF position when instrument is not is use.

BREATHALYZER® OPERATIONAL CHECK LIST

Name of subject _____ Date _____

Time (of test) _____ Blood Alcohol 0 _____ % Ampul Control No. _____

Operator _____ Witness _____

Instrument _____ No. _____

✓

1. ☐ Observe subject for twenty minutes prior to testing to prevent oral intake of any material.

PREPARATION

2. ☐ Throw SWITCH to "ON", wait until THERMOMETER shows 50° ± 3° C.
3. ☐ Gauge REFERENCE AMPUL, then insert in left-hand holder.
4. ☐ Gauge TEST AMPUL, open, insert BUBBLER and connect to outlet.

PURGE

5. ☐ Turn to TAKE, flush out, turn to ANALYZE.
6. ☐ When RED empty signal appears, wait 1½ minutes, turn on LIGHT, BALANCE.
7. ☐ Set BLOOD ALCOHOL POINTER on START line.

ANALYSIS

8. ☐ Turn to TAKE, take breath sample, turn to ANALYZE, (record time).
9. ☐ When RED empty signal appears, wait 1½ minutes, turn on LIGHT BALANCE.

Record answer, dispose of test ampul, TURN CONTROL KNOB to "OFF"

THEORY OF OPERATION
(Refer to Figures 1 and 2)

Each Breathalyzer® test begins with a balanced condition as indicated by the galvanometer located on the top panel of the instrument. The balanced condition refers to a photometric balance of the test ampoule against the reference ampoule. A balanced photometric condition is achieved by adjusting the position of the light carriage assembly and hence the photometer lamp on an axis between two photocell surfaces. The physical adjustments are accomplished by rotating the knurled thumb wheel located on the instrument top panel. This rotation is mechanically linked to a screw adjustment which in turn moves the light source (photometer lamp) back and forth between the two photocells. When the instrument is balanced, equal illumination from the photometer lamp is falling on each photocell surface. This causes identical electrical outputs from the two photocells, which can be seen by the resultant centering of the galvanometer. With the instrument in a balanced condition as indicated by the galvanometer on the top panel, the alcohol scale pointer is then aligned with the zero point on the instrument scale.

When a sample enters the instrument (selector knob in TAKE), it passes through the clear sample tube, the large bore tubing in the top header assembly, the metal distributor tube, and into the cylinder through the bottom header assembly. The pressure of the incoming sample lifts the piston upwards in the cylinder until vents at the top of the cylinder are uncovered, thus allowing the first portion of the breath to escape. When the incoming sample pressure stops, the piston drops to a predetermined position, covering the vents, and is held from further downward travel by the alignment of a permanent magnet and iron studs which protrude slightly through the top header assembly and into the sample chamber. The piston also completes an electrical circuit through the top contact, illuminating the piston-up lamp located on the top panel of the instrument. When the selector knob is rotated to the ANALYZE position, the permanent magnet disaligns, and the piston begins to descend under its own weight, forcing the air sample to travel back through the metal distributor tube, through the small bore tubing in the top header assembly and into the test ampoule. When the piston descends to the bottom of the cylinder, an electrical circuit is completed (through the bottom contact) illuminating the piston-down lamp on the top panel of the instrument.

If oxidation reduction has occurred in the test ampoule during the 90 second analyze time, the yellow coloring will have decreased. This will cause an increase in the transmittence of light through the test ampoule to the surface of the test photocell. Thus, more light will fall on the test photocell surface than on the reference photocell surface. This photometric imbalance can be seen in the deflection of the galvanometer needle. When the light source is moved towards the reference ampoule, causing an increase in the light falling on the reference photocell, and a corresponding decrease in light falling on the test photocell, the photometer will begin to approach a balanced condition as indicated by the movement of the galvanometer needle. The linear distance the light carriage has moved to restore the photometric balance is directly related to the quantity of alcohol in the breath sample, and results in a proportional travel of the scale pointer across the BAC scale. Once a photometric null has again been established, the test result can be read directly on the instrument scale.

268/Municipal Court

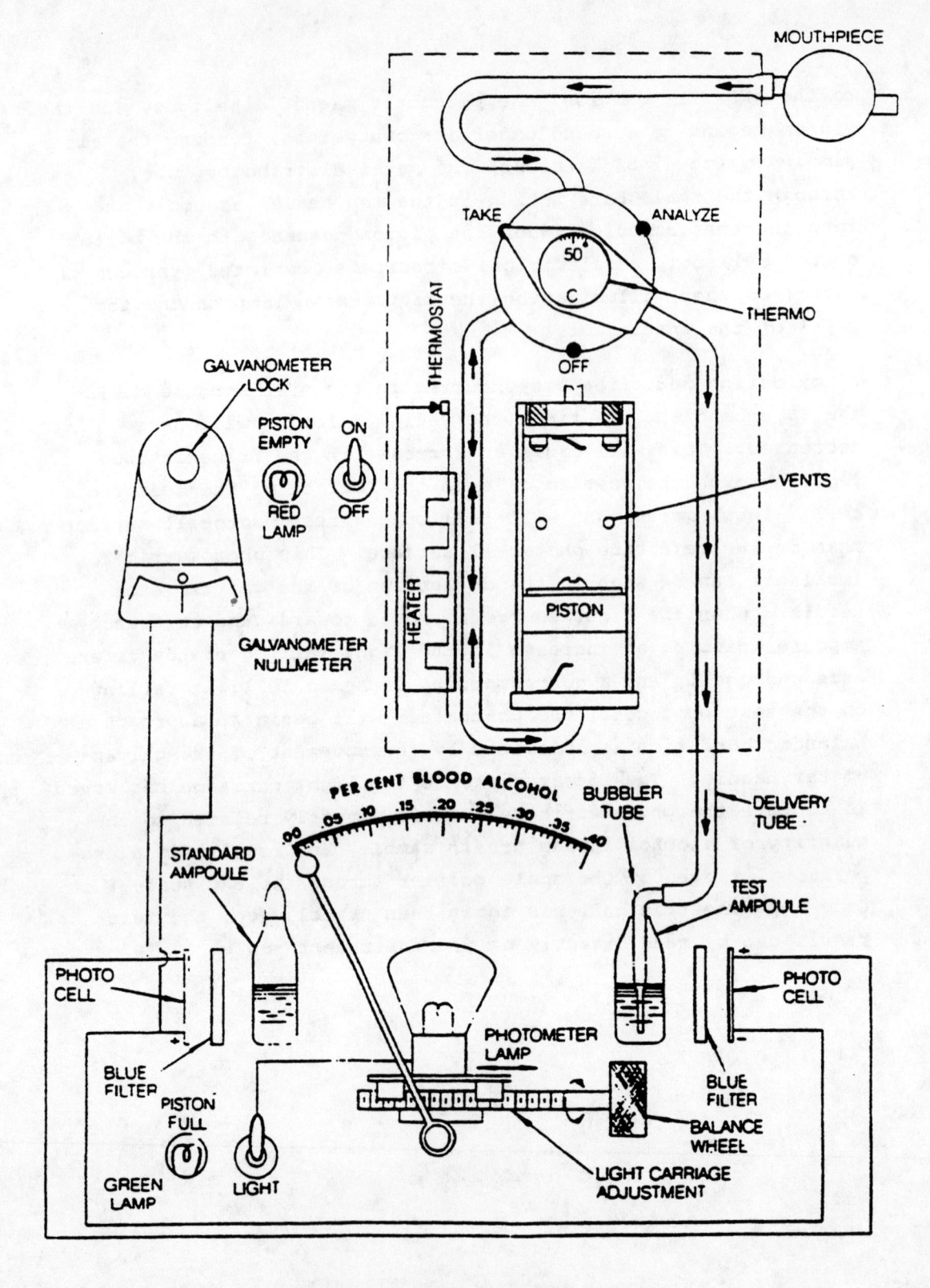

Figure 9. Breathalyzer Schematic

PREPARATION - THE KEY TO SUCCESSFUL DWI PROCESSING

Achieving the objective of successful DWI prosecution involves not only proper use of the Model 900, but also careful observation and detailed recording of the subject's behavior. The handling of a driver suspected of being under the influence should be serious. It is very common for police officers to joke with the driver and to laugh at his comical remarks and antics. In still other cases, the requests and remarks of the driver are completely ignored. All of these deviations from a business-like approach have a definite effect on the development of case material substantiating the charge for which the subject has been detained.

The Alcoholic Influence Report Form, as recommended by the National Safety Council, or your department's version of this form, should be used. The original can be used for reference on the witness stand by the officer who filled it out. In the section of the report entitled "observations", the first four headings call for impressions of the subject's appearance and behavior. The examiner should check the factors that form an accurate description of the subject at the time of testing. The choice of terms to be checked should be factual as observed. More than one term may be checked under each heading and additional ones may be added, if necessary.

In the section of the Alcoholic Influence Report Form titled "interview", the questions are quite clear, and the first answer of the subject to each question should be recorded exactly, even if it is known to be inaccurate. This section of the Alcoholic Influence Report Form provides the officer and the court with verbatim responses of the subject to the questions most commonly used as defense mechanisms. Effective reporting in this section will prove to be an invaluable tool in the prosecution of your case.

MODEL 900 CONSUMABLES/ACCESSORIES

Certified Test Kits, Part Number 003-0006-00

A test kit comprises one certified Breathalyzer® ampoule, one glass bubbler, one mouthpiece, one checklist, and one test record ticket. Test kits may be ordered in quantities of 25, 200, 1200, 6000, 12000, and 24000.

Breathalyzer® Operational Checklist, Part Number 003-0013-00

Each pad of Breathalyzer® operational checklists contains 25 sheets. One checklist is used for each Breathalyzer® test. Operator's checklists are ordered per pad.

Test Record Tickets, Part Number 470-3276-00

One test record ticket is used per Breathalyzer® test and each pad contains 50 tickets. Test record tickets are ordered per pad.

Mark IIA Alcohol Simulator, Part Number 003-0279-00

The NATIONAL DRAEGER, INC. Mark IIA Simulator is an electronically controlled alcohol reference standard. The Simulator solution consists of specified amounts of alcohol and water. The Simulator converts the prepared solution to a vapor resembling a human breath sample in density and temperature. Thus, the Simulator, when used in conjunction with a Breathalyzer®, provides a predictable alcohol reading, with which calibration and certification procedures may be performed.

DEPARTMENT OF
Law and Public Safety
VOID
This is to certify that

IS QUALIFIED AND COMPETENT TO CONDUCT CHEMICAL BREATH ANALYSES PURSUANT TO
CHAPTER 142 OF THE LAWS OF 1966 IN THE OPERATION OF THE
A METHOD TO DETERMINE INTOXICATION

GIVEN UNDER MY HAND AT TRENTON, NEW JERSEY THIS _____ DAY OF
_____ ONE THOUSAND NINE HUNDRED AND _____

ORIGINAL COURSE DATES _____

Refresher Course

	DATE	PLACE	INSTRUCTOR
1	_____	_____	_____
2	_____	_____	_____
3	_____	_____	_____
4	_____	_____	_____
5	_____	_____	_____
6	_____	_____	_____
7	_____	_____	_____
8	_____	_____	_____
9	_____	_____	_____

SP - 293B

272/Municipal Court

STATE OF NEW JERSEY
DEPARTMENT OF LAW AND PUBLIC SAFETY
DIVISION OF STATE POLICE
BREATH TESTING INSTRUMENT INSPECTION CERTIFICATE

Periodic Inspection ☐   Number
Other Inspection ☐   Date

Instrument	Serial Number	Department	County

Cylinder Output	Ampoule Control Number	Optical System	Balance Lost Motion	Instrument Temperature	Simulator Solution Percentage	Instrument Test Percentage Results

INSTRUMENT LOCATION

Background Check	Effect	No Effect	Remarks

☐ ABOVE INSTRUMENT IS NOT RFI SENSITIVE

RADIO TRANSMISSION TESTING

OPERATING FREQUENCY	CHANNEL DESIGNATION	BASE STATION	MOBILE (Distance)	PORTABLE (Distance)	REMARKS

REMARKS:

The above instrument has been ☐ repaired and ☐ inspected and found to be in satisfactory working condition.

"I am a Breath Test Coordinator Instructor, empowered by the Attorney General of the State of New Jersey, pursuant to the provisions of P. L. 1966 c. 142 S3 as amended (C. 39:4-50.3) and rules and regulations adopted thereunder, to perform inspection and maintenance of approved instruments for performing chemical analysis of a person's breath. I hereby affirm that I have inspected the approved instrument designated on this certificate. I further attest that this document contains a true, accurate and complete record of the inspection and maintenance performed herein; including random sample testing of ampoules used in the operation of this approved instrument as is evidenced by the ampoules control number (s) designated on this certificate. The original document of this inspection is on file at Division Headquarters of the New Jersey State Police, P.O. Box 7068, West Trenton, New Jersey 08628-0068."

Date

Signature

Name and Badge Number (Print)

LEGEND: N/E — NO EFFECT   N/A — NOT APPLICABLE

S.P. 343 (Rev. 6-86)   WHITE COPY — (N.J.S.P. File)   YELLOW COPY — (Remains with Instrument)   PINK COPY — (Coordinator)

STA./UNIT CODE NUMBER	NEW JERSEY STATE POLICE DRINKING - DRIVING REPORT	(1) DEFENDANT First Name Initial Last Name
		(2) Age	(3) Sex	(4) Weight	(5) Eye Color	(6) Race
		1	2			3

(7) Street Address	(8) City and State	(9) Summons Number (39:4-50 or 39:4-14.3g ONLY)
(10) Drivers License Number and State	(11) Day of Week	Violation Date	Time of Day A.M. P.M.
		5	6	7
(12) Make of Vehicle Used	(13) Year - Model - Color	(14) License Number and State
(15) Name of Vehicle Owner	(16) Address of Owner	
(17) Municipality of Violation	Code No.	(18) Roadway or Location	(19) County
8	9		
(20) Arrested By — Badge Number — Station	(21) Tested By — Badge Number — Station
10	11	12

(22) 13 ACCIDENT INVOLVED   (23) 14 EXAMINATION   (24) 15 SUMMONS ISSUED FOR

- ☐ 1 NONE
- ☐ 2 PEDESTRIAN
- ☐ 3 FATAL
- ☐ 4 INJURY
- ☐ 5 1 VEHICLE
- ☐ 6 2 VEHICLES OR MORE

- ☐ 1 CHEM. BREATH TEST
- ☐ 2 BREATH TEST REFUSED
- ☐ 3 OBSERVATION
- ☐ 4 DOCTOR'S EXAMINATION
- ☐ 5 BLOOD TEST
- ☐ 6 NARCOTICS, HABIT PRODUCING DRUGS, OR HALLUCINOGENIC

- ☐ 139:4-50 INFLUENCE
- ☐ 239:4-14.3g INFLUENCE (Moped)
- ☐ 3 OR ALLOWING ....
- ....
- TO OPERATE

16 BLOOD ALCOHOL RESULTS ....%
17 SUMMONS NUMBER (39:4-50.2 REFUSAL ONLY)
....
18 SUMMONS NUMBER (39:4-14.3g REFUSAL ONLY)
....

OBSERVATIONS WERE: LABORATORY ☐ YES   ☐ NO   REPORT # ....

(25) ABILITY TO WALK
- ☐ UNABLE TO
- ☐ FALLING
- ☐ ON HANDS AND KNEES
- ☐ MOVED IN CIRCLES
- ☐ SWAYING
- ☐ SAGGING
- ☐ GRASPING FOR SUPPORT
- ☐ STAGGERING

(26) ABILITY TO STAND
- ☐ SWAYING
- ☐ RIGID
- ☐ UNABLE TO STAND
- ☐ SAGGING KNEES
- ☐ CONTINUAL LEANING FOR BALANCE
- ☐ FEET WIDE APART FOR BALANCE

(27) SPEECH
- ☐ SHOUTING
- ☐ RAMBLING
- ☐ SLOBBERING
- ☐ INCOHERENT
- ☐ BOISTEROUS
- ☐ WHISPERING
- ☐ SLURRED
- ☐ HOARSE
- ☐ WHINING
- ☐ CRYING
- ☐ STUTTERING
- ☐ ACCENT
- ☐ SLOW

(28) DEMEANOR
- ☐ FIGHTING
- ☐ EXCITED
- ☐ INDIFFERENT
- ☐ HILARIOUS
- ☐ ANTAGONISTIC
- ☐ COOPERATIVE
- ☐ POLITE
- ☐ CALM
- ☐ SLEEPY
- ☐ CRYING

(29) ACTIONS
- ☐ PUNCHING
- ☐ KICKING
- ☐ RESISTING
- ☐ PROFANITY
- ☐ THUMBING NOSE
- ☐ THREATENING
- ☐ DIFFICULT TO AWAKEN

(30) EYES
- ☐ BLOODSHOT
- ☐ GLASS EYE?
- ☐ WATERY
- ☐ RIGHT
- ☐ DROOPY LIDS
- ☐ LEFT
- ☐ WEARING GLASSES
- ☐ NOT WEARING GLASSES?

(31) CLOTHING
- ☐ MUSSED
- ☐ DIRTY
- ☐ PARTLY DRESSED
- ☐ VOMITED ON
- ☐ DEFECATED IN SAME
- ☐ URINATED IN SAME

(32) MOVEMENT OF HANDS
- ☐ FUMBLING
- ☐ SLOW

(33) FACE
- ☐ FLUSHED
- ☐ PALE

(34) ODOR OF ALCOHOLIC BEVERAGE ON BREATH
- ☐ NONE
- ☐ YES

(35) REMARKS: (IF NEEDED, TO CLARIFY OBSERVATIONS)

PAGE _____ of _____ PAGES

S.P. 317 (Rev. 9-84)

(36) **ARRESTING OFFICER MUST READ THE FOLLOWING TO THE DEFENDANT:** I have probable cause to believe you have operated a motor vehicle while under the influence of intoxicating liquor or drugs. Therefore, I wish to inform you that:

1. You have been arrested for a violation of N.J.S.A. 39:4-50 (operating a motor vehicle while under the influence of intoxicating liquor or drugs)

2. You are required by law (N.J.S.A. 39:4-50.2) to consent to the taking of samples of your breath for purposes of conducting breath tests to determine the content of alcohol in your blood.

3. Upon your request, a copy of the results of the breath tests will be given to you.

4. The warnings previously given to you concerning your right to remain silent and right to consult with an attorney do not apply to the taking of breath samples and do not give you the right to refuse to give samples of your breath for purposes of conducting breath tests. You have no legal right to consult with an attorney, physician or anyone else, or have any of these individuals present, for purposes of taking the breath samples. If you refuse to give the required breath samples, such a refusal will be used against you on a charge of refusing to submit to breath tests. (N.J.S.A. 39:4-50.2)

5. After you take the required breath tests, you have the right to have a person or physician of your own selection take independent samples and conduct independent chemical tests of your breath, urine or blood.

6. If you refuse to consent to the taking of samples of your breath for purposes of conducting breath tests, you will be issued a separate summons for violating N.J.S.A. 39:4-50.2 in addition to any summons issued for operating a motor vehicle under the influence of intoxicating liquor or drugs.

7. If the municipal court finds you guilty of refusing to submit to breath tests when requested to do so, you will be fined a sum of not less than $250.00 or more than $500.00 and your right to operate a motor vehicle shall be revoked for six (6) months. However, if your refusal is in connection with a second or subsequent offense under this law, the revocation shall be for a period of two (2) years (N.J.S.A. 39:4-50.4a).

8. This revocation for refusing to take the breath tests will run consecutively and in addition to any revocation imposed for driving while under the influence of intoxicating liquor or drugs because the refusal is a separate offense.

9. If you are found guilty of refusing to submit to breath tests, you must, in addition to a fine and license revocation, satisfy the requirements of a program of alcohol education or rehabilitation.

I repeat, you are required by law to take the breath tests. Now, will you take the breath tests? Answer _____

If defendant remains silent or states that he/she refuses to answer on the grounds that he/she has a right to remain silent or that he/she first wishes to consult an attorney, physician, or other person, the arresting officer should read the following:

I have previously informed you that the warnings given to you concerning your right to remain silent and right to consult an attorney do not apply to the taking of breath tests and do not give you a right to refuse to take the breath tests. If you either (1) do not respond to my question or (2) tell me that you refuse to take the breath tests, you will be charged with refusing to submit to breath tests in violation of N.J.S.A. 39:4-50.2

Once again, I ask you, will you take the breath test? Answer _____

(37) **NARRATIVE OF INVESTIGATION** - Number, capitalize and underline the following paragraph titles in the sequence of events. Be brief, record events in order to refresh recollection at a later time. (1) **OPERATION OF THE MOTOR VEHICLE:** (2) **WHEN STOPPED OR ARRIVAL AT SCENE:** if an accident. (3) **ENROUTE TO STATION:** or wherever going (4) **AT THE STATION:** or wherever taken, i.e., doctor's office, hospital, etc. (Add bond paper if more space is needed) (5) List other **TRAFFIC OFFENSES** by summons number and statute number.

1. OPERATION OF THE MOTOR VEHICLE:

_____
_____
_____
_____
_____
_____
_____
_____
_____
_____
_____
_____
_____
_____
_____

(38) Title	Signature	Badge Number	(39) Reviewed By
(40) Date To Appear	(41) Amended Court Dates	(42) Refusal Disposition & Date	(43) Influence Disposition & Date

Municipal Court/275

NEW JERSEY STATE POLICE DRINKING-DRIVING REPORT CONTINUATION PAGE	Troop	Station	Date	Case Number
	Sequential File Number	Defendant		

NARRATIVE OF INVESTIGATION (Continued)

Title	Signature	Badge Number	Reviewed By:

S.P. 317-1 (9-84)

(36) ARRESTING OFFICER MUST READ THE FOLLOWING TO THE DEFENDANT: I have probable cause to believe you have operated a motor vehicle while under the influence of intoxicating liquor or drugs. Therefore, I inform you that:

1. You have been arrested for operating a motor vehicle while under the influence of intoxicating liquor or drugs.

2. You are required by law, N.J.S.A. 39:4-50.2, to submit to the taking of samples of your breath for the purpose of conducting chemical tests to determine the content of alcohol in your blood.

3. A record of the taking of the samples, including the date, time and results, will be made and, upon your request, a copy of that record will be made available to you.

4. The warnings previously given to you concerning your right to remain silent and right to consult with an attorney do not apply to the taking of breath samples and do not give you the right to refuse to give, or to delay giving, samples of your breath for the purpose of conducting chemical tests to determine the content of alcohol in your blood. You have no legal right to have an attorney, physician, or anyone else present, for the purpose of taking the breath samples. If you refuse to give the required breath samples, your refusal will be used against you on a charge of refusing to submit to breath tests, a violation of N.J.S.A. 39:4-50.2.

5. After you have provided samples of your breath for chemical testing, you have the right to have a person or physician of your own selection and at your own expense, take independent samples and conduct independent chemical tests of your breath, urine or blood.

6. If you refuse to provide samples of your breath for the purpose of conducting chemical tests to determine the content of alcohol in your blood, you will be issued a separate summons charging you with a violation of N.J.S.A. 39:4-50.2 in addition to any summons issued to you for operating a motor vehicle while under the influence of intoxicating liquor or drugs.

7. If a court of law finds you guilty of refusing to submit to chemical tests of your breath, then according to N.J.S.A. 39:4-50.4a you will be fined a sum not less than $250.00 or more than $500.00 and your right to operate a motor vehicle shall be revoked by the court for six (6) months. However, if your refusal is in connection with a subsequent offense under this section, your current refusal conviction will subject you to a fine of not less than $250.00 or more than $500.00 and your right to operate a motor vehicle shall be revoked by the court for two (2) years.

8. Revocation for refusing to submit to chemical tests of your breath is a separate offense and will run consecutively and in addition to any revocation imposed for operating a motor vehicle while under the influence of intoxicating liquor or drugs.

9. In addition, if you are found guilty and your right to operate a motor vehicle is revoked for refusing to submit to chemical tests of your breath, you must satisfy the requirements of a program of alcohol education or rehabilitation.

10. I repeat, you are required by law to submit to the taking of samples of your breath for purposes of conducting chemical tests to determine the content of alcohol in your blood. Now, will you submit the samples of your breath?

Answer: _____.

IF THE DEFENDANT REMAINS SILENT OR STATES THAT HE/SHE REFUSES TO ANSWER ON THE GROUNDS THAT HE/SHE HAS A RIGHT TO REMAIN SILENT OR THAT HE/SHE FIRST WISHES TO CONSULT AN ATTORNEY, PHYSICIAN OR OTHER PERSON, THE ARRESTING OFFICER SHALL READ THE FOLLOWING:

I have previously informed you that the warnings given to you concerning your right to remain silent and right to consult with an attorney do not apply to the taking of breath samples and do not give you a right to refuse to give, or to delay giving, samples of your breath for purposes of conducting chemical tests to determine the content of alcohol in your blood. If you either (1) do not respond to my question about submitting breath samples, or (2) tell me that you refuse to answer this question because you have a right to remain silent or first wish to consult with an attorney, physician or any other person, or (3) tell me that you will not submit breath samples because you have a right to remain silent or first wish to consult with an attorney, physician or any other person, you will be charged with refusing to submit to breath tests, a violation of N.J.S.A. 39:4-50.2.

Once again, I ask you, will you submit to giving samples of your breath? Answer: _____.

New Jersey State Police ALCOHOL INFLUENCE REPORT

(1) Defendant (First Name) (Initial) (Last Name)

(2) Age (3) Sex (4) Weight (5) Eyes (6) Summons Number

(7) Tested by and Station

(8) Arrested by and Station or Police Department

CHEMICAL TEST INFORMATION 14 - 1

	(9) Date and Time Samples Taken	(10) Instrument Used and Full Serial Number	(11) Ampoule Control Number	(12) Blood Alcohol % Result
Test 1				
Test 2				
Test 3				

BREATHALYZER OPERATIONAL CHECK LIST   MODEL 900 ☐ 900A ☐

Test 1 Test 2 Test 3

Preparation
1. Throw SWITCH to "ON", wait until THERMOMETER shows 50° — plus or minus 3°C.
2. Gauge REFERENCE AMPOULE and insert in left-hand holder.
3. Gauge TEST AMPOULE open, insert in right-hand holder, insert BUBBLER and connect to outlet.
4. Turn on LIGHT, BALANCE, set BLOOD ALCOHOL POINTER on START line.

Purge
5. Turn to TAKE, FLUSH OUT, turn to ANALYZE.
6. When RED empty signal appears, wait 1½ minutes, turn on LIGHT and BALANCE.
7. RECORD RESULT: Test 1,0. ___%; Test 2,0. ___%; Test 3,0. ___%.
8. Set BLOOD ALCOHOL POINTER on START line.

Analysis
9. Turn to TAKE, take BREATH SAMPLE, turn to ANALYZE, (Record Time).
10. When RED empty signal appears, wait 1½ minutes, turn on LIGHT and BALANCE.
11. Record answers, turn control knob to "OFF", dispose of test ampoule (after each test).

QUESTIONS:

(13) The following Questions were asked.

On _____, 19___ At _____ ☐ AM ☐ PM

(14) Occupation?

(15) Are you Sick? If Yes, Explain

(16) Are you under the care of a Doctor? If so, Who and His Address

(17) Last Visit Date: Time: ☐ AM ☐ PM

(18) Are you taking Medicine? If so, What and What for?

(19) Last Dose? Date Time ☐ AM ☐ PM

(20) Do you have Diabetes?

(21) Are you taking Insulin?

(22) Last Dose? Date Time ☐ AM ☐ PM

(23) Are you Injured?

(24) Where?

(25) Are your Injuries Affecting you now? If so, What and How?

(26) Note any Physical Injuries or Deformities observed.

ADVISE SUBJECT OF MIRANDA WARNING:

(27) What kind of Alcoholic Drinks have you had?

(28) How many?

(29) Where?

(30) What was the time between each drink?

(31) When did you have your First Drink? Date Time ☐ AM ☐ PM

(32) When did you finish your Last Drink? Date Time ☐ AM ☐ PM

(33) What time did you finish eating?

(34) What did you Eat?

(35) Remarks:

(36) (Rank) (Signature) (Badge No)

(37) Copy given to Subject On _____, 19___

SP 111 (Rev. 3.85)

CHAPTER 51
CHEMICAL BREATH TESTING

Authority
N.J.S.A. 39:4-50.3, 39:3-10.25 and 12:7-56.

Source and Effective Date
R.1991 d.505, effective September 16, 1991.
See: 23 N.J.R. 2248(b), 23 N.J.R. 3032(c).

Executive Order No. 66(1978) Expiration Date
Chapter 51, Chemical Breath Testing, expires on September 16, 1996.

Chapter Historical Note

Chapter 51, Chemical Breath Testing, was filed and became effective prior to September 1, 1969. Amendments to the original filing were adopted as R.1970 d.84, effective July 9, 1970. See: 2 N.J.R. 50(f), 2 N.J.R. 67(e). R.1972 d.10, effective January 24, 1972. See: 3 N.J.R. 267(a), 4 N.J.R. 27(b). R.1973 d. 354, effective December 17, 1973. See: 5 N.J.R. 390(a), 6 N.J.R. 21(c). R.1980 d.8, effective January 7, 1980. See: 11 N.J.R. 21(a), 12 N.J.R. 91(a). Amendments that replaced the entire text with new language were adopted as R.1982 d.187, effective June 21, 1982. See: 14 N.J.R. 376(a), 14 N.J.R. 660(a).

Pursuant to Executive Order No. 66(1978), Chapter 51 was readopted as R.1987 d.229, effective April 27, 1987. See: 19 N.J.R. 444(b), 19 N.J.R. 882(b). Pursuant to Executive Order No. 66(1978), Chapter 51 was readopted as R.1991 d.505. See: Source and Effective Date.

See section annotations for specific rulemaking activity.

CHAPTER TABLE OF CONTENTS

SUBCHAPTER 1. BREATH TESTING OPERATORS
13:51-1.1	Purpose of subchapter
13:51-1.2	Definitions
13:51-1.3	Certification
13:51-1.4	Prerequisite for application for certification
13:51-1.5	Application for operator's certification
13:51-1.6	Requirements for certification
13:51-1.7	Duration of certification
13:51-1.8	Suspension and reinstatement of operator's certification
13:51-1.9	Revocation of certificate
13:51-1.10	Hearing and determination on a request or recommendation for revocation
13:51-1.11	Restoration of revoked certifications
13:51-1.12	Return, loss and/or replacement of replica
13:51-1.13	Administration

SUBCHAPTER 2. BREATH TEST COORDINATOR/INSTRUCTORS
13:51-2.1	Eligibility requirements
13:51-2.2	Training and functional qualifications

SUBCHAPTER 3. APPROVED INSTRUMENTS AS METHODS OF CHEMICAL BREATH TESTING
13:51-3.1	Purpose of subchapter
13:51-3.2	Application for approval
13:51-3.3	Training Breath Test Coordinator/Instructors
13:51-3.4	Periodic inspection of approved instruments
13:51-3.5	Approved instruments for performing chemical analysis of a person's breath
13:51-3.6	Approved methods for performing chemical analysis of a person's breath utilizing an approved instrument

SUBCHAPTER 1. BREATH TESTING OPERATORS

13:51-1.1 Purpose of subchapter

This subchapter prescribes the requirements for certification of a person to conduct chemical analysis of the breath of a person arrested pursuant to N.J.S.A. 39:4-50 et seq., N.J.S.A. 39:3-10.13, N.J.S.A. 39:3-10.20, N.J.S.A. 39:3-10.24, N.J.S.A. 39:3-10.25, N.J.S.A. 12:7-34.19, N.J.S.A. 12:7-46, N.J.S.A. 2A:4A-23 or N.J.S.A. 12:7-54 et seq., the conditions under which certification can occur and the general rules for holders of certificates, pursuant to the statutory requirements of P.L. 1966, c.142, Sec. 3, as amended by P.L. 1971, c.273, Sec. 1 (N.J.S.A. 39:4-50.3), hereinafter denoted as N.J.S.A. 39:4-50.3; or P.L. 1990, c.103, Sec. 17 (N.J.S.A. 39:3-10.25), hereinafter denoted as N.J.S.A. 39:3-10.25; or P.L. 1986, c.39, Sec. 8 (N.J.S.A. 12:7-56), hereinafter denoted as N.J.S.A. 12:7-56.

Amended by R.1987 d.229, effective May 18, 1987.
See: 19 N.J.R. 444(b), 19 N.J.R. 882(b).
   Added list of N.J.S.A. cites.
Amended by R.1991 d.505, effective October 7, 1991.
See: 23 N.J.R. 2248(b), 23 N.J.R. 3032(c).
   Added to list of N.J.S.A. citations.
Administrative correction.
See: 24 N.J.R. 857(a).

13:51-1.2 Definitions

For the purpose of this chapter, and subchapters 1, 2 and 3 thereof, the terms set forth herein are defined as follows:

"Approved instrument" shall mean a device or instrument approved by the Attorney General at N.J.A.C. 13:51-3.5 for use in the chemical analysis of the breath of a person arrested pursuant to the provisions of N.J.S.A. 39:4-50 et seq., N.J.S.A. 39:3-10.13, N.J.S.A. 39:3-10.20, N.J.S.A. 39:3-10.24, N.J.S.A. 12:7-34.19, N.J.S.A. 12:7-46 or N.J.S.A. 2A:4A-23.

"Approved methods" shall mean those steps or operations approved by the Attorney General at N.J.A.C. 13:51-3.6 for use in the chemical analysis of the breath of a person arrested pursuant to the provisions of N.J.S.A. 39:4-50 et seq., N.J.S.A. 39:3-10.13, N.J.S.A. 39:3-10.20, N.J.S.A. 39:3-10.24, N.J.S.A. 12:7-34.19, N.J.S.A. 12:7-46 or N.J.S.A. 2A:4A-23 on an approved instrument.

"Approved school" shall mean police training academies and schools as approved by the Police Training Commission pursuant to N.J.S.A. 52:17B-67, et seq. It shall also include the Training Academy of the Division of State Police and any similar such academy, training center or school operated by or for the Department of Defense of the United States of America.

"Breath Test Coordinator/Instructor" is a person who meets the eligibility requirements as set forth at N.J.A.C. 13:51-2 and is duly appointed thereunder.

"Calendar year" shall mean all days of a year commencing with and including January 1 of a specific year and continuing through to and including December 31 of the same year.

"Certification" shall mean the approval by the Attorney General of a person as an operator, as herein defined, and shall mean said person is qualified and competent to perform chemical breath test analysis utilizing an approved method and an approved instrument as defined in this subchapter and as set forth at N.J.A.C. 13:51-3 as authorized by N.J.S.A. 39:4-50.3, N.J.S.A. 39:3-10.25 or N.J.S.A. 12:7-56.

"Operation of an approved instrument" shall mean operation of an approved instrument (as defined herein) by approved methods (as defined herein) for the operation of that approved instrument.

"Operator" shall mean a person who is certified as a Chemical Breath Test Operator to perform analysis of an arrested person's breath utilizing an approved method and an approved instrument, as defined in this subchapter and as set forth at N.J.A.C. 13:51-3 and pursuant to the provisions of N.J.S.A. 39:4-50.3, N.J.S.A. 39:3-10.25 or N.J.S.A. 12:7-56.

"Operator's certificate" shall mean a certificate issued under the authority of the Attorney General which bears the signatures or facsimile signatures of the Attorney General and the Superintendent of State Police.

"Organized police department" shall include all police and law enforcement agencies of the State of New Jersey; and all municipal and county police agencies of the various municipalities and counties of the State of New Jersey as established by law; and police agencies established by the laws of the United States of America within the Department of Defense.

"Recertification" shall mean the extension of the certification of an operator upon compliance with the training as required by this subchapter.

"Replica" shall mean a document which is an operator's certificate as defined in this section and which shall bear the signatures or facsimile signatures of the Attorney General and the Superintendent of State Police and which is of a size that permits it to be carried in the pocket, purse, wallet, etc., and includes replacements thereof as set forth at N.J.A.C. 13:51-1.12(c).

"Satisfactory completion of training" shall mean demonstrated competence of operation of chemical breath test analysis methods and devices or instruments approved by the Attorney General as set forth at N.J.A.C. 13:51-3, maintenance of a passing course average and passing a written examination.

Amended by R.1987 d.229, effective May 18, 1987.
See: 19 N.J.R. 444(b), 19 N.J.R. 882(b).
   Added N.J.S.A. cites to "approved instrument", "approved methods", "calendar year", "operator" and "replica".
Amended by R.1991 d.505, effective October 7, 1991.
See: 23 N.J.R. 2248(b), 23 N.J.R. 3032(c).
   Added N.J.S.A. cites to "approved instrument", "approved methods", "certification", "operator".

13:51-1.3 Certification

(a) For the purpose of prosecution, no operator may conduct a valid analysis of an arrested person's breath under the provisions of N.J.S.A. 39:4-50.3, N.J.S.A. 39:3-10.25 or N.J.S.A. 12:7-56, unless such operator has been issued a valid operator's certificate which is current at the time of the analysis of an arrested person's breath and which attests that such operator is then qualified and competent to conduct such analysis utilizing an approved method and an approved instrument as set forth at N.J.A.C. 13:51-3.

(b) Certification of a person as an operator shall be by recommendation of the Superintendent of the State Police to the Attorney General upon the satisfactory completion of training as more fully set forth at N.J.A.C. 13:51-1.6.

Amended by R.1987 d.229, effective May 18, 1987.
See: 19 N.J.R. 444(b), 19 N.J.R. 882(b).
   Added N.J.S.A. 12:7-56.
Amended by R.1991 d.505, effective October 7, 1991.
See: 23 N.J.R. 2248(b), 23 N.J.R. 3032(c).
   In (a), added "N.J.S.A. 39:3-10.25".

13:51-1.4 Prerequisite for application for certification

An applicant for certification as an operator must be a sworn, full-time member of an organized police department for a minimum of one year after graduation from an approved school; except that members of a police or law enforcement agency of the Department of Defense of the United States of America may apply at any time after graduation from an approved school.

13:51-1.5 Application for operator's certification

Application shall be made in writing to the Division of State Police by the Chief of Police or other executive head of the organized police department of which the applicant is a sworn full-time member.

13:51-1.6 Requirements for certification

(a) Initial certification requires satisfactory completion of training consisting of a minimum of five days of training prescribed and conducted by the Division of State Police. Such training shall include:

1. Instruction in the metric system;
2. Instruction in mathematical calculations as required;
3. Statutory and case law;
4. Instruction and training in the operation of the approved instrument;
5. Laboratory practice with air samples passed through test solutions of alcohol and air samples taken from human subjects;
6. A written examination and a test for competency.

(b) Certification of an applicant upon an approved instrument other than that which the applicant was previously trained and certified, requires that the applicant be a certified breath test operator and whose certification is both current and valid and requires satisfactory completion of training consisting of a minimum of two days of training prescribed and conducted by the Division of State Police. Such training shall include:

1. Statutory and case law, instruction and training in the operation of the approved instrument;
2. Instruction and training in the operation of the approved instrument;
3. Laboratory practice with air samples passed through test solutions of alcohol;
4. A written test and a test for competency.

(c) A person who has received a post graduate degree from an institution of higher education in the field of chemistry or biochemistry or a person licensed as a doctor of medicine shall be deemed to have met the requirements of satisfactory completion of training and may be recommended for certification, provided said person also passes a test for competency in the operation of the approved instrument as administered by a Breath Test Coordinator/Instructor of the Division of State Police.

(d) Recertification of an operator, whose certification is not subject to suspension for any reason or revoked, requires satisfactory completion of training consisting of a minimum one day of training as prescribed and conducted by the Division of State Police. Such training shall include:

1. Statutory and case law;
2. Instruction and training in the operation of the approved instrument;
3. Laboratory practice with air samples passed through test solutions of alcohol;
4. A written examination and a test for competency.

(e) Reinstatement and recertification of an operator whose certification is suspended pursuant to N.J.A.C. 13:51-1.8(a) and to whom the requirements as set forth at N.J.A.C. 13:51-1.8(b) apply requires satisfactory completion of training as set forth at N.J.A.C. 13:51-1.6(d).

(f) Reinstatement and special recertification of an operator whose certification is suspended pursuant to N.J.A.C. 13:51-1.8(a) and to whom the requirements as set forth at N.J.A.C. 13:51-1.8(c) apply requires satisfactory completion of training consisting of a minimum of three days of training prescribed and conducted by the Division of State Police. Such training shall include:

1. Statutory and case law;

2. Instruction and training in the operation of the approved instrument;

3. Laboratory practice with air samples passed through test solutions of alcohol;

4. A written examination and a test for competency.

13:51-1.7 Duration of certification

(a) An operator's certification will be documented by the issuance of a certificate and replica which shows that said operator has completed the required course of training, including the date of the course completion and type of approved instrument upon which the operator has been certified. Said certification as evidenced by the certificate and replica shall be valid throughout the remainder of the calendar year corresponding to the date of course completion and shall remain valid throughout the next two calendar years.

(b) An operator's certification will be deemed continued as valid upon the satisfactory completion of training for recertification as described at N.J.A.C. 13:51-1.6(d). Recertification shall be valid throughout the remainder of the calendar year corresponding to the completion date of the recertification course and shall remain valid throughout the next two calendar years.

(c) The certification of an operator which has been suspended pursuant to N.J.A.C. 13:51-1.8(a) and who has been reinstated and recertified pursuant to N.J.A.C. 13:51-1.8(b) or N.J.A.C. 13:51-1.8(c) will be deemed to be valid for all purposes as of and from the date of reinstatement and recertification. This reinstatement and recertification shall thereafter be valid throughout the remainder of the calendar year corresponding to the date of reinstatement and recertification and shall remain valid throughout the next two calendar years.

(d) The recertification and/or reinstatement and recertification of an operator pursuant to N.J.A.C. 13:51-1.6(d), N.J.A.C. 13:51-1.6(e) or N.J.A.C. 13:51-1.6(f), whichever applies, is considered validated when the replica is signed and dated by a Breath Test Coordinator/Instructor.

13:51-1.8 Suspension and reinstatement of operator's certification

(a) The certification of an operator will be automatically suspended on the date set for expiration of the operator's present valid certification as set forth at N.J.A.C. 13:51-1.7 if said operator has not satisfied the requirement for recertification as set forth at N.J.A.C. 13:51-1.6(d) before the expiration of said valid certification.

(b) An operator whose certification is suspended for failing to be recertified as set forth at N.J.A.C. 13:51-1.6(d) and who has been automatically suspended for less than one year from the date of the automatic suspension must attend and satisfy the requirements of the reinstatement and recertification course as set forth at N.J.A.C. 13:51-1.6(e) conducted by the Division of State Police. Reinstatement and recertification under this subsection must be completed before one year from the date of automatic suspension otherwise the operator must satisfy the requirements as set forth at N.J.A.C. 13:51-1.8(c).

(c) An operator whose certification is suspended for failing to be recertified as set forth at N.J.A.C. 13:51-1.6(d) or N.J.A.C. 13:51-1.6(e) and who has been automatically suspended for one year or more from the date of the automatic suspension must attend and satisfy the requirements of a reinstatement and special recertification course as set forth at N.J.A.C. 13:51-1.6(f) conducted by the Division of State Police.

(d) Any test conducted to analyze a person's breath pursuant to procedures and methods contained in this chapter by an operator whose certification is suspended or automatically suspended, at the time such test is conducted, shall be considered invalid for presentation in evidence or testimony in a court of law or administrative hearing.

13:51-1.9 Revocation of certificate

(a) The Attorney General may revoke an operator's certification after consideration of a request or recommendation for revocation by the Superintendent of State Police.

(b) A request or recommendation for revocation will be made to the Attorney General when an operator is determined to be ineffective or incompetent by the Superintendent of State Police.

(c) A request or recommendation that an operator's certification be revoked must be in writing and addressed to the Superintendent of State Police and must state the reason(s) for the request or recommendation for revocation. The replica certificate of the operator who is the subject of the request or recommendation must accompany the request or recommendation for revocation unless it is otherwise unobtainable.

(d) The following persons are authorized to initiate a request or recommendation for revocation:

1. A Breath Test Coordinator/Instructor; or

2. Chief of Police of the organized police department of which the operator is a sworn member; or

3. Executive head of the organized police department of which the operator is a sworn member.

(e) Upon receipt of a request or recommendation for revocation, the Superintendent of State Police shall cause a written Notice of Suspension to be delivered to the operator who is the subject of the request or recommendation. A copy of the Notice of Suspension shall also be delivered to the Chief of Police or executive head of the organized police department of which the operator is a sworn member. The Notice of Suspension shall state:

1. The effective date of suspension;

2. The reason(s) revocation has been requested or recommended;

3. The name and title of the person originating the request or recommendation for revocation; and

4. Information that the operator may request a hearing on the request or recommendation for revocation by serving the Superintendent of State Police with written notice of such request within 30 days of the date the notice of suspension was signed and dated by the Superintendent of State Police.

(f) Failure to request a hearing as set forth at N.J.A.C. 13:51-1.9(e) within the time alloted shall be considered an absolute waiver of any right to a hearing.

13:51-1.10 Hearing and determination on a request or recommendation for revocation

(a) The purpose of a hearing is to assist the Superintendent of State Police in arriving at a determination on the request or recommendation for revocation as set forth at N.J.A.C.

13:51-1.9(b). Where no hearing is conducted the Superintendent of State Police may make his determination based on the written documentation supplied in the request or recommendation to revoke or other materials supplied in support or opposition thereto.

(b) The hearing will be conducted by the Superintendent of State Police or by an officer designated by him. The hearing officer may, at his discretion, cause the operator to be given a written or oral examination or a competency test or any combination of such tests to arrive at a determination. Such tests may be given by a Breath Test Coordinator/Instructor or other person so designated by the Superintendent or the hearing officer.

(c) Upon conclusion of the hearing or review when no hearing is requested, the Superintendent of State Police will recommend, in writing, to the Attorney General whether the operator's certification should be revoked, including the reasons to support such recommendation; or if the operator's certification should be reinstated and the reasons in support thereof. Reinstatement may be conditioned upon the suspended operator satisfying certain training or other requirements. The Attorney General shall determine, in his sole discretion, what conditions or other requirements must be met before reinstatement can become effective.

(d) An operator recommended for reinstatement with conditions or other requirements as set forth at N.J.A.C. 13:51-1.10(c), who fails to satisfy and successfully complete said conditions or other requirements within a reasonable period of time, may be recommended by the Superintendent of State Police to the Attorney General for revocation of the operator's certification.

13:51-1.11 Restoration of revoked certifications

The Attorney General may restore a revoked certification when he is satisfied that the cause for revocation has been removed. An operator whose certification is revoked may apply for a new operator's certification after the expiration of 12 months from the date of revocation, or final judgment thereon, whichever is later. Application shall be pursuant to the provisions of N.J.A.C. 13:51-1.4 and N.J.A.C. 13:51-1.5, but shall be subject to review by the Superintendent of State Police. The applicant must complete the training as set forth at N.J.A.C. 13:51-1.6(a); but may not commence such training until any other requirements imposed by the Superintendent of State Police are satisfied. Upon satisfactory completion of training and any other prerequisites, the Superintendent of State Police may recommend certification of the applicant to the Attorney General.

13:51-1.12 Return, loss and/or replacement of replica

(a) If an operator's certification is suspended or revoked pursuant to N.J.A.C. 13:51-1.9 and/or N.J.A.C. 13:51-1.10, or if the operator resigns, retires or leaves the police department for any reason, it shall be the responsibility of the Chief of Police or other executive head of the organized police department or law enforcement agency where the operator serves or served to retrieve the replica certificate from the operator and return the same to the Division of State Police with a notation of the reason for the return.

(b) If a replica has been lost or is otherwise in need of replacement, the operator or Chief of Police or other executive head of the organized police department of which the operator is a member shall notify the Breath Test Unit of the Division of State Police in writing of such loss or need of replacement. Lost replicas must be reported immediately.

(c) A replica will be replaced for an operator when the operator's replica has been lost and duly reported as lost, pursuant to N.J.A.C. 13:51-1.12(b) or is otherwise in need of replacement. The replacement replica will bear the date of issuance of the replacement and bear the signatures or facsimile signatures of the Attorney General and the Superintendent of State Police. The reverse side of the replacement replica will show the date of the operator's original certification and the date of the operator's most recent recertification.

13:51-1.13 Administration

Administrative files will be maintained by the Division of State Police and will include the present and past status of all persons certified as operators.

SUBCHAPTER 2. BREATH TEST COORDINATOR/INSTRUCTORS

13:51-2.1 Eligibility requirements

(a) To be eligible as a Breath Test Coordinator/Instructor a person must be a sworn member of the New Jersey State Police, hold a current and valid Breath Test Certificate and be a holder of:

    1. A certificate in police training issued by the New Jersey Police Training Commission; or

    2. An instructor certificate issued by the United States Armed Forces; or

    3. Certification from a duly accredited school of education; or

    4. Instructor certificate issued by the Division of State Police, Training Bureau.

(b) The Attorney General may waive the instructor certification requirement, if he is satisfied such person has equivalent background and experience to instruct breath test applicants and operators.

(c) The Attorney General's approval will be in the form of a letter to the person approved as a Breath Test Coordinator/Instructor and will be reflected on the operator's replica certificate by the words Breath Test Coordinator/Instructor.

13:51-2.2 Training and functional qualifications

(a) A Breath Test Coordinator/Instructor will have specialized training as prescribed by the Division of State Police and have the knowledge to properly perform the following functions:

    1. Preparation and checking of chemicals used for testing;

    2. Presentation of the scientific theory of approved instruments and approved methods;

    3. Inspection and maintenance of approved instruments;

    4. Instruction in courses for operators and applicants;

    5. Make a request or recommendation for revocation of an operators certification;

    6. Validate replica certificates held by certified breath test operators as provided at N.J.A.C. 13:51-1.7 (Duration of certification).

SUBCHAPTER 3. APPROVED INSTRUMENTS AS METHODS OF CHEMICAL BREATH TESTING

13:51-3.1 Purpose of subchapter

Pursuant to the provisions of P.L. 1966, c.142, Sec. 3, as amended by P.L. 1971, c.273, Sec. 1 (N.J.S.A. 39:4-50.3), P.L. 1990, c.103, Sec. 17 (N.J.S.A. 39:3-10.25) and P.L. 1986, c.39, Sec. 8 (N.J.S.A. 12:7-56); hereinafter denoted N.J.S.A. 39:4-50.3, N.J.S.A. 39:3-10.25 or N.J.S.A. 12:7-56, respectively, the provisions of this subchapter set forth the instruments and methods approved by the Attorney General for the chemical analysis of the breath of a person arrested pursuant to the provisions of N.J.S.A. 39:4-50, et seq., N.J.S.A. 39:3-10.13, N.J.S.A. 39:3-10.20, N.J.S.A. 39:3-10.24, N.J.S.A. 12:7-34.19, N.J.S.A. 12:7-46 or N.J.S.A. 2A:4A-23.

Amended by R.1987 d.229, effective May 18, 1987.
See: 19 N.J.R. 444(b), 19 N.J.R. 882(b).
   Added N.J.S.A. cites.
Amended by R.1991 d.505, effective October 7, 1991.
See: 23 N.J.R. 2248(b), 23 N.J.R. 3032(c).
   Added to list of N.J.S.A. cites.

13:51-3.2 Application for approval

(a) The Superintendent of State Police is designated by the Attorney General as the official to whom all applications for approval of instruments, methods and operational functions shall be made.

(b) Primarily, evaluation will be dependent upon test results reflecting reliability for satisfactory specificity, precision and accuracy. The instrument and component parts necessary for operation shall be supplied at the expense of the applicant.

(c) Any evaluating reports by the applicant or independent investigating groups shall be forwarded with the instrument along with operating servicing and maintenance manuals, schematic drawings and other detailed information.

(d) Upon completion of evaluation of an instrument, method and/or operational function, the Superintendent shall recommend approval or rejection of the same to the Attorney General. The Attorney General, upon review of the recommendations, shall approve or reject the instrument, method and/or operational function pursuant to law (N.J.S.A. 39:4-50.3, N.J.S.A. 39:3-10.25 or N.J.S.A. 12:7-56).

Amended by R.1987 d.229, effective May 18, 1987.
See: 19 N.J.R. 444(b), 19 N.J.R. 882(b).
   Added N.J.S.A. 12:7-56.
Amended by R.1991 d.505, effective October 7, 1991.
See: 23 N.J.R. 2248(b), 23 N.J.R. 3032(c).
   In (d), added "N.J.S.A. 39:3-10.25".

13:51-3.3 Training Breath Test Coordinator/Instructors

(a) Upon approval of an instrument, method and/or operational function as described in N.J.A.C. 13:51-3.2, factory personnel shall train an initial class consisting of Breath Test Coordinator/Instructors (see N.J.A.C. 13:51-2) at the expense of the applicant.

(b) The initial training course shall include the history of the instrument, nomenclature of the operational controls, detailed operating instructions, nomenclature of all parts and their functions, maintenance and repair of the instrument and class participation in the operation of the device including laboratory practice with air passed through test solutions of alcohol of strengths known and unknown to the class participants.

13:51-3.4 Periodic inspection of approved instruments

Periodic inspection of all approved instruments used in this State in connection with the prosecution of a person pursuant to the provisions of N.J.S.A. 39:4-50 et seq., N.J.S.A. 39:3-10.13, N.J.S.A. 39:3-10.20, N.J.S.A. 39:3-10.24, N.J.S.A. 12:7-34.19, N.J.S.A. 12:7-46 or N.J.S.A. 2A:4A-23 shall be made by a Breath Test Coordinator/Instructor. The results of such periodic inspections shall be recorded on forms provided by the Superintendent of State Police and the originals thereof shall be maintained by the Division of State Police.

Amended by R.1987 d.229, effective May 18, 1987.
See: 19 N.J.R. 444(b), 19 N.J.R. 882(b).
    Added N.J.S.A. cites.
Amended by R.1991 d.505, effective October 7, 1991.
See: 23 N.J.R. 2248(b), 23 N.J.R. 3032(c).
    Added to list of N.J.S.A. cites.

13:51-3.5 Approved instruments for performing chemical analysis of a person's breath

(a) The Breathalyzer, Model 900, is an instrument approved by the Attorney General pursuant to P.L. 1966, c.142, Sec. 3, as amended by P.L. 1971, c.273, Sec. 1 (N.J.S.A. 39:4-50.3), P.L. 1990, c.103, Sec. 17 (N.J.S.A. 39:3-10.25) and P.L. 1986, c.39, Sec. 8 (N.J.S.A. 12:7-56) and this subchapter, for the testing of a person's breath by chemical analysis.

(b) The Breathalyzer, Model 900A, is an instrument approved by the Attorney General pursuant to P.L. 1966, c.142, Sec.3, as amended by P.L. 1971, c.273, Sec. 1 (N.J.S.A. 39:4-50.3), P.L. 1990, c.103, Sec. 17 (N.J.S.A. 39:3-10.25) and P.L. 1986, c.39, Sec. 8 (N.J.S.A. 12:7-56) and this subchapter, for the testing of a person's breath by chemical analysis.

(c) The Dominator Albreath is an instrument approved by the Attorney General pursuant to P.L. 1966, c.142, Sec. 3 as amended by P.L. 1971, c.273, Sec. 1 (N.J.S.A. 39:4-50.3), P.L. 1990, c.103, Sec. 17 (N.J.S.A. 39:3-10.25) and P.L. 1986, c.39, Sec. 8 (N.J.S.A. 12:7-56) and this subchapter, for the testing of a person's breath by chemical analysis.

(d) The Alco-Tector is an instrument approved by the Attorney General pursuant to P.L. 1966, c.142, Sec. 3, as amended by P.L. 1971, c.273, Sec. 1 (N.J.S.A. 39:4-50.3), P.L. 1990, c.103 Sec. 17 (N.J.S.A. 39:3-10.25) and P.L. 1986, c.39 Sec. 8 (N.J.S.A. 12:7-56) and this subchapter, for the testing of a person's breath by chemical analysis.

Amended by R.1985 d.441, effective September 3, 1985.
See: 17 N.J.R. 1531(a), 17 N.J.R. 2141(b).
    Deleted (e).
Amended by R.1987 d.229, effective May 18, 1987.
See: 19 N.J.R. 444(b), 19 N.J.R. 882(b).
    Added N.J.S.A. cites.
Amended by R.1991 d.505, effective October 7, 1991.
See: 23 N.J.R. 2248(b), 23 N.J.R. 3032(c).
    Added to list of N.J.S.A. cites in (a), (b), (c), (d).

13:51-3.6 Approved methods for performing chemical analysis of a person's breath utilizing an approved instrument

(a) Breathalyzer, Model 900 and Model 900A:

1. The Breathalyzer, Model 900 and 900A, both being approved instruments, have been demonstrated to contain functional and operational components that are the same or perform the same or similar operations or functions and operate utilizing the same principal or theory of chemical breath analysis and utilize the same chemical compounds interchangeably in the analysis process. The term "Breathalyzer" as utilized in this chapter shall mean both the Breathalyzer, Model 900 and Model 900A.

    i. Any operator or Breath Test Coordinator/Instructor whose certificate specifies Breathalyzer is deemed trained and certified on the Breathalyzer Model 900 and Breathalyzer, Model 900A.

2. A Breathalyzer check off list may be used with this device and may be prepared by either the manufacturer of the Breathalyzer or the organization using the Breathalyzer. The check off list, if used, shall contain at least the following items:

    i. Preparation:

        (1) Turn Switch to "on"; wait until thermometer shows 50 degrees Centigrade plus or minus three degrees;

(2) Gauge reference ampoule and place in left hand holder;

(3) Gauge test ampoule; open; insert bubbler and connect to outlet.

ii. Purge:

(1) Turn to "take"; flush; turn to "analyze";

(2) When red empty signal appears, wait 90 seconds, turn on light, balance.

iii. Analysis:

(1) Set scale Pointer on start line;

(2) Turn to "take"; take breath sample; turn to "analyze";

(3) When red empty signal appears, wait 90 seconds, turn on light; balance;

(4) Record answer; dispose of test ampoule; turn to "off".

(b) Dominator Albreath:

1. The Dominator Albreath, being an approved instrument, has been determined to contain operational and functional components that are the same or perform the same or similar operations or functions as the Breathalyzer as described at N.J.A.C. 13:51-3.6(a)1. It is further determined that this instrument operates upon the same principal or theory as the Breathalyzer and utilize the same chemical compounds in the analysis process as the Breathalyzer.

2. The steps of operation in the check off list applicable to the Breathalyzer as found at N.J.A.C. 13:51-3.6(a)2 shall also apply to the operation of the Dominator Albreath when a check off list is employed.

(c) Alco-Tector:

1. The Alco-Tector, being an approved instrument, has been determined to operate on the same basic principle or theory and utilizes the same chemical compounds in the analysis process as the Breathalyzer as described at N.J.A.C. 13:51-3.6(a)1.

2. An operational check off list may be used with this device and may be prepared by either the manufacturer of the Alco-Tector or the organization using the Alco-Tector. The check off list, if used and prepared by an organization other than the manufacturer herein, shall contain, at least, the following information:

i. Preparation:

(1) Turn switch to "on", depress standby button, wait for thermometer to reach operating temperature of 120 to 130 degrees Fahrenheit;

(2) Gauge reference ampoule and place in left holder;

(3) Gauge test ampoule, open, insert bubbler, connect to outlet.

ii. Purge:

(1) Depress purge button number 1 for flush, wait 30 or 45 seconds, depress bubbler button number 2;

(2) When red empty signal appears, wait 90 seconds, depress balance button number 3 and balance.

iii. Analysis:

(1) Set blood alcohol pointer on start line;

(2) Depress sample button number 4, take breath sample, depress bubbler button number 5, record time;

(3) When red empty signal appears, wait 90 seconds, depress read button number 6 and balance;

(4) Record answer; dispose of test ampoule, depress number 1 button for 30 to 45 seconds, depress number 2 button until red light appears, depress standby button.

Amended by R.1985 d.441, effective September 3, 1985.
See: 17 N.J.R. 1531(a), 17 N.J.R. 2141(b).
    Deleted (d).
Correction: (a)2i(3): added "open;".
See: 21 N.J.R. 171(e).

290/Municipal Court

INTOXICATED DRIVER PENALTY PROVISIONS COURT ORDER STATE OF NEW JERSEY

MUNICIPAL COURT | **COUNTY**
ADDRESS | **CITY** | **ZIP**

DEFENDANT INFORMATION

DEFENDANT'S NAME	SEX ☐ M ☐ F	BIRTHDATE	TELEPHONE (Area Code)	EYE COLOR / CODE

ADDRESS	CITY	STATE	ZIP

DRIVER'S LICENSE NUMBER	LICENSING STATE	VIOLATION DATE	CONVICTION DATE

DWI ☐ Alcohol ☐ Drugs	BLOOD ALCOHOL CONTENT %	DOCKET NUMBER	SUMMONS NUMBER

PENALTY PROVISIONS (Complete as applicable)

The Defendant has been convicted of operating a motor vehicle under the influence as described above. Pursuant to N.J.S.A. 39:4-50 and Program Requirements of the Intoxicated Driver Resource Centers (IDRC) and Bureau of Alcohol Countermeasures, this ORDER imposes the following penalty provisions.

	FINE	COSTS	ENFORCEMENT SURCHARGE	DETENTION / IMPRISONMENT / ABATEMENT REHABILITATION	COMMUNITY SERVICE	LICENSE SUSPENSION
First Offense	$	$	$	☒ IDRC (12–48 hrs.) ☐ Inpatient Rehabilitation ☐ Imprisonment ____ Days		_____ Months
Second Offense	$	$	$	☐ IDRC (48 hrs.) ☐ Inpatient Rehabilitation ____ Days (48 HOURS MINIMUM) ☐ Jail or Workhouse ____ Days (48 HOURS MINIMUM)	☒ 30 Days	☒ 2 Years
3rd & Subsequent Offense	$	$	$	☐ Imprisonment ____ Days ☐ Inpatient Rehabilitation ____ Days	____ Days	☒ 10 Years

Other sentence description (Use reverse if additional space required)

_____
_____
_____
_____
_____
_____
_____
_____
_____

Defendant must satisfy screening, evaluation, educational or treatment referral, and program requirements of the Bureau of Alcohol Countermeasures and Intoxicated Driver Resource Center. Defendant's failure to attend the IDRC when notified or failure to satisfy any of the above requirements shall result in license suspension until such requirements are met and 2 days imprisonment in county jail.

JUDGE'S NAME (Print)	JUDGE'S SIGNATURE	ORDER DATE

DEFENDANT CERTIFICATION

I understand the consequences of failure to meet the requirements of the above-referenced program. I further certify the above-described Defendant Information is correct and acknowledge receipt of a copy of and understand this ORDER.

DEFENDANT'S SIGNATURE	DATE

white Court file   canary Defendant   pink County Probation Department   goldenrod Division of Motor Vehicles, Bureau of Court Reports & Fines